Verifiable Autonomous Systems

How can we provide guarantees of behaviours for autonomous systems such as driverless cars? This tutorial text for professionals, researchers, and graduate students explains how autonomous systems, from intelligent robots to driverless cars, can be programmed in ways that make them amenable to formal verification. The authors review specific definitions, applications, and the unique future potential of autonomous systems, along with their impact on safer decisions and ethical behaviour. The topics discussed in this book include the use of rational cognitive agent programming from the Beliefs–Desires–Intentions paradigm to control autonomous systems, and the role of model-checking in verifying properties of this decision-making component. Several case studies concerning both the verification of autonomous systems and extensions to the framework beyond the model-checking of agent decision-makers are included, along with complete tutorials for the use of the freely available verifiable cognitive agent toolkit Gwendolen, written in Java.

DR LOUISE A. DENNIS is leader of the Autonomy and Verification research group at The University of Manchester and conference coordinator for the ACM Special Interest Group for Artificial Intelligence (AI). She studied mathematics and philosophy at the University of Oxford and received her PhD from the University of Edinburgh in using AI techniques to prove mathematical theorems; her interest in the overlap between mathematics, philosophy, and AI has continued ever since. Her current research encompasses the programming of autonomous systems, the development of agent programming languages, reasoning about systems and programs via formal mathematical techniques, and the ethical implications of AI. Beyond the university setting, Dr Dennis is active in public engagement and spends a lot of time taking Lego Robots into schools to introduce robotics programming to children.

DR MICHAEL FISHER is a professor of Computer Science at The University of Manchester. He holds a Royal Academy of Engineering Chair in Emerging Technologies and is a fellow of both the British Computer Society and the Institution of Engineering and Technology. He was previously a professor of logic and computation in the Department of Computing & Mathematics at Manchester Metropolitan University and a professor of computer science at University of Liverpool. Dr Fisher's research concerns autonomous systems, particularly software engineering, formal verification, safety, responsibility, and trustworthiness. He has been involved in over 200 journal and conference papers and authored the book *An Introduction to Practical Formal Methods Using Temporal Logic* (Wiley) in 2011.

Verifiable Autonomous Systems

Using Rational Agents to Provide Assurance about Decisions Made by Machines

LOUISE A. DENNIS
University of Manchester

MICHAEL FISHER
University of Manchester

CAMBRIDGE
UNIVERSITY PRESS

CAMBRIDGE
UNIVERSITY PRESS

Shaftesbury Road, Cambridge CB2 8EA, United Kingdom

One Liberty Plaza, 20th Floor, New York, NY 10006, USA

477 Williamstown Road, Port Melbourne, VIC 3207, Australia

314–321, 3rd Floor, Plot 3, Splendor Forum, Jasola District Centre, New Delhi – 110025, India

103 Penang Road, #05-06/07, Visioncrest Commercial, Singapore 238467

Cambridge University Press is part of Cambridge University Press & Assessment, a department of the University of Cambridge.

We share the University's mission to contribute to society through the pursuit of education, learning and research at the highest international levels of excellence.

www.cambridge.org
Information on this title: www.cambridge.org/9781108484992
DOI: 10.1017/9781108755023

First published 2023

A catalogue record for this publication is available from the British Library.

Library of Congress Cataloging-in-Publication Data
Names: Dennis, Louise, author. | Fisher, Michael, 1962- author.
Title: Verifiable autonomous systems : using rational agents to provide assurance about decisions made by machines / Louise A. Dennis, University of Manchester, Michael Fisher, University of Manchester.
Description: Cambridge, United Kingdom ; New York, NY, USA : Cambridge University Press, 2023. | Includes bibliographical references and index.
Identifiers: LCCN 2023006704 | ISBN 9781108484992 (hardback) | ISBN 9781108755023 (ebook)
Subjects: LCSH: Robust control. | Automatic control. | Machine learning. | Computer programs–Verification.
Classification: LCC TJ217.2 .D46 2023 | DDC 629.8–dc23/eng/20230302
LC record available at https://lccn.loc.gov/2023006704

ISBN 978-1-108-48499-2 Hardback

This book is dedicated to Gwendolen Sellers.
The original, you might say.

Contents

Acknowledgements

Thanks are due to the many people who worked with us on the material in this book: Davide Ancona, Martin Mose Bentzen, Rafael Bordini, Paul Bremner, Neil Cameron, Rafael C. Cardoso, Marie Farrell, Angelo Ferrando, Mike Jump, Maryam Kamali, Nick Lincoln, Felix Lindner, Alexei Lisitsa, Matt Luckuck, Viviana Mascardi, Owen McAree, Marija Slavkovik, Sandor Veres, Matt Webster, and Alan F. Winfield. Thanks also to Chris Anderson for proof reading the early chapters.

1

Introduction

While the idea of an 'Autonomous System', a system that can make complex decisions without human intervention, is both appealing and powerful, actually developing such a system to be safe, reliable, and trustworthy, is far from straightforward. An important aspect of this development involves being able to verify the decision-making that forms the core of many truly autonomous systems. In this book, we will introduce a particular approach to the formal verification of agent-based autonomous systems, leading the reader through autonomous systems architectures, agent programming languages, formal verification, agent model-checking, and the practical analysis of autonomous systems.

In this introductory chapter we will address the following aspects.

- What is an *Autonomous System*?
  $\longrightarrow$ from automatic, to adaptive, then on to autonomous systems

- Why are *Autonomous Systems* used?
  $\longrightarrow$ with increased flexibility, wider applicability, and significant future potential

- Why apply *Formal* Verification?
  $\longrightarrow$ provides a strong mathematical basis and increased confidence in systems

- What it means in *Practice*?
  $\longrightarrow$ with an impact on safer decisions, ethical behaviour, certification, and so on

1.1 What is an Autonomous System?

1.1.1 From Automatic, through Adaptive, on to Autonomous

The concept of *Autonomy* can be characterised as

the ability of a system to make its own decisions and to act on its own, and to do both without direct human intervention.

We want to distinguish this from both automatic and adaptive systems. An **automatic** system follows a pre-scripted series of activities, with very little (if any) potential for deviation. An **adaptive** system will modify its behaviour, but does so rapidly in order to adapt to its environment (Sastry and Bodson, 1994). This means that its behaviour is tightly based on the inputs or stimuli from its environment and adaptation is typically (especially in adaptive control systems) achieved through continuous feedback loops usually described using differential equations. These are common features of adaptive systems, with continuous feedback control responding to changes in the environment.

Example. Consider a legged robot walking in a straight line across some ground that varies between a hard tarmac surface, a smooth icy surface, and a soft sandy surface. If the robot is controlled by an adaptive system, then as the properties of the ground change, the system can adapt the control of the legs: taking smaller, slower steps on the icy surface, or lifting the legs higher on the sandy surface.

While the behaviour of this system varies flexibly based on the environment it encounters, we would tend not to consider this adaptation to be decision-making and would not describe the system as autonomous unless it also had the capacity to turn aside from its straight line in order to, for instance, examine some object of interest.

By contrast, an **autonomous** system does more than simply react and adapt to its environment. It may have many different reasons for making a choice, and often these are not at all apparent to an external observer. The important thing is that an autonomous system might not be directly driven by immediate factors in its environment. It is often natural to talk of an autonomous system having goals that it is trying to achieve and seeing its behaviour as influenced both by its goals and its current environment.

It should be noted that the distinction between a system that makes its own decisions and one that is purely automatic or adaptive is often difficult to draw, particularly if you do not want the definition to depend upon the specifics of how the system is implemented. In general, the greater the ability of system to behave flexibly in dynamic, uncertain environments and cope well with scenarios that may not have been conceived of, or only partially specified, when the system was designed, the more autonomous the system is usually considered to be. This book concerns itself with one particular methodology for providing greater autonomy – agent programming – and how the autonomy provided in this way may be verified.

1.1.2 Variable Autonomy

In practical applications there are many levels of autonomy. While fully autonomous systems still remain quite rare, there are many systems that involve a mixture of human and system control. These can range from direct human (e.g., operator/pilot/driver) control of *all* actions all the way through to the system controlling decision-making and action with only very limited (if any) human intervention. This spectrum of *variable autonomy* is so common that several taxonomies have been developed; below is one such classification, called 'PACT' (Bonner et al., 2004), often used in aerospace scenarios.

Level 0: 'No Autonomy'
> → *Whole task is carried out by the human except for the actual operation*

Level 1: 'Advice only if requested'
> → *Human asks system to suggest options and then human makes selection*

Level 2: 'Advice' → *System suggests options to human*

Level 3: 'Advice, and if authorised, action'
> → *System suggests options and also proposes one of them*

Level 4: 'Action unless revoked'
> 4a: *System chooses an action and performs it if the human approves*
> 4b: *System chooses an action and performs it unless the human disapproves*

Level 5: 'Full Autonomy'
> 5a: *System chooses action, performs it, and informs the human*
> 5b: *System does everything autonomously*

An interesting aspect of this, and a current research topic, concerns the mechanism by which a system changes between these levels. Not only when can the operator/pilot/driver give the system more control, but when can the system relinquish some/all control back to the human?

Aside. Consider a convoy (or 'road train') of cars on a motorway. The driver chooses to relinquish control to his/her vehicle and sits back as the car coordinates with other vehicles in the convoy. Some time later, the driver decides to take back control of the vehicle. In principle the vehicle should let him/her do this, but what if the vehicle assesses the situation and works out that allowing the driver to take control in this way will very likely lead to an accident. Should the car refuse to let the driver have control back? Should the car only let the driver have *partial* control back? And what are the legal/ethical considerations?

1.2 Why Autonomy?

Higher levels of autonomy are increasingly appearing in practical systems. But why? There are traditionally several reasons for this trend, and we begin with *distant* or *dangerous* environments. If a system needs to be deployed in a *remote* environment, then direct human control is likely to be infeasible. For example, communications to planetary rovers take a *long* time, while communications to deep sea vehicles can be prone to failure. Perhaps more importantly, the remote control of an autonomous system is notoriously difficult. Even with unmanned aircraft, as soon as the vehicle goes out of sight, its direct control by a human operator on the ground is problematic. Similarly, there are many *dangerous* situations where humans cannot be nearby, and so cannot easily assess the possibilities and confidently control the system. Such environments include space and deep sea, as above, but can also include closer environments such as those involving nuclear or chemical hazards.

In some cases, the environment is neither distant nor dangerous, yet a human is not able to effectively control the system as his/her reactions are just not quick enough. Imagine an automated trading system within a stock market – here the speed of interactions is at the millisecond level, which is beyond human capabilities. In some scenarios there are just too many things happening at once. Possibly a human can remotely control a single unmanned air vehicle, as long as it remains in the controller's line of sight. But what if there are two, or twenty, or two hundred such vehicles? A single human controller cannot hope to manage all their possible interactions.

There are increasingly many cases where a human *could* carry out various tasks, but finds them just too dull. In the case of a robot vacuum cleaner, we could clearly sweep the floor ourselves but might find the task boring and mundane. Instead, we utilise the robot vacuum cleaner and use the time to tackle something more interesting.

Finally, it may well be that using an autonomous system is actually *cheaper* than using a human-controlled one. With training, safety regulations, and ongoing monitoring required for human pilots, drivers, or operators, possibly an autonomous solution is more cost effective.

Applications

Unsurprisingly, there are very many potential applications for autonomous systems. Few have yet made it to reality and, those that have, rarely employ full autonomy. So, below, we explore some of the possibilities, both existing and future.

Before doing that, however, we note that there is clearly a whole class of purely software applications that have autonomy at their heart. Typically, these are embedded within internet algorithms, e-commerce applications, stock trading systems, and so on. However, for the rest of this section, we will ignore such applications, focussing on those that have more of a physical embodiment.

Embedded Applications. While many applications are explicitly autonomous (e.g., robots, unmanned aircraft) where it is clear to users as well as programmers that the system makes its own decisions, there are perhaps more that are implicit, with autonomous behaviour being embedded within some other system and not necessarily obvious to users. Particularly prominent are the range of *pervasive* or *ubiquitous* systems, typically characterised by multiple computational entities and multiple sensors all situated within an open communications framework. Examples include *communications networks* where some form of autonomy is used for reconfiguration or re-routing or *autonomous sensor networks* where the sensing task is autonomously organised by the sensor nodes. Embedded autonomy also appears within smart cities, smart homes, and so on (see Figure 1.1), where the monitoring aspects are linked to decisions about the system, for example, controlling traffic flow, controlling the environment, deciding what to do in exceptional situations, and so on. More generally, these examples are all varieties of *pervasive* or *ubiquitous* systems.

Autonomous Vehicles. Vehicles of various forms (automotive, air, space, underwater, etc.) increasingly incorporate at least adaptive behaviour and sometimes autonomous behaviour. The 'driver-less car' is one, particularly high profile, example. While both driving in a single lane and obstacle avoidance are

Figure 1.1 'Smart' home
Source: DrAfter123/DigitalVisionVectors via Getty Images. Used with permission

essentially adaptive, the role of the human driver in terms of high-level decisions is increasingly being carried out by software on the vehicle that can make decisions about which route to take and could even foreseeably choose destinations such as petrol stations, supermarkets, and restaurants. While, at the time of writing, there are a number of technological and regulatory obstacles in the way of fully autonomous vehicles, automotive manufacturers are quickly moving towards convoying or 'road train' technology. However, as described earlier, there are clearly some legal/regulatory and ethical questions surrounding even this limited form of autonomous behaviour, especially when the system must decide whether to allow control to be given back to the driver or not.

Moving from ground vehicles, the motivation for utilising autonomy becomes stronger. When vehicles are to move through the air, underwater, or in space, direct pilot/driver control can become difficult. Some of these environments are also potentially dangerous to any human in the vehicle. It is not surprising then that autonomy is increasingly being built into the controlling software for such vehicles. For example, choices made without human intervention are an important element in many aerospace applications, such as *unmanned air vehicles* (Figure 1.2a) or cooperative *formation flying satellites* (Figure 1.2b).

Robotic Assistants. The use of industrial robotics, for example in manufacturing scenarios, is well established. But we are now moving towards the use of

(a) Unmanned Aircraft
Source: Stocktrek Images/Stocktrek
Images via Getty. Used with
permission.

(b) 'Formation Flying' Satellites
Source: Stocktrek/Stockbyte via Getty.
Used wtih permission.

Figure 1.2 Autonomous vehicles

Figure 1.3 Care-o-Bot 4 robotic home assistant
Source: Fraunhofer IPA: www.care-o-bot.de/en/. Used with permission

more flexible, autonomous robotic assistants not only in the workplace but in
our homes. Robotic cleaning devices, such as the Roomba,[1] already exist but it
is much more autònomous *Robotic Assistants* that are now being designed and
developed. Initially intended for the elderly or incapacitated, we can expect to
see such robots as domestic assistants in our homes quite soon (see Figure 1.3).

[1] www.irobot.com/uk/Roomba.

As we get towards this stage, and as these robotic assistants are required to exhibit increasing levels of autonomy, we might see these robots less like 'servants' and more as 'friends' or 'team-mates'! It is not surprising, therefore, that there is considerable research into *human–robot teamwork*; not only how to facilitate such teamwork, but how to ensure that the team activity is effective and reliable. It is recognised that sophisticated human–robot interaction scenarios will be with us very soon.

1.3 Why use *Formal* Verification?

While there are many potential applications for autonomous systems, few current systems involve full autonomy. Why? Partly this is because the regulatory frameworks often do not *permit* such systems to be deployed; partly this is because we (developers or users) do not *trust* such systems. In both these cases, the ability to *formally verify* properties of an autonomous system will surely help. Mathematical proof that a system has certain 'safe' behaviour might be used in certification or regulation arguments; the certainty of such proofs can also help alleviate public fears and provide designers with increased confidence.

1.3.1 What is *Verification*?

In this book we will distinguish between validation and verification. We use the term *validation* for a process that aims to ensure that whatever artefact we have produced meets the 'real' world needs we have. We will use *Verification*, on the other hand, to refer to any process used to check that the artefact matches our specification or requirements. Such verification might often be carried out using methods such as *testing* or *simulation*.

1.3.2 Formal Approach

On the other hand, *formal* verification utilises strong mathematical techniques, particularly logical proof, to assess the system being produced against its specification. One or both of the system and specification may be described using formal logic and then formal verification will attempt to show either that the system satisfies the given specification or, if it does not, provide an example system execution that violates the specification. There are a wide range of formal verification techniques, from formal proof carried out by hand through to automated, exhaustive exploration of the execution possibilities of the system. It is the latter type that we consider in this book, specifically in Chapters 4 and 6.

1.3.3 Why?

Formal verification is difficult and time-consuming, and formal verification techniques are not at all common in the development of autonomous systems. So, why bother? What do such techniques give us that is important enough to expend all this effort on?

As we have seen, autonomous systems are on the increase, and are set to be widespread in the future. One place where formal verification is widely used is in the development of safety-critical systems, particularly in aircraft where its use is often required by regulators. Unsurprisingly, we can anticipate that in order to be *legal* some of these systems may need to have been verified.

The use of formal verification techniques, with their strong mathematical basis, can not only provide formal evidence for certification and regulation processes, but can potentially increase the public's confidence and *trust* in these systems (Chatila et al., 2021). More generally, formal verification gives us much greater certainty about the decision-making that is at the heart of autonomous systems. Before these systems came along, engineers were principally concerned with the questions 'what does the system do?' and 'when does the system do it?'. But, now, we must address the key question relating to autonomy: 'why does the system choose to do this?'. As we will see later, having viable formal verification techniques impacts upon a wide range of areas: safety, ethics, certification, and so on.

In the following chapters, we will describe *hybrid agent architectures* where high-level decision-making in an autonomous system is carried out by a type of software component referred to as a *cognitive agent*. This architecture and the use of cognitive agents enable us to perform formal verification of the system's decision-making.

Part I

Foundations

2

Autonomous Systems Architectures

In this chapter, we provide an introduction to *architectures* for autonomous systems, specifically the software managing all the components within, and interactions between components of, an autonomous system. The description here is in no way comprehensive, and there are many other sources, for example Brooks (1999) and Winfield (2012), that provide much more detail. We will touch upon some of the theoretical aspects, such as layered/behavioural versus symbolic/component views or continuous control versus discrete control, will discuss practical architectural styles, such as hierarchical control systems and hybrid architectures, and will highlight practical robotic middle-ware, such as the *Robot Operating System* (ROS) (Quigley et al., 2009).

This background will help to motivate and explain the development of *hybrid agent architectures*. This style of autonomous system architecture will then be the one we primarily use throughout the rest of this book.

2.1 Architectures for Autonomous Systems

Embodied autonomous systems comprise many different physical components. Typically, these are *sensors* (such as cameras, infrared detectors, and motion trackers), components for *propulsion* (such as wheels, engines, legs, and wings), *communication* (such as Bluetooth, GPS, screens, and voice), and more general *actuators* (such as arms, magnets, and lifting aids). All these must be brought together and controlled to achieve the tasks associated with the overall system and, as is standard in Engineering, each of these physical components will likely have some form of software *control system* that manages its behaviour. Predominantly, *feedback* control systems (which use sensors to monitor the state of the system and then adjust actuators based on how far the sensor readings are from some ideal) are used at this level to adapt the behaviour of the component to that of its function and its environment.

Once we have such control components, they can be organised into numerous different architectures, some of which are briefly described.

Symbolic Artificial Intelligence: Sense–Plan–Act. A straightforward and modular approach, rooted in methods for logical reasoning by machines (often referred to as symbolic artificial intelligence), is that of the *sense–plan–act* architecture. Here, *sensing* is carried out to gather information about the system's environment, typically by invoking the system's sensors. This is then used to construct an internal 'world model', and then symbolic *planning* is invoked upon this world model in order to attempt to achieve the system's goals. The plan constructed is subsequently transformed into *actions* that are sent to the lower-level components to undertake. And then the activity cycles back to sensing.

Engineering: Hierarchical Control Systems. Once we have a collection of controllers managing the system's physical interactions, we can, in turn, generate a control system that, itself, manages a set of such sub-components. We can think of the basic control systems as sitting at the bottom of some layered data structure. Above these are the first layer of controllers, each of which manages some subset of the systems at the bottom layer. Further control elements, in the next layer up, handle sets of manager controllers, and so on. These layers can be viewed as a mathematical tree structure, with 'leaves' in the bottom layer each connected to only one controller 'node' in the layer above, and these nodes are connected to a single node in the layer above them. Each controller handles data/activity from the layer below, packages these up, and then sends them up to the node above. Similarly, a node interprets commands from above and delegates them to subordinate nodes below. It is typical that nodes nearer to the root of this tree deal with higher-level, more abstract, behaviours, while leaf nodes typically characterise detailed sensor or actuator control.

Robotics: Subsumption Architecture. The above idea of an abstraction hierarchy also influences *subsumption architectures* that are popular in robotics. As in hierarchical control systems, the higher layers represent more abstract behaviours than lower layers. Individual layers in a subsumption architecture form finite state machines, all of which take input directly from the sensors. Data is transmitted between the nodes of each layer in order to form a behaviour. A higher layer can *subsume* a lower layer by inserting new information into the data connections between its nodes (Brooks, 1986). So, for example, any decision made by a node may take into account decisions from nodes above it because of data inserted by the higher-level node, but if no information comes

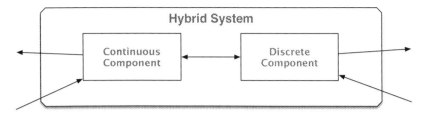

Figure 2.1 Hybrid agent architecture

from higher up, a node acts independently. As this approach was developed in part as a response to top-down planning approaches (such as sense–plan–act, mentioned earlier in the chapter), there is no identifiable planning node. Instead, behaviours at a node are activated through a combination of sensor inputs and behaviours from above.

To some extent, we can see the aforementioned sense–plan–act and subsumption approaches as mirror structures; each is hierarchical: one being driven primarily by the control/input aspects, the other being driven primarily by abstract/planning aspects. Neither of these approaches is without problems. The sense–plan–act approach, in its simplest form, can potentially be too slow when limited computational resources are available since it represents a centralised approach to reasoning about the current situation in its entirety. The tightly constrained cycle can restrict flexibility and efficiency, especially if the system becomes embroiled in time-consuming planning over complex models. Subsumption architectures are typically more efficient, but are often seen as being quite *opaque*; decisions are made somewhere in the hierarchy, but the reasons for these decisions can be hard to isolate.

There are a range of variations and approaches that attempt to take elements from each of these. These can often be classed under the umbrella term *hybrid architectures* (Figure 2.1), which typically involve the interaction between *continuous* components that deal with reasoning with numbers often involving differential equations and produce outputs that are numbers and that are often continuous in a mathematical sense – meaning that similar inputs generate similar outputs. Discrete components deal with more logical reasoning over whether facts are true or false and whether their outputs tend to be zeros and ones (or trues and falses).

Artificial Intelligence: Three–Layer Architectures. These architectures are again hierarchical, with the higher level being concerned with abstract planning and deliberation, while the lowest-level layer is concerned with feedback control mechanisms (Firby, 1990). The activity within the layers of a three-layer architecture tends to be much more autonomous than that prescribed by the fixed sense–plan–act cycle. So, sensing can be going on while deliberation occurs and both might be occurring in the background while external communication is being undertaken.

Engineering: Hybrid Control Systems. In a traditional hierarchical control system, all layers use continuous control controllers. *Hybrid* control systems typically mix continuous and discrete components. The continuous nodes are feedback control systems, as often with mathematically continuous behaviour. The discrete nodes control activity amongst the continuous nodes and, often, provide *discontinuous* changes in behaviour switching between quite different continuous controllers depending upon the situation – so two similar sets of inputs may produce very different behaviours. This kind of behaviour is difficult to produce using hierarchies of continuous controllers. Continuous controllers tend to be efficient at optimising with respect to the system's environment but, if the situation changes radically, this optimisation might be inappropriate. The discrete component gives the possibility of making a significant change, potentially between distinct continuous control regimes, either provoked by a big change in the environment or possibly by an internal choice.

These hybrid architectures are both flexible and very popular, but again have problems. From our viewpoint, their primary problem is that, as with subsumption architectures, the reasons for decisions are often very hard to discern. Recently, and particularly in autonomous vehicles, the use of *hybrid* **agent** *architectures* has increased.

2.2 Agent Architectures

An 'agent' is an abstraction developed to capture autonomous behaviour within complex, dynamic systems (Wooldridge, 2002). It is defined by Russell and Norvig (2003) as something that 'can be viewed as **perceiving** its environment through **sensors** and **acting** upon that environment through **effectors**'. There are many versions of the 'agent' concept (Franklin and Graesser, 1996), including ones in which the environment it perceives and acts upon is a software system, but the basic concept lends itself naturally to robotic and autonomous systems in which a decision-making component must perceive and act upon some external environment.

In agent architectures for autonomous systems, we encapsulate decision-making as a component programmed as an agent within the larger system.

Since the core new aspect of such a system is autonomous decision-making we can see how this decision-making agent component has a key role in this type of architecture. The agent must make decisions based on the perceptions it has from its environment (which is often dynamic and unpredictable) and under hard deadlines. In principle, the agent might *learn* new high-level behaviours besides making choices about behaviours. As suggested by Wooldridge (2002), an agent must fundamentally be capable of *flexible autonomous action*. Since we are encapsulating decision-making within these components, we require them to be, as much as possible, *rational* agents. These are loosely defined as agents that 'do the right thing' (Russell and Norvig, 2003).

Since the 1980s, the agent approach, and the concept of rational agents in particular, has spawned a *vast* range of research (Bond and Gasser, 1988; Bratman et al., 1988; Cohen and Levesque, 1990; Davis and Smith, 1983; Durfee et al., 1989; Shoham, 1993), not only regarding the philosophy behind autonomous decision-making but also programming languages/frameworks and practical industrial exploitation.[1] It has become clear that the agent metaphor is very useful in capturing many practical situations involving complex systems comprising flexible, autonomous, and distributed components.

Yet, it turns out that the 'rational agent' concept on its own is still not enough! Continuous control systems, neural networks, genetic algorithms, and so on, can all make decisions (and in many cases are designed to make these decisions rationally) and so are autonomous. However, while agents comprising such components can indeed act autonomously, the reasons for their choice of actions are often opaque. Consequently, these systems are very hard to develop and control. From our point of view, they are also difficult to formally analyse, and hence difficult to use where reliability and transparency are paramount.

In reaction to these issues, the *beliefs–desires–intentions* model of agency has become more popular as a mechanism for implementing decision-making. Agents following this model are sometimes referred to as *cognitive* agents. Again, there are many variations on this (Bratman, 1987; Rao and Georgeff, 1992; Wooldridge and Rao, 1999), and we will examine these further in Chapter 3, but we consider a cognitive agent to be one which

must have explicit reasons for making the choices it does, and should be able to explain these if necessary.

---

[1] IFAAMAS — The International Foundation for Autonomous Agents and Multiagent Systems – www.ifaamas.org.

Rational cognitive agents typically provide

1. *pro-activeness*

   that is, the agent is not driven solely by events and so it takes the initiative and generates, and attempts to achieve, its own goals

2. *social activity*

   that is, the agent interacts with other (sometimes human) agents and can cooperate with these in order to achieve some of its goals

3. *deliberation*

   that is, the agent can reason about its current state and can modify its subsequent actions and future goals according to its knowledge about situation.

Crucially, rational cognitive agents adapt their autonomous behaviour in an analysable fashion to cater for the dynamic aspects of their environment, requirements, goals, and knowledge.

Example 2.1 Spacecraft Landing

Imagine a cognitive agent controlling a spacecraft that is attempting to land on a planet. The agent has:

control of dynamic activity . . . . for example, thrust, direction, and so on;

information (i.e., 'knowledge'/'belief') . . . . for example, about the terrain and target landing sites;

motivations (i.e., 'goals') . . . for example, to land soon, and to remain aloft until safe to land.

The cognitive agent must dynamically

- *assess*, and possibly *revise*, the information held
- *generate* new motivations or *revise* current ones
- *decide* what to do, that is, *deliberate* over motivations/information

---

So, the requirement for *reasoned* decisions and explanations has refined the basic *hybrid agent architecture* approach (Figure 2.2) in order to require that the discrete agent component is actually a *cognitive* agent. These autonomous systems are based on the hybrid combination of

1. *cognitive agent* for **high-level** autonomous (discrete) decisions and

2. traditional *control systems* for **low-level** (continuous) activities.

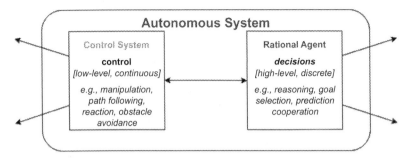

Figure 2.2 Hybrid agent architecture

These can be easier to *understand, program,* and *maintain* and, often, be much more *flexible.*

It is important to note that, while there is typically just one cognitive agent, as autonomous (and particularly robotic) systems have become more complex, such architectures have involved an increasing number of other components. These could be multiple sensor control systems (including sophisticated image classification systems for perception), learning systems, planners, schedulers, monitors, navigation components, and so on. These will not all be traditional control systems, but can be composed of neural networks, genetic algorithms, or any mechanism for finding solutions to adaptive problems. We will touch on the wider issue of verification of these complex modular systems in Chapter 5.

Aside: Governor/Arbiter Agents. While these hybrid agent architectures are increasingly popular, many autonomous systems are still constructed using complex control hierarchies. We will see later that the possibility of identifying a high-level decision-making component can be advantageous for deep analysis, particularly where legal, safety, or ethical arguments need to be made. However, even for more opaque control architectures, there is a useful option. If the idea of an agent is not built into the architecture, we can, in some cases, add an agent to the system as an arbiter or governor (Figure 2.3). Here, the agent decides whether to *approve* or *reject* any proposed course of action for the autonomous system. This means, for example, that decisions about the safety, legality, or ethics of any course of action are assessed in a discrete (and analysable) way.

This is the approach taken by Arkin in his proposed *ethical governor* (Arkin, 2008) used in military uncrewed aerial vehicle (UAV) operations. This governor conducts an evaluation of the ethical appropriateness of a plan prior to

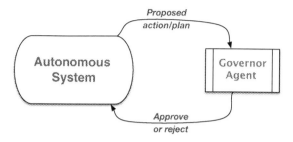

Figure 2.3 Governor architecture

its execution, prohibiting plans deemed unethical. Similarly, Woodman et al. (2012) developed a *protection layer*, which aims to filter out unsafe actions.

Though not explicitly constructed with an agent at its core, we can still view these system–agent pairs as hybrid agent systems.

We will see examples of these governor architectures in Chapters 10 and 13.

2.3 Modularity in Modern Robotic Software

It is widely recognised that robotic systems need to be programmed in a modular fashion, allowing software packages from different suppliers to be integrated into a single system. There are a number of technologies available to support this integration. One of the better known of these technologies is the Robot Operating System (ROS) (Quigley et al., 2009). This system enables individual software components, termed *nodes*, to specify their behaviour in terms of the messages they exchange with other parts of the system and provides support for nodes to communicate via ROS *core* nodes. The ROS distribution provides APIs for programming nodes in C and Python, and there is also support for programming ROS nodes in other languages (Crick et al., 2011).

The Robot Operating System does not impose any particular architecture upon a system built using it. Nodes may operate in publisher–subscriber or client–server modes (or both at once for different functionalities). Links may be made freely between any nodes in the system, as it is the structure of these links that will determine the particular architecture of any system built using ROS. However, the abstraction imposed by ROS upon an autonomous system – that of self-contained nodes that communicate via messages – has proved powerful and appealing, enabling the easy reuse of particular components for, for instance, image processing across multiple systems.

2.4 Practical Systems

In this book, we discuss the development of rational cognitive agent languages for programming autonomous systems, particularly in aerospace and robotics, and so we focus on the use of hybrid agent architectures. The cognitive agent can be programmed in any of the many agent programming languages, almost all of which have interpreters implemented in Java. Examples of such systems include

Autonomous Convoying System The autonomous convoy is a queue of vehicles in which the first is controlled by a human driver, but subsequent vehicles are controlled autonomously (Kamali et al., 2017).[2] The autonomously controlled 'follower' vehicles maintain a safe distance from the vehicle in front. When a human driving a vehicle wishes to join a convoy, they signal their intent to the convoy lead vehicle, together with the position in the convoy they wish to join. Autonomous systems in the lead vehicle then instructs the vehicle that will be behind the new one to drop back, creating a gap for it to move into. When the gap is large enough, the human driver is informed that they may change lane. Once this is achieved, autonomous systems take control and move all the vehicles to the minimum safe convoying distance. Similar protocols are followed when a driver wishes to leave the convoy.

Maintenance of minimum safe distances between vehicles is handled by two low-level control systems. When the convoy is in formation, control is managed using distance sensors and wireless messages from the lead vehicle. These messages inform the convoy when the lead vehicle is braking or accelerating and so allow smooth responses from the whole convoy to these events. This reduces the safe minimum distance to one where fuel efficiency gains are possible. In some situations control uses sensors alone (e.g., during leaving and joining). In these situations the minimum safe distance is larger.

A cognitive agent system manages the messaging protocols for leaving and joining, and switches between the control systems for distance maintenance. For instance, if a communication breakdown is detected, the agent switches to safe distance control based on sensors alone. A simulation of the vehicle control systems was created in MATLAB[3] and connected to the TORCS[4] racing car simulator.

---

[2] Software available from `github.com/VerifiableAutonomy`.
[3] `uk.mathworks.com`.
[4] `torcs.sourceforge.net`.

We will discuss this system in more detail with a focus on its verification in Chapter 11.

An Autonomous Robotic Arm The autonomous robotic arm system performs sort and segregate tasks such as waste recycling or nuclear waste management[5] (Aitken et al., 2014, 2017). The system is required to view a set of items on a tray and identify those items. It must determine what should be done with each one (e.g., composted, used for paper recycling or glass recycling) and then move each item to a suitable location.

The system integrates computer vision, a robot arm, and agent-based decision-making. It is implemented in ROS (Quigley et al., 2009). Computer vision identifies items on a tray (Shaukat et al., 2015). Their identities and locations are communicated to the agent that makes decisions about what should be done with each object. These decisions involve, for instance, sending anything that is plant matter to be composted, paper for recycling, and bricks for landfill. These decisions are then enacted by control systems.

Satellite Formations Traditionally, a satellite is a large and very expensive piece of equipment, tightly controlled by a ground team with little scope for autonomy. Recently, however, the space industry has sought to abandon large monolithic platforms in favour of multiple, smaller, more autonomous, satellites working in teams to accomplish the task of a larger vehicle through distributed methods. The system described here embeds existing technology for generating feedback controllers and configuring satellite systems within an agent-based decision-maker. The agent relies on *discrete* information (e.g., 'a thruster is broken'), while system control uses *continuous* information (e.g., 'thruster fuel pressure is 65.3').

In the example a group of satellites can assume and maintain various formations while performing fault monitoring and recovery. This allows them to undertake collaborative surveying work in environments such as geostationary and low Earth orbits and among semi-charted asteroid fields. The system and scenarios are described more fully in Lincoln et al. (2013). We describe its verification in Chapter 8.

Lego Rovers The LEGO Rovers system (Figure 2.4) was developed to introduce the concepts of abstraction and cognitive agent programming to

---

[5] The robotic arm system involves proprietary software developed jointly by the universities of Liverpool, Sheffield, and Surrey and National Nuclear Labs. Requests for access to the code or experimental data should be made to Profs Fisher, Veres, or Gao.

Figure 2.4 The LEGO Rovers system. Image courtesy of Phil Jimmieson and Sophie Dennis. Used with permission

school children.[6] It is used in science clubs by volunteer members of the STEM Ambassador scheme,[7] and has also been used in larger-scale events and demonstrations. The activity introduces the user to a teleoperated LEGO robot and asks them to imagine it is a planetary rover. The robot's sensors are explained; the user is shown how the incoming data is abstracted into beliefs such as *obstacle* or *path* using simple thresholds and can then create simple rules for a software agent, using a GUI, which dictates how the robot should react to the appearance and disappearance of obstacles, and so on. Aspects of the LEGO Rovers architecture are described in Dennis et al. (2016).

---

[6] legorovers.csc.liv.ac.uk/ software available at github.com/legorovers.
[7] www.stemnet.org.uk/ambassadors/.

3

Agent Decision-Maker

In this chapter we overview the concept of an agent and in particular the concept of a *rational cognitive agent* that can make decisions as part of an autonomous system. To do this we will briefly introduce ideas from logic programming and show how they can be extended to model the *beliefs*, *desires*, and *intentions* of a software agent.

We will then introduce the GWENDOLEN agent programming language that uses these ideas to write programs that run within some environment created using the Java-based *agent infrastructure layer*.

3.1 Agents and Cognitive Agents

How do we describe and implement the 'intelligent' decision-making component we described in Chapter 2? In the past this has often been conflated with the dynamic control subsystems, the whole being described using a large, possibly hierarchical control system, genetic algorithm, or neural network. However, we provide an architecture in which this autonomous, 'intelligent' decision-making component is captured as an agent.

But: what is an 'agent'? First, a little background. The development and analysis of autonomous systems, particularly autonomous software, is different to 'traditional' software in one crucial aspect. In designing, analysing, or monitoring 'normal' software we typically care about

- *what* the software does, and
- *when* the software does it.

Since autonomous software has to *make its own decisions*, it is usually important to be able to analyse not only what the software does and when it does it, but also

- *why* the software did something.[1]

This need – the ability to describe why a system chooses one course of action over another – provides new entities to be analysed. A very useful abstraction for capturing such autonomous behaviour within complex, dynamic systems turns out to be the concept of an *agent* (Franklin and Graesser, 1996) that we introduced in Chapter 2. It has become clear that this agent metaphor is extremely useful for capturing many practical situations involving complex systems comprising flexible, autonomous, and distributed components. In essence, agents must fundamentally be capable of *flexible autonomous action* (Wooldridge, 2002). Since work on agents came into prominence in the 1980s, there has been *vast* development within both academia and industry (Bond and Gasser, 1988; Cohen and Levesque, 1990; Durfee et al., 1989; Shoham, 1993).

However, the basic concept of an 'agent' is still not enough for us and so we utilise the enhanced concept of a *rational cognitive agent*. Again, there are many variations (Bratman, 1987; Rao and Georgeff, 1992; Wooldridge and Rao, 1999) but we can consider this to be an agent which

> *has explicit* reasons *for making the choices it does, and is able to explain these if necessary.*

It is crucial, both for transparency and for the allocation of responsibility, that such a rational cognitive agent can be examined to discover *why* it chose a certain course of action. These agents are often programmed and analysed by describing their *motivations* (e.g., 'goals'), their *information* (e.g., 'knowledge' or 'belief'), and how these change over time (see Section 3.2). Rational cognitive agents can then adapt their autonomous behaviour to cater for the dynamic aspects of their environment, their requirements, and their knowledge. Typically, they can also modify their decision-making as computation proceeds.

The predominant form of rational cognitive agent architecture is that provided through the *Beliefs*, *Desires*, and *Intentions* (BDI) model of agency (Rao and Georgeff, 1991, 1992). Here, the *beliefs* represent the agent's (probably incomplete, possibly incorrect) information about itself, other agents, and its environment, *desires* represent the agent's long-term goals, and *intentions* represent the goals that the agent is actively pursuing. The BDI approach has been enormously influential, not only in academia (Rao and Georgeff, 1995) but also in real applications (Muscettola et al., 1998).

---

[1] It should be noted that we do not include some concept of explicit explainability as part of the definition of an autonomous system – however, we do note that the high-level decision-making capabilities possessed by many autonomous systems tend to introduce questions of *why* during debugging, testing, and assurance processes.

3.2 Agent Programming

We will use a rational cognitive agent to provide the core autonomous decision-making component within an autonomous system. But, how can cognitive agents be programmed? Commonly, programming languages for cognitive agents (Bordini et al., 2005, 2009) utilise:

- a set of *beliefs*, representing the information the agent has;
- a set of *goals*, representing the motivations the agent has (in BDI approaches these map to the agent's desires);
- a set of *rules/plans*, representing the agent's options for achieving its goals;
- a set of *actions*, corresponding to the agent's external acts (that are often delegated to other parts of the system); and
- deliberation mechanisms for deciding between alternative goals/plans/ actions.

The majority of cognitive agent programming languages, essentially those based on the BDI approach, are provided as extensions of the logic programming language Prolog so, to understand how these programming languages work we will begin with a brief survey of the logic programming paradigm. It is not our intention to provide a detailed tutorial on formal specification, logics, or proof. We provide this background to help clarify later discussions on agent programming and verification. We assume basic familiarity with classical propositional and first-order logic.

3.2.1 Classical Logic and Horn Clauses

We can view logic as a language that allows us to describe, or model, some abstraction of objects or actions that occur in reality. Of course, logic is not the only choice we have for such a language; an obvious alternative being English. However, as we wish to be precise and unambiguous, we require a more 'formal' language with well-defined semantics and a consistent reasoning mechanism. In spite of this, even if logic is used to model practical scenarios, we must recognise that a logic represents a particular abstraction. Naturally, if we want to represent a more complex or more detailed view of the world, a more refined formal system must be used. As Ambrose Bierce so elegantly put it, logic is 'the art of thinking and reasoning in strict accordance with the limitations and incapacities of human misunderstanding' (Bierce, 2001).

An analogy of this occurs in the field of mechanics. For several centuries, *Newtonian Mechanics* was believed to describe all the mechanical properties of real-world objects. Indeed, it seemed to work easily for any of the practical examples that people tried. However, in the twentieth century, physicists discovered situations where Newtonian Mechanics did not give the correct answers (e.g., objects moving *very* quickly). Thus, a more detailed abstraction of the world was required and *Relativistic Mechanics* was devised. So, in order to describe more aspects of the real world, a simple system that was easily applicable to everyday situations was replaced by a more complex system in which calculations about everyday situations were hopelessly intricate.

There are a wide variety of logical systems that have been developed. Fortunately, all have several things in common. Each consists of two parts: a *model theory*, which is concerned with the statements in the logic model and provides semantics for such statements; and a *proof theory*, which is concerned with how statements in the language can be combined and reasoned about.

A simple logic with which the reader is hopefully familiar is classical, *propositional*, logic. Here, we construct logical statements solely from the constructs *and, if....then, or, not* (written $\wedge$, $\Rightarrow$, $\vee$, $\neg$), together with a set of propositional variables that can only have the value **true** or **false**.

We now turn to how can we adapt propositional logic so that we can use it as a way of programming reasoning in an approach referred to as logic programming.

Horn Clauses. There are various ways to organise propositional formulae, one particularly useful one being *Conjunctive Normal Form (CNF)*. A propositional formula in CNF is a conjunction ('$\wedge$') of disjunctions ('$\vee$' – referred to as clauses or conjuncts) of propositional *literals* (either propositional variables or negated propositional variables).

While normal forms such as CNF are widely used, there are variations that have improved computational properties and, hence, even wider application.

Definition 3.1 A *Horn Clause* is a clause (i.e., a disjunction of literals) containing at most one positive literal.

Definition 3.2 A Horn Clause is *definite* if it contains a positive literal; otherwise it is a *negative* Horn Clause.

Example 3.1 Below are simple examples of different classes of Horn Clause.

$a \vee \neg b \vee \neg c$ is a definite Horn Clause.
$\neg a \vee \neg b \vee \neg c$ is a negative Horn Clause.
a is a definite Horn Clause, but it is also a unit clause.
$a \vee \neg b \vee c$ is not a Horn Clause.

Rule Interpretation of Horn Clauses. One useful way to represent Horn Clauses is as *rules*, *facts*, or *goals*. The analogy between this rule form and the clausal form is as follows.

- A definite clause, such as

$$a \lor \neg b \lor \neg c$$

 is equivalent to the implication

$$(b \land c) \Rightarrow a.$$

Thus, the negative literals represent some *hypothesis* while the positive literal can be considered as the conclusion.

 We can also write such an implication as a *rule*, that is, in the form

$$a \leftarrow b, c.$$

This can be interpreted as, for instance, 'to do a you need to do b and c' or 'to produce a you need to produce b and c'.

- A positive Horn Clause, such as

$$d$$

 can be represented as a *fact* ('d' is definitely *True*).
- A negative Horn Clause, such as

$$\neg a$$

 can be represented as the implication

$$a \Rightarrow \textbf{false}$$

 and then as the *goal* ('the system needs to do a')

$$\leftarrow a.$$

Note that where we have an implication: $A \Rightarrow C$ we often refer to the formula before the arrow as the *antecedent* and the formula after the arrow as the *consequent*.

 This is the essential form of clause structure that underlies logic programming and hence many cognitive agent programming languages.

3.2.2 First-Order Logic

One of the main limitations of propositional logic is that it cannot reason over complex structures. This is achieved in first-order (predicate) logic by allowing propositional symbols to have arguments ranging over the elements of these structures. These proposition symbols are then called *predicate* symbols.

Further expressivity also stems from the availability of quantifiers and variables. These allow us to state facts about elements of the structure without enumerating the particular elements.

Language of First-Order Logic. The language of first-order logic consists of the symbols from propositional logic, together with symbols for variables, constants, functions, and predicates.

The set of *terms* are the constants and variables plus expressions built by applying function symbols to other terms (e.g., $john$, $jane$, $father(john)$ (john's father), and so on).

The set of *atomic formulae* are the propositional symbols, **true**, **false**, and expressions built by applying predicate symbols to terms (e.g., $is\_parent(john, father(john))$).

The set of *well-formed formulae* (WFF) consists of the atomic formulae, expressions constructed by applying propositional connectives to WFFs and $\forall x.A$ and $\exists x.A$, where x is a variable and A is a WFF (e.g., $\forall x.is\_parent(x, father(x))$).

A variable can occur in a formula without an enclosing quantifier. When used in this way, a variable is said to be *free*, whereas a variable that occurs in a formula and in an enclosing quantifier is said to be *bound*.

If a formula has no free variables, it is called a *closed* formula. If it has neither free nor bound variables, it is called a *ground* formula.

Now we can revisit our definition of Horn Clauses to provide a first-order analogue. Deduction within such clauses provides the basis for logic programming (Kowalski, 1979; Sterling and Shapiro, 1987).

Definition 3.3 A *Horn Clause* is a universally quantified logical implication consisting of a conjunction of atomic formulae and negated atomic formulae as the antecedent and a single atomic formula as the consequent.

3.2.3 Logic Programming and Prolog

Logic programming grew out of attempts to automate formal human reasoning. It represents programs as a set of *Horn Clauses*.

In Prolog, Horn Clauses are written with the consequent first, then the symbol ' : – ' representing the implication, and then the conjuncts that form the antecedent are listed separately by commas.

Example 3.2   The following are all logical formulas as they would be written in Prolog.

```
h  :- t1, t2, ... , tn.
t1 :- z1.
t2 :- z2.
...
z1.
z2.
...
```

The execution of a Prolog program attempts to determine the truth of some formula by evaluating and simplifying the system based on rules and facts.

Example 3.3   Continuing with Example 3.2, if Prolog were executed to discover the truth of 'h' then the program would check first if t1 were true (which it is because z1 is true), then check if t2 were true (again, it is), and so on eventually returning the answer yes.

Implementations of logic programming have built-in search capabilities (so if there are a number of ways some formula might be true, the underlying implementation will search through all of these), allowing a programmer to focus on capturing the information describing the problem, rather than programming the search for the solution.

Prolog enables the computation of values with the use of variables. Variables represent the logical concept of 'for all' in positive clauses and 'exists' in negative clauses and are represented as capital letters. Quantifiers themselves are omitted from Prolog programs. Prolog instantiates the variables in a solution using a process called *unification* which matches capital letters representing variables to ground terms. We will not cover the full details of unification here but will illustrate it with an example.

Example 3.4   The logical formula

$$\forall x.\, q(x) \rightarrow p(x)$$

would be represented in Prolog as

```
p(X) :- q(X).
```

where X is a variable to be instantiated by unification. Consider a larger program

```
p(X) :- q(X).
q(a).
```

A goal is a negative literal and so the Y in a goal p(Y) is existentially quantified meaning the goal is asking if there exists some value for Y that makes p(Y) true. If the above Prolog program were executed with the goal p(Y) then Prolog would match (unify) the Y in the goal with the X in p(X) :- q(X). Then it would check to see if q(X) were true, and would see that it is as long as X is instantiated to 'a'. So if X = a and Y = X then the goal is true so Prolog would return

```
Y = a
```

naming the instantiation that makes the goal true.

Logic programming languages such as Prolog are exemplars of *declarative programming* whereby a problem is stated in a high-level (often logical) language and the underlying computational mechanism uses sophisticated search algorithms to find a solution to the problem.

3.2.4 Logic Programming for Agents: Events, Beliefs, and Goals

Cognitive agent programming languages seek to extend logic programming with the concepts of beliefs and goals and, in some cases, events. They are generally based on the BDI paradigm with the events, beliefs, and goals (desires) controlling the creation of intentions that are then executed. The extensions vary in many ways though there are some features that are common to most, including:

- use of traditional Prolog to reason about beliefs (and goals);
- limiting search capabilities (especially where there are external actions);

- using the consequent of each Horn Clause to react to events; and
- using *guards* to restrict the applicability of clauses.

In general the Horn Clauses of logic programming become *plans* in BDI agent programming, and these plans are used to represent the implementation of intentions. In most of these languages, an agent can maintain several *intentions* and even be working on separate plans within each intention.

Beliefs and Goals. Nearly all cognitive agent languages utilise the concepts of beliefs and goals. Beliefs are propositions that the agent believes to be true and are stored in a *belief base*. Goals are states of the world the agent wants to bring about and are stored in a *goal base*. Beliefs and Goals may be added to the bodies of plans and checked for in guards on plans. Beliefs may also be added because of information provided from elsewhere, such as from external perception.

Actions. Actions are things the agent can do. In most cases we assume they have some effect on the external environment which the agent may subsequently need to assess. In languages which use them, actions are executed in the bodies of plans. In some cases actions may have explicit pre- and post-conditions which capture part of how the environment is modelled.

Plans. In agent programming languages, plans typically look similar to *Guarded Horn Clauses* (Ueda, 1985). They provide a logical guard, expressed in terms of beliefs (and goals), and then (a list of) deeds to be carried out when the guard is satisfied. Deeds can include actions, belief updates, and goal updates. In many languages plans are triggered by events.

The Reasoning Cycle. Much as Prolog is driven by a built-in (depth-first) search mechanism, logic-based agent languages have a built-in *reasoning cycle*. The reasoning cycle controls when events are reacted to, searching is invoked, plans are selected, executed, and so on.

The Environment. Unlike many programming languages, we assume, following the definition of an agent, that agent programs execute within some external environment. This environment may itself be a software entity representing/simulating the context in which the agent resides or it may be the real world. In autonomous systems it is often a combination of the two, consisting of sensors and actuators for some physical system as well as other nodes in the architecture. An agent programming language's reasoning cycle controls when external perceptions and messages arrive at the agent from the environment and when (and in some cases how) an agent's actions affect the environment. As we will see later, the environment in our case (as well as comprising other agents) will often be a software simulation of the 'real world' written in Java.

3.2.5 Operational Semantics

Most BDI agent programming languages have an explicit formal definition given in terms of an *operational semantics* (Plotkin, 1981). The operational semantics describes the execution of the program on some formalised, abstract machine. An agent's state is represented as a tuple of mathematical objects in this abstract machine and transition rules describe how an agent in one state can change to be in a different state. This completely describes the possible executions, upon this abstract machine, of any agent written in the programming language.

Example 3.5   Below is an example semantic rule describing how the agent reacts when the next item (within the current intention structure) is the addition of a belief:

$$\frac{\text{head}_d(i) = +b}{\langle ag, B, i, I \rangle \rightarrow \langle ag, \quad B \cup b, \quad \text{tail}_i(i) \quad I \rangle}$$

The tuple representing the agent state is here represented as an identifier, ag, a set of beliefs B, a current intention i, and a set of other (ongoing, but not active) intentions I (in this particular example we do not worry about goals or plans). Above the line there is a condition for the semantic rule to apply, in this case that the 'head' item (known as a 'deed') within the intention must be the addition of a belief, b. The expression below the line shows how the rule changes the state of the agent from $\langle ag, B, i, I \rangle$ to a state where b is now in the belief base $B \cup b$ and it has been removed from i leaving only the 'tail' of the intention.

We will see in Chapter 6 how the operational semantics of our BDI programming language is central to its formal verification.

3.3 GWENDOLEN Programming Language

In this book we will be considering examples written in the GWENDOLEN programming language, a typical BDI language designed for use with the AJPF

model-checker. GWENDOLEN and AJPF are both part of the MCAPL framework (Dennis, 2018)[2].

For those familiar with the input languages for model-checkers, it should be
noted that GWENDOLEN programs are intended for the *actual programming*
of cognitive agents. Input languages for most model-checkers are normally
designed to encourage abstractions (in particular the omission of details that
may be important to the actual execution of the program but are irrelevant to
the truth of the properties under consideration), and often have limited flexibility, in terms of program structuring, in order to maximise the efficiency
of model-checking. While GWENDOLEN does contain optimisations to aid
model-checking these appear in the implementation of its interpreter in Java
not as restrictions to constructs available to a programmer to use.

Documentation for GWENDOLEN appears in Appendix A. This includes instructions for running GWENDOLEN programs and a set of tutorials explaining
the language. This documentation is also available with the MCAPL distribution. In this section we will provide a brief introduction to GWENDOLEN,
primarily through a range of examples, the interested reader should refer to
Appendix A for full details.

GWENDOLEN Reasoning Cycle. We will begin with the general reasoning
cycle employed in GWENDOLEN. This is shown graphically in Figure 3.1. Execution starts at A where an intention is selected for processing. If no intentions
are available then the agent checks the environment for updated perceptions
and new messages (E) and then processes its inbox (F) – both of these steps
may generate new intentions. Once an intention has been selected then the
agent generates the plans that could be applied to achieve that intention (B).
This includes both new plans for handling a new event and processing the plan
already associated with the intention. The agent then selects a plan (C) and
then executes the top deed on the intention (D).

Syntax. GWENDOLEN uses many syntactic conventions from BDI agent languages: +b indicates the addition of the belief b; while −b indicates the removal of the belief; +!g [type] indicates the addition of the goal g of
type where the type can be either achieve (which means the goal persists
until the agent believes g – i.e., it believes it has successfully achieved making
g the case) or perform (which means that the goal is dropped once a plan
triggered by it is executed, even if the agent does not believe g is the case after
the execution of the plan).

---

[2] The MCAPL framework is available from
https://autonomy-and-verification.github.io/tools/mcapl and
archived at Zenodo (DOI: 10.5281/zenodo.5720861.svg).

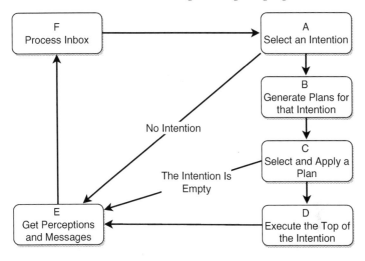

Figure 3.1 The GWENDOLEN reasoning cycle

Plans each have three components:

$$trigger \ : \ guard \ <- \ body.$$

Here, the 'trigger' is usually the addition of a goal or a belief (beliefs may be acquired thanks not only to external perception but as a result of internal deliberation), the 'guard' states what conditions about the agent's beliefs and goals must be true before the plan can be invoked, and the 'body' is a stack of 'deeds' the agent should perform in order to execute the plan. These deeds typically involve the addition and deletion of both goals and beliefs as well as *actions* (such as move_to(X1, Y1)) referring to code that is delegated to external, non-agent components.

Below is our first, very simple, GWENDOLEN program.[3]

Example 3.6   There is one agent called ag1 that starts with the initial belief 'empty' and an initial *achieve* goal 'pickup'. The agent has one plan, stating that if the agent acquires the goal 'pickup' as an event, and it believes 'empty_gripper' (the *guard*) then it should add the belief 'pickup', delete the belief 'empty_gripper' and then print 'done' (note that normally

---

[3] The examples in this chapter can be found in MCAPL distribution at folder
src/examples/verifiableautonomoussystems/chapter3.

we would expect an autonomous agent to perform some kind of action followed by a perception check before adding a belief that something had succeeded. We will introduce this kind of behaviour in later examples).

```
:name: ag1                                                          1
                                                                    2
:Initial Beliefs:                                                   3
                                                                    4
empty_gripper                                                       5
                                                                    6
:Initial Goals:                                                     7
                                                                    8
pickup [achieve]                                                    9
                                                                   10
:Plans:                                                            11
                                                                   12
+!pickup [achieve] : {B empty_gripper} ←                           13
    +pickup, −empty_gripper, print(done);                          14
```

When this program is executed the initial belief (`empty_gripper`) is added to the agent's belief base and the initial goal (`pickup`) is added to its goal base. Both of these additions are posted as events. Because the plan is triggered when the goal is posted *and* its guard is true (because of the initial belief), the plan body is executed. '`done`' is printed, as expected.

Communication. Of course, as well as an agent interacting with its (physical) environment, we can have multiple agents (each interacting with their environment) communicating together. Agents can communicate with each other using messages. In particular, the action

`.send(Agent, Performative, Content)`

sends a message to `Agent`, with a `Performative` type of instruction, and with content `Content`. An agent can then have plans specifically for dealing with particular sorts of messages using the special event

`+.received(Performative, Content).`

Each `Performative` is a speech act (Searle, 1969), such as *tell* or *perform*, commonly used in agent communication (FIPA, 2002), while `Content` is an atomic first-order formula.

Example 3.7 describes a simple program in which two agents, `ag1` and `ag2`, communicate about a block that one of them is holding.

Example 3.7 Agent `ag1` initially believes it is holding a block, `hold(block)` and wants to achieve the state 'empty_gripper'. It has four plans. The first tells it to add a belief if it receives a message with the `:tell` performative, and the second to add a goal if receives a message with the `:perform` performative. (In both cases, there is a guard that is always true — ⊤.) The third says it can achieve the `empty_gripper` state by asking `ag2` to take the block and then waiting until it is taken (the syntax *b means 'wait for b'). Finally, if it believes that some agent has taken the block then it adds the belief 'empty_gripper'.

Meanwhile `ag2` has identical plans for handling messages but also has a plan to react to a `take` goal by sending a message to the other agent to say that it has taken the block.

```
:name:  ag1                                                      1
                                                                 2
:Initial  Beliefs:                                               3
hold( block )                                                    4
                                                                 5
:Initial  Goals:                                                 6
empty_gripper  [ achieve ]                                       7
                                                                 8
:Plans:                                                          9
+.received (: tell , B): { ⊤ } ← +B;                            10
+.received (: perform , G): { ⊤ } ← +!G [ perform ];           11
+!empty_gripper [ achieve ]  :  {B hold ( block )} ←           12
        .send( ag2 , : perform , take( ag1 , block )),          13
        *take( ag2 , block );                                    14
+take( Ag, block )  :  { ⊤ } ← +empty_gripper;                 15
                                                                 16
                                                                 17
:name:  ag2                                                      18
                                                                 19
:Initial  Beliefs:                                               20
:Initial  Goals:                                                 21
                                                                 22
:Plans:                                                          23
+.received (: tell , B): { ⊤ } ← +B;                            24
+.received (: perform , G): { ⊤ } ← +!G [ perform ];           25
+!take( Ag, block ) [ perform ]  :  { ⊤ } ←                    26
        .send( Ag, : tell , take( ag2 , block ));                27
```

If we execute this in a configuration that prints out agent actions (see Sections A.2 and B.1 for more details on configuration and logging) we can see the agents exchanging messages in this program.

```
ag1 done send(2:take(ag1,block), ag2)
ag2 done send(1:take(ag2,block), ag1)
```

GWENDOLEN can reason using Prolog about the statements that appear in the guards of plans. This reasoning is captured as *Reasoning Rules*, and can be described using the following, longer, example. In Example 3.8 robots will collaborate to find 'survivors' in a simulated disaster rescue scenario.

Example 3.8   Here, a simple (simulated) robot is searching for a human in a grid. It does this by exploring all the squares in the grid and annotating each one as either 'empty' or as possibly containing a human. The agent (controlling the robot) has initial beliefs concerning the locations of the squares in the grid. It also has two reasoning rules (Reasoning rules can be applied to both beliefs and goals in GWENDOLEN, that is, an agent believes an area is empty if it believes there are no non-empty squares, but it can also have a goal to make the area empty if it has a goal that there should be no nonempty squares. In this simple program the reasoning rules are only applied to beliefs.):

- It deduces that an area is empty if it is not the case, ˜, that there is a square, square(X,Y), which it is not empty. In simpler language, the agent deduces an area is empty if it believes all the squares are empty.
- It also deduces that a grid square is unchecked, unchecked(X,Y), if there is a square, square(X,Y), and the agent is not at that square, the square is not empty and there is no human at that square.

The agent's goal is to leave the area, and it has five plans that can help it achieve this goal. The first is an initialisation plan. If the agent does not believe it is at some square then it should move to an unchecked square and add the belief that it is at that square. The second plan says that if it has not yet found a human, ˜B human, nor does it believe the area is empty, and there is an unchecked square then it should note that the current square is empty, move to the unchecked square and update its belief base accordingly. If it does not believe there is an unchecked square (third plan) then it simply notes this one is empty and removes its belief about its location. If it believes that there is a human in the current square then it adds a belief that it has found the human, and lastly if it believes the area is empty then it adds the belief that it can leave (thus achieving the goal).

Finally, when the agent adds the belief that it has found the human then it sends messages to a lifting robot informing it that it has found the human and then adds the belief that it can leave the area.

```
: Initial  Beliefs :                                               1
 square(0,0), square(0,1), square(0,2)                             2
 square(1,0), square(1,1), square(1,2)                             3
 square(2,0), square(2,1), square(2,2)                             4
                                                                   5
: Reasoning  Rules :                                               6
 emptyarea :-  ~(square(X,Y), ~empty(X,Y));                        7
 unchecked(X,Y) :- square(X,Y), ~at(X,Y),                          8
                   ~empty(X,Y), ~human(X,Y);                       9
                                                                   10
: Initial  Goals :                                                 11
 leave[achieve]                                                    12
                                                                   13
+! leave[achieve]: {~B at(X1,Y1), B unchecked(X,Y)}               14
   ← +at(X,Y),                                                     15
          move_to(X,Y);                                            16
+! leave[achieve]: {B at(X,Y), ~B human,                          17
                    ~B emptyarea, B unchecked(W,Z)}               18
   ← +empty(X,Y),                                                  19
        -at(X,Y),                                                  20
        +at(W,Z),                                                  21
        move_to(W,Z);                                              22
+! leave[achieve]: {B at(X,Y), ~B human,                          23
                    ~B emptyarea, ~B unchecked(W,Z)}              24
   ← +empty(X,Y),                                                  25
        -at(X,Y);                                                  26
+! leave[achieve]: {B at(X,Y), B human } ←   +found;             27
+! leave[achieve]: {B emptyarea} ←   +leave;                     28
+found : {B at(X,Y)}                                               29
   ← .send(lifter , :tell , human(X,Y)),                          30
     +sent(lifter , human(X,Y)),                                   31
     +leave;                                                       32
```

Since we are looking at collaboration we have a second robot in the multi-agent system which can lift rubble to free a human. This has the following plans:

```
: Plans :                                                          1
+.received(:tell , Msg): {~B Msg} ← +Msg, +rec(msg);             2
                                                                   3
+human(X,Y): {⊤} ←  +! free(human)[achieve];                     4
                                                                   5
+! free(human)[achieve] : {B human(C,Y), ~B at(C,Y),             6
                           ~B have(human)}                        7
   ← move_to(C, Y),                                                8
     +at(C, Y);                                                    9
```

```
+! free(human)[achieve]  :  {B human(X,Y), B at(X,Y),      10
                               ~B have(human)}               11
    ←  lift(human),                                          12
       +have(human);                                         13
+! free(human)[achieve]  :  {B have(human)}                 14
    ←  +free(human);                                         15
```

The output from these two programs when logging actions depends upon where the human is found in the grid (which is randomly determined). However it will look something like the following:

```
searcher done move_to(0,0)
searcher done move_to(0,1)
searcher done move_to(0,2)
searcher done move_to(1,0)
searcher done send(1:human(1,0), lifter)
lifter done move_to(1,0)
lifter done lift(human)
Sleeping agent lifter
```

We begin to see, in examples such as this, how search capabilities from logic programming are combined with intentional reasoning, communication, and perception.

3.4 Agent Environments

As well as at least one agent, a multi-agent system generally contains an *environment* within which the agent works. The varieties of autonomous system we are concerned with generally act within the physical world. However, we frequently want to assess these agents in simulation and nearly always (in both simulation and deployment on physical systems) delegate parts of an agent's operation to standard software components which are treated as part of the environment. For example, the *lifting* capability in the previous agent will have involved software controllers as well as physical interactions with the real environment.

The *Agent Infrastructure Layer* (AIL), which is part of the MCAPL framework, is a toolkit for implementing interpreters for BDI agents. It was used to implement the GWENDOLEN interpreter. It also provides support for implementing the environments in which agents operate, and allows such environments to be coded in Java. These environments can comprise abstract representations of the 'physical environment', simulations of the real world, or components that get input from sensors or control actuators either directly or via some middleware such as ROS. The agent interacts with the environment by executing actions and perceiving effects.

Example 3.9 The code below provides a very simple example environment. It subclasses the AIL's `DefaultEnvironment` class which implements procedures for message passing and manages the items agents can 'see'. This environment overwrites one method from that class, `executeAction` and specifies that if an agent picks up an object, then that object can no longer be seen, and if an agent puts down an object then the object again becomes visible. All other actions are delegated to the super class for handling.

```
public class SimpleEnv extends DefaultEnvironment
{
    public SimpleEnv() { super(); }

/** When a pickup action is executed the environment
 ** stores new perceptions for the agent - that it
 ** has picked something up and that its hands are
 ** no longer empty.
 **/
    public Unifier executeAction(String agName, Action act)
      throws AILexception
        {
        Unifier theta = new Unifier();

        if (act.getFunctor().equals("pickup"))
            { Predicate object = (Predicate) act.getTerm(0);
                removePercept(object); }
        else if (act.getFunctor().equals("putdown"))
            { Predicate object = (Predicate) act.getTerm(0);
                addPercept(object); }

        try { theta = super.executeAction(agName, act); }
            catch (AILexception e) { throw e; }

        return theta;
        }
}
```

We discuss the creation of environments further in Chapter 6 and full details can be found in the tutorials in Appendix B. Any Java environment can be provided, as long as it implements the relevant AIL API.

4

Formal Agent Verification

Later, we will be formally verifying autonomous systems, specifically those constructed using cognitive agents within a hybrid agent architecture. But, what do we mean by 'verifying'? And what do we mean by 'formally verifying'? In this chapter we provide brief background to these terms and their associated techniques. We will discuss the basic varieties of *formal verification*, such as logical proof, model-checking, program-checking, and so on, as well as the logical foundations concerning the properties that we might verify, typically: temporal logics, modal logics, BDI logics.

Within the broad range of formal verification techniques we will primarily use techniques from *model-checking* and so will spend some time explaining the core principles of (explicit-state) model-checking. This involves exploration of finite automata over infinite strings, specifically *Büchi Automata* (Emerson, 1990b), and the automata-theoretic approach to model-checking (Sistla et al., 1987; Vardi and Wolper, 1994). In practice, there are a range of techniques for implementing model-checking, but we particularly highlight the 'on the fly' approach (Gerth et al., 1996). This, in turn, leads us on to *program* model-checking (Visser et al., 2003) where actual *code*, rather than a mathematical model of the code's behaviour, is analysed.

Finally, we can outline practical program model-checking systems, such as Java PathFinder (JPF) for Java programs (Mehlitz et al., 2013; Visser and Mehlitz, 2005).[1] Our own approach, which will be explained in detail in later chapters, extends JPF with structures for representing cognitive agent programs (Dennis et al., 2012) and provides extended program model-checking techniques for handling cognitive agent implementations (Dennis et al., 2012; Dennis et al., 2016c; Fisher et al., 2013).

---

[1] https://github.com/javapathfinder.

4.1 What is Verification?

We begin with some dictionary definitions.[2] Verification is the act or process of *verifying*:

Verify: *to prove, show, find out, or state that (something) is true or correct*

Verification [of a system]:

Establishing that the system under construction conforms to the specified requirements.

So, we want to carry out *verification* to *show that our system matches its requirements*. But, why do we want to verify systems at all? Some systems are clearly *safety critical* – if they fail, safety is compromised, for example, aerospace control, hardware design, industrial control processes. We obviously must be as sure as possible that such systems behave as required.

Though not so dangerous, other systems may be *business critical* – if they fail the viability of the business is compromised, for example through financial, security, or privacy issues. We need to be *very* sure that such systems will not do any *bad* things in any context.

In both cases, testing specific scenarios, no matter how many, is unlikely to be sufficient. We need, where possible, to consider *all* possible behaviours and to be sure that our requirements are satisfied on every one.

There is, however, a need for verification beyond either safety critical systems or business critical systems. It is often important that system software works as expected, even in 'non-critical' applications. In such areas, software failure can still have quite severe effects, such as *bad publicity*, *legal aspects*, *product recall*, or even significant additional *revision and testing*. All of these are to be avoided and so increased verification *before* deployment should be carried out.

4.2 From Testing to Formal Verification

The basic approach to *testing* is to select a range of scenarios and inputs, run the particular system in all these configurations, and assess how well the system achieves the expected outcomes. In a realistic system, the number of potential scenarios and inputs can be *very* large, and potentially infinite. So, in choosing a finite set of configurations, there is considerable skill in selecting

---

[2] *Merriam-Webster Dictionary* online – www.merriam-webster.com.

a finite subset that characterises enough of the input space to provide confidence. Yet this confidence is always tempered by uncertainty over coverage measurement.

Increasingly, developers require *formal* verification techniques to increase confidence, find bugs early, improve efficiency, and so on. Such verification can be carried out on both the design and the code itself. Essentially, formal verification is used to increase the trust and confidence of both programmers and users.

Again, back to the dictionary.

Formal Verification:[3]

> *the act of proving or disproving the correctness of intended algorithms underlying a system with respect to a certain formal specification or property, using formal methods of mathematics.*

So, with formal verification, we utilise mathematical techniques to establish correctness of a system with respect to specific requirements. In contrast to testing, the mathematical proof covers *all* possible behaviours. Clearly, however, if the number of possibilities is very large, or even infinite, then we need a concise way to characterise these.

4.3 Varieties of Formal Verification

We will see later that there is a wide range of logical dimensions with relevance to our requirements, such as time, location, uncertainty, intention, belief, resources, and so on. Yet, even before this, there are quite a number of different mechanisms for carrying out formal verification. Imagine that we have a *formal requirement*, perhaps given as a logical formula, R. This is to be matched against the system we are interested in (Figure 4.1).

There is a range of possibilities for formal verification.

- **Proof:** where the behaviour of the system is itself described by the logical formula, S, and verification involves *proving* $\vdash S \Rightarrow R$.

    Typically, this requires (ideally, automated) deductive methods able to cope with the logical complexity within S and R.

- **Model-Checking:** where R is checked against a representation of all possible execution paths within the system.

    All these executions of S are usually described using a finite state structure, typically an automaton A.

[3] http://en.wikipedia.org/wiki/Formal_verification.

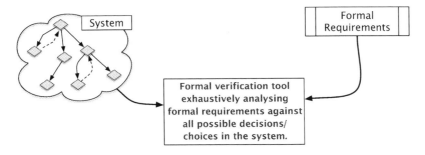

Figure 4.1 Checking a system against its requirements

Our system satisfies R so long as for every path σ through the automaton $\mathscr{A}$, we can show that σ satisfies R (i.e., $\sigma \models R$ for each σ through $\mathscr{A}$).

- **Dynamic Fault Monitoring (aka Runtime Verification):** where executions *actually* generated by the system are checked against R.

  A finite-state automaton, representing the property R, can be used to iteratively scan any execution produced by the system to check that it indeed satisfies R.

- **Program Model-Checking:** where, instead of assessing R against a *model* of the system (e.g., $\mathscr{A}$ above), R is checked against all executions of the *actual* code.

  This depends on being able to generate <u>all</u> the program executions and typically requires quite sophisticated *symbolic execution* techniques.

Note that we will be particularly concerned with this last variety since it allows us to be confident that we are formally verifying the actual code used, rather than any approximate model of its behaviour.

4.4 Understanding Program Model-Checking

The simplest way to explain program model-checking is to start by explaining 'traditional' model-checking and work from that. In turn, the simplest way to explain model-checking is to use *finite automata*. However, the finite automata that we use accept *infinite* strings – they are called Büchi Automata (Emerson, 1990b). The details are not so important, the key aspects being

1. these are finite structures and
2. they represent sets of infinite strings.

These strings will be used to represent both execution sequences of the system we have in mind and models of logical (typically, temporal/modal logic)

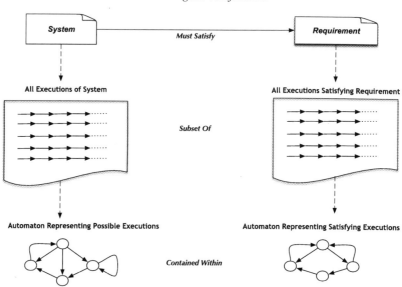

Figure 4.2 Model-checking. Reprinted by permission from John Wiley and Sons.
Fisher M. (2011) *An Introduction to Practical Formal Methods Using Temporal
Logic*, by Fisher M. © 2011

formulae. Figure 4.2 shows us a simple view that appears in Fisher (2011).
Here, if we have some system (e.g., our target program) together with a formal
requirement that it should satisfy then we can (at least in principle) generate
all possible executions of our system, and generate all executions that satisfy
our formal requirement. Then we just require that

$$\begin{matrix} \text{the set of all executions} \\ \text{of our system} \end{matrix} \quad \subseteq \quad \begin{matrix} \text{the set of executions} \\ \text{satisfying our formal requirement} \end{matrix}$$

If this is *not* the case, then this means there is at least one execution of our
system that does **not** satisfy our requirement.

Now the problem with this approach is that we are dealing with a large, potentially infinite, set of sequences each of which, in turn, could well be infinite.
This is quite unwieldy, so the automata-theoretic approach aims to use a finite
state automaton (technically, a Büchi Automaton) to capture all the relevant
sequences in a finite way. So, instead of the set of all executions of our system we use an automaton, say B_S, capturing all these. Similarly, instead of
the set of executions that satisfy our formal requirement, we use an automaton, say B_R. Now, since each such automaton is describing a language (a set

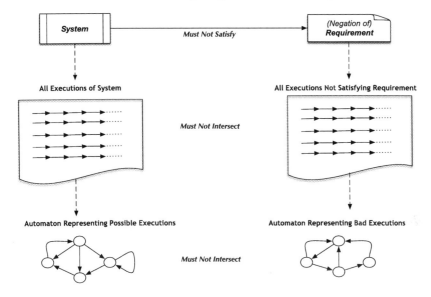

Figure 4.3 Checking the system does not satisfy the negation of our requirement

of strings), then we just need to check that the language described by B_S is contained within the language described by B_R (Vardi and Wolper, 1994).

While we are moving in the right direction, in that we are now dealing with finite objects, the containment check between automata is still likely to be quite complex. So, let us follow similar ideas, but from a slightly different hypothesis. Rather than being concerned with whether the system, S, satisfies the formal requirement, R, let us try to check that the system, S, does **not** satisfy the negation of our requirement, $\neg R$. And so, the process is as shown in Figure 4.3.

This might seem like we are making little progress but, with these automata, there is a useful shortcut, namely

$$accepted\_by(B_S) \cap accepted\_by(B_{\neg R}) \quad = \quad accepted\_by(B_S \times B_{\neg R}).$$

So, rather than checking that there is no intersection between the languages accepted by B_S and $B_{\neg R}$, we can construct the *product* of the two automata and then check the emptiness of the structure produced, that is, we check whether

$$accepted\_by(B_S \times B_{\neg R}) \quad = \quad \varnothing.$$

The important aspect here is that the product automaton $B_S \times B_{\neg R}$ only accepts sequences that are simultaneously accepted by each of the constituent automata (Sistla et al., 1987). So, if a sequence is accepted, then it must not only be a run of the system (i.e., B_S accepts it) but it must also have the *bad* property (i.e., $B_{\neg R}$ accepts it). So, ideally, the product automaton accepts no sequences. If it does actually accept at least one sequence, then such sequences give exact counter-examples to our check that S satisfies R.

And, indeed, most model-checkers use this approach (at least in principle).

Example 4.1   To see how this approach works in practice, let us recap a simple example, similar to one given in Fisher (2011). Consider the program:

```
int x = random(0,3);    /* randomly choose 0, 1, 2, or 3 */

while (x != 1)
do
    if  (x < 1) then x:=x+1; fi
    if  (x > 1) then x:=x-1; fi
od
```

The possible execution sequences of the above program are:

```
x = 0, x = 1, x = 1, x = 1, x = 1, ...
x = 1, x = 1, x = 1, x = 1, x = 1, ...
x = 2, x = 1, x = 1, x = 1, x = 1, ...
x = 3, x = 2, x = 1, x = 1, x = 1, ...
```

Example 4.2   Example Property for Example 4.1: our requirement is that

'At some moment in the future x will have the value 1'

Formal property to check is: $\Diamond(x = 1)$. However, as described above, we negate this formula, giving: $\Box(x \neq 1)$. Sequences that satisfy $\Box(x \neq 1)$ include

```
x = 0, x = 0, x = 0, x = 0, x = 0, ...
x = 0, x = 0, x = 3, x = 0, x = 2, ...
x = 3, x = 2, x = 2, x = 3, x = 3, ...
x = 2, x = 2, x = 2, x = 2, x = 2, ...
.....
```

And so on. Essentially any combination that never involves 'x=1' anywhere.

Example 4.3   Example automata for $B_{program}$ (the automaton describing program runs) and $B_{\Box(x \neq 1)}$ (the automaton describing sequences satisfying $\Box(x \neq 1)$).

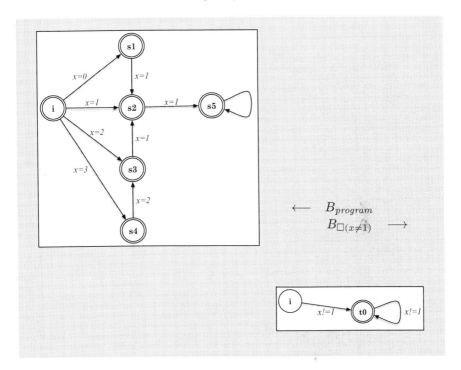

Recall that we wish to check that

$$sequences\_of(B_{program}) \cap sequences\_of(B_{\square(x \neq 1)}) = \varnothing.$$

So that: *no execution of the program also satisfies* $\square(x \neq 1)$.

Taking intersections is not so convenient and so, as described above, we go further and change the above to a check that

$$sequences\_of(B_{program} \times B_{\square(x \neq 1)}) = \varnothing.$$

In other words there is no sequence accepted by the combined automaton; thus, a key aspect of many model-checkers is constructing products such as $B_{program} \times B_{\square(x \neq 1)}$.

Example 4.4 Product of Automata: When we construct $B_{program} \times B_{\square(x \neq 1)}$ then we cannot have a transition labelled by *both* $x = 1$ and $x! = 1$ and so such transitions are removed. This gives:

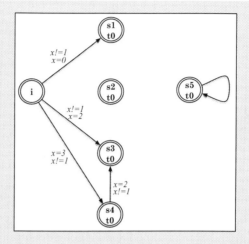

Note here that there is **no** accepting run for this automaton, namely no infinite sequence, starting from the initial state, i, and reaching an infinite accepting state (specifically, $s5t0$). Thus the above automaton is empty (accepts no appropriate infinite sequences) and so the product $B_{program} \times B_{\Box(x \neq 1)}$ is empty, meaning that all runs through the program satisfy $\Diamond(x = 1)$.

4.5 Program Model-Checking with Java PathFinder

4.5.1 'On the Fly' Product Construction

Constructing automata products such as

$$B_S \times B_{\neg R}$$

can be *very* expensive. For example, the number of states in the product automaton may be *HUGE*. So, rather than combining the two automata explicitly, the *'on the fly'* approach (Gerth et al., 1996) explores *all* the paths through B_S and, as we do so, simultaneously checks whether any path satisfies $B_{\neg R}$.

Essentially, we *symbolically execute* our system/program and, at each step, take a transition in the parallel automaton (see Figure 4.4). If we finish an execution, having successfully traced out a path in the 'bad' automaton, then this describes a counter-example to our required property. If we fail to find a route through the 'bad' automaton then the symbolic execution of the system/program backtracks and begins tracing out an alternative path. And so on. If we have explored all possible execution paths through the 'system' automaton,

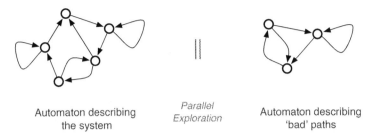

Automaton describing the system

Parallel Exploration

Automaton describing 'bad' paths

Figure 4.4 Parallel exploration

and none of them match a path through the 'bad' automaton, then the required property holds for all executions of the system/program.

4.5.2 Program Model-Checking

What do we need in order to be able to implement the on-the-fly model-checking approach? Essentially we require:

1. a mechanism for extracting *all possible* runs of a system;
2. some way to step the monitoring automaton forwards, as each run proceeds; and
3. a way of recognising *good/bad* looping situations.

Within model checkers such as SPIN (Holzmann, 2003), these were achieved by (1) an automaton representing all system executions, (2) a *monitoring* process running synchronously with the main program execution, and (3) an algorithm for recognising Büchi acceptance.

Now that we wish to tackle a high-level programming language such as Java we need these again.

The particular approach we consider here is implemented as the Java Path-Finder (JPF) system, which is an explicit-state open source model-checker for Java programs (Mehlitz et al., 2013; Visser and Mehlitz, 2005).[4] The key aspects that allow JPF to achieve (1), (2), and (3) above are that

a) it incorporates a modified virtual machine and that
b) *listener* threads are used.

Programs in Java are compiled to a set of *bytecodes* which are then executed, when required, by a *virtual machine*, called the Java Virtual Machine

---

[4] https://github.com/javapathfinder.

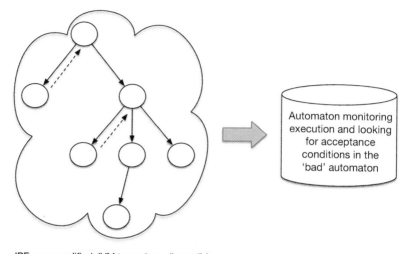

JPF uses modified JVM to explore all possible
execution branches for the bytecodes, not only
by forward execution but through backtracking

Figure 4.5 A pictorial view of JPF

(JVM) (Downing and Meyer, 1997). In order to allow this execution to be controlled, and indeed backtracked if necessary, JPF provides a special, modified
JVM which can explore all executions including all non-deterministic choices,
thread inter-leavings, and so on. Importantly, this new JVM records all the
choices made and can backtrack to explore previous choice points.

Note that this modified JVM is actually implemented in Java and so runs on
top of a standard JVM.

Now, JPF uses a *listener*[5] in order to provide a representation of an automaton that is attempting to build a model based on the program execution. As the
program proceeds, the listener recognises state changes in the execution and
checks this against its automaton representation. At certain times the listener
may be reset, forcing the JVM to backtrack. If the listener recognises an execution sequence, then it reports this. Since we define the listeners to correspond
to our automaton capturing 'bad' sequences, then the reported sequences are
counter-examples.

A general, pictorial, view of JPF is shown in Figure 4.5. Thus, JPF essentially combines (backtracking) symbolic execution and a monitoring automaton.

---

[5] A Java listener is a mechanism within the Java language allowing the programmer to 'listen'
for events.

4.5.3 Efficiency

JPF is now quite well developed and is used for many Java applications (Mehlitz et al., 2013). While extremely useful, JPF is inherently quite slow. It is built upon Java itself so, for example, code that is running executes on the modified JVM, which in turn runs on the standard JVM. In order to improve efficiency, JPF employs a variety of sophisticated techniques. As well as standard partial-order reduction (Peled, 1993) used in many model-checkers, two additional aspects are interesting.

1. Rather than just exploring the runs through a program in arbitrary order, the user can specify a '*choice generator*' which will explore branches in a specific order.
2. The other main enhancement involves ensuring that the listener is only forced to move forward if *important* changes occur in the Java execution.

    Thus, 'unimportant' state changes/operations are collected together into one 'important' step. The *Model Java Interface* (MJI) is a feature of JPF that effectively allows code blocks to be treated as atomic/native methods. Consequently, since new states are *not* built by JPF for calls to atomic/native methods, these code blocks are effectively hidden from the listener and cannot force a step forward in this listener.

We will see later how JPF provides the basis for our agent verification, but can summarise the description here as follows.

- Verification is important, in order to be certain about the program/system behaviours.
- Program model-checking allows us to directly verify the program code.
- The key aspects that allow JPF to achieve 'on the fly' checking are that it incorporates a modified virtual machine (capable of symbolic execution and backtracking) and that *listener* threads are used (to monitor executions).
- Program model-checking is *significantly* slower than standard model-checking applied to models of the program execution, since it requires symbolic execution.
- However, JPF provides a strong basis for our verification of agent programs.

4.6 Logical Agent Requirements

In describing the requirements of our agents we take a formal approach, using a *logical* specification to describe exactly what the agent should achieve. While it is not our intention to provide a detailed tutorial on formal specification, logics, and proof, we will provide a little background to begin with.

4.6.1 Modal and Temporal Logics

Classical propositional logic, as we saw in Section 3.2.1, is typically used to capture *static* and unchanging situations. To describe more dynamic situations with more complex possibilities, we can turn to modal or temporal logics. When we use these logics any evaluation of formulae takes place within a *set* of worlds, rather than a fixed world. Thus, **it is Friday** may be true in some worlds, but not in others.

The general study of *modal logic* concerns different interpretations of *accessibility* between these worlds. Consequently, modal logic is a vast area of research describing the general forms of logic based on the notion of propositions having distinct truth values in different states/worlds/points and using *modal operators* to navigate between these worlds (Blackburn et al., 2006; Bull and Segerberg, 1984; Gabbay et al., 2003; Hughes and Cresswell, 1984). Typically, modal logics have just two operators: one capturing the notion that a propositional formula is true 'in all accessible worlds'; the other being the dual of this, capturing 'in some accessible world'. We will see later that some of the logics we use are modal logics, typically logics of *belief* and logics of *knowledge* (Fagin et al., 1996).

Example 4.5 [Logic of Knowledge] The formula '$K_a p \Rightarrow K_b q$' means that if agent *a knows* p is true then agent *b knows* q is true. (Note that 'K_a' is the 'in all worlds accessible by *a*' modal operator, where accessibility characterises the *knowledge* of agent *a*.)

Alternatively, we can interpret this modal navigation between worlds as a *temporal* relation. So, as we move from one world to another, the intuition is now that we are moving *through time*. For example, propositional, discrete, linear *temporal* logic extends the descriptive power of classical propositional logic in order to be able to describe sequences (hence: *linear*) of distinct (hence: *discrete*) worlds, with each world being similar to a classical (propositional) model (Emerson, 1990a; Fisher, 2011).

Example 4.6 [Propositional Temporal Logic] The formula '$p \wedge \bigcirc q \wedge \Diamond r$' means that p is true now (in the current world/state), q is true in the next world/state (accessible from this one), and r is true at *some* accessible world/state in the 'future'.

4.6.2 Logical Theories for Cognitive Agents

Clearly, for describing requirements of a cognitive agent, we should choose an appropriate logic. One that provides a level of abstraction close to the key concepts of the system. However, as we have already seen, there are many options. Indeed, we have only just scratched the surface as there is a vast variety of logics we could use, each capturing some aspect of the agent/environment. For example, we might use any of the following logics that have been developed to describe particular types of system:

- dynamic communicating systems $\longrightarrow$ *temporal logics* (Demri et al., 2016; Fisher, 2011; Manna and Pnueli, 1992)
- systems managing information $\longrightarrow$ *logics of knowledge* (Fagin et al., 1996)
- autonomous systems $\longrightarrow$ *logics of motivation* (Lorini and Herzig, 2008; Rao, 1998)
- situated systems $\longrightarrow$ *logics of belief, contextual logics* (Baltag et al., 2019; Ghidini and Serafini, 2014)
- timed systems $\longrightarrow$ *real-time temporal logics* (Ferrère et al., 2019)
- stochastic systems $\longrightarrow$ *probabilistic logics* (Halpern, 2003)
- cooperative systems $\longrightarrow$ *cooperation/coalition logics* (Berthon et al., 2021; Pauly, 2002; van der Hoek and Wooldridge, 2005)

However, none of these will exactly capture a cognitive agent and so, in realistic scenarios, we will need to *combine* several logics. Consequently, logical theories for rational cognitive agents typically consist of several logical dimensions, as least involving representations of

Dynamism – often, temporal or dynamic logic,
Information – often, modal/probabilistic logics of belief/knowledge, and
Motivation – often, modal logics of goals, intentions, desires.

For example, the BDI approach discussed in Chapter 3 comprises

- a (branching) temporal/dynamic logic,
- a modal logic of *belief*,
- a modal logic of *desire*, and
- a modal logic of *intention*.

Combining logics can become very complex, very quickly. Not only in terms of readability and understandability, but in terms of computational complexity when we come to the formalisation of proof or model-checking (Gabbay et al., 2003).

Just to show how complex the formal requirements concerning these agents might become, here is one example. This is still quite a simple example, in principle, yet its full verification is beyond us at present.

Example 4.7   Sample Logical Specification

'If the robot believes, with over 75% probability that at some point in the future the opponent's goal will be to create danger, then robot intends to leave the area within 5 seconds'.

$B_{robot}^{>0.75}$ ....robot believes with over 75% probability

$\Diamond$ .... at some point within the future

$G_{opponent}$ ....opponent's goal

I_{robot} ....robot intends

$\Diamond^{<5s}$ ....within 5 seconds

$$B_{robot}^{>0.75} \Diamond G_{opponent} \, create\_danger \; \Rightarrow \; I_{robot} \Diamond^{<5s} leave\_area$$

We do not yet have the tools to be able to cope with such complex logical combinations. So, an important aspect is to limit the requirements we have to occur within as small/simple fragment as possible. Though not always possible, many requirements are indeed relatively straightforward. For example, here is a typical statement we might have concerning human–robot interaction.

> *if a robot 'believes' that a human is directly in front of it, and it has a goal to get to a room beyond the human, then it should never deliberately choose a plan that brings it into close proximity with the human, unless there is no alternative, in which case the robot may even decide to wait for the person to move or instead may decide to drop or revise its goal.*

Such a typical statement will then be formalised in a logical form, most likely in a logic combing time, intention, and belief. This, then, provides a formal requirement that we can check of our robot. Consequently, in our logical systems later, we just use (a) simple linear temporal logic combined with (b) modal logics of belief and intention, both referring to goals and plans that the agent has. However, in Chapter 11, we will consider how this comparatively simple logic can be combined with a logic that involves real-time considerations in order to extend the guarantees we can give of system behaviour.

4.7 Discussion

So autonomous systems are important. But are they any different to 'traditional' systems? In one way, the answer is 'no' since they can be seen as traditional systems, for example distributed object-based software, in many cases. However, autonomous systems, particularly autonomous software, is different in one crucial aspect. In designing, analysing, or monitoring 'normal' software we typically care about

- *what* the software does, and
- *when* the software does it.

Autonomous software has to *make its own decisions* and then enact them in a dynamic and uncertain environment. This is challenging to the task of verification. In particular the robot may decide to take the correct course of action, but nevertheless fail to achieve the desired outcome (for instance it may drop and break something it is attempting to pick up). In order to understand and debug such errors it is important to know whether the robot intended to break the object (so something had gone wrong with its decision-making) or whether it intended to pick something up (and either there was something wrong with the programming of its grasping action or it was simply unlucky). Furthermore when attempting to verify the code that controls the decisions made by the robot it may make more sense to ask what decision it would make given certain states of the world than what action would actually result.

Therefore in verifying an autonomous decision-maker we often want to know:

- *what* the software does,
- *when* the software does it, and also
- *why* the software chose to do it?

This requirement to describe why a system chooses one course of action over another provides new entities to be analysed. But how shall we describe these new entities? It is here that the novel concepts describing *intention* come into play. This leads towards the need for rational cognitive agent approaches such as the BDI approach.

5

Verifying Autonomous Systems

Autonomous systems are clearly important for applications in distant or dangerous environments. But they are increasingly being used for mundane tasks in our everyday lives. It seems likely that interacting in some way with an autonomous system will soon (if not already) be a regular occurrence. However, while systems that clean our floors while we sleep or take over speed control for our car as we cruise on the motorway both seem safe enough, we are reaching the stage where the public are becoming more suspicious of the power of this enhanced autonomy. Decades of films and books about duplicitous machines, together with a constant 'drip feed' of articles about 'killer robots' in the media, lead the public to uncertainty, anxiety, and even hostility.

Separate from these social aspects are the legal aspects associated with such systems. If truly autonomous systems are to be deployed even in the above, seemingly mundane, situations then their safety assurance (and certification) must be considered seriously. How do we know autonomous systems will be safe? How can we assess this, not only before deployment, but as the system progresses? And how should legal and regulatory frameworks be adapted to cope with increasing levels of autonomy?

As we move from systems directly controlled by humans to increasingly autonomous systems, we clearly lose several elements. The most important are the *senses* that the human can deploy, for example vision, hearing, touch, and the conscious *decision-making* that the human carries out. In moving to fully autonomous systems we attempt to mitigate the loss of a human's senses by incorporating additional sensors and sophisticated analysis of the data generated by those sensors. We also need to supply a *software* component that autonomously makes decisions, rather than the human making these.

This is at the core of both the anxiety many people feel about such systems and the problems with safety assurance and certification. What typically worries us is that when a human pilot, driver or operator is replaced by software that makes its own choices about what to do, then we lack any *trust* in this software (Chatila et al., 2021). Similarly, when we wish to *certify* an autonomous system, we must be sure that its decision-making is as safe as necessary.

Example 5.1 In air travel, an autopilot system can keep an aircraft flying on a certain path, but there is a human pilot deciding which path to take, when to divert, and how to deal with unexpected situations. Similarly, cruise control, lane control and, soon, 'convoying' will allow our road vehicles to carry out path-following activities though drivers will continue to make the bigger decisions. But once we move to truly autonomous systems, software will play a much more significant role. We will no longer need a human to decide when to change the route of an aircraft or when to turn our car off the motorway onto a side road.

It is at this point that the public become concerned. If a machine can truly make its own decisions then how do we know it is safe? After seeing movies such as *Terminator* and *I, Robot*, we wonder how we can trust machines not to double-cross us. For many, the idea of boarding an aeroplane with no human pilot is unnerving, let alone the thought of allowing an autonomous robotic assistant into their home. Often this leads to two, extreme, options: either we must blindly trust these machines or we should refuse to allow the use of any autonomous systems at all!

However, the formal verification approach described in this book presents a third option. It allows us to assess the choices the system makes and, in particular, the intentions or aims that it has when it makes them.

Example 5.2 We often depend on other people. Yet, when we deal with another human being, we cannot be sure what they will decide to do. While we can make assumptions based on what we think of them, for example whether that person has lied to us in the past or has a record for making mistakes, we cannot truly be certain about any of our assumptions as the other person could still be deceiving us. Essentially, we do not know, for certain, what their *intentions* are.

With autonomous systems, on the other hand, we are in a much better situation. As these systems are essentially controlled by software then, once we isolate the software making all the high-level decisions then we can exhaustively analyse the detailed working of these programs. This is clearly not possible with a human brain.

So, using the techniques described in this book we can do exactly this. We isolate the software agent making the high-level decisions – those decisions that a human would have made – within our autonomous systems, and can then analyse the detailed working of these programs through formal verification. This formal verification can, in some cases, allow us to prove that the agent controlling our autonomous system will *never* make bad decisions. In other cases it can at least highlight situations in which such bad decisions might potentially occur.

In the longer term we believe that this approach can help alleviate public fears about autonomous systems. By asserting that a given system's decision-making has been *proved* to be 'correct' and that any bad situation that occurs was *not* deliberately planned by the system, then we can begin to increase public trust and help make people more comfortable with the use of such technologies.

Example 5.3 A robot is holding a hammer, but then drops it on a person's head. Either this was a *deliberate* act and the robot aimed to injure the person, or it was an accident and was due to some failure in, for example, its gripper control. From the viewpoint of public trust, the difference between these two options is *huge*. So, if we can formally verify the robot's decision-making processes to show that it will *never* deliberately decide to take an action it believes will cause harm, then this is a significant step on the path to increasing public confidence in this technology.

While this might make us believe that formal verification techniques can prove that an autonomous system is always *safe*, it is important to realise that they cannot. The environments in which our systems work are both complex and uncertain and, since there are always some things we cannot predict, then accidents can still occur. However, we *can* at least verify that the system always *tries* to avoid them. This might seem insufficient, but it allows us to tackle some of our concerns, particularly about deceitful robots. While we cannot say that a robot will never accidentally harm someone, through formal verification we can prove that the robot never intentionally causes harm. In particular, once we can look at the system's internal programming, we can assess not just what the robot decides to do, but *why* it decided to do it.

Although people may still be wary of robots and autonomous systems, if they know that the system is not actively intending to double-cross them, then they will hopefully be more likely to trust such systems. Similarly, with the legal aspects. Once we have some way to assess and evaluate the autonomous decision-making then we can be more certain of what the system will try to do.

In subsequent chapters we will look at some of these scenarios; for example in Chapter 9 we will use our formal verification techniques to assess whether the agent's decisions in controlling an uncrewed aircraft match what a pilot *should* do when controlling the same vehicle. In this case, the expectations of pilot behaviour are written down in a 'Rules of the Air' document that all (human) pilots must learn and apply. More generally, however, establishing these requirements becomes difficult and the main problem typically becomes finding *what* to prove, rather than actually proving it. For example, what requirements do we have of an assistive robot? We might try to prove that the robot never deliberately chooses to harm a human. But what about robots working in surgical or law-enforcement contexts? A medical robot might try to resuscitate someone, for example by exerting pressure on their chest. But that might inadvertently harm them. A police robot is charged with protecting the public but what if a criminal is shooting a gun at someone? Can the robot harm the criminal in order to avert the greater danger? We look at the question of ethical behaviour and what we might be able to prove about it in Chapter 10.

While we are clearly moving on from technical questions towards philosophical and ethical questions about what behaviour we find acceptable and what ethical behaviour our robots should exhibit, having a clear view of how our autonomous systems are programmed to make decisions will help us in assessing whatever requirements we specify.

5.1 Modular Architectures for Autonomous Systems

As autonomous systems have become more complex over the past decade so have their architectures. An agent architecture can no longer simply be divided into a discrete agent reasoner and a continuous control system but may include many other components that support autonomy such as sophisticated motion-planning systems supported by statistical techniques for simultaneous localisation and mapping, planners, and schedulers for determining when and in what order tasks should be performed, and health monitoring processes to determining if all the system components are functioning as they should. The agent decision-maker coordinates information and control between these various systems.

For example, a typical uncrewed air system might incorporate an aircraft, a set of control systems and planners encapsulated within an autopilot, and a high-level decision-maker that makes the key 'choices'. Once a destination has been decided, a planner will determine an appropriate route given the current fuel and weather conditions, then the continuous dynamic control, in the form of the autopilot, will be able to fly there. The high-level 'intelligence' only becomes involved if either an alternative destination is chosen, or if some fault or unexpected situation occurs.

5.2 Overview

While *formal verification* techniques have been developed for many aspects of hybrid architectures, for example, control systems, we will focus in this book on formal verification of the cognitive agent. When doing this, we verify the system's *decision-making*, not the real-world outcome of the actions it takes. Consequently, we verify

what the autonomous system chooses to do, given its beliefs

rather than

what effect the autonomous system has on the world

Although we do not focus upon the wider verification in this book we note that we want to employ distinct techniques for different aspects. For instance, in our work we have variously used

- *simulation* of the whole system (Webster et al., 2011) and individual components such as motion planning (Dinmohammadi et al., 2018);
- *testing* (often large-scale, via HPC) to assess the range/correctness of the continuous control part (Webster et al., 2011).

In Chapter 11 we will discuss the use of *compositional verification* to combine results about individual modules into guarantees of system behaviour (Cardoso et al., 2020b; Farrell et al., 2019).

We have also examined how formal verification, simulation and testing can be used in a corroborative fashion to support each other (Webster et al., 2020) Other work in the field has looked at

- formal verification and testing techniques for analysing the behaviour of image classifiers and other components based on deep neural networks (Huang et al., 2020), and
- deductive approaches to verifying the behaviour of planning systems (Lacerda et al., 2019).

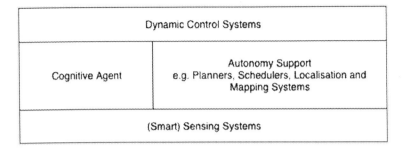

Figure 5.1 Typical modern agent autonomous system architecture

One key aspect of the approach described in this book is that the formal verification is carried out on the *code* of the rational cognitive agent and this code is exactly that used to drive both simulations and the real autonomous system. This gives increased confidence as there is no additional modelling step to justify.

5.3 Verifying Autonomous Choices

Now we return to our original question: how do we go about *verifying* decision-making in autonomous systems? Recall the architecture in Figure 5.1. For the 'traditional' parts there are well known, recognized, and trusted approaches, such as testing for real-world interaction and analytic techniques for continuous dynamics and emerging approaches to verifying the autonomy support. But what about the agent that makes high-level, 'intelligent' choices about what to do? As we will explain next, it is our approach to use *formal verification* of the potential choices the agent can take. This is feasible since, while the space of possibilities covered by the continuous dynamics is huge (and potentially infinite), the high-level decision-making within the agent typically involves reasoning within a discrete state space. The agent rarely, if ever, bases its choices directly on the *exact* values of sensors, etc. It might base its decision on values reaching a certain threshold, but relies on its continuous dynamics to alert it of this, and such alerts are typically binary valued (either the threshold has been reached or it has not). Thus, we propose a mixture of techniques to provide the basis for formal verification of autonomous systems.

Example 5.4 To some (limited) extent, our agent here captures high-level (conscious) human decision-making. We rarely base our actions on anything

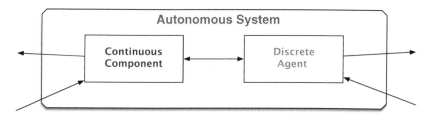

Figure 5.2　Decision-making within a discrete agent

more complex than Boolean decisions. Typically, '*elapsed_time* >55', or '*average_so_far = 93*' or '*speed* <20'.

Recap: Separating Decision-Making　Recall that in a simple agent architecture we separate out the *decision-making* aspect of the system, capturing it within a 'discrete agent' as shown in Figure 5.2. The cognitive agent is typically non-deterministic, but finite. The 'continuous control' part is typically

1. deterministic, in that it has a predictable feedback interaction with its environment, but
2. potentially infinite, as the environment can be arbitrary/uncertain.

Note that we have a range of possibilities for carrying out verification of the 'control' part:

- we could use *formal verification* for hybrid systems (Alur et al., 1995; Henzinger et al., 1997; Platzer, 2010);
- we could use *approximation techniques* for the differential equations describing the continuous interaction;
- we could use analytical *mathematical proof* if viable, on abstractions or equations as above; or
- we can use *testing* (Ammann and Offutt, 2008; Hierons et al., 2009).

We typically use the last of these where components are opaque and hard to analyse in detail or where they are embedded in inherently complex environments whose interactions are impossible to predict.

How shall we verify autonomous decision-making, as captured by the cognitive agent? Our main proposal is to use program model-checking to demonstrate that the core agent always *endeavours* to act in line with our requirements and never *deliberately* chooses options that it believes will lead to bad situations (e.g., ones where the agent believes something is unsafe). Thus, we do not try to verify all the 'real-world' outcomes of the agent's choices, but instead verify the *choices* themselves. In particular, we verify that the agent always tries to achieve its goals/targets to the best of its knowledge/beliefs/ability. Thus, the agent achieves situations it *believes* to be good and avoids situations it *believes* to be bad and, consequently, any guarantees here concern the autonomous system's decisions, not its overall effects.

This lets us distinguish between a cognitive agent *knowingly* choosing a dangerous/insecure option and a cognitive agent *unknowingly* doing so based on an imperfect representation of the actual environment. Indeed, we argue that the most crucial aspect of autonomous system verification, for example concerning safety, is to identify that the agent never deliberately makes a choice that leads it into what it *believes* to be an unsafe state of the world. We wish to ensure that if an unsafe situation arises this is because of unforeseen consequences of an agent's actions (i.e., its model of the environment was too weak, or its assessment of physical control was incomplete) not because the agent chose an option it should have foreseen would lead to a bad outcome.

Aside: Accidental or Deliberate? Are all dangerous situations equally bad? What if a robot *deliberately* took an action that it knew would cause danger? Is this more serious than a robot *accidentally* causing this danger? This distinction can be important, not least to the public, and if a robot is being 'vindictive', then few safeguards can protect us. Importantly, our approach allows us to distinguish between these cases. We can verify whether the agent's beliefs were simply not accurate enough (in which case, the agent is 'innocent') or whether the agent knew about the danger and decided to proceed anyway.

One reason for taking this approach of verifying what the agent chooses, based on its beliefs, is the purely practical issue of trying to model the 'real world'. We can *never* have a precise model of the 'real world' and so can never say, for certain, what the effect of any action the system could choose might be. We might construct increasingly precise models approximating the 'real world', but they will clearly always be imperfect.

A second reason is to treat the agent, to some extent, as we might treat a human. In assessing human behaviour, we are trusting if someone *is competent and tries their best* to achieve something. In particular, we consider someone as exhibiting 'safe' behaviour, if they have taken all the information they have access to into account and have then competently made the safest decision they consider possible. Just as with humans, an agent's beliefs capture its partial knowledge about the 'real world'. The agent's beliefs might be wrong, or incorrect, **but** we only verify that the agent never *chooses* a course of action that it should have been able to reason would lead to what it *believes* to be bad situation. The agent's beliefs could be wrong and, of course, these beliefs might be refined/improved providing a better (more accurate) approximation of the real situation.

We can contrast this with the traditional approach to formal (temporal) verification where we verify that bad things *never* happen and good things *eventually* happen (Manna and Pnueli, 1992). Instead, we only need to verify that the agent *believes* this to be the case. This also has an impact upon the agent's selection of intentions/goals. As the agent is required to believe that no bad thing should occur, then it should never select an intention that it believes will lead to something bad, for example,[1]

$$\mathbf{B}(\varphi \Rightarrow \mathsf{bad}) \ \Rightarrow \ \Box\neg\mathbf{I}\varphi.$$

So, if the agent believes that achieving 'φ' implies something bad, it will never intend to undertake φ. N.B.: this is clearly an over-simplification as the agent may often have to 'juggle' several 'bad' options and choose the least bad – we discuss this further in Chapter 10.

In the context of the verification discussed in this book, we use the property specification language that is provided with AJPF (Dennis et al., 2012). This language is propositional linear temporal logic (PLTL), extended with specific modalities for checking the contents of the agent's belief base (**B**), goal base (**G**), actions taken (**A**) and intentions – goals which are associated with a deed stack – (**I**). We discuss this further in Chapter 6.

This approach is clearly a simplification as we can carry out verification without comprehensive modelling of the 'real world'. We verify the (finite) *choices* the agent has, rather than all the 'real world' effects of those choices. Clearly, some parts of an agent's reasoning are still triggered by the arrival of information from the real world and we must deal with this appropriately. So, we first analyse the agent's program to assess what these incoming *perceptions* can be and then explore, via the AJPF model-checker, all possible combinations of these inputs. This allows us to be agnostic about how the real world might actually behave and simply verify how the agent behaves *no matter what* information it receives. Furthermore, this allows us to use hypotheses that explicitly describe how patterns of perception may occur in reality. Taking such an approach clearly gives rise to a large state space because we explore

---

[1]　Here, '**B**' means 'the agent believes', '$\Box$' means 'at all future moments in time', and '**I**' means 'the agent intends'.

all possible combinations of inputs to a particular agent. In some cases we will restrict this state-space to make the exploration manageable. There are several examples of this in the applications chapters of this book and we discuss an approach to detecting potential errors this may introduce in Chapter 12.

The approach also allows us to investigate a multi-agent system in a compositional way. Using standard computational approaches (such as *assume-guarantee* or *rely-guarantee* (Jones, 1986; Manna and Pnueli, 1992)), we need only check the internal operation of a single agent at a time and can then combine the results from the model-checking using deductive methods to prove theorems about the system as a whole.

5.4 Onward

To exemplify our approach we will, in the subsequent chapters, describe a variety of different scenarios that have been implemented using GWENDOLEN and verified formally using *Agent JPF* (AJPF), a program model-checker for GWENDOLEN programs. In all these examples, the agent makes a decision, passes on to the continuous control to implement the fine detail, and then monitors the activity. The agent only becomes involved again if a new situation is reached, if a new decision is required, or if the agent notices some irregularity in the way the continuous control is working.

6

Agent-Based Autonomous System Verification

In this chapter we introduce the MCAPL framework (Dennis et al., 2012) that provides a route to the formal verification of cognitive agents and agent-based autonomous systems using JPF.

The MCAPL framework has two main sub-components: the AIL toolkit for implementing interpreters for BDI agent programming languages and the AJPF model-checker. Interpreters for BDI languages are programmed by instantiating the language's operational semantics using the Java-based *AIL toolkit*. An agent system can be programmed in the normal way for a language but runs in the AIL interpreter which, when performing model-checking, runs on the JPF virtual machine.

Agent JPF (AJPF) is a customisation of JPF that is optimised for AIL-based language interpreters. Agents programmed in languages that are implemented using the AIL toolkit can thus be model-checked in AJPF. Furthermore if they run in an environment programmed in Java, then the whole agent system can be model-checked. Common to all language interpreters implemented using the AIL are the AIL-agent data structures for *beliefs, intentions, goals*, and so on, which are subsequently accessed by the model-checker and on which the modalities of a *property specification language* are defined.

In Chapter 4 we described how JPF provides a basis for the formal verification of actual Java code. In this chapter we concentrate on three aspects:

1. how we implement a cognitive agent programming language in Java for use with JPF;

2. the *property specification language*, based on temporal logic, and specialised to cognitive agent programs; and

3. the AJPF approach to model-checking of agent-controlled autonomous systems.

6.1 From Operational Semantics to Model-Checking

Recall from Chapter 4 that JPF employs *listeners* that detect changes in program state and can then check properties when these changes occur.

Where we have an operational semantics for a programming language (as descibed in Chapter 3), such as is common for many BDI agent programming languages then it is natural to think of a transition in this operational semantics as a transition from one state to the next. So a transition rule:

$$\frac{\cdot}{s_1 \rightarrow s_2} \tag{6.1}$$

appearing in the operational semantics becomes a transition from state, s_1, to state s_2 in the automaton representing the program constructed by JPF.

The AIL-toolkit thus provides support for implementing representations of BDI program states, transitions between these states and links these transitions to a listener that can be used by JPF. We will describe some of the details of how the listeners build program automata and how this is checked against properties in Chapter 13 where we discuss how this information can be extracted from AJPF and used in other model-checking systems.

6.2 The Property Specification Language

Once we have a representation of runs of the program as an automaton we need some way to describe properties of interest. The MCAPL Property Specification Language is based on LTL with 'modalities' for agent concepts.

Syntax. The syntax for property formulæ ϕ is as follows, where ag is an 'agent name' referring to a specific agent in the system, and f is a ground first-order atomic formula (although it may use '_', as in Prolog, to indicate variables which may match any value):

$$\phi ::= \quad \mathbf{B}_{ag}\, f \mid \mathbf{G}_{ag}f \mid \mathbf{A}_{ag}f \mid \mathbf{I}_{ag}f \mid \mathbf{ID}_{ag}f \mid \mathbf{P}\, f \mid$$
$$\phi \vee \phi \mid \phi \wedge \phi \mid \neg \phi \mid \phi \, \mathsf{U} \, \phi \mid \phi \, \mathsf{R} \, \phi \mid \Diamond \phi \mid \Box \phi.$$

Here, $\mathbf{B}_{ag}\, f$ is true if ag believes f to be true, $\mathbf{G}_{ag}f$ is true if ag has a goal to make f true, and so on (with $\mathbf{A}$ representing actions, $\mathbf{I}$ representing intentions, $\mathbf{ID}$ representing the intention to take an action, and $\mathbf{P}$ representing percepts, that is, properties that are true in the environment).

Semantics. We next summarise semantics of property formulæ. Consider a program, P, describing a multi-agent system and let MAS be the state of the multi-agent system at one point in the run of P. MAS is a tuple consisting of the local states of the individual agents and of the environment. Let $ag \in MAS$ be the state of an agent in the MAS tuple at this point in the program execution. Then

$$MAS \models_{MC} \mathbf{B}_{ag} \mathsf{f} \quad \text{iff} \quad ag \models \mathbf{B}_{ag} \mathsf{f},$$

where $\models$ is logical consequence as implemented by the agent programming language. The semantics of $\mathbf{G}_{ag}\mathsf{f}$, $\mathbf{I}_{ag}\mathsf{f}$, and $\mathbf{ID}_{ag}\mathsf{f}$ similarly refer to internal implementations of the language interpreter.[1] The interpretation of $\mathbf{A}_{ag}\mathsf{f}$ is:

$$MAS \models_{MC} \mathbf{A}_{ag}\mathsf{f}$$

if, and only if, the last action changing the environment was action f taken by agent ag. Finally, the interpretation of $\mathbf{P}\,\mathsf{f}$ is given as:

$$MAS \models_{MC} \mathbf{P}\,\mathsf{f}$$

if, and only if, f is a percept that holds true in the environment.

The other operators in the AJPF property specification language have standard LTL semantics (Emerson, 1990a) and are implemented as Büchi Automata as described in Courcoubetis et al. (1992) and Gerth et al. (1996). Thus, the classical logic operators are defined by:

$$MAS \models_{MC} \varphi \vee \psi \quad \text{iff} \quad MAS \models_{MC} \varphi \text{ or } MAS \models_{MC} \psi$$
$$MAS \models_{MC} \neg\phi \quad \text{iff} \quad MAS \not\models_{MC} \phi.$$

The temporal formulae apply to runs of the programs in the JPF model-checker. A run consists of a (possibly infinite) sequence of program states $MAS_i, i \geq 0$ where MAS_0 is the initial state of the program (note, however, that for model-checking the number of *different* states in any run is assumed to be finite).

Let P be a multi-agent program, then:

$MAS \models_{MC} \quad \varphi \cup \psi \quad$ iff $\quad$ in all runs of P there exists a state MAS_j such that $MAS_j \models_{MC} \psi$ and for all $0 \leq i < j \quad MAS_i \models_{MC} \varphi$.

$MAS \models_{MC} \quad \varphi \mathsf{R} \psi \quad$ iff $\quad$ either $MAS_i \models_{MC} \varphi$ for all i or there exists MAS_j such that $MAS_i \models_{MC} \varphi$ for all $0 \leq i \leq j$ and $MAS_j \models_{MC} \varphi \wedge \psi$.

Conjunction $\wedge$ and the common temporal operators $\Diamond$ (eventually) and $\Box$ (always) are, in turn, derivable from $\vee$, $\cup$, and R in the usual way (Emerson, 1990a).

---

[1] We briefly cover the GWENDOLEN implementation in Appendix C.1.6.

6.2.1 Examples

The following are all examples of properties of agents in a multi-agent system, such as that might be found in a system for controlling cars on a motorway.

1. Eventually *car* believes *at_speed_limit* is true.

$$\Diamond \mathbf{B}_{car} \text{ at\_speed\_limit}$$

2. Eventually *car* has the goal *at_speed_limit*.

$$\Diamond \mathbf{G}_{car} \text{at\_speed\_limit}$$

3. Eventually the *car* believes *started* and eventually car_1 believes *at_speed_limit*.

$$\Diamond \mathbf{B}_{car} \text{ started} \land \Diamond \mathbf{B}_{car_1} \text{ at\_speed\_limit}$$

4. If *car* has the intention to be *at_speed_limit* then eventually *car* will invoke *accelerate*.

$$(\mathbf{I}_{car} \text{at\_speed\_limit}) \Rightarrow (\Diamond \mathbf{A}_{car} \text{accelerate})$$

5. It is always the case that if *car* invokes *accelerate* then *at_speed_limit* becomes perceptible.

$$\Box (\mathbf{A}_{car} \text{accelerate} \Rightarrow \mathbf{P} \text{ at\_speed\_limit})$$

6. Eventually *car* intends to do *accelerate*

$$\Diamond \mathbf{ID}_{car} \text{accelerate}$$

7. Eventually car_1 intends to send car_2 an achieve request (performatives are represented by numbers – in this case achieve is represented by the number 3) to be *at_speed_limit*.

$$\Diamond \mathbf{ID}_{car_1} \text{send}(car_2, 3, \text{at\_speed\_limit})$$

6.3 Where Does the Automaton Representing a BDI Agent Program Branch?

A key part of model-checking is the full exploration of the state space of a program (or model). Its value is therefore in situations where there are branching points in the possible execution of a program. A program that simply prints out the numbers from 1 to 10, for instance, needs only to be tested once to see if it actually does this since there is only one possible execution of the program. In general BDI agent programming languages do not implement any randomness within the language itself so branching in the execution of a program generally occurs at two points.

Firstly, in a multi-agent system, individual agents may act in different orders. Consider two agents, a_1 and a_2 each with a simple program which means that a_1 does act_1 and a_2 does act_2. Then there is potentially a run of this system in which act_1 happens before act_2 and another in which act_2 happens before act_1. The AIL toolkit provides support for different scheduling policies among agents. These scheduling policies govern which agent gets to make a state transition at any one time and can, for instance, enforce strict turn taking among agents or, alternatively, select the next agent to make a transition entirely at random. Depending upon the policy used then there may be branching points created in the automata checked by AJPF. At present no language in AJPF allows two agents to make a transition at exactly the same time, but this is not in principle excluded.

The second place in which branching may occur is in the information received by the agent from perception or messages. Sometimes this information is generated by other agents in the system and so branching points are caused by the scheduling policy which dictates when agents perform actions or send messages. However, we may also wish to represent non-determinism in the environment within which the agents operate – for instance, we might want to introduce the possibility that messages get lost. In that case we can use randomness when we program our Java environment to create such branching. The AIL toolkit provides specific support for this randomness in order both to assist the model-checking process and to allow replay of specific paths through a program execution if a bug is detected.

6.4 The Problem with Environments

This desire to represent non-deterministic behaviour in the agents' environment leads us to one of the key features of our approach to model-checking. When we model check an agent in AJPF (or indeed any model-checking system) we *have to* model check it in the context of a purely Java environment that we have placed it in. However, the reason we may be representing non-determinism in that environment (e.g., message loss) is because we believe that in the 'real' environment in which it will actually be deployed different things may occur and we wish to understand the effect of this on the system behaviour.

So when model-checking an autonomous hybrid agent system in AJPF we have to construct a Java environment that represents a simulation of some 'real' world. We can encode assumptions about the behaviour of the 'real' world in this simulation, but we would prefer to minimize such assumptions. For much of our autonomous systems work we try to have minimal assumptions where the environment asserts or retracts percepts and messages on an entirely random basis. By this we mean that we do not attempt to model assumptions about the effects an agent's actions may have on the world, or assumptions about the sequence in which perceptions may appear to the agent. This approach is not without its cost in terms of state space and the efficiency of model-checking. As a result we often do have to build in assumptions about the real world and examples of these can be seen throughout Part II of this book. We will discuss an approach to mitigating the potential issues introduced by making assumptions in Chapter 12.

The process for verifying an agent in this way, is to first analyse the agent program in order to identify all the perceptions that have an effect on the program. In multi-agent systems it is also necessary to identify all messages that the agent may receive from other agents in the environment. Once a list of perceptions and messages has been identified, an environment is constructed for the agent alone in such a way that every time the agent takes an action the set of perceptions and messages available to it are created *at random*. When model-checking, the random selection causes the search tree to branch and the model checker to explore all environmental possibilities (Dennis et al., 2016c).

We will illustrate this process with multiple examples in the case studies addressed in later chapters, but we will begin with a simpler, but instructive, example.

6.5 Example: Cars on a Motorway

We explain our approach to model-checking autonomous systems via an example of two cars on a motorway.[2]

Example 6.1 We will consider an intelligent cruise control for a car, focussing simply on when to accelerate and when to maintain its speed. The GWENDOLEN code for this is shown below. There are two cars, `car1` and `car2` and, in both cases, when the car has a goal to reach the speed limit, `+! at_speed_limit [achieve]`, it accelerates and then waits until the goal is achieved (The '*' symbol is the GWENDOLEN syntax for 'waiting'). The first car then also sends a message to *car2*. Once the cars have reached the speed limit they perform a **maintain_speed** action followed by a **finished** action. *Car1* gets the goal to be at the speed limit when it

---

[2] Examples from this chapter can be found in `src/examples/verifiableautonomoussystems/chapter5` within the MCAPL distribution. The motorway simulator can be found in `src/examples/motorwaysim`.

perceives that it has started, while $car2$ gets the goal only when it receives a message to achieve the goal.

```
:name:  car₁                                                    1
                                                                2
 :Initial  Beliefs:                                             3
                                                                4
 :Initial  Goals:                                               5
                                                                6
 :Plans:                                                        7
 +started:  { T } ←  +!at_speed_limit[achieve];                 8
                                                                9
 +! at_speed_limit [achieve]  :  { T } ←                       10
         accelerate ,                                           11
         *at_speed_limit ,                                      12
         .send(car₂ , :achieve , at_speed_limit );             13
                                                                14
 +at_speed_limit:  { T } ←                                     15
         maintain_speed ,                                       16
         finished ;                                             17
                                                                18
 :name:  car₂                                                   19
                                                                20
 :Initial  Beliefs:                                             21
                                                                22
 :Initial  Goals:                                               23
                                                                24
 :Plans:                                                        25
 +.received(:achieve , G):  { T } ←  +!G [achieve];            26
                                                                27
 +! at_speed_limit [achieve]  :  { T } ←                       28
         accelerate ,                                           29
         *at_speed_limit ;                                      30
                                                                31
 +at_speed_limit:  { T } ←                                     32
         maintain_speed ,                                       33
         finished ;                                             34
```

6.5.1 Exccuting the Program

In order to execute the above program, it needs to be connected either to physical vehicles or simulations. Figure 6.1 shows the output in a very simple vehicle simulator. The simulator has two cars each in their own motorway lane. The lanes loop around so when one car reaches the end of its lane it loops back to the start. The simulator reports both the speed of each car and their distance from the start of the motorway.

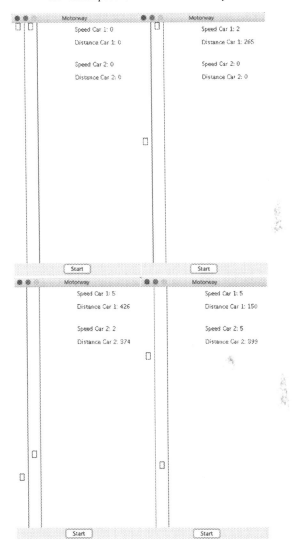

Figure 6.1 Simulating two cars on a motorway. Images from left to right show:
(a) two cars waiting at the start; (b) the first car accelerating; (c) as the first car reaches a speed of 5 it messages the second car which begins accelerating; until (d) both cars are moving at a speed of 5.

The agents are connected to the simulator via a Java environment which communicates using a standard socket mechanism. It reads the speeds of the cars from the sockets and publishes values for required acceleration to the socket. If a car's speed becomes larger than 5, then the environment adds a perception that the car is at the speed limit. If a car agent performs the `accelerate` action, then the environment publishes an acceleration of 0.1 to the socket. If a car agent performs the `maintain_speed` action, then the environment publishes an acceleration of 0 to the socket.

6.5.2 Verification: Building a Model by Examining the Environment

Suppose we wish to use AJPF to verify our agents for controlling the two cars. We cannot include the whole of the motorway simulator program in our formal verification since it is an external program. We need to replace the socket calls to this simulator in our Java environment with some model of its behaviour.

A naive way to set about this might be to capture the obvious behaviour of the simulator. We could use a scheduler to alternately execute a method, generally called `do_job` in AIL-supporting environments, in the simulator to calculate the position of each car and then to execute one step in the reasoning cycle of each car. If a car agent executes `accelerate` then each call of `do_job` increases the car's speed by 1. If the car agent executes `maintain_speed` then the car's speed remains constant. As in the Java environment that communicated with the simulator, once the speed has reached 5 this is set as a percept, `at_speed_limit`, that the agent can receive.

Such a model is, in fact, entirely deterministic (like the program that counted to 10 in Section 6.3) because of the turn-based control of the environment and the two agents. All the properties considered in Section 6.2.1 are satisfied on this model and we can determine that truth simply by executing the program – there is no need for more sophisticated model-checking.

Obviously we can make our model more complex – for instance, we could introduce a random element into whether the car detects that it has reached the speed limit, or exactly how much acceleration is created. There are some limitations to this, however. For instance, we need our model to contain a reasonable number of states, so we cannot simply vary the acceleration by a random double since that would introduce a very large search space, creating a search branch for each possible double value that could be used at that point.

Similarly as the world we wish to model becomes more complicated, such environments inevitably become harder and harder to craft in ways that behave with appropriate fidelity.

6.5.3 Verification: Building a Model by Examining the Agents

The alternative to trying to create a Java model to accurately describe the behaviour of the real world is to analyse instead the inputs in terms of perceptions and messages received by the agent program. This is our approach. We construct a model in which, every time the agent program queries the environment for perceptions, the environment returns a random subset of these. In the case of `car1` there are only two perceptions `at_speed_limit` and `started` and so we need an environment that generates inputs from these two.

The MCAPL framework provides support for creating these kinds of environments for GWENDOLEN programs through an abstract

`VerificationofAutonomousSystemsEnvironment`

class that can, in turn, be sub-classed. The sub-classes simply have to sub-class the methods for generating random perceptions, `generate_percepts`, and random messages, `generate_messages`.

Example 6.2

```
public Set<Predicate> generate_percepts ()                         1
{                                                                  2
    Set<Predicate> beliefs = new HashSet<Predicate>();            3
                                                                   4
    boolean at_speed_limit =                                       5
        random_bool_generator.nextBoolean ();                      6
    boolean started =                                              7
        random_bool_generator.nextBoolean ();                      8
    if (at_speed_limit)                                            9
    {                                                             10
        beliefs.add(new Predicate("at_speed_limit"));            11
        AJPFLogger.info(logname, "At_Speed_Limit");              12
    }                                                             13
                                                                  14
    if (started)                                                  15
    {                                                             16
        beliefs.add(new Predicate("started"));                  17
        AJPFLogger.info(logname, "Started");                    18
    }                                                             19
    return beliefs;                                               20
}                                                                 21
```

Here, we show the `generate_percepts` method. Two booleans are generated at random and are used to decide whether or not a percept is added to the set returned to the agent. For our car example, the two percepts in question are `at_speed_limit` and `started`. A similar mechanism can be used to generate messages at random. A logging mechanism `AJPFLogger` prints output about the perceptions generated for a user to see.

Using this environment *none* of the properties from Section 6.2.1 are true, not even ones such as *'if car_1 accelerates, eventually it will be at the speed limit'*. This is because the environment does not link the acceleration action in any way to the car's speed. In fact the actions taken by the agent in such an environment have no causal link to the perceptions that are returned. Essentially, we cannot make any assumptions about whether the software and machinery involved in making acceleration happen are working, nor whether the sensors for detecting the car's speed are working.

To prove useful properties with this kind of environment we typically prove properties of the general form

'If whenever the agent does X eventually the agent believes Y then...'.

So for instance we can prove, using the above environment, that 'provided that, if car1 invokes acceleration then eventually car1 believes it is at the speed limit, then eventually car1 will invoke finished', that is:

$$\Box(\mathbf{A}_{car_1}\mathsf{accelerate} \rightarrow \Diamond\mathbf{B}_{car_1} \mathsf{at\_speed\_limit}) \rightarrow \Diamond\mathbf{A}_{car_1}\mathsf{finished}.$$

There are many properties of this form discussed in the case studies in subsequent chapters.

Just as we could make our model based on examination of the environment more complex and so increase the state space, we can reduce the state space for models based on examination of the agents by linking the generation of percepts to actions. By default we only randomly generate new sets of perceptions after an action has been invoked – any other time the agent polls the environment for perceptions it receives the same set it was sent last time it asked. While this does introduce assumptions about the behaviour of the real world – that changes in perceptions only occur after an agent has taken some action, it is normally comparatively safe if you can assume that agent deliberation is very fast compared to the time it takes to execute an action and for changes in the world to occur. This reduces the possibilities and the complexity of the model-checking problem.

It is also possible to make application-specific assumptions to constrain the generation of sets by the environment: for instance that the `at_speed_limit` perception cannot be included in a set until after the `accelerate` action has been performed at least once. This does increase the risk that the environment used for verification may exclude behaviours that would be observed in the real environment and we will discuss this further in Chapter 12.

The applications we discuss in the next part of this book take a variety of approaches to the question of environments both in terms of the actual system and its verification.

6.6 Moving on to Applications

In the next part of this book we will look at a variety of case studies, showing how the principles described so far can be applied to the verification of a range of different autonomous systems. The case studies we give are deliberately from very different application areas and often involve combinations of techniques: *environmental abstraction*; *single agent verification*; *communication*; *complex properties*; *multi-agent systems*; and so on.

Through all these case studies we aim to follow a similar pattern, tackling

1. *What is the system?*
   that is, what is the autonomous system we want to verify, is it virtual or physical, what is its purpose, and so on?
2. *What do we want to establish?*
   that is, what properties and/or requirements do we wish to verify?
3. GWENDOLEN *code*
   we provide at least key fragments of the GWENDOLEN code for the system.
4. *Environments*
   that is, what structural work is needed to link this to real-world systems – note that in some, purely virtual, scenarios this might be very little – and how is this reflected in the environment we use for verification.
5. *Example verification*
   that is, we show how the formal verification of (3) with respect to (2) has been carried out, highlighting any peculiarities.
6. *Issues*
   that is, we highlight any issues that arise from this case study, in modelling, requirements, abstraction, or verification.

Part II

Applications

7

Multi-Agent Auctions

This work was carried out with Matt Webster, who was involved in both implementation and verification, and was reported initially in Webster et al. (2009) then subsequently as part of Dennis et al. (2012) in broader work with Rafael Bordini.

7.1 What is the System?

We will begin with a *very* simple multi-agent system. This comprises purely software agents and, furthermore, contains very few agents! However, this exploration will show how standard software agents, and multi-agent systems, can be formally verified using AJPF.

In these examples we do not tackle the problem of how we can model the real world by generating perceptions at random. We will leave examples of this technique to later chapters.

7.1.1 Simple Agent Auctions

Auctions (Klemperer, 2004; Vickrey, 1961), as well as being central to the study of Economics, are widely used in multi-agent scenarios (Boutilier et al., 1997). They are fundamental within many agent-based e-commerce applications (Collins et al., 2009; Fortnow et al., 2008), and are often implicit within many *market-based* approaches to agent computation (Walsh and Wellman, 1998). These auctions are especially useful when either resource allocation or task allocation is required, for example in electricity supply management (Corera et al., 1996), telecommunications (Haque et al., 2005), agent mobility (Bredin et al., 2003), logistics (Dash et al., 2007), or scheduling (Reeves et al., 2005).

While significant work has been, and continues to be, carried out on the deep analysis of auction mechanisms, such as through formal mechanism design

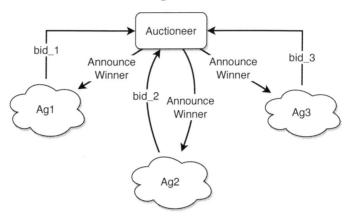

Figure 7.1 Initial auction scenario. Reprinted by permission from Springer Nature. Dennis, L.A., Fisher, M., Webster, M.P. *et al.* 2012. Model checking agent
programming languages. *Automated Software Engineering*, 19, 5-63, © 2012

(Wooldridge et al., 2007), the formal analysis of *implementations* of auction
mechanisms is less well developed. While there has been *some* work on the
formal verification of implemented auctions, such as Doghri (2008), typically
this does not incorporate an *agent* perspective. By contrast, our examples here
will utilise more sophisticated agent aspects such as goals, intentions, and beliefs within an auction context.

The basic version of this study is initially very simple. We will first describe this basic scenario and then, in subsequent sections, develop (slightly)
more sophisticated variants, each becoming increasingly (though never totally)
realistic.

7.1.2 An Initial Basic Auction

The idea here is simple. A number of agents (in Figure 7.1, three) make bids of
some value to an `auctioneer` agent. When the `auctioneer` agent has the
three bids, it will then award the 'contract' to the highest bidder, and will subsequently announce this. This cycle can then repeat, if required (note, however,
that in our verified scenarios, the bidding process does *not* cycle).

Here, all agents believe what they are told. The `auctioneer` agent essentially records bids from the other agents, and when bids have been received from the other three agents (`ag1`, `ag2`, and `ag3`) notifies the agents
of the winner. (Note that we have simplified this to assume that bids are either 100, 150, or 200, with the agent bidding 200 winning – we will describe

changes to this later.) The bidding agents (ag1, ag2, and ag3) essentially have the same behaviours, though with different bidding values. Each has a (perform) goal to make a bid (+!bid [perform]), and one plan to achieve this. This plan just allows each agent to make a bid of either 100, 150, or 200.

Versions of this scenario with increasing numbers of agents (Figure 7.2) were implemented in GWENDOLEN. The code for the four-agent version can be found Section 7.3 while the verification carried out on this basic scenario is reported in Section 7.5.

Auction Coalition Scenario. The basic auction scenario is, as the name suggests, not very sophisticated. So, we will now extend this to incorporate the possibility of *coalitions* (Konishi and Ray, 2003; Sandholm and Lesser, 1997). Here, a coalition occurs when several agents collaborate by pooling their bids in order to win the auction. For example, if three agents ag1, ag2, and ag3 bid 100, 150, and 200, respectively, then ag3 ought to win every time. However, if ag1 and ag2 form a coalition, their collective bid of 250 should then be enough to win the auction.

A simple coalition scenario was developed with an auctioneer and a variable number of bidders. Here, most of the agents make their bids straight away, but one agent instead attempts to form a simple coalition by communicating with one of the other bidding agents. The bidding agent who has been contacted then agrees to form the coalition, and so informs the coalition instigator of the amount that is available to be pooled. The instigator can then combine its own bidding amount with that of its coalition partner and can subsequently submit this pooled bid to the auctioneer. As usual, once the auctioneer has received all the bids, it announces the winner.

In the diagram in Figure 7.3, agent ag2 instigates the coalition: The main difference in the implementation of this scenario, as compared with our earlier one, is that one agent, ag2, has an additional goal to form a coalition. In tackling this goal, agent ag2 contacts ag1 and proposes a coalition. If ag1 agrees then ag2 can now bid a winning 250 (i.e., 100 + 150). Clearly, we would like to verify that this approach does, indeed, lead to agent ag2 winning the auction. This is one of the properties we verify in Section 7.5.

We can then proceed to develop increasingly sophisticated variations, a few of which are outlined below.

Dynamic Auction Coalition Scenario. In the previous scenario, a coalition was instigated immediately, but we next consider a variant on the auction coalition scenario where this only occurs once results have been discovered. First,

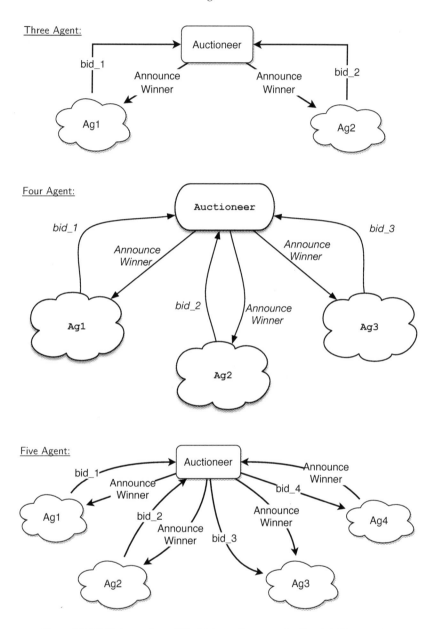

Figure 7.2 Multiple versions of the basic auction scenario. Reprinted by permission from Springer Nature. Dennis, L.A., Fisher, M., Webster, M.P. et al. 2012. Model checking agent programming languages. *Automated Software Engineering*, 19, 5-63, © 2012

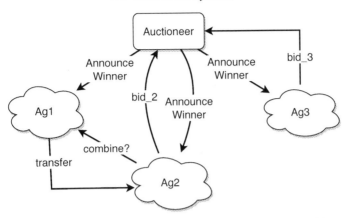

Figure 7.3 The simple coalition scenario. Reprinted by permission from Springer Nature. Dennis, L.A., Fisher, M., Webster, M.P. et al. 2012. Model checking agent programming languages. *Automated Software Engineering*, 19, 5-63, © 2012

a round of bidding takes place in which all agents bid. Then, after an agent discovers that it has lost the auction, it sends a message to one of the other agents (but not the previous winner) in order to form a coalition. Then, the agents bid again with the *pooled* resources, as above.

Coalition Trust Scenario. This scenario is also similar to that described already, but coalition forming agent now has a *belief* about which other agent(s) it can *trust*, that is, the other agents with which it would *prefer* to form a coalition. This trust aspect is static, that is, the coalition-forming agent starts the auction with belief(s) about which agents it can trust, and these do not change during the auction.

The interesting difference here is that when one agent, ag1, acquires a goal to form a coalition, it consults its beliefs to learn the identity of an agent it trusts, ag3 say. Agent ag1 then contacts ag3 and proposes a coalition. If ag3 agrees then ag1 can now make a winning bid. Again, we would like to verify that this approach does, indeed, lead to ag1 winning the auction. This is also one of the properties we aim to verify in Section 7.5.

Dynamic Trust Scenario. Our final scenario builds directly on the trust scenario above. Now, if the coalition-forming agent loses the initial auction, it tries to form a coalition with an agent it trusts as before. If this coalition is successful in winning the auction, it stops. However, if this coalition is *unsuccessful* then the instigating agent no longer believes that it can trust the other agent in the coalition, and will try to form another coalition with another agent it trusts. Again, sample code for this scenario can be seen in Section 7.3.

7.2 What *Properties* Do We Want to Establish?

The basic property that will be verified is

$$\Diamond \mathbf{B}_{ag_b} \text{ win,}$$

where ag_b is the agent with the highest bid, '**B**' is the *belief* operator, and '$\Diamond$' means 'at some time in the future'. In other words, the agent with the highest bid will eventually believe it has won. We will use this to assess which agent wins in the various multi-agent auction scenarios.

Later we will also verify

$$\Diamond \mathbf{G}_{ag_c} \text{coalition,}$$

where ag_c was the (last) coalition forming agent. Here, '**G**' is the 'goal' operator. In verifying this, we are not checking that the agent necessarily achieved any win, but that it (at some point in its execution) adopted the goal to form a coalition.

7.3 GWENDOLEN Code

We present GWENDOLEN code for the auction scenarios.[1] Many GWENDOLEN constructs should already be familiar from where we introduced the language in Chapter 3. However the code here also uses +.lock and -.lock. When a GWENDOLEN program has multiple intentions it normally executes one deed on each intention in turn. However this can mean that intentions can interfere with each other. For instance in the code for the dynamic coalition example the auctioneer agent changes its beliefs about the current winner as the bids come in from the individual agents. So it may be processing several bids in parallel and since it removes its belief about the previous current winner before adding its belief about the new current winner could potentially get into a state where it does not believe there is a current winner even though some bids have been received.

To overcome this GWENDOLEN has a special deed, .lock which 'locks' an intention in place and forces GWENDOLEN to execute deeds from that intention *only* until the intention is unlocked. The syntax +.lock locks an intention

---

[1] The examples in this chapter can be found in the folder
src/examples/gwendolen/auctions of the AJPF distribution.

and the syntax −.lock unlocks the intention. In the case of the dynamic co-alition scenario this means that the auctioneer fully updates its beliefs about the current winner before processing a different intention.

The use of locking is discussed more fully in Appendix A.6.2.

7.3.1 Basic Auction Scenario

The GWENDOLEN code for the four agent (one auctioneer agent and three *bidding* agents) system is given below. Here, all agents believe what they are told. Agent auctioneer, who takes the role of the auctioneer, essentially records bids from the other agents and, when bids have been received from the other three agents (ag1, ag2, and ag3) notifies the agents of the winner. (Note that we have simplified this to assume that bids are either 100, 150, or 200.) The bidding agents (ag1, ag2, and ag3) are essentially the same. Each has a (perform) goal to make a bid (+! bid [perform]), and one plan to achieve this. This plan just allows each agent to make a bid of either 100, 150, or 200.

In some of these examples, the auctioneer can perform an action, win(A, Z), which the environment treats as a public announcement and makes the perception that agent, A, as won the auction by bidding Z, available to all the agents.

```
:name: auctioneer                                           1
                                                            2
:Initial  Beliefs:                                          3
                                                            4
:Initial  Goals:                                            5
                                                            6
:Plans:                                                     7
                                                            8
+.received(:tell , B): {⊤} ← +B;                            9
+bid(Z, A) : {B bid(X1, ag1), B bid(X2, ag2),              10
  B bid(X3, ag3), B bid(200, Ag),                          11
  ~.sent(Ag, auctioneer , :tell , win)}                    12
  ← .send(Ag, :tell , win);                                13
                                                            14
:name: ag1                                                  15
                                                            16
:Initial  Beliefs:                                          17
                                                            18
my_name(ag1)                                                19
                                                            20
:Initial  Goals:                                            21
                                                            22
bid [perform]                                               23
                                                            24
:Plans:                                                     25
                                                            26
```

```
+.received (: tell ,  B):  { T }  ←  +B;                           27
+!bid [perform]  :  {B my_name(Name),                             28
   ~ . sent ( auctioneer ,  Name,  : tell ,  bid (100,  Name))}   29
   ←  . send ( auctioneer ,  : tell ,  bid (100,  Name));        30
                                                                  31
:name:  ag2                                                       32
                                                                  33
:Initial  Beliefs:                                               34
                                                                  35
my_name(ag2)                                                     36
                                                                  37
:Initial  Goals:                                                 38
                                                                  39
bid  [perform]                                                    40
                                                                  41
:Plans:                                                          42
                                                                  43
+.received (: tell ,  B):  { T }  ←  +B;                           44
+!bid [perform]  :  {B my_name(Name),                             45
   ~ . sent ( auctioneer ,  Name,  : tell ,  bid (200,  Name))}   46
   ←  . send ( auctioneer ,  : tell ,  bid (200,  Name));        47
                                                                  48
:name:  ag3                                                       49
                                                                  50
:Initial  Beliefs:                                               51
                                                                  52
my_name(ag3)                                                     53
                                                                  54
:Initial  Goals:                                                 55
                                                                  56
bid  [perform]                                                    57
                                                                  58
:Plans:                                                          59
                                                                  60
+.received (: tell ,  B):  { T }  ←  +B;                           61
+!bid [perform]  :  {B my_name(Name),                             62
   ~ . sent ( auctioneer ,  Name,  : tell ,  bid (150,  Name))}   63
   ←  . send ( auctioneer ,  : tell ,  bid (150,  Name));        64
```

7.3.2 Auction Coalition Scenario

A version of the code for the basic coalition scenario with four agents is shown below:

```
GWENDOLEN                                                         1
                                                                  2
:name:  auctioneer                                               3
                                                                  4
:Initial  Beliefs:                                               5
                                                                  6
                                                                  7
```

```
: Initial  Goals :                                                    8
                                                                      9
: Plans :                                                            10
                                                                     11
+. received (: tell , B): { ⊤ } ← +B;                               12
+bid(Z, A)  :  {B  bid(X1,  ag1),  B  bid(X2,  ag2),               13
   B  bid(X3,  ag3),  B  bid(250, Ag),                             14
   ∼ .sent(Ag,  Me,  : tell ,  win)}                               15
   ←  .send(Ag,  : tell ,  win );                                  16
                                                                     17
: name :  ag1                                                        18
                                                                     19
: Initial  Beliefs :                                                 20
                                                                     21
my_name( ag1 )                                                       22
                                                                     23
: Initial  Goals :                                                  24
                                                                     25
coalition  [ perform ]                                              26
                                                                     27
: Plans :                                                           28
                                                                     29
+. received (: tell , B): { ⊤ } ← +B;                               30
+!bid  [ perform ]  :  {B  my_name(Name),                          31
   ∼ .sent(auctioneer ,  Name,  : tell ,  bid(250,  Name))}        32
   ←  .send(auctioneer ,  : tell ,  bid(250,  Name));              33
+!coalition  [ perform ]  :  {B  my_name(Ag),                      34
   ∼ .sent(ag3,  Ag,  : tell ,  coalition(Ag))}                    35
   ←  .send(ag3,  : tell ,  coalition(Ag));                        36
+agree(A, X)  :  { ⊤ } ← +!bid  [ perform ];                       37
                                                                     38
: name :  ag2                                                        39
                                                                     40
: Initial  Beliefs :                                                 41
                                                                     42
my_name( ag2 )                                                       43
                                                                     44
: Initial  Goals :                                                  45
                                                                     46
bid  [ perform ]                                                    47
                                                                     48
: Plans :                                                           49
                                                                     50
+. received (: tell , B): { ⊤ } ← +B;                               51
+!bid  [ perform ]  :  {B  my_name(Name),                          52
   ∼ .sent(auctioneer ,  Name,  : tell ,  bid(200,  Name))}        53
   ←  .send(auctioneer ,  : tell ,  bid(200,  Name));              54
                                                                     55
: name :  ag3                                                       56
                                                                     57
: Initial  Beliefs :                                                58
```

```
my_name(ag3)                                                          59
                                                                     60
                                                                     61
:Initial  Goals:                                                     62
                                                                     63
bid [perform]                                                        64
                                                                     65
:Plans:                                                              66
                                                                     67
+.received (:tell , B): {⊤} ← +B;                                    68
+!bid [perform]  : {B my_name(Name),                                 69
    ~.sent(auctioneer, Name, :tell , bid(150, Name))}               70
    ← .send(auctioneer , :tell , bid(150, Name));                   71
+coalition(A)  : { B my_name(Name),                                 72
    ~.sent(A, Name, :tell , agree(Name, 150))}                      73
    ← .send(A, :tell , agree(Name, 150));                           74
```

7.3.3 Dynamic Auction Coalition Scenario

A version of the code for the dynamic coalition scenario with four agents is shown below:

```
GWENDOLEN                                                             1
                                                                     2
:name: auctioneer                                                    3
                                                                     4
:Initial  Beliefs:                                                   5
                                                                     6
my_name(auctioneer)                                                 7
                                                                     8
:Reasoning  Rules:                                                   9
                                                                    10
allbids  :— bid_processed(ag1), bid_processed(ag2),                 11
    bid_processed(ag3);                                             12
                                                                    13
:Initial  Goals:                                                   14
                                                                    15
:Plans:                                                            16
                                                                    17
+.received(:tell , bid(D, From))  : {B bid(E, From)}               18
    ← −bid(From, E), +bid(From, D);                                19
+.received(:tell , bid(D, From))  : {~B bid(E, From)}              20
    ← +bid(From, D);                                               21
+bid(Z, A)  : {B current_winner(Ag1, Amw), Amw < A,                22
    B allbids}                                                     23
    ← +.lock, −current_winner(Ag1, Amw), +ann_winner,             24
      +current_winner(Z, A), win(Z, A), −.lock;                    25
+bid_processed(Ag)  : {B current_winner(Agw, Amw),                 26
    B allbids , ~B ann_winner}                                     27
    ← +.lock, +ann_winner, win(Agw, Amw), −.lock;                 28
+bid(Ag, Am)  : {~B current_winner(Ag2, Amw)}                      29
```

```
 ← +current_winner(Ag, Am), +bid_processed(Ag);                    30
+bid(Ag, Am) : {B current_winner(Agw, Amw),                        31
  ∼Am < Amw, ∼B allbids}                                           32
   ← +.lock, +current_winner(Ag, Am),                              33
     +bid_processed(Ag), −current_winner(Agw, Amw),                34
     −.lock;                                                       35
+bid(Ag, Am) : {B current_winner(Agw, Amw), Am < Amw,             36
  ∼B allbids}                                                      37
   ← +bid_processed(Ag);                                           38
                                                                   39
+!bp(Ag) [perform] : {⊤} ← +bid_processed(Ag);                    40
                                                                   41
:name: ag1                                                         42
                                                                   43
:Initial Beliefs:                                                  44
                                                                   45
my_name(ag1)                                                       46
collaborator(ag3)                                                  47
cash(150)                                                          48
                                                                   49
:Initial Goals:                                                    50
                                                                   51
bid [perform]                                                      52
                                                                   53
:Plans:                                                            54
                                                                   55
+.received(:tell, B): {⊤} ← +B;                                   56
+!bid [perform] : {B my_name(Name), B cash(C),                    57
  ∼.sent(auctioneer, Name, :tell, bid(C, Name))}                  58
   ← .send(auctioneer, :tell, bid(C, Name));                      59
+agree(A, X): {B cash(C), B my_name(Name)}                        60
   ← .send(auctioneer, :tell, bid((C + X), Name));                61
+win(Ag, X): {B my_name(Name), ∼B win(Name, Any),                 62
  B collaborator(Coll)}                                            63
   ← +!coalition(Coll) [achieve];                                 64
+!coalition(Coll) [achieve] : {B my_name(Ag),                     65
  ∼.sent(Coll, Ag, :tell, coalition(Ag))}                         66
   ← .send(Coll, :tell, coalition(Ag)),                           67
     +coalition(Coll);                                             68
                                                                   69
:name: ag2                                                         70
                                                                   71
:Initial Beliefs:                                                  72
                                                                   73
my_name(ag2)                                                       74
cash(200)                                                          75
                                                                   76
:Initial Goals:                                                    77
                                                                   78
bid [perform]                                                      79
                                                                   80
```

```
: Plans :                                                        81
                                                                 82
+.received (:tell , B): { ⊤ } ← +B;                              83
+!bid [perform] : {B my_name(Name), B cash(C),                   84
    ∼.sent(auctioneer, Name, :tell, bid(C, Name))}               85
    ← .send(auctioneer, :tell, bid(C, Name));                    86
                                                                 87
:name: ag3                                                       88
                                                                 89
: Initial Beliefs :                                              90
                                                                 91
my_name(ag3)                                                     92
cash(150)                                                        93
                                                                 94
: Initial Goals :                                                95
                                                                 96
bid [perform]                                                    97
                                                                 98
: Plans :                                                        99
                                                                100
+.received (:tell , B): { ⊤ } ← +B;                             101
+!bid [perform] : {B my_name(Name), B cash(C),                  102
    ∼.sent(auctioneer, Name, :tell, bid(C, Name))}              103
    ← .send(auctioneer, :tell, bid(C, Name));                   104
+coalition(A) : {B my_name(Name), B cash(C),                    105
    ∼.sent(A, Name, :tell, agree(Name, C))}                     106
    ← .send(A, :tell, agree(Name, C));                          107
```

7.3.4 Coalition Trust Scenario

A version of the code for the coalition trust scenario with four agents is shown below:

```
GWENDOLEN                                                         1
                                                                  2
:name: auctioneer                                                 3
                                                                  4
: Initial Beliefs :                                               5
                                                                  6
                                                                  7
: Initial Goals :                                                 8
                                                                  9
: Plans :                                                        10
                                                                 11
+.received (:tell , bid(D, From)) : {B bid(From, E)}             12
    ← −bid(From, E), +bid(From, D);                              13
+.received (:tell , bid(D, From)) : { ∼B bid(From, E)}           14
    ← +bid(From, D);                                             15
+bid(Z, A) : {B bid(ag1, X1), B bid(ag2, X2),                    16
    B bid(ag3, X3), ∼B winning_amount(Am),                       17
    X2 < X1, X3 < X1}                                            18
```

```
    ← +winning_amount(X1),  win(ag1,  X1);                          19
+bid(Z, A)  :  {B bid(ag1,  X1),  B bid(ag2,  X2),                  20
   B bid(ag3,  X3),  ∼B winning_amount(Am),                         21
   X1 < X2,  X3 < X2}                                               22
    ← +winning_amount(X2),  win(ag2,  X2);                          23
+bid(Z, A)  :  {B bid(ag1,  X1),  B bid(ag2,  X2),                  24
   B bid(ag3,  X3),  ∼B winning_amount(Am),                         25
   X2 < X3,  X1 < X3}                                               26
    ← +winning_amount(X2),  win(ag3,  X3);                          27
+bid(Z, A)  :  {B winning_amount(Am),  Am < A}                      28
    ← −winning_amount(Am),                                          29
   +winning_amount(A),                                              30
   win(Z,  A);                                                      31
                                                                   32
:name:  ag1                                                         33
                                                                   34
:Initial  Beliefs:                                                 35
                                                                   36
my_name(ag1)                                                       37
trust(ag3)                                                          38
                                                                   39
:Initial  Goals:                                                   40
                                                                   41
bid  [perform]                                                     42
                                                                   43
:Plans:                                                            44
                                                                   45
+.received(:tell,  B):  {⊤}  ← +B;                                 46
+!bid  [perform]  :  {B my_name(Name),                            47
   ∼.sent(auctioneer,  Name,  :tell,  bid(150,  Name))}           48
    ← .send(auctioneer,  :tell,  bid(150,  Name));                49
+win(A,  X)  :  {B my_name(Name),  ∼B win(Name,  Y),             50
   B trust(Ag),                                                    51
   ∼.sent(Ag,  Name,  :tell,  coalition(Name))}                   52
    ← .send(Ag,  :tell,  coalition(Name));                        53
+agree(A,  X)  :  {⊤}                                             54
    ← .send(auctioneer,  :tell,  bid(300,  ag1));                55
                                                                   56
:name:  ag2                                                        57
                                                                   58
:Initial  Beliefs:                                                59
                                                                   60
my_name(ag2)                                                      61
                                                                   62
:Initial  Goals:                                                  63
                                                                   64
bid  [perform]                                                    65
                                                                   66
:Plans:                                                           67
                                                                   68
+.received(:tell,  B):  {⊤}  ← +B;                                69
```

```
+!bid [perform] : {B my_name(Name),                           70
    ~.sent(auctioneer, Name, :tell, bid(200, Name))}          71
    ← .send(auctioneer, :tell, bid(200, Name));               72
                                                              73
:name: ag3                                                    74
                                                              75
:Initial Beliefs:                                             76
                                                              77
my_name(ag3)                                                  78
                                                              79
:Initial Goals:                                               80
                                                              81
bid [perform]                                                 82
                                                              83
:Plans:                                                       84
                                                              85
+.received(:tell, B): {⊤} ← +B;                               86
+!bid [perform] : {B my_name(Name),                           87
    ~.sent(auctioneer, Name, :tell, bid(150, Name))}          88
    ← .send(auctioneer, :tell, bid(150, Name));               89
+coalition(A) : { B my_name(Name),                            90
    ~.sent(A, Name, :tell, agree(Name, 150))}                 91
    ← .send(A, :tell, agree(Name, 150));                      92
```

7.3.5 Dynamic Trust Scenario

A version of the code for the dynamic trust scenario with five agents is shown below:

```
GWENDOLEN                                                      1
                                                               2
:name: auctioneer                                              3
                                                               4
:Initial Beliefs:                                              5
                                                               6
                                                               7
:Initial Goals:                                                8
                                                               9
:Plans:                                                        10
                                                               11
+.received(:tell, bid(D, From)) : {B bid(From, E)}             12
    ← −bid(From, E),                                           13
        +multiple_bidder(From),                                14
        +bid(From, D);                                         15
+.received(:tell, bid(D, From)) : {~B bid(From, E)}            16
    ← +bid(From, D);                                           17
+bid(Z, A) : {B bid(ag1, Am1), B bid(ag2, Am2),               18
    B bid(ag3, Am3), B bid(ag4, Am4),                          19
    ~B winning_amount(Am),                                     20
    Am2 < Am1, Am3 < Am1, Am4 < Am1}                           21
    ← +winning_amount(Am1), win(ag1, Am1);                     22
```

```
+bid(Z, A)  :  {B bid(ag1, Am1), B bid(ag2, Am2),          23
   B bid(ag3, Am3), B bid(ag4, Am4),                        24
   ~B winning_amount(Am),                                   25
   Am1 < Am2, Am3 < Am2, Am4 < Am2}                         26
   ← +winning_amount(Am2), win(ag2, Am2);                   27
+bid(Z, A)  :  {B bid(ag1, Am1), B bid(ag2, Am2),          28
   B bid(ag3, Am3), B bid(ag4, Am4),                        29
   ~B winning_amount(Am),                                   30
   Am2 < Am3, Am1 < Am3, Am4 < Am3}                         31
   ← +winning_amount(Am3), win(ag3, Am3);                   32
+bid(Z, A)  :  {B bid(ag1, Am1), B bid(ag2, Am2),          33
   B bid(ag3, Am3), B bid(ag4, Am4),                        34
   ~B winning_amount(Am),                                   35
   Am2 < Am4, Am1 < Am4, Am3 < Am4}                         36
   ← +winning_amount(Am4), win(ag4, Am4);                   37
+bid(Z, A)  :  {B winning_amount(Am), Am < A}              38
   ← -winning_amount(Am), +winning_amount(A), win(Z, A);   39
+bid(Z, A)  :  {B multiple_bidder(Z),                      40
   B winning_amount(Am), A < Am}                            41
   ← .send(Z, :tell, failed_bid);                          42
                                                            43
:name: ag1                                                 44
                                                            45
:Initial Beliefs:                                          46
                                                            47
my_name(ag1)                                               48
trust(ag3)                                                 49
trust(ag4)                                                 50
                                                            51
:Initial Goals:                                            52
                                                            53
bid [perform]                                              54
                                                            55
:Plans:                                                    56
                                                            57
+.received(:tell, B): {⊤} ← +B;                            58
+!bid [perform]  :  {B my_name(Name),                      59
   ~.sent(auctioneer, Name, :tell, bid(150, Name))}        60
   ← .send(auctioneer, :tell, bid(150, Name));             61
+win(A, Am)  :  {B my_name(Name), ~B win(Name, Y),        62
   B trust(Ag), ~B formed_coalition(AgB),                  63
   ~.sent(Ag, Name, :tell, coalition(Name))}               64
   ← .send(Ag, :tell, coalition(Name)),                    65
   +formed_coalition(Ag);                                  66
+failed_bid  :  {B my_name(Name), ~B win(Name, Y),        67
   B trust(Ag), B formed_coalition(AgB),                   68
   ~.sent(Ag, Name, :tell, coalition(Name))}               69
   ← .send(Ag, :tell, coalition(Name)),                    70
   +formed_coalition(Ag),                                  71
   -trust(AgB);                                            72
+agree(A, Am)  :  {⊤}                                      73
```

```
        ←  .send(auctioneer ,  :tell ,  bid((Am + 150), ag1));    74
                                                                  75
  :name:  ag2                                                     76
                                                                  77
  :Initial  Beliefs:                                             78
                                                                  79
  my_name(ag2)                                                    80
                                                                  81
  :Initial  Goals:                                               82
                                                                  83
  bid  [perform]                                                  84
                                                                  85
  :Plans:                                                         86
                                                                  87
  +.received(:tell , B): {⊤} ← +B;                               88
  +!bid [perform]  :  {B my_name(Name),                          89
    ~.sent(auctioneer , Name, :tell , bid(200, Name))}           90
       ←  .send(auctioneer ,  :tell ,  bid(200, Name));          91
                                                                  92
  :name:  ag3                                                     93
                                                                  94
  :Initial  Beliefs:                                             95
                                                                  96
  my_name(ag3)                                                    97
                                                                  98
  :Initial  Goals:                                               99
                                                                  100
  bid  [perform]                                                 101
                                                                  102
  :Plans:                                                        103
                                                                  104
  +.received(:tell , B): {⊤} ← +B;                              105
  +!bid [perform]  :  {B my_name(Name),                         106
     ~.sent(auctioneer , Name, :tell , bid(25, Name))}          107
       ←  .send(auctioneer ,  :tell ,  bid(25, Name));          108
  +coalition(A)  :  { B my_name(Name),                          109
     ~.sent(A, Name, :tell , agree(Name, 25))}                  110
       ←  .send(A, :tell , agree(Name, 25));                    111
                                                                  112
  :name:  ag4                                                    113
                                                                  114
  :Initial  Beliefs:                                            115
                                                                  116
  my_name(ag4)                                                   117
                                                                  118
  :Initial  Goals:                                              119
                                                                  120
  bid  [perform]                                                 121
                                                                  122
  :Plans:                                                       123
                                                                  124
```

```
+.received(:tell, B): {⊤} ← +B;                                    125
+!bid [perform] : {B my_name(Name),                                126
    ~.sent(auctioneer, Name, :tell, bid(150, Name))}               127
    ← .send(auctioneer, :tell, bid(150, Name));                    128
+coalition(A) : { B my_name(Name),                                 129
    ~.sent(A, Name, :tell, agree(Name, 150))}                      130
    ← .send(A, :tell, agree(Name, 150));                           131
```

7.4 Environments

In these scenarios the environment has very little role to play beyond passing messages between the agents. We could have implemented the possibility of messages getting lost but chose not to – if we had done this then we would have needed to make the agent code more complex in order to involve handshakes to confirm that messages had been received.

There is one action, win(A, Z), that the auctioneer takes in some examples which represents a broadcast announcement. Again, instead of treating this as if it could succeed or fail, we assumed that it always succeeded – that is, that all agents would receive the news of the winner the next time their reasoning cycle checked for perceptions.

We used this environment both for running/testing the system and for verification.

It is possible to imagine a single system of this kind in which the agents in the system all run within the one unified software environment, such as we used here. These agents might represent particular users who activate the agents within the system and set them up with the user's desired bid. However many such auction systems will be distributed with agents spread across many computers and communicating with each other. In such systems we would indeed want to expand our verification in order to consider issues such as message loss and thus the verification would need to consider non-determinism in the environment and we would need to start using our techniques for verifying a single agent in order to show its decisions are correct no matter what information is being sent and in what order. In such a scenario we would want to consider both the protocols used by the auctioneer (does it eventually assign the winner to the highest bidder – and how should it decide when no more bids will arrive) and by the agents (do their protocols still work if the agent with which they are attempting to form a coalition may not receive their message?)

7.5 Example Verification

We now discuss the results of verifying several of the auction scenarios described earlier. Recall that our use of AJPF necessitates heavy resource use;

the underlying JPF JVM is relatively slow, while our AIL layer introduces significant additional computation. So, while the verifications described here are not fast, they showcase what AJPF can achieve, beyond most other agent verification systems.

7.5.1 Properties of the *Basic Auction* Scenario

The following property was verified:

$$\Diamond \mathbf{B}_{ag_b} \text{ win}$$

meaning that the agent with the highest bid will eventually believe it has won. This scenario was tackled with 3, 4, and 5 agents, with the following statistics (here, timings are given in the form *hours:minutes:seconds* for the system running on a 3GHz Dual Processor Macbook Pro).

	1 auctioneer; 2 bidders	1 auctioneer; 3 bidders	1 auctioneer; 4 bidders
Elapsed time	0:00:11	0:00:50	0:04:58
Size of state space	443	2.258	12,685
Max memory	703MB	707MB	707MB

7.5.2 Properties of the *Auction Coalition* Scenario

In this scenario, we again verified the property

$$\Diamond \mathbf{B}_{ag_c} \text{ win},$$

where ag_c is the coalition-forming agent. Recall that here, two agents who could not win on their own attempt to form a coalition; the verification shows that they are, indeed, successful.

	1 auctioneer; 3 bidders; 1 coalition	1 auctioneer; 4 bidders; 1 coalition
Elapsed time	0:02:40	17:36
Size of state space	8,121	44,393
Max memory	707MB	707MB

7.5.3 Properties of the *Dynamic Auction Coalition* Scenario Variant

Recall that, in this scenario, the coalition formation was not 'hard-wired' from the start. Agents bid and, when they find they have lost, might then attempt to form a coalition for the next auction. We tackled a number of variants of this, both in terms of the number of bidding agents (3 or 4), the number of coalitions that can be formed amongst the bidders (1 or 2), and the property verified. In particular we verified both properties involving time and belief (as previously) and time and *goals*.

Belief Property. The property verified again was

$$\Diamond \mathbf{B}_{ag_c} \text{ win,}$$

where ag_c is the agent that forms the winning coalition.

	1 auctioneer; 3 bidders; 1 coalition	1 auctioneer; 3 bidders; 2 coalitions	1 auctioneer; 4 bidders; 1 coalition	1 auctioneer; 4 bidders; 2 coalitions
Elapsed time	0:10:55	0:18:16	1:05:47	1:30:05
Size of state space	30,329	48,347	199,173	290,344
Max memory	1,510MB	2,581MB	1,501MB	2,280MB

Goal Property. The property verified was

$$\Diamond \mathbf{G}_{ag_c} \text{coalition,}$$

where ag_c was the (last) coalition forming agent. Here, '**G**' is the 'goal' operator. In verifying this, we are not checking that the agent necessarily achieved any win, but that it (at some point in its execution) adopted the goal to form a coalition.

	1 auctioneer; 3 bidders; 1 coalition	1 auctioneer; 3 bidders; 2 coalitions	1 auctioneer; 4 bidders; 1 coalition	1 auctioneer; 4 bidders; 2 coalitions
Elapsed time	0:03:00	0:09:40	0:21:33	1:05:37
Size of state space	7,648	30,372	50,631	199,1353
Max memory	706MB	1,495MB	1,671MB	1,494MB

7.5.4 Properties of the *Coalition Trust* Scenario

We now turn to the scenarios involving *trust*. In this scenario, the agent would only form a coalition with a trusted agent, and its idea of trust was prescribed initially. Four agents were used in the first example: an auctioneer, and three bidding agents a_1, a_2, a_3 with bids 100, 200, 25, and 150. The property verified was

$$\Diamond \mathbf{B}_{a_1} \text{ win},$$

where agent a_1 forms a coalition with a_3 after losing the auction to a_2. In the second example, five agents were used: an auctioneer, and four bidding agents a_1, a_2, a_3, a_4 with bids 100, 200, 150 and 150. The property verified was

$$\Diamond \mathbf{B}_{a_1} \text{ win},$$

where agent a_1 forms a coalition with one of the trusted agents, a_4 and a_5, after losing the auction to a_2. The results were:

	1 auctioneer; 3 bidders	1 auctioneer; 4 bidders
Elapsed time	0:03:40	30:39
Size of state space	8,711	39,202
Max memory	1,472MB	2,261MB

7.5.5 Properties of the *Dynamic Trust* Scenario

Finally, we have the dynamic trust scenario, where an agent loses trust in another agent if they fail in a coalition together. Again, five agents were used: an auctioneer, and four bidding agents a_1, a_2, a_3, a_4 with bids 100, 200, 25, and 150. The property verified was

$$\Diamond \mathbf{B}_{a_1} \text{ win},$$

where a_1 forms a coalition with one of the trusted agents after losing the auction to a_2. If it chooses a_4 first, it wins and stops. If it chooses a_3 first, it loses the auction and distrusts that agent, trying subsequently with a_4. It then wins the auction. The results were:

	1 auctioneer; 4 bidders	1 auctioneer; 5 bidders
Elapsed time	0:43:22	7:45:50
Size of state space	65,816	403,019
Max memory	3,515MB	4,496MB

7.6 Issues

The simplicity of the examples we examined here mean that, although we are using program model checking, we are still really verifying a protocol as opposed to an implementation (because, as noted above) we have not considered issues of communication unreliability, or even how the amounts that agents bid are decided which would be necessary in a deployed system with genuine utility.

Already some features of model-checking should be obvious though. For instance we need the model-checking to be finite state so we could not consider the case of an arbitrary number of agents and we needed to fix the amount each agent bid. In the next chapter we will discuss some techniques for how verification might tackle these problems.

We have focussed on a series of scenarios of increasing complexity in order to demonstrate that it is a realistic proposition to model-check the properties of interesting multi-agent implementations within a reasonable time but it should be obvious from the results that even with fairly simple protocols our ability to model-check a system containing a large number of agents, if we model each agent in full, is quite limited as the state space and time taken increase.

8

Autonomous Satellite Control

The examples in the previous chapter involved relatively simple GWENDO-LEN code, with no external/physical interaction.* While this served to illustrate our methodology on single and multiple agents, we now need to embed these agents in an autonomous system. So we will now look at how the *hybrid agent* architecture we described earlier can be used in autonomous space systems, and then how the agent within such a system can be verified. Specifically, we will look at code developed as part of a project to investigate agent-based control of autonomous, multi-satellite systems (Lincoln et al., 2013); note that this code was not initially developed with formal verification in mind, it was meant to provide high-level, explainable, and justifiable autonomous system control.

8.1 What is the System?

Satellites are, traditionally, large (and expensive) items of equipment whose positions and directions are closely controlled by flight engineers in ground stations. However, both of these are changing: it has become a goal of the space industry to develop and deploy a greater number of smaller, and more autonomous, satellites that can work cooperatively to carry out the missions previously handled by large, monolithic platforms. This improves both cost and reliability. Cost, since producing small satellites is significantly cheaper; reliability, since failures in one satellite will likely not mean the mission is aborted. However, with these benefits comes the significant problem of how to

---

* Verification of agent-based autonomous satellites was carried out as part of a wider project on *Engineering Autonomous Space Software* (Dennis et al., 2010b, c). That project, and the paper in which the verification was reported (Dennis et al., 2016c), was developed in collaboration with Nick Lincoln, Alexei Lisitsa, and Sandor Veres. In particular, Nick and Sandor are Control Engineers who developed the practical control aspects for both real and simulated satellites.

coordinate multiple satellites to work together in order to achieve the mission's tasks.

Our aim was to construct a hybrid agent architecture to control, coordinate and re-organise such multi-satellite systems. Subsequently, we became interested in verifying the agent's behaviour both within an individual satellite and in providing control for broader multi-satellite formations, in part because the agent was implemented in GWENDOLEN which gave us access to AJPF.

The nature of these satellite systems, having a genuine need for co-operation and autonomy, mission critical aspects and interaction with the real world in an environment that is, in many respects, simpler than a terrestrial one, makes them a good test-bed for our approach to analysing autonomous systems.

8.1.1 Autonomous Satellites in Low Earth Orbit

A *Low Earth Orbit* (LEO) is an orbit with altitude varying between that of the Earth's upper atmosphere, approximately 250 km, and an upper bound of 2,000 km; the LEO may be inclined to the equator, and may or may not be elliptical. LEOs are used predominantly by Earth observation missions requiring high resolution images, such as weather, military, and mineral resource satellites.

LEO satellites travel at high speed, completing an Earth orbit within approximately 90 minutes. Orbiting at these great speeds presents an issue concerning the control and monitoring of LEO satellites: ground station visibility is restricted to between 5 and 15 minutes per overhead passage of a ground station. Whilst multiple ground stations, or space-based relay satellites orbiting at higher altitudes, may be switched between to enable greater communication periods, this growth in infrastructure is disadvantageous. As a result there is a need to increase the autonomous control of such systems; clearly, there is also a need for verification to ensure increased levels of predictability and reliability.

The Scenario. We developed a model of satellite formations in LEO. Each agent controls one satellite and these satellites would communicate to maintain certain formations in which they could achieve their tasks. Each satellite was provided with thrusters in three body axes (X, Y, and Z) and each also utilised two fuel lines. In addition to controlling movement, the agent could control which fuel line was in use, enabling it to switch in the event of a rupture (which is detected by a drop in fuel pressure). In the simple case examined here, the satellites were expected to move to pre-generated locations in a formation, correcting for a single fuel line breakage, if it occurred. The satellite software

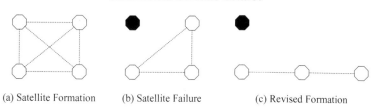

Figure 8.1 Satellite formation changes

includes a planning algorithm which can plan the control needed for a satellite to move from one orbital location to a location in a formation.

8.1.2 Multiple Satellites, Communication, and Formations

While initially verifying individual satellite/agent behaviour, we subsequently extended the scenario into one which involves multiple agents and communication. In the original scenario the agent knew which pre-determined position in a formation it was to assume. For this example a further 'lead agent' is introduced. This is a purely software agent whose role is to decide which position in some formation each of the four satellites are to assume and communicate that information to the agents controlling the spacecraft. It can place the satellites in a line or a square formation and can react to an abort from one of the satellites (e.g., because of thruster failure) to modify the formation if possible (i.e., moving from a square to a line); see Figure 8.1. Section 8.3 shows the code for this lead agent.

8.2 What *Properties* Do We Want to Establish?

We wish to verify that each individual satellite's decision-making agent component is 'correct' *independent* of any environmental interactions and the modelling of other parts of the system. As discussed in Chapter 6 this means that the verification will be exploring all possible incoming perceptions and therefore we need properties of the form:

if whenever the agent does X then eventually it believes Y then ...

Agent Operation without Thruster Failure or Outside Communication.
We first chose to investigate the operation of the agent in a situation where no thrusters fail and no messages are received from outside. This simple agent started with the goal of assuming its position in a formation, and that the position it was to assume was in the `middle` of a line of satellites.

We start by identifying two properties of actions of the form *if whenever the agent does X then eventually it believes Y*, which we will use as hypotheses in several of the properties we want to prove:

if the agent requests a plan to get to some position, then it eventually believes it has received a suitable plan.

$$\mathsf{PlanningSucceeds}(Pos) \equiv$$
$$\Box(\mathbf{A}_{ag1}\mathsf{query}(\mathsf{get\_close\_to}(\mathsf{Pos}, \mathsf{P})) \Rightarrow \Diamond\mathbf{B}_{ag1}\mathsf{ have\_plan}(\mathsf{Pos}, \mathsf{plan}))$$
$$(8.1)$$

and

if the agent executes a plan then eventually it believes it has reached the desired position.

$$\mathsf{PlanExecutionSucceeds}(Pos) \quad \equiv$$
$$\Box(\mathbf{A}_{ag1}\mathsf{perf}(\mathsf{execute}(\mathsf{plan})) \Rightarrow \Diamond\mathbf{B}_{ag1}\mathsf{ in\_position}(\mathsf{Pos})). \qquad (8.2)$$

Now, we aim to verify, using AJPF, that:

if the agent receives a plan, and the execution of that plan will take it to the middle position in a line, then eventually the agent will believe it is maintaining a position in the middle of the line.

In logical form, this can be characterised as:

$$\mathsf{PlanningSucceeds}(middle) \land \mathsf{PlanExecutionSucceeds}(middle) \Rightarrow$$
$$\Diamond\mathbf{B}_{ag1}\mathsf{ maintaining}(\mathsf{middle}). \qquad (8.3)$$

Note how we only verify internal aspects of the agent such as its beliefs about its environment.

Now, if we wish to relax our assumptions about the properties of actions, we can also try to verify that

if plan execution always succeeds, then either the agent will eventually believe it is in its desired position, or it never believes it possesses a plan for getting there.

$$\mathsf{PlanExecutionSucceeds}(middle) \Rightarrow$$
$$\Diamond\mathbf{B}_{ag1}\mathsf{ maintaining}(\mathsf{middle}) \lor \Box\neg\mathbf{B}_{ag1}\mathsf{ have\_plan}(\mathsf{middle}, \mathsf{plan}). \qquad (8.4)$$

Investigating the Response to Thruster Failure. If we include the possibility of thruster failure into our analysis then we would like to show that *if the planning process succeeds then either the agent eventually believes it is maintaining its position or it believes it has a broken thruster (either the X, Y, or Z thruster).*

$$(\text{PlanningSucceeds}(middle) \wedge \text{PlanExecutionSucceeds}(middle)) \Rightarrow$$
$$\Diamond \mathbf{B}_{ag1} \text{ maintaining}(\text{middle}) \vee$$
$$\mathbf{B}_{ag1} \text{ broken}(\text{x}) \vee \mathbf{B}_{ag1} \text{ broken}(\text{y}) \vee \mathbf{B}_{ag1} \text{ broken}(\text{z}).$$

$$(8.5)$$

We can improve on this result still further by adding extra properties for actions:

whenever the agent switches a fuel line then eventually it believes the thruster is working (i.e. no longer 'broken') again.

$$\text{ChangingLineSucceeds}(T) \quad \equiv$$
$$\Box(\mathbf{A}_{ag1} \text{perf}(\text{change\_line}(\text{T})) \Rightarrow \Diamond \neg \mathbf{B}_{ag1} \text{ broken}(\text{T})),$$

$$(8.6)$$

where T is the thruster affected. A second failure hypothesis is

broken thrusters never lead to an abort because of thruster failure.

$$\text{NoIrrepairableBreaks}(T) \quad \equiv$$
$$\Box(\mathbf{B}_{ag1} \text{ broken}(\text{T}) \Rightarrow \Box \neg \mathbf{B}_{ag1} \text{ aborted}(\text{thruster\_failure})).$$

$$(8.7)$$

Finally, the combined property (8.8) states that

if planning for the middle position succeeds, the x thruster is always believed to be fixable and changing a fuel line means eventually the agent believes the thruster is no longer broken, then eventually the agent will believe it is maintaining its position in the middle of the formation.

$$\text{PlanningSucceeds}(middle) \wedge \text{PlanExecutionSucceeds}(middle)$$
$$\wedge \text{ChangingLineSuceeds}(x) \wedge \text{NoIrrepairableBreaks}(x)$$
$$\Rightarrow \Diamond \mathbf{B}_{ag1} \text{ maintaining}(\text{middle})$$

$$(8.8)$$

Single Formation. We now move on to investigate properties for our formations of multiple agents. First, we aim to verify the behaviour of both the leader agent and the follower agents in the situation where there is only one simple formation, a line, to be adopted. In this case we require a new assumption about the performance of the environment, stating that:

once the leader believes it has informed an agent that it should assume a position in a line formation then, eventually, it will believe it has received a message telling it that the (informed) agent is maintaining that position.

$$\text{AlwaysResponds}(AgName, Pos) \equiv$$
$$\Box(\mathbf{B}_{aglead} \text{ informed}(\text{AgName}, \text{Pos}) \Rightarrow \Diamond \mathbf{B}_{aglead} \text{ maintaining}(\text{AgName})).$$
$$(8.9)$$

Once we have this assumption, we are able to verify that

if all agents respond, the lead agent eventually believes the agents have assumed a linear formation.

$$\text{AlwaysResponds}(ag1, line) \wedge \text{AlwaysResponds}(ag2, line) \wedge$$
$$\text{AlwaysResponds}(ag3, line) \wedge \text{AlwaysResponds}(ag4, line) \quad (8.10)$$
$$\Rightarrow \Diamond \mathbf{B}_{aglead} \text{ in\_formation}(line).$$

We also verified certain *safety* properties, for example:

the leader never believes it has assigned an agent to two positions at the same time.

$$\Box \left[\begin{array}{c} \mathbf{B}_{aglead} \text{ position}(ag1, left) \Rightarrow \\ \neg(\mathbf{B}_{aglead} \text{ position}(ag1, middle) \wedge \mathbf{B}_{aglead} \text{ position}(ag1, right)) \end{array} \right] \quad (8.11)$$

the leader never believes it has assigned two agents to the same position.

$$\Box \left[\begin{array}{c} \mathbf{B}_{aglead} \text{ position}(ag1, left) \Rightarrow \\ \neg(\mathbf{B}_{aglead} \text{ position}(ag2, left) \vee \\ \mathbf{B}_{aglead} \text{ position}(ag3, left) \vee \mathbf{B}_{aglead} \text{ position}(ag4, left)) \end{array} \right]. \quad (8.12)$$

The follower agent uses the code investigated in our single agent case, but when it is interacting with a multi-agent system we want to verify that the messages it sends to the leader agent accurately portray its beliefs. So, we also need to show that

under the assumption that planning and plan execution are successful for the relevant formation and position, the follower will eventually believe it has informed the leader that it is maintaining its position in the formation.

For example, in the case of the 'middle' position in a line:

$$\text{PlanningSucceeds}(middle) \wedge \text{PlanExecutionSucceeds}(middle) \Rightarrow$$
$$\Box(\mathbf{B}_{ag1} \text{ handling}(assuming\_formation(line)) \wedge \mathbf{B}_{ag1} \text{ my\_position\_}$$
$$\text{is}(middle) \Rightarrow \Diamond \mathbf{B}_{ag1} \text{ sent}(aglead, maintaining(ag1)).$$
$$(8.13)$$

We can also verify that

followers only send messages if they believe they are maintaining the positions they have been assigned.

$$\Box(\mathbf{A}_{ag1}\text{send}(\text{aglead}, \text{maintaining}(ag1)) \Rightarrow$$
$$\mathbf{B}_{ag1}\text{ my\_position\_is}(\text{middle}) \wedge \mathbf{B}_{ag1}\text{ maintaining}(\text{middle}). \tag{8.14}$$

Changing Formations. Finally we can investigate the behaviour of the leader agent in situations where the formation could change. For example, if the system is to change from a *square* formation to a *line* formation:

if all agents respond, then eventually the leader agent will believe a square formation has been achieved.

$$\text{AlwaysResponds}(ag1, square) \wedge \text{AlwaysResponds}(ag2, square) \wedge$$
$$\text{AlwaysResponds}(ag3, square) \wedge \text{AlwaysResponds}(ag4, square) \tag{8.15}$$
$$\Rightarrow \Diamond(\mathbf{B}_{aglead}\text{ in\_formation}(\text{square}))$$

if all agents respond, and if the leader agent believes all the agents to be in square formation, then it will eventually believe they are in a line formation.

$$\text{AlwaysResponds}(ag1, line) \wedge \text{AlwaysResponds}(ag2, line) \wedge$$
$$\text{AlwaysResponds}(ag3, line) \wedge \text{AlwaysResponds}(ag4, line) \tag{8.16}$$
$$\Rightarrow \Box(\mathbf{B}_{aglead}\text{ in\_formation}(\text{square}) \Rightarrow \Diamond(\mathbf{B}_{aglead}\text{ in\_formation}(\text{line}))).$$

8.3 GWENDOLEN Code

We show the GWENDOLEN code for our two agents of interest: the agent that interacts with underlying control systems and the lead (software only) agent.*

As well as the actions the agents can perform that we discussed in the previous section, they can also perform a 'null' action, `perf(null)`. Which shuts down thrusters and attempts to manoeuvre, in order to await new instructions.

8.3.1 Full Code for an Agent that Interacts with the Underlying Control Systems

```
:name: ag1                                          1
                                                    2
:Initial Beliefs:                                   3
                                                    4
leader(aglead)                                      5
my_name(ag1)                                        6
```

---

* The examples in this chapter can be found in the folder
  `src/examples/eass/verification/leo` of the AJPF distribution.

```
maintaining (none)                                              7
                                                                8
my_position_is (middle)                                         9
                                                               10
                                                               11
: Reasoning  Rules:                                            12
                                                               13
repairable (X,  with (change_line (X)))  :−                    14
     thruster_line (X,  1);                                    15
                                                               16
: Initial  Goals:                                              17
                                                               18
assuming_formation (line)  [perform]                           19
                                                               20
: Plans:                                                       21
+.received (:perform,  LG):  {∼B handling (LG)}                22
     ← +handling (LG),  +!LG [perform],  −handling (LG);       23
+.received (:achieve,  LG):  {∼B handling (LG),  ∼B LG}        24
     ← +handling (LG),  +!LG [achieve],  −handling (LG);       25
+.received (:tell,  LG):  {∼B LG} ← +LG;                       26
                                                               27
// Initial goal can either be provided on start−up, or         28
// communicated to the agent                                   29
+!assuming_formation (F) [perform]  :                          30
     {∼B assuming_formation (F)}                               31
     ← +!initialise (F) [perform],                             32
        +!my_position_is (X) [achieve],                        33
        +!maintaining (X) [achieve];                           34
+!assuming_formation (F) [perform]  :                          35
     {B assuming_formation (F)};                               36
                                                               37
// May get told to abandon the current formation               38
+! drop_formation (F) [perform]  :                             39
     {B assuming_formation (F)}                                40
     ← −! assuming_formation (F) [perform],                    41
        +! clear_position [perform],                           42
        +! cleanup [perform],                                  43
        perf (null);                                           44
+! drop_formation (F) [perform]  :                             45
     {∼B assuming_formation (F)} ←                             46
     −! assuming_formation (F) [perform],                      47
     perf (null);                                              48
+! clear_position [perform]  : {B my_position_is (X)} ←        49
     + .lock,                                                  50
     −my_position_is (X),                                      51
     −position (X),                                            52
     −.lock;                                                   53
+! clear_position [perform]  : {∼B my_position_is (X)};        54
                                                               55
+!initialise (F) [perform]  : {B maintaining (Pos)} ←          56
     +.lock,                                                   57
```

```
   -maintaining(Pos),                                              58
   +assuming_formation(F),                                         59
   -.lock;                                                         60
+!initialise(F) [perform] : {~B maintaining(Pos)} ←               61
   +assuming_formation(F);                                         62
                                                                   63
+position(X) : {~B my_position_is(Y)} ←                           64
   +my_position_is(X);                                             65
+my_position_is(none) : {~B maintaining(none)} ←                  66
   +maintaining(none);                                             67
                                                                   68
+!my_position_is(X) [achieve] : {~B my_position_is(X),            69
   B leader(Leader), B my_name(Name)}                             70
   ← .send(Leader, :perform, send_position(Name)),               71
      * my_position_is(X);                                        72
                                                                   73
                                                                   74
+! in_position(Pos) [achieve] : {~B in_position(Pos),            75
   ~B have_plan(Pos, Plan)}                                       76
   ← query(get_close_to(Pos, P)),                                77
      +have_plan(Pos, P),                                         78
      perf(execute(P)),                                           79
      *close_to(Pos),                                             80
      +in_position(Pos);                                          81
+! in_position(Pos) [achieve] : {~B in_position(Pos),            82
   B have_plan(Pos, P)}                                           83
   ← perf(execute(P)),                                           84
      *close_to(Pos),                                             85
      +in_position(Pos);                                          86
                                                                   87
+! maintaining(Pos) [achieve] : {B in_position(Pos),             88
   B assuming_formation(F), ~B aborted(Reason),                   89
   ~B broken(X)}                                                  90
   ← perf(maintain_path),                                        91
      +maintaining(Pos),                                          92
      +!cleanup [perform];                                        93
+! maintaining(Pos) [achieve] : {~B in_position(Pos),            94
   B assuming_formation(F), ~B aborted(Reason),                   95
   ~B broken(X)}                                                  96
   ← +! in_position(Pos) [achieve],                              97
      perf(maintain_path),                                        98
      +maintaining(Pos),                                          99
      +!cleanup [perform];                                       100
+! maintaining(Pos) [achieve] :                                 101
   {B broken(X), ~B aborted(Reason)}                             102
   ← *fixed(X),                                                  103
      -fixed(X);                                                 104
+! maintaining(Pos) [achieve] :                                 105
   {~B assuming_formation(F)} ←                                   106
      -! maintaining(Pos) [achieve];                             107
+! maintaining(Pos) [achieve] : {B aborted(Reason),             108
```

```
B assuming_formation(F)}                                          109
  ←  −! assuming_formation(F)  [perform];                         110
                                                                  111
+maintaining(Pos)  :  {B leader(Leader),  B my_name(Name)}        112
  ←  .send(Leader,  :tell,  maintaining(Name)),                   113
     +sent(Leader,  maintaining(Name));                           114
                                                                  115
+!cleanup  [perform]  :  {∼B have_plan(Pos,  P),                  116
  B in_position(Pos),  B perform_cleanup,                         117
  B assuming_formation(F)}                                        118
  ←  +.lock,                                                      119
     −assuming_formation(F),                                      120
     −in_position(Pos),                                           121
     −.lock;                                                      122
+!cleanup  [perform]  :  {∼B have_plan(Pos,  P),                  123
  B in_position(Pos),  B perform_cleanup,                         124
  ∼B assuming_formation(F)}                                       125
  ←  +.lock,                                                      126
     −in_position(Pos),                                           127
     −.lock;                                                      128
+!cleanup  [perform]  :  {∼B have_plan(Pos,  P),                  129
  ∼B in_position(Pos1),  B perform_cleanup,                       130
  B assuming_formation(F)}                                        131
  ←  +.lock,                                                      132
     −assuming_formation(F),                                      133
     −.lock;                                                      134
+!cleanup  [perform]  :  {B have_plan(Pos,  P),                   135
  B perform_cleanup,  B assuming_formation(F)}                    136
  ←  +.lock,                                                      137
     −assuming_formation(F),                                      138
     −have_plan(Pos,  P),                                         139
     −in_position(Pos),                                           140
     −.lock;                                                      141
+!cleanup  [perform]  :  {B have_plan(Pos,  P),                   142
  B perform_cleanup,  ∼B assuming_formation(F)}                   143
  ←  +.lock,                                                      144
     −have_plan(Pos,  P),                                         145
     −in_position(Pos),                                           146
     −.lock;                                                      147
+! cleanup  [perform]  :  {∼B perform_cleanup};                   148
                                                                  149
+broken(X):  {B aborted(thruster_failure)}  ←                    150
  −fixed(X);                                                      151
                                                                  152
+broken(X):  {B repairable(X, with(Y)),                          153
  ∼B aborted(thruster_failure),                                   154
  ∼B fixed(X)}  ←                                                 155
     perf(Y);                                                     156
                                                                  157
+broken(X):  {∼B repairable(X, Y),                               158
  ∼B aborted(thruster_failure)}  ←                                159
```

```
 −fixed(X),                                                    160
 +! abort(thruster_failure) [perform];                         161
                                                               162
+broken(X): {B repairable(X, Y), B fixed(X),                   163
   ∼B aborted(thruster_failure)} ←                             164
 −fixed(X),                                                    165
 +! abort(thruster_failure) [perform];                         166
                                                               167
−broken(X): {⊤} ←                                              168
 +fixed(X);                                                    169
                                                               170
+!abort(R) [perform]: {B leader(Leader), B my_name(Name),      171
   G maintaining(Pos) [achieve]} ←                             172
 +aborted(R),                                                  173
 −! maintaining(Pos) [achieve],                                174
 .send(Leader, :tell, aborted(R, Name)),                       175
 +sent(Leader, aborted(R, Name)),                              176
 perf(null);                                                   177
+!abort(R) [perform]: {B leader(Leader), B my_name(Name),      178
   ∼G maintaining(Pos) [achieve]} ←                            179
 +aborted(R),                                                  180
 .send(Leader, :tell, aborted(R, Name)),                       181
 +sent(Leader, aborted(R, Name)),                              182
 perf(null);                                                   183
```

Listing 8.1 Code for a LEO agent that interacts with an abstraction engine

It is worth noting that many of the possible goals and beliefs that this agent could acquire have multiple plans associated with them, each plan with a slightly different guard condition. The need for many of these plans was only discovered during verification where particular edge cases were highlighted by exploration of potential runs through the system driven by model-checking.

8.3.2 Full Code for the Leader Agent

```
:name: aglead                                                   1
                                                               2
:Initial Beliefs:                                              3
                                                               4
agent(ag1)                                                      5
agent(ag2)                                                      6
agent(ag3)                                                      7
agent(ag4)                                                      8
                                                               9
pos(line, left)                                                10
pos(line, right)                                               11
pos(line, middle)                                              12
pos(square, topleft)                                           13
pos(square, topright)                                          14
```

```
pos ( square ,   bottomleft )                                      15
pos ( square ,   bottomright )                                     16
                                                                   17
: Reasoning  Rules :                                               18
                                                                   19
all_positions_assigned ( Formation )  :—                           20
~  ( pos ( Formation ,   Pos ) ,  ~  position ( Ag ,  Pos ) ) ;    21
inform_start  :—                                                   22
    ~  ( position ( Ag ,  Pos ) ,  ~  informed ( Ag ,  F ) ) ;     23
in_formation ( F )  :—  ~  ( pos ( F ,  P ) ,  ~  agent_at ( P ) ) ; 24
agent_at ( Pos )  :—    position ( Ag ,  Pos ) ,  maintaining ( Ag ) ; 25
some_formation  :—                                                 26
    desired_formation ( F1 ) ,   in_formation ( F1 ) ;             27
aformation  :—  in_formation ( line ) ;                            28
aformation  :—  in_formation ( square ) ;                          29
desired_formation ( line )   :—  in_formation ( square ) ;         30
desired_formation ( line )   :—  in_formation ( line ) ;           31
desired_formation ( square )  :—  ~  aformation ;                  32
                                                                   33
// Only  one  way  to  conclude  a  satellite  is  broken .        34
broken ( Ag )  :—  aborted ( thruster_failure ,  Ag ) ;            35
                                                                   36
// Beliefs  used  for  clean  up  phases .                         37
formation_clear ( F )  :—  ~  ( pos ( F ,  P ) ,  position ( Ag ,  P ) ) ; 38
agent_pos_clear  :—  ~  maintaining ( AG ) ;                       39
informed_clear ( F )  :—  ~ informed ( Ag ,  F ) ;                 40
                                                                   41
: Initial  Goals :                                                 42
some_formation  [ achieve ]                                        43
                                                                   44
: Plans :                                                          45
+ . received ( : tell ,  LG ) :  { ~B  LG }  ←  +LG ;              46
+ . received ( : perform ,  LG ) :  { ~B  handling ( LG ) }  ←     47
    +handling ( LG ) ,  +!LG  [ perform ] ,  −handling ( LG ) ;    48
                                                                   49
+! some_formation  [ achieve ]  :                                  50
    { ~B  formation ( F ) ,  B  desired_formation ( Form ) }       51
    ←  +!  in_formation ( Form )  [ achieve ] ;                    52
+! some_formation  [ achieve ]  :  { B  formation ( F ) ,          53
    B  desired_formation ( F ) }                                   54
    ←  +!  in_formation ( F )  [ achieve ] ;                       55
+! some_formation  [ achieve ]  :  { B  formation ( F1 ) ,         56
    ~B  desired_formation ( F1 ) ,                                 57
    B  desired_formation ( Form1 ) }                               58
    ←  +!cleanup_initialisation ( F1 )  [ perform ] ,             59
    +!cleanup_formation ( F1 )  [ perform ] ,                      60
    +!  in_formation ( Form1 )  [ achieve ] ;                      61
                                                                   62
+!  in_formation ( F )  [ achieve ]  :  { ⊤ }  ←                   63
    +formation ( F ) ,                                             64
    +!  all_positions_assigned ( F )  [ achieve ] ,               65
```

```
+! inform_start [achieve] ,                                      66
*in_formation (F) ,                                             67
+! cleanup_initialisation (F) [perform] ;                      68
                                                                69
+! all_positions_assigned (Formation) [achieve] :              70
  {B agent(Ag) , ~B position (Ag, X) ,                          71
   B pos(Formation , Y) , ~B position (Ag2, Y) ,                72
   ~B broken(Ag)}                                               73
  ←  .send(Ag, :tell , position (Y)) ,            .             74
  +position (Ag, Y) ;                                           75
                                                                76
+! inform_start [achieve] :                                     77
  {B position (Ag, X) , B formation (F) ,                       78
   ~B informed (Ag, F)}                                         79
  ←  .send(Ag, :achieve , assuming_formation (F)) ,             80
  +informed (Ag, F) ;                                           81
                                                                82
// Information or Requests from other agents                    83
+ aborted (Reason , Ag) : {B position (Ag, X) ,                 84
  G some_formation [achieve] , ~B maintaining (Ag)}  ←          85
  +.lock ,                                                      86
  −position (Ag, X) ,                                           87
  −informed (Ag, F) ,                                           88
  −.lock ,                                                      89
  .send(Ag, :perform , drop_formation (F)) ,                    90
  −! some_formation [achieve] ;                                 91
                                                                92
+! send_position (Ag) [perform] : {B position (Ag, X)}          93
  ←  .send(Ag, :tell , position (X)) ;                          94
+! send_position (Ag) [perform] : {~B position (Ag, X)}         95
  ←  .send(Ag, :tell , position (none )) ;                      96
                                                                97
// plans for cleaning up after a formation is achieved.         98
+! formation_clear (F) [achieve] :                              99
  {B pos(F, P) , B position (Ag, P)}  ←                        100
  −position (Ag, P) ;                                          101
+! agent_pos_clear [achieve] : {B maintaining (Ag)}  ←         102
  −maintaining (Ag) ;                                          103
+! informed_clear (F) [achieve] : {B informed (Ag, F)}        104
  ←  .send(Ag, :perform , drop_formation (F)) ,               105
  −informed (Ag, F) ;                                          106
                                                                107
+! cleanup_initialisation (F) [perform] : {⊤}  ←              108
  +! informed_clear (F) [achieve] ;                           109
+! cleanup_formation (F) [perform] : {⊤}  ←                   110
  −formation (F) ,                                            111
  +! formation_clear (F) [achieve] ,                          112
  +! agent_pos_clear [achieve] ;                              113
```

Listing 8.2 Code for the Leader Agent

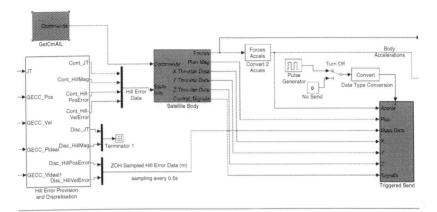

(a) MATLAB Simulation Environment.

(b) Satellite Test Facility. Image from Dennis et al.
2016b) courtesy of Sandor Veres.

Figure 8.2 Environments used for demonstrations of autonomous agent implementations

8.4 Environments

We developed a hybrid agent architecture to allow for both *simulated* and *real* satellites: simulated satellites were provided through a MATLAB model, which would simulate all the physical aspects of the satellite (its orbit, thrusters, communications, etc; see Figure 8.2a); physical satellites were provided on a 2D very low friction test-bed, initially at the University of Southampton and subsequently at the University of Sheffield; see Figure 8.2b).

The Architecture. The hybrid agent architecture used here is more complex than the examples we have seen already. It contains not only the BDI agent, in

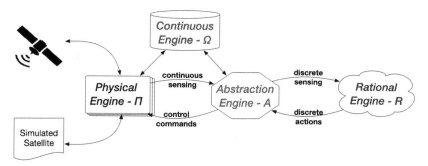

Figure 8.3 Continuous Engine in the Architecture

this work called the *Reasoning Engine*, but also the control environment consisting of feedback control systems and either physical models or real hardware, here called the *Physical Engine*. In addition, two further elements are used: an abstraction engine, whose role is to link between the continuous world of the Physical Engine and the discrete world of the Reasoning Engine; and a *Continuous Engine*, which provides the agent with an auxiliary computational model of the environment that can be used for prediction, calculation, and so on. The Continuous Engine is an example of an autonomy support component as discussed in Chapter 5. A key role of the Continuous Engine was to synthesize plans for particular satellite movements (Lincoln and Veres, 2006), which could then be deployed by the Reasoning Engine (the agent) in the real environment. Figure 8.3 provides a diagrammatic representation of the main components.

The abstraction engine provides the bridge between the Reasoning Engine and its environment; in particular, the abstraction engine provides all the (discrete) beliefs related to input, output, and control. It does this by asserting and retracting a special data structure treated as a *shared belief*. Inspecting the abstraction engine code thus allows us to determine the beliefs shared between Abstraction and Reasoning engines and in turn the perceptions we want to exhaustively explore during verification. We implemented the abstraction engine for this example in GWENDOLEN (although we later also used a Java-based abstraction engine in a different case study (Dennis et al., 2016a)). A fragment of this code is provided in Listing 8.3 and the listing for the Reasoning Engine can be found in Listing 8.1. Here, $+_\Sigma b$ and $-_\Sigma b$ are used to indicate when the abstraction engine asserts or removes a shared belief.

```
+bound(yes)  :  { B heading_for(Pos),  ∼B close_to(Pos)}          1
    ← +Σ(close_to(Pos));                                          2
+bound(no)   :  { B heading_for(Pos),  B close_to(Pos)}          3
    ← −Σ(close_to(Pos));                                          4
                                                                  5
+thruster(X,L1,L2,P,C,V):                                         6
    { B thruster_bank_line(X,N,L),  ∼B broken(X),  P < 1}        7
    ← +Σ(broken(X));                                              8
+thruster(X,L1,L2,P,C,V):                                         9
    { B thruster_bank_line(X,N,L),  B broken(X),  1 < P }       10
    ← −Σ(broken(X));                                             11
                                                                 12
−broken(X)  :                                                    13
    { B thruster_bank_line(X,N,L),                               14
      B thruster(X,L1,L2,P,C,V),  P < 1 }                       15
    ← +Σ(broken(X));                                             16
```

Listing 8.3 Abstraction engine for the LEO Agent

The lead agent has no abstraction engine since it is not controlling a physical system directly and so does not actually receive any information in the form of shared beliefs. It receives all its inputs as messages from other agents.

8.4.1 Implementation

We built a hybrid system using the architecture described in Section 8.1.1 consisting of a Reasoning Engine, R, an abstraction engine, A, a Physical Engine, Π, and a Continuous Engine, Ω. Figure. 8.3 shows the full architecture for our system (Dennis et al., 2010c).

Real-time control of the satellite is governed by a traditional feedback controller which forms the Physical Engine (Π). This engine communicates with the abstraction engine that filters and discretizes information. To do this A may use a Continuous Engine (which contains a simulation of the satellite and its environment) to make calculations. The Reasoning Engine is the rational agent whose code we have seen in Listing 8.1. Actions involve either calls to the Continuous Engine, Ω, for instance to calculate new flight paths or instructions to the Physical Engine, Π, for instance to change these flight paths. These instructions are passed through the abstraction engine, A, to the agent.

Semantics of Interaction

We developed a semantics for interaction between the components of the architecture (Dennis et al., 2010a) (updated in Dennis et al. (2016a)) which operates via shared sets of which, for our purposes, the most interesting is the set of *shared beliefs*, Σ, used by both A and R to describe their shared, discrete, understanding of the world. R may also make specific requests for calculations to be performed by Ω or actions to be performed by Π. These requests are sent via A. Among other things, A takes any (potentially continuous) results returned by Ω and discretises these as a shared belief for R. Overall, the role of A is to interface between R and the other engines. This helps avoid data overload by replacing large 'chunks' of streaming data with key discrete predicates.

In this semantics all perceptions that arrive via sensors from the real world are filtered through A, which converts them into discrete shared beliefs, Σ. Therefore, from a model-checking perspective, if we are interested in how the external world can affect the internal beliefs of the Reasoning Engine, R, then we are primarily interested in the possible compositions of Σ.

Testing

This architecture and interaction semantics have been implemented within a simulation environment, where the Physical and Continuous engines (Π and Ω) are implemented in MATLAB, while A and R are written in the customised EASS variant of the GWENDOLEN programming language (described in Appendix A.10). This extended language includes constructs for explicitly calling Π and Ω and a Java environment interface that supports such calls. This Java environment handles the shared data sets, in particular the shared beliefs which are used by A and R, and also controls communication with MATLAB via sockets. In other work we have experimented with using other languages for the abstraction engine while obeying the interaction semantics (Dennis et al., 2016a).

The architecture has been deployed on multiple satellites within the satellite hardware test facility as well as within a number of simulated environments. A range of satellite scenarios has been devised and tested, involving assuming and maintaining various formations, fault monitoring and recovery and collaborative surveying work in environments such as geostationary and low Earth orbits and among semi-charted asteroid fields. The system and scenarios are described more fully in Lincoln et al. (2013).

In simulation a 'gremlin' agent was introduced that could, at specified points, insert hardware failures into the satellite system. In physical testing it was possible to simulate failures in 'path following' by physically moving the satellites from their chosen course.

8.4.2 Verification Environment

The architecture proved particularly conducive to the verification methodology described in Chapter 6. Since programmers had to explicitly program up the abstractions to be used with the abstraction engine it became possible to 'read off' from the code for an abstraction engine all the shared beliefs that could possibly be asserted in response to changing perceptions. This in turn allows us to pre-determine the possible configurations of the set of shared beliefs. Similarly we were able to analyse the messages that agents sent to determine which messages might be received by other agents in the system. Since the only external inputs to the reasoning engine come from shared beliefs and messages it was easy to clearly define the set of inputs needed for verification.

Recall that we need to implement verification environments that observe the agent to be verified's interface to the rest of the system and supply random sets of inputs to the agent. In this case, these environments consisted entirely of asserting and retracting these shared beliefs and messages. Each time an agent took an action in the environment a new set of shared beliefs and a new set of messages were generated at random. Each time the agent requested the shared beliefs a random shared belief set was sent to it (similarly with messages). During model-checking the calls to random number generation caused the model-checker to branch and to explore all possible outcomes that could be generated. In order to limit the search space we took the (simplifying) view that reasoning happens instantaneously, while action has a duration. Therefore the only times at which the system randomly changes the perceptions/shared beliefs and messages available to the reasoning engine are when the reasoning engine takes some form of action (i.e., a request for a calculation from the Continuous Engine). The model-checker will then explore *all possible* combinations of shared beliefs and messages that might be available at that point, modelling essentially both the times an action results in the expected outcome and those when it does not.

We are interested both in verifying the behaviour of the agents that interact with the lower-level satellite control systems via an abstraction engine and with verifying behaviour of the software-only lead agent that determines formations.

For the agent that interacts using an abstraction engine, we can analyse the shared beliefs and use these to construct the random sets of perceptions that will be sent to the agent during verification. Reading off the uses of these constructs in Listing 8.3 tells us that the shared beliefs that can be used are

- `close_to(Pos)` (meaning that the satellite is close to position, `Pos`), and
- `broken(X)` (meaning thruster `X` is broken).

Also appearing in the full code shown in listing 8.1 are `thruster_bank_line(X, B, L)` (meaning thruster X, is currently in bank B and using fuel line L) and `get_close_to(Pos, P)` (meaning that P is a plan for moving to position, `Pos`).

All of these have parameters. We know from the physical satellite set-up that the thruster 'name', X, could be x, y or z and its bank, B (not used in these examples), and line, L, could be 1 or 2, respectively, depending upon the formation under consideration, `Pos`, could be `none`, `right`, `middle`, `left`, `topright`, `topleft`, `bottomright` or `bottomleft`. `get_close_to` also has the name of a plan, P, as a parameter. This name was generated and supplied by the Continuous Engine. We determined that the actual name used was not relevant to the correctness of the system – the agent merely passes it on to the underlying control system and so we used a placeholder name, `plan`, for this parameter.

Messages are passed directly between rational agents rather than being processed by their abstraction engines. So as well as analysing the abstraction engine for an agent we also need to analyse the messages that other agents in the system send. However, this does not allow us to verify the system against the presence of unknown agents, or message corruption. It is important to note, therefore, that we are explicitly *not* investigating this in the context of a system where malicious agents may send conflicting messages. In fact the properties we establish would not hold if messages were lost.

We determine the following messages that may be received by agents in the system. `aglead` may receive the message `maintaining(AgName)` in which agent, `AgName`, asserts that is is maintaining its position and the message `aborted(thruster_failure,AgName)` in which agent, `AgName` states that it has aborted its current maneouvre because of thruster failure. The satellite agents (as represented by `ag1`) can receive three messages:

- `assuming_formation(F)` which tells them that the group will be assuming some formation, F;
- `position(Pos)` which informs them that they should assume position, Pos within the formation; and
- the instruction `drop_formation(F)` which tells the agent to abandon the attempt to assume the formation F.

In the system under consideration, AgName can be ag1, ag2, ag3 or ag4. F is one of `line` or `square`, and Pos could be `none`, `right`, `middle`, `left`, `topright`, `topleft`, `bottomright` or `bottomleft`. For reasons of efficiency, we do not consider the issue of thruster failure in the multi-agent system so we will not use values of `aborted(thruster_failure, AgName)` in what follows.

Table 8.1 Results for analysis of a single agent with no thruster failure

Inputs:

Property	close_to	broken	thruster_bank_line	get_close_to
(8.3)	middle	×	×	(middle, plan)
(8.4)	middle	×	×	(middle, plan)

Results:

Property	States	Time
(8.3)	33	12s
(8.4)	33	12s

8.5 Example Verification

Note. For most verification experiments in this section it is necessary to limit the number of possibilities. However, the analysis does allow us to state clearly which inputs are being considered, as is shown in Tables 8.1–8.4.

Agent Operation without Thruster Failure or Outside Communication.
Table 8.1 shows the environment provided for each property (**Inputs**), and the size of the generated product automata (in states) and the time taken in hours, minutes and seconds on a dual core 2.8GHz Mac-book with 8GB of memory running MacOS X 10.9.2* (**Results**). The columns on the left of the Inputs chart show the arguments that were supplied to each of the potential percepts (i.e., every time it took an action the agent could potentially gain the perception `get_close_to(middle, plan)` or not, but could not, for instance, get the perception `get_close_to(left, plan)`). In Table 8.1, × indicates that the percept was not supplied at all.

The important aspect to note is that the theorem resulting from the model-checking process explicitly states its assumptions about the real world (i.e., that plans are always produced and are always accurate) rather than concealing these assumptions within the coding of the model. Since it is, in reality, unlikely that we could ever guarantee that plan execution would always succeed it might be necessary to combine the model-checking with probabilistic results to obtain an analysis of the likely reliability of the agent (see both the dis-

---

* It can be seen (particularly, for instance, by comparison of Tables 8.2 and 8.4) that time taken does not scale consistently with the number of states in the product automata. This is because the time taken to generate the automata was sensitive to the complexity of generating new states within the agent code – for instance, where a lot of Prolog-style reasoning was needed there was a significant slowdown in the generation of new program states.

Table 8.2 Results of the analysis of a single agent with thruster failures

Inputs:

Property	close_to	broken	thruster_bank_line	get_close_to
(8.5)	middle	x, y, z	(x, 1, 1), (y, 1, 1), (z, 1, 1)	middle
(8.8)	middle	x	(x, 1, 1)	middle

Results:

Property	States	Time
(8.5)	16,609	1h,18m,42s
(8.8)	2,754	9m,04s

cussion of compositional verification approaches in Chapter 11 and the use of AJPF with the probabilistic model-checker PRISM discussed in Chapter 13).

Investigating the Response to Thruster Failure. Recall that Property (8.5) states that

if the planning process succeeds then either the agent eventually believes it is maintaining the position or it believes it has a broken thruster.

while Property (8.8) states that

if planning succeeds for the middle position, and the x thruster is always believed to be fixable and changing a fuel line means eventually the agent believes the thruster is no longer broken, then eventually the agent will believe it is maintaining its position.

Property (8.8) is obviously only true if the y and z thrusters do not also break. Unfortunately expressing these conditions for the additional thrusters made the verification process too slow (however, see 'aside' below). As a result this property was checked only with the option of sending the agent the predicate broken(x) not with the option of broken(y) or broken(z). However this restriction is clear from the presentation of results in Table 8.2.

Single Formation. Recall that the particular properties we are verifying here are as follows.

- Property (8.10):
  if all agents respond, the lead agent eventually believes the agents have assumed a linear formation.

- Property (8.11):
  the leader never believes it has assigned an agent to two positions at the same time.

Table 8.3   Analysis of a multi-agent system with no thruster failure
attempting to form into a line

Leader Agent

Property	maintaining	aborted	States	Time
(8.10)	ag1, ag2, ag3, ag4	×	1,381	18m, 6s
(8.11)	ag1, ag2, ag3, ag4	×	2,751	25m, 07s
(8.12)	ag1, ag2, ag3, ag4	×	2,751	26m, 47s

Follower Agent (Inputs)

Property	close_to	get_close_to	assume_formation	position	drop_formation
(8.13)	middle	(middle, plan)	line	×	line
(8.14)	middle	(middle, plan)	line	×	line

Follower Agent (Results)

Property	States	Time
(8.13)	602	5m,33s
(8.14)	602	4m,41s

- Property (8.12):

  the leader never believes it has assigned two agents to the same position.

- Property (8.13):

  under the assumption that planning and plan execution are successful for the relevant formation and position, the follower will eventually believe it has informed the leader that it is maintaining its position.

- Property (8.14):

  followers only send messages if they believe they are maintaining the positions they have been assigned.

The results of this analysis are shown in Table 8.3.

Changing Formations. Finally, we investigated the behaviour of the leader agent in situations where the formation could change. Here the relevant properties are as follows.

- Property (8.15):

  if all agents respond, then eventually the leader agent will believe a square formation to have been achieved.

Table 8.4   Analysis of results of a multi-agent system with no failures but
changing formations

Property	maintaining	States	Time
(8.15)	ag1, ag2, ag3, ag4	1,892	29m, 58s
(8.16)	ag1, ag2, ag3, ag4	3,333	1h, 5m, 21s

- Property (8.16):

  if all agents respond, then whenever the leader agent believes all the agents to be in square formation it will eventually believe them to be in a line formation.

The results of this are shown in Table 8.4

We can, of course, continue with further verification. However, it should be clear to the reader by now how this proceeds, combining model-checking of the behaviour for individual agents in the presence of a random environment, together with straightforward temporal/modal reasoning that can be carried out by hand or by appropriate automated proof tools.

8.6 Issues

Once again we see that program verification in AJPF is *very* slow. The efficiency of AJPF can be improved using well-known abstraction techniques such as property-based slicing (Winikoff et al., 2019). Following work by Hunter et al. (2013), we have also investigated the use of AJPF to generate models of the program that can be exported into other model-checking systems such as SPIN, NuSMV, or PRISM and this is discussed in Chapter 13.

Related to this, it might be useful to incorporate a more refined *probabilistic* analysis of environmental interactions. For instance, it is highly probable that no guarantee can be supplied that data incoming from sensors is correct, yet it is highly likely that the sensor will come with a probabilistic guarantee of reliability. It is therefore desirable to extend the kind of analysis we have done here to theorems of the form 'Assuming data from sensors is correct 98% of the time, and actions succeed 98% of the time, then 97% of the time the agent never believes it has reached a bad state'. This compositional approach is discussed in Chapter 11 and the extraction of probabilistic results from AJPF is discussed in Chapter 13.

9

Certification of Unmanned Air Systems

9.1 What is the System?

The increased role of autonomous systems in modern society is clear.* Nowhere is this as obvious as the use of 'drones' or unmanned air systems (UASs, see Figure 1.2a) both in military and civilian applications.[1] These air vehicles should be able to fly on their own, avoid hazards on their own and, essentially, follow the air regulations on their own. Without this last ability particularly, such air vehicles will surely not be allowed to fly autonomously in civilian airspace. So, in order to be used for civil applications, unmanned air systems must gain regulatory approval through the process known as *certification*. At the time of writing, however, truly autonomous air systems are not certified for flight in civilian airspace, and the process for certifying such systems is unclear.

The application described in this chapter forms part of an attempt to remedy this. If we have a high-fidelity simulation of both the aircraft and the environment in which it will fly, then we can test the air system out in a wide range of conditions and situations. This requires detailed models of the airframe, airflow, weather, and so on, all of which were provided by Neil Cameron, Mike Jump and the Virtual Engineering Centre in the UK.[2] Yet this is only one part of any certification process. It is also vital that an unmanned air system make similar decisions to those made by a human-piloted air system and, in particu-

---

* This work involved Matt Webster, who undertook the verification, together with Neil Cameron and Mike Jump, and was reported initially in Webster et al. (2011) and subsequently in Webster et al. (2014). Neil and Mike are Aerospace Engineers who provided both the control and air system simulation framework, and the aerospace (and pilot) expertise in general.

[1] Note, though, that we are only concerned with civilian uses of such systems.

[2] www.virtualengineeringcentre.com – providing visualisation, HPC, and simulation facilities.

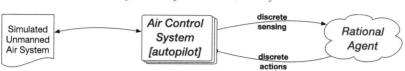

Figure 9.1 An agent-based unmanned air system linked to a high-fidelity flight simulation

lar, that the unmanned air system should follow the same rules and regulations that human pilots must adhere to.

So the context for the work here is that we again have an agent-based autonomous system, this time an unmanned air system, and wish to show that the agent will follow the same rules that a human pilot should. Note that this verification does not concern low-level flying skills – the aircraft's *autopilot* will take care of those – but instead concerns high-level issues such as what to do if another aircraft approaches, what to do in an emergency, when to contact air traffic control, and so on.

We here aim to formally verify that the agent controlling the unmanned air system conforms to the 'Rules of the Air' (Civil Aviation Authority, 2010), for example air traffic control clearance rules or rules corresponding to emergency avoidance scenarios. A prospective (human) pilot is examined against these rules and we will use AJPF to assess how well the agent controlling the air system adheres to these rules. Consequently, an agent-based unmanned air system was developed and linked into a high-fidelity flight simulation, as in Figure 9.1. We did not verify that the agent made decisions corresponding to *all* the 'Rules of the Air' but instead chose a small subset to assess and evaluate. This provided a 'proof of concept' that such verification *could*, in principle, be achieved. Initially there was doubt about whether this would be possible, as many saw this as verifying that the agent corresponded to a human. However, it should be clear that we only verify the agent against the rules that a human pilot *should* follow. Of course, this is only a small, though necessary, part of any certification process. Indeed, we did formalise and verify several additional *airmanship* requirements derived from interviews with subject matter experts, some of which we also discuss here. For further details on the broader certification context see Cameron et al. (2011) and Patchett et al. (2015).

We have modified the UAS agent used in the results reported in Webster et al. (2011) and Webster et al. (2014) to account for updates in the MCAPL system, to simplify some aspects of the system for ease of presentation, and to reflect our growing understanding of how best to integrate an agent-based decision-maker into a more complex autonomous system and verify that agent. While we believe this has resulted in a clearer and better-engineered system we have not been able to re-validate its performance within the high-fidelity simulated environment provided by the Virtual Engineering Centre although we have been able to reverify its performance with respect to the Rules of the Air. We will comment as we proceed, concerning some of the updates to the system.[3]

Aside. What is the key *difference* between an unmanned and a manned aircraft? Clearly the human pilot has flight skills, visual capabilities and strong situational awareness. But, beyond this, those high-level decisions usually made by a pilot, such as

1. where to tell the autopilot to fly to,
2. what to do in air traffic situations,
3. what to do in an emergency, and so on,

are now going to be made by software. For example, a typical rule (from the 'Rules of the Air') that we expect a human pilot to obey is

when two aircraft are approaching head-on ... and there is danger of a collision, each shall alter its course to the right.

In the case of a manned aircraft the pilot is responsible for this. In the unmanned case, we need to verify that the agent also does this; if it detects another aircraft coming towards it, it will invoke an action to fly to the right. So our long-term aim is to verify that the cognitive agent flying the unmanned air system behaves just as a pilot should. In other words, is the agent *equivalent to*, and possibly indistinguishable from, the pilot in this narrow sense?

The UAS agent is implemented to perform a mission to take-off from one airfield, fly to a destination and land. In order to do this it needs to taxi to the correct runway, hold at that runway, line up on the runway, take off, and once airborne it performs simple navigation and sense/avoid actions. Finally, it lands and taxis to a stand. While on the ground it must request permission to taxi, line up and take-off from air traffic control although air traffic control permission for approach, landing and taxying at the destination airport is given along with permission to take off and so need not be requested again. It must also request its navigation system calculate routes both for taxying and flying and instruct the auto-pilot to store those routes for enaction. In this system

---

[3] The code for this re-implementation can be found in the
`src/examples/gwendolen/verifiableautonomoussystems/chapter9.`
directory of the MCAPL distribution. A version of the agent reported in Webster et al. (2011) and Webster et al. (2014) can be found, for comparison, in the
`src/examples/gwendolen/uavs/certification` directory.

the auto-pilot automatically engages a particular route when it detects that the correct *flight phase* has begun. Determining the flight phase is a shared task between the agent which specifies when taxying, line up, take off and landing approach begin and also updates the flight phase to 'landed' once it detects the aircraft is on the ground and the underlying system which detects when the plane is in the runway hold position, has successfully lined up, and moved to the 'cruise' phase of flight. This underlying system also reports to the agent, when it has landed, but does not send this as a flight phase change. At any point the agent may detect that an object is approaching and, in flight phases such as cruise and taxying where the aircraft is in motion, it must instruct the system to perform an emergency avoidance manoeuvre.

Thus, missions are divided up into a number of flight phases representing the behaviour of the air vehicle at different points of its mission:

1. Waiting at the airport ramp (leading to the runway).
2. Taxying.
3. Holding at end of runway.
4. Lining up on the runway prior to take-off.
5. Lined up and ready for take-off.
6. Take-off.
7. Cruise at selected altitude.
8. Emergency avoid.
9. Airfield approach.
10. Landing and stopping.
11. Taxying from runway back to the ramp (i.e., at the destination).

The architecture of the system comprises the cognitive agent, named `executive`, together with a range of subsystems that it interacts with. Typical subsystems include the following.

- An air traffic control (ATC) communication subsystem, responsible for communication with ATC during the flight.
- A detect-and-avoid sensor (DAS), responsible for the detection of nearby aircraft.
- An environment reporting subsystem (Env), responsible for providing the cognitive agent with information on various aspects of the unmanned air system's environment. Specifically, in our case, the flight phase changes controlled by the environment.
- A fuel subsystem (Fuel), responsible for monitoring the vehicle's fuel levels.
- A navigation subsystem (Nav), responsible for providing the location of the vehicle.

- A vehicle subsystem monitor (Veh), responsible for providing information on the 'health' of the vehicle's systems, including reporting when the vehicle has landed, and when it has reached its destination.
- A route planner (Planner), responsible for generating detailed routes through civil airspace.

The agent's beliefs are formed using sensor inputs into the above subsystems, distilled from continuous 'real-world' data – so each subsystem acts like a specialised abstraction engine, as introduced in Chapter 8 – however, in this case, this abstraction layer is left implicit and the subsystems communicate with the agent via messages, which the agent then transforms into beliefs.

9.2 What *Properties* Do We Want to Establish?

There are a vast range of 'Rules of the Air'. Many are difficult to formalise, since they are imprecise or require pilot knowledge to disambiguate. There are relatively straightforward rules such as those concerning permission, for example:

'An aircraft shall not taxi on the apron or the manoeuvring area of an aerodrome [without permission]'

However, some of the 'Rules of the Air' appear contradictory. Consider the following.

- *'... when two aircraft are approaching head-on, or approximately so, and there is danger of a collision, each shall alter its course to the right'.*
- *'[An aircraft in the vicinity of an aerodrome must] make all turns to the left unless [told otherwise]'*

Clearly, if an aircarft is approaching, and we are in the vicinity of an aerodrome, then pilot expertise is needed for disambiguation and resolution of this potential conflict!

We consider here a small number of properties for illustrative purposes. A much larger selection can be found in Webster et al. (2011) and Webster et al. (2014).

1. **Detect and Avoid 1**
   Requirement: 'When two aircraft are approaching head-on, or approximately so, in the air and there is a danger of collision, each shall alter its course to the right'.

Formalisation:

$$\Box(\mathbf{B}_{exec} \text{ objectApproaching} \land \mathbf{B}_{exec} \text{ flightPhase(cruise)} \land$$
$$(\Box \mathbf{A}_{exec} \text{requestEmergencyAvoid} \Rightarrow \Diamond \mathbf{B}_{exec} \text{ enacting(emergencyAvoid)})) \Rightarrow$$
$$\Diamond(\mathbf{B}_{exec} \text{ flightPhase(emergencyAvoid)} \lor \neg\mathbf{B}_{exec} \text{ objectApproaching}).$$

$$(9.1)$$

This formalisation says that it is always the case that if the agent believes that there is an object on a collision course and it is currently cruising and if it requests emergency avoidance action from the underlying system then the system eventually responds to say that this is happening, then it will eventually believe that it has shifted the unmanned aircraft into an 'emergency avoid' flight phase or it will believe that the object is no longer approaching.

Note that we added the second disjunction ($\neg\mathbf{B}_{exec}$ objectApproaching) to account for occasions where the situation resolves itself before the emergency avoid is enacted. This requirement emerged during the model-checking process where this combination of events could occur because of the random exploration of perceptions while in the various simulations used for testing it was assumed that the object would always continue approaching the aircraft unless an emergency avoid manoeuvre was undertaken.

In our re-engineered system, we also had to add the additional condition that the property only holds in situations where requests for emergency avoid actions are answered. In the verification environment used with the original agent it was assumed that emergency avoid requests were always immediately responded to with a message confirming the manoeuvre was being enacted. We chose to engineer a verification environment in which there could be a (potentially infinite) delay between request and response and thus were forced to add the caveat that a response was eventually received in order for the property to be true. We will discuss this issue further at the end of the chapter.

This formalisation is an adequate translation of the requirement as once the emergencyAvoid flight phase is selected, the Planner will be used to calculate an emergency avoidance route which will steer the aircraft to the right around the intruder aircraft.

In fact the assumptions made here about the behaviour of the Planner during the emergency avoid flight phase mean that the same formalism is adequate to cover two further requirements from the Rules of the Air:

- **Detect and Avoid 2**
  Requirement: 'Notwithstanding that a flight is being made with air traffic control clearance it shall remain the duty of the commander of an aircraft to take all possible measures to ensure that his aircraft does not collide with any other aircraft'.
- **Detect and Avoid 3**
  Requirement: 'An aircraft shall not be flown in such proximity to other aircraft as to create a danger of collision'.

2. **ATC Clearance**
   Requirement: 'An aircraft shall not taxi on the apron or the manoeuvring area of an aerodrome without the permission of either: (a) the person in charge of the aerodrome; or (b) the air traffic control [ATC] unit or aerodrome flight information service unit notified as being on watch at the aerodrome'.
   Formalisation:

$$\Box(\mathbf{B}_{exec}\, \text{flightPhase(taxiing)} \wedge \neg\mathbf{B}_{exec}\, \text{landed} \Rightarrow \mathbf{B}_{exec}\, \text{taxiClearanceGiven})$$

$$\Box(\mathbf{B}_{exec}\, \text{flightPhase(lineUp)} \Rightarrow \mathbf{B}_{exec}\, \text{lineUpClearanceGiven})$$

$$\Box(\mathbf{B}_{exec}\, \text{flightPhase(takeOff)} \Rightarrow \mathbf{B}_{exec}\, \text{takeOffClearanceGiven}).$$

Notes: The agent's beliefs about the flight phase it is in correspond to the agent performing some manoeuvre, such as taxiing, lining up, etc. These formalisations state that the agent will not believe that it is doing *act* (in the relevant flight phase) unless it believes that it has clearance to do *act*. Clearly we assume that the Planner (which plans routes around the aerodrome) will only generate routes for which clearance is granted, and that the flight control system (which implements the routes) will not err in its implementation of these routes. Note that because our system receives taxi clearance for its destination on takeOff we only check for this when the aircraft is taxiing at the start of its journey and not after it has landed.

3. **500-feet rule**
   Requirement: 'Except with the written permission of the CAA, an aircraft shall not be flown closer than 500 feet to any person, vessel, vehicle or structure'.
   Formalisation:

$$\Box(\mathbf{B}_{exec}\, \text{alert500} \wedge \mathbf{B}_{exec}\, \text{flightPhase(cruise)}) \wedge$$
$$(\Box\mathbf{A}_{exec}\text{requestEmergencyAvoid} \Rightarrow \Diamond\mathbf{B}_{exec}\, \text{enacting(emergencyAvoid)}) \Rightarrow$$
$$\Diamond(\mathbf{B}_{exec}\, \text{flightPhase(emergencyAvoid)} \vee \neg\mathbf{B}_{exec}\, \text{alert500})$$

Notes: This formalisation of the requirement states that if the agent believes that the detect-and-avoid sensor (das) has raised an alert that the aircraft is in danger of flying within 500 feet of another airspace user, and if the agent believes that it is cruising, then it will eventually change its flight phase to emergencyAvoid. This rule formalisation is largely the same as for the detect and avoid rule.

9.2.1 Properties Based on Airmanship

Airmanship properties are derived from requirements based on interviews with subject matter experts, and represent rules that should be followed by aircraft operating in civil airspace, but which are not explicitly written in the Rules of the Air.

In the original version of the UAS system, the agent persistently polled the subsystems for information about their current status. It should be recalled, however, that the current version of the GWENDOLEN language regularly checks for messages and perceptions and so this explicit polling behaviour was unnecessary. A number of the airmanship properties discussed in Webster et al. (2011) and Webster et al. (2014) encapsulated the idea that a pilot should continuously monitor the aircraft sub-systems and these were represented by properties stating that it was always the case that each subsystem would eventually be polled. These properties become redundant on the assumption that the agent regularly checks messages as part of the reasoning cycle, though for high levels of assurance this behaviour would need certifying.

However, there are nevertheless a number of airmanship properties that still pertain to our system.

1. **Complete mission**
   Requirement: 'During the operation of an aircraft, the commander of an aircraft should endeavour to complete the stated mission until that mission is complete'.
   Formalisation:

$$\Box\Diamond \mathbf{G}_{exec}\mathsf{completeMission} \vee$$
$$\Box\Diamond (\mathbf{G}_{exec}\mathsf{missionComplete} \ \mathsf{U} \ \Box\Diamond \mathbf{B}_{exec} \ \mathsf{completeMission}).$$

Notes: This requirement concerns the agent's behaviour towards the completion of its mission. The formalisation of the requirement states that the Executive (agent) must always eventually have a goal to complete its mission until it believes the mission is complete or it simply always eventually has the goal (in the event that the mission does not complete – for instance if take off clearance is never given by ATC). We might expect this property to state that the agent always has the goal, until this requirement is released by the acquisition of the corresponding belief but, as will be seen when we examine the code, the goal $\mathbf{G}_{exec}$completeMission is represented by an achievement goal. When attempting to achieve such a goal, a GWENDO-LEN agent selects and executes a plan to achieve the goal, removes the goal from its goal base, and then checks to see if the goal has been achieved[4] so in execution the goal missionComplete is continuously deleted and then re-attempted as the agent works through the flight phases of the mission – hence this is formalised as 'always eventually' the agent has the goal.

This is a relatively strict requirement as it does not allow for the agent to delete its goal to complete the mission after deciding that the goal is impossible to achieve. It may be preferable to allow the agent to 'give up' in trying to complete its mission, but in this case we do not permit this.

2. **No further activity after mission is complete**
   Requirement: 'Once the mission is complete, the commander of an aircraft does not need to try to complete the mission any longer'.
   Formalisation:

$$\Box \left(\begin{array}{c} \mathbf{B}_{exec}\text{ missionComplete} \implies \\ \Diamond\Box(\neg\mathbf{G}_{exec}\text{completeMission} \vee \neg\mathbf{I}_{exec}\text{completeMission}) \end{array} \right).$$

Notes: This requirement sounds very abstract for a human commander of an aircraft; it is obvious to state that once a person has achieved what they set out to do that they no longer need to try to achieve it. However, in the case of an autonomous system these kinds of facts cannot be considered obvious, and must be listed as system requirements.

This requirement states that once the Executive believes that the mission is complete, then it will eventually be the case that the Executive will never have a goal to complete the mission, and will never have an intention to complete the mission. This, in effect, states that once the Executive believes that its mission is complete then it will eventually stop trying to complete the mission. Of course, this assumes that the Executive will only ever have one mission per execution run. If it were desirable for the agent to have multiple missions, then this requirement would need to be modified. (Another alternative to multiple missions for the agent would be to have a single 'overriding' mission which is to complete a set of sub-missions, in which case this requirement could be kept as-is.)

---

[4] This is obviously a quirk of the GWENDOLEN semantics that is not entirely desirable, it would be better if the goal were not deleted until definitively achieved.

3. **Check fuel before taxi**

   Requirement: 'The commander of an aircraft should check the current fuel level before starting to taxi'.

   This can be refined into a specific requirement for the Executive: 'It is always the case that when the Executive sends a message to the planner to calculate a taxi route, then it informs it of the current fuel level'.

   Formalisation:

   $$\Box(\mathbf{A}_{exec}\mathsf{requestTaxiRoute}(\_, \_, \_, 200) \Rightarrow \mathbf{B}_{exec}\,\mathsf{fuel}(\mathsf{level}, 200)).$$

   Notes: This is derived from the polling requirements for the original system. However, unlike many of those, it makes sense to expressly check that the planner has up-to-date information when it is asked to plan a route. Note that although we want this property to hold true for *any* fuel level, we only check it for 200, which is the value our verification environment returns for all fuel status check requests. In the expression we use the '$\_$' notation to indicate that we do not care what the value of that argument is (the three arguments in question are a route number and the aircraft's current latitude and longitude) – so we check all `requestTaxiRoute` actions performed by the system where the required fuel level is 200.

   The correctness of this property also relies on the assumption that old fuel level beliefs are regularly updated, otherwise the executive could pass out-of-date fuel information to the planner. We can ameliorate this issue somewhat by checking an additional quality that – until it lands – the aircraft regularly removes fuel beliefs:

   Formalisation:

   $$\Box(\mathbf{B}_{exec}\,\mathsf{fuel}(\mathsf{level}, \_) \land \neg\mathbf{B}_{exec}\,\mathsf{veh}(\mathsf{landed}, \_)) \Rightarrow \Diamond\neg\mathbf{B}_{exec}\,\mathsf{fuel}(\mathsf{level}, \_).$$
   $$(9.2)$$

   Even this does not perfectly capture the idea that fuel beliefs should always be current, but it brings us closer to that requirement. It can be viewed as a property that reduces the possibility of an error but cannot entirely guarantee it.

4. **Check fuel before cruise**

   Requirement: 'The commander of an aircraft should check the current fuel level before starting to cruise'.

   Formalisation:

   $$\Box(\mathbf{A}_{exec}\mathsf{requestRoute}(\_, \_, \_, 200) \Rightarrow \mathbf{B}_{exec}\,\mathsf{fuel}(\mathsf{level}, 200)).$$

Notes: This is similar to requirement 3 though it is worth noting that the agent program requests both the route for cruising and the route for taxying at the same time. The informal statement of this property invites us to imagine the pilot checking the fuel gauge after take off at the point of starting the cruise portion of the mission (possibly to see if there had been an unusual reduction in fuel during the take off manoeuvre). This property instead guarantees that the planner has been passed the correct fuel level when it computed the cruise route.

5. **Check fuel before approach**
   Requirement: 'The commander of an aircraft should check the current fuel level before starting to approach for landing'.
   Formalisation:

$$\Box(\mathbf{A}_{exec}\text{requestApproach}(200) \Rightarrow \mathbf{B}_{exec}\text{ fuel}(level, 200)).$$

Notes: This requirement is also similar to requirement 9.2.1

9.3 GWENDOLEN Code

The UAS agent is the most complex agent that we will present in this book. As such we will focus on specific aspects of it and the interested reader can review the full code in the MCAPL distribution.

We start with the plans used to handle the messages sent to the agent by the various subsystems. These are shown in Listing 9.1. These plans can be divided into plans for reacting to messages from the detect and avoid sensor that either an object is approaching or the 500 feet rule has been violated. In these cases the plans determine whether the craft needs to react to the alert (by adopting a goal to do so) or just needs to note the existence of the alert – for instance in situations when the craft is on the ground and stationary. There are a few details here – such as the use of the `alertnoted` belief to register when the agent is about to react to the alert but has not yet actually adopted the plan to do so (the need for this arises when alerts are changing at a rapid rate and the interleaved execution of plans means the situation has changed – an edge case revealed during the model-checking). The next set of plans handle message from the detect and avoid sensor that the object that was approaching or was within 500 feet has now passed – these plans clean up any beliefs or goals related to the previous alert.

The next set of plans are for when the environment sends a message that the craft has entered a new flight phase. Some flight phases – such as `linedup` are initiated by the environment and some, such as `lineup` are initiated by the agent. Where the agent has initiated the flight phase it simply treats the message from the environment as an acknowledgement that the flight phase change has been accomplished. Where the flight phase was not initiated by the agent then it needs to update its own beliefs about the flight phase. There is one plan which tells the agent to ignore confirmation messages that the underlying system is enacting an emergency avoidance manoeuvre if it is no longer reacting to an alert. Lastly all other messages from the system, such as air traffic control confirmations, are converted to beliefs.

```
+.received (: tell ,  das ( objectApproaching ))  :              1
        { ~B  flightPhase ( emergencyAvoid ) ,  ~B  stationary ,   2
         ~B  das_alert ,   ~G  reactToAlert  [ perform ] ,         3
         ~B  alertnoted }  ←                                       4
                +.lock ,                                           5
                +das ( objectApproaching ) ,                      6
                +alertnoted ,                                      7
                −.lock ,                                          8
                +!reactToAlert  [ perform ];                       9
+.received (: tell ,  das ( objectApproaching ))  :             10
        {B  stationary ,   ~B  das ( objectApproaching )}  ←      11
                +das ( objectApproaching );                      12
+.received (: tell ,  das ( objectApproaching ))  :             13
        {G  reactToAlert  [ perform ] ,                          14
         ~B  das ( objectApproaching )}  ←                        15
                +das ( objectApproaching );                      16
+.received (: tell ,  das ( objectApproaching ))  :             17
        {B  alertnoted ,   ~B  das ( objectApproaching )}  ←      18
                +das ( objectApproaching );                      19
+.received (: tell ,  das ( alert500 ))  :                      20
        { ~B  flightPhase ( emergencyAvoid ) ,  ~B  on_ground ,   21
         ~B  das_alert ,   ~G  reactToAlert  [ perform ] ,        22
         ~B  alertnoted }  ←                                      23
                +.lock ,                                          24
                +alertnoted ,                                     25
                +das ( alert500 ) ,                               26
                −.lock ,                                         27
                +!reactToAlert  [ perform ];                     28
+.received (: tell ,  das ( alert500 ))  :                      29
        {B  on_ground ,   ~B  das ( alert500 )}  ←                30
                +das ( alert500 );                                31
+.received (: tell ,  das ( alert500 ))  :                      32
        {G  reactToAlert  [ perform ] ,   ~B  das ( alert500 )}  ← 33
                +das ( alert500 );                                34
+.received (: tell ,  das ( alert500 ))  :                      35
        {B  alertnoted ,   ~B  das ( alert500 )}  ←               36
                +das ( alert500 );                                37
                                                                 38
+.received (: tell ,  das ( objectPassed ))  :                  39
        {B  flightPhase ( emergencyAvoid ) ,                     40
         B  store ( flightPhase , F )}  ←                         41
```

```
        +.lock ,                                              42
        -alertnoted ,                                         43
        -! reactToAlert [perform],                            44
        -das(objectApproaching),                              45
        -das(alert500),                                       46
        -enacting(emergencyAvoid),                            47
        +! changeFlightPhase(F) [perform],                    48
        -.lock;                                               49
+.received(:tell , das(objectPassed)) :                       50
    { ~B flightPhase(emergencyAvoid) } ←                      51
        +.lock ,                                              52
        -alertnoted ,                                         53
        -! reactToAlert [perform],                            54
        -das(objectApproaching),                              55
        -das(alert500),                                       56
        -enacting(emergencyAvoid),                            57
        -.lock;                                               58
                                                              59
+.received(:tell , veh(status , NewFP)):                       60
    {B flightPhase(OldFlightPhase),                           61
     B environment_flight_phase(NewFP),                       62
     ~B waiting_confirmation(NewFP)} ←                        63
        +.lock ,                                              64
        +!changeFlightPhase(NewFP) [perform],                65
        -.lock;                                               66
+.received(:tell , veh(status , NewFlightPhase)):             67
    {B waiting_confirmation(NewFlightPhase)} ←               68
        -waiting_confirmation(NewFlightPhase);               69
                                                              70
+.received(:tell , enacting(emergencyAvoid)) :                71
    { ~G reactToAlert [perform]};                            72
                                                              73
+.received(:tell , M):                                        74
    { ~B flightPhase_message(M),                             75
     ~B das_message(M)} ←                                    76
        +M;                                                  77
```

Listing 9.1 UAS Agent Message Handling Plans

The set of plans for handling the perform goal changeFlight
Phase(To) are omitted. In theory these are straightforward – simply updat-
ing the belief, flightPhase appropriately. They are complicated by the fact
that such requests can be initiated either by the agent or by a message from the
environment. Where the agent is initiating a flight phase change it needs to take
an updateFlightPhase action to inform the rest of the aircraft systems of
the new flight phase. Furthermore, when changing to the emergencyAvoid
flight phase, the agent needs to store the previous flight phase so that it can return to it once the emergency avoidance behaviour is concluded. Lastly when
changing out of the emergencyAvoid flight phase we need to extract the

previous flight phase from the store and clean up various housekeeping beliefs. While all this was quite fiddly to get correct, the overall concept is hopefully fairly straightforward to understand.

Listing 9.2 shows the plans for progressing the agent through the various flight phases in normal operation (i.e., when there are no alerts from the detect and avoid sensor). Most of these are triggered by attempts to achieve missionComplete and get the agent to collect the information it needs in each flight phase in order to progress to the next. Sometimes, when information arrives, such as proposed routes for taxying and cruise, this immediately triggers an action to store the route for later enaction. Similarly when the agent is informed that it is now in the location of the destination airfield, this triggers immediate requests for updated fuel and latitute/longitude information.

```
+flightPhase(waitingAtRamp):  {  ~B  missionComplete}  ←      1
                requestFuelStatus ,                            2
                requestPosition ;                             3
                                                              4
+!missionComplete  [achieve]  :                               5
        {B  flightPhase(waitingAtRamp),                       6
        ~B  fuel(level ,  F)}  ←                              7
                *fuel(level ,  F);                            8
                                                              9
+!missionComplete  [achieve]  :                              10
        {B  flightPhase(waitingAtRamp),                      11
        ~B  position(Lat,  Lon,  Alt)}  ←                    12
                *position(Lat,  Lon,  Alt);                  13
                                                             14
+!missionComplete  [achieve]  :                              15
        {B  flightPhase(waitingAtRamp),                      16
        ~B  atc(taxiClearanceGiven(R))}  ←                   17
                −atc(N),                                      18
                requestTaxiClearance ,                       19
                *atc(M);                                      20
                                                             21
+!missionComplete  [achieve]  :                              22
        {B  flightPhase(waitingAtRamp),  B  destination(D),  23
        B  fuel(level ,  F),  B  position(Lat,  Lon,  Alt),  24
        B  atc(taxiClearanceGiven(R)),                       25
        ~B  routes_stored_for_enaction}  ←                   26
                requestTaxiRoute(R,  Lat,  Lon,  F),         27
                requestRoute(D,  Lat,  Lon,  F),             28
                *enactRoute(taxi ,  NT),                     29
                *enactRoute(cruise ,  NC);                   30
                                                             31
+route(taxi ,  N,  T,  F,  S)  :  {⊤}  ←                     32
                requestEnactRoute(taxi ,  N);                33
+route(cruise ,  N,  T,  F,  S)  :  {  ⊤  }  ←               34
                requestEnactRoute(cruise ,  N);              35
```

```
+!missionComplete [achieve] :                              36
    {B flightPhase(waitingAtRamp),                         37
     B atc(taxiClearanceGiven(R)),                         38
     B enactRoute(taxi, Num),                              39
    ~B das(objectApproaching)} ←                           40
            +.lock,                                        41
            +!changeFlightPhase(taxying) [perform],        42
            −.lock,                                        43
            *flightPhase(holding);                         44
                                                           45
                                                           46
                                                           47
+!missionComplete [achieve] :                              48
    {B flightPhase(holding), B enactRoute(cruise, N),      49
    ~B atc(lineUpClearanceGiven)} ←                        50
            −atc(M1),                                       51
            requestLineUpClearance,                        52
            *atc(M);                                        53
                                                           54
+!missionComplete [achieve] :                              55
    {B flightPhase(holding),                               56
     B atc(lineUpClearanceGiven), ~B das_alert} ←          57
            +.lock,                                        58
            +!changeFlightPhase(lineup) [perform],         59
            −.lock,                                        60
            *flightPhase(linedup);                          61
                                                           62
+!missionComplete [achieve] :                              63
    {B enactRoute(cruise, R), B flightPhase(linedup),      64
    ~B atc(takeOffClearanceGiven)} ←                       65
            −atc(N),                                        66
            requestTakeOffClearance,                       67
            *atc(M);                                        68
                                                           69
+!missionComplete [achieve] :                              70
    {B enactRoute(cruise, R), B flightPhase(linedup),      71
     B atc(takeOffClearanceGiven), ~B das_alert} ←         72
            +.lock,                                        73
            +!changeFlightPhase(takeOff) [perform],        74
            −.lock,                                        75
            *flightPhase(cruise),                          76
            +.lock,                                        77
            −enactRoute(cruise, R),                        78
            −enactRoute(taxi, N),                          79
            −route(taxi, N, T, F, S),                      80
            −route(cruise, R, T1, F1, S1),                 81
            −atc(takeOffClearanceGiven),                   82
            −.lock;                                        83
                                                           84
+!missionComplete [achieve] :                              85
    {B flightPhase(cruise), B destination(L),              86
```

```
            ~B location(L), ~B das_alert} ←           87
                *location(L);                          88
                                                       89
// Reached destination                                 90
+veh(location ,L) : {B destination(L)} ←               91
                +.lock ,                                92
                -veh(location ,L),                      93
                +location(L),                           94
                -fuel(level , F),                       95
                -position(Lat, Lon, Alt),              96
                requestFuelStatus ,                     97
                requestPosition ,                       98
                -.lock ;                                99
                                                       100
+!missionComplete [achieve] :                          101
        {B flightPhase(cruise), B destination(L),      102
        B location(L), ~B fuel(level , F),             103
        ~B das_alert} ←                                104
                *fuel(level , F);                       105
                                                       106
+!missionComplete [achieve] :                          107
        {B flightPhase(cruise), B destination(L),      108
        B location(L), ~B position(Lat, Lon, Alt),     109
        ~B das_alert} ←                                110
                *position(Lat, Lon, Alt);              111
                                                       112
+!missionComplete [achieve] :                          113
        {B flightPhase(cruise), B destination(L),      114
        B location(L), B fuel(level , F),              115
        B position(Lat, Lon, Alt),                     116
        ~B appr(N, T, F1, S), ~B das_alert} ←          117
                requestApproach ,                       118
                *appr(N, T, F1, S);                     119
                                                       120
+!missionComplete [achieve] :                          121
        {B flightPhase(cruise), B destination(L),      122
        B location(L), B appr(N, T, F, S),             123
        ~B enactAppr(N), ~B das_alert} ←               124
                enactApproach(N),                       125
                *enactAppr(N);                          126
                                                       127
+!missionComplete [achieve] :                          128
        {B flightPhase(cruise), B destination(L),      129
        B location(L), B enactAppr(N), ~B das_alert} ← 130
                +.lock ,                                131
                -appr(N, T, F, S),                      132
                -enactAppr(N),                          133
                +!changeFlightPhase(approach) [perform], 134
                -.lock ;                                135
                                                       136
+!missionComplete [achieve] :                          137
```

```
{B flightPhase(approach), B destination(L),              138
  ~B das_alert} ←                                        139
        *veh(landed,L),                                  140
        +.lock,                                          141
        −fuel(level, F),                                 142
        −position(Lat, Lon, Alt),                        143
        +!changeFlightPhase(landed) [perform],           144
        −.lock,                                          145
        requestFuelStatus,                               146
        requestPosition;                                 147
                                                         148
+!missionComplete [achieve]  :                           149
    {B flightPhase(landed), ~B fuel(level, F)} ←         150
        *fuel(level, F);                                 151
                                                         152
+!missionComplete [achieve]  :                           153
    {B flightPhase(landed),                              154
      ~B position(Lat, Lon, Alt)} ←                      155
        *position(Lat, Lon, Alt);                        156
                                                         157
+!missionComplete [achieve]  :                           158
    {B flightPhase(landed), B fuel(level, F),            159
     B position(Lt, Ln, Alt),                            160
      ~B route(taxi, Num, Time, Fuel, Safety)} ←         161
        requestTaxiRoute(destination, Lt, Ln, F),        162
        *enactRoute(taxi, Num);                          163
                                                         164
+!missionComplete [achieve]  :                           165
    {B flightPhase(landed), B enactRoute(taxi, Num),     166
     ~B das_alert} ←                                     167
        +.lock,                                          168
        +!changeFlightPhase(taxying) [perform],          169
        −.lock,                                          170
        *flightPhase(waitingAtRamp);                     171
```

Listing 9.2 UAS Flight Phases

Lastly the plans in Listing 9.3 are for handling alerts from the detect-and-avoid sensor. Normally, when there is an alert, the agent should request emergency avoidance behaviour and, once notifed that this is now being enacted, it should change the flight phase to `emergencyAvoid`. However because of the way model-checking explores edge cases where alerts can change rapidly, it is necessary to check that there is still an alert, `B das_alert`, and that it is relevant (i.e., the aircraft is not on the ground). If there is no longer an alert or it is irrelevant, then the 'react to alert' process should be stopped (the `reactToAlert` goal is dropped) and relevant beliefs should be cleaned up. Meanwhile, while reacting to an alert, behaviour aimed at achieving `missionComplete` should be suspended.

```
+!reactToAlert [perform] :                                            1
     {B das_alert , ∼B das_alert_irrelevant} ←                       2
     +.lock ,                                                         3
     −alertnoted ,                                                    4
     requestEmergencyAvoid ,                                          5
     −.lock ,                                                         6
     *enacting(emergencyAvoid),                                       7
     +.lock ,                                                         8
     +! changeFlightPhase(emergencyAvoid) [perform],                 9
     −.lock ;                                                         10
                                                                      11
+!reactToAlert [perform] : {∼B das_alert};                           12
+!reactToAlert [perform] :                                            13
     {B das_alert , B das_alert_irrelevant };                        14
                                                                      15
+enacting(emergencyAvoid) :                                           16
     {∼B store(flightPhase , F),                                     17
     B enacting(emergencyAvoid)} ←                                   18
          enacting(emergencyAvoid);                                   19
+enacting(emergencyAvoid) :                                           20
     {B das_alert_irrelevant ,                                       21
     G reactToAlert[perform]} ←                                      22
          +.lock ,                                                    23
          −alertnoted ,                                               24
          −! reactToAlert [perform],                                 25
          −enacting(emergencyAvoid),                                 26
          −.lock ;                                                    27
+enacting(emergencyAvoid) :                                           28
     {B das_alert_irrelevant , B alertnoted} ←                      29
          +.lock ,                                                    30
          −alertnoted ,                                               31
          −! reactToAlert [perform],                                 32
          −enacting(emergencyAvoid),                                 33
          −.lock ;                                                    34
                                                                      35
+!missionComplete [achieve] :                                        36
     {B das_alert , B store(flightPhase , F),                        37
     ∼B flightPhase(F)} ←                                            38
          *flightPhase(F);                                           39
+!missionComplete [achieve] :                                        40
     {B flightPhase(emergencyAvoid),                                  41
     B store(flightPhase , F)} ←                                     42
          *flightPhase(F);                                           43
+!missionComplete [achieve] :                                        44
     {B das(objectApproaching)} ←                                    45
          *∼das(objectApproaching);                                  46
+!missionComplete [achieve] : {B das(alert500)} ←                    47
          *∼das(alert500);                                           48
```

Listing 9.3 Detect and Avoid Behaviour

9.4 Environments

As can be seen the UAS system is complex. It interacts with seven subsystems via its environment each of which can return messages, it is assumed in response to specific requests. According to our methodology we could have attempted a verification in which we ignored this structure and simply returned some random subset of the possible messages these sub-systems could generate. However in order to control the state space we chose in turn to fix some of the subsystems to generate specific messages – for instance we fixed the fuel subsystem to report a fuel level of 200 on all requests.

We also fixed the environment so that responses to requests for information or air traffic control clearance only arrived once, and only after requested. In some situations we allowed the response to be immediate (e.g., the next time the agent polled for messages it would get the response; this happened in the case of requests for fuel and position information, and for confirmation that routes were stored for interaction all of which we judged to be operations that could be assumed to reliably give swift responses), in other cases – requests to Air Traffic Control and calculation of possible routes, we allowed the response to be delayed - potentially infinitely. When clearance was requested from Air Traffic Control for various manoeuvres we set the system to return at random either clearance or a denial.

The detect-and-avoid sensor (DAS) returned either `objectApproaching`, `alert500` or nothing. If its last message was an alert then it would randomly return ether `objectPassed` or nothing.

Lastly, we considered the flight phase changes that were controlled by the environment – the move to `holding` after the aircraft has taxied at its start location, the move to `linedup` after `lineup`, the move to `cruise`, after take off, and the move to `waitingAtRamp` after the aircraft has taxied at its destination. Again, we did not allow these flight phases to be returned completely at random. When in the relevant agent-supplied flight phase (e.g., `lineup`) the environment could at random send a message that the new taerget was reached or not. Lastly, during the `approach` flight phase the environment could randomly return `landed`.

So here we have a very constrained verification environment, with the random behaviour tightly controlled, in most cases, by the flight phase the agent is in and responses to requests for information being returned at most once. Even so it takes over two hours to verify the agent behaviour in most cases.

Many of the rules of the air include physical quantities e.g. '500 feet' in the **500 feet rule** which it is difficult for our verification machinery to handle. In the existing model we could only verify that the aircraft would perform an emergency avoid if alerted to its possibility. However we also tested the original version of this agent in simulation, with models of aircraft flight behaviour and sensor ranges, where it was possible to determine that the aircraft maintained this distance in all the scenarios examined. Was it possible to bring model-checking and simulation closer together in order to explore all possible paths through some scenario in a way that contained enough detail to analyse separation distances?

To do this a higher fidelity environment was created. This environment contained an explicit model of an intruder aircraft (with behaviour governed by a simple finite state machine) and an abstraction of the airspace into a two-dimensional grid in which it was assumed the aircraft would maintain a steady altitude. The actions of the GWENDOLEN agent were converted into specific manoeuvres in this space (in contrast to the idea that anything might happen in response to the agent taking an action) – in particular emergency avoidance behaviour was implemented. The behaviour of the GWENDOLEN agent was model-checked within this higher fidelity model against properties related to detect and avoid behaviour. Model-checking within this higher fidelity environment verified that the aircraft could maintain a safe separation (more than 500 feet) from the intruder aircraft. However it was also possible to perform more detailed analysis to discover the minimum separation that could occur between the two aircraft. We discuss this further in Section 9.5.1.

9.5 Example Verification

Under the assumptions about the environment outlined above, we were able to verify the properties we had generated from the Rules of the Air the properties related to airmanship. As noted above, even with the very restricted environment we used, most of these properties took over two hours to verify.

We noted when we discussed the code for our satellite agent in Chapter 8 (Code Listing 8.1) that many of the cases appearing in the code were the result of detecting edge cases while debugging.

A similar process occurred in the development of our UAS and we discuss one case here. The system was only model-checked after testing a virtual prototype using a flight simulator. Most properties were found to hold, but some did not. In the case where they did not, the model checker reported an error that the property was violated. One such property was our formalisation of the requirement that an agent should regularly clean out its fuel level beliefs from Equation (9.2). Meaning there were situations where the agent did not clean out old fuel beliefs and was therefore operating under incorrect beliefs about the current fuel level.

Importantly, this error was not found during simulated flight trials as the virtual prototype was always equipped with enough fuel for each scenario tested. The bug could have been found during simulation if a scenario had been specifically created to test behaviour if there was insufficient fuel (in which case the agent might have failed to detect this because of the failure to clear away the initial fuel belief).

9.5.1 Verification in the Higher Fidelity Model

Recall that the original agent implementation was also verified in a grid-based environment in which emergency avoidance behaviour was modelled. In this environment it was found that the minimum separation distance from the unmanned aircraft to the intruder aircraft was 1,129 feet when the detect-and-avoid sensor range was set to 20,000 feet. Analysis of the flight simulation of the same scenario showed that the minimum separation distance between the unmanned aircraft and the intruder aircraft was 820 feet. A difference between the two models of 309 feet!

Investigation revealed that, in the higher fidelity environment model, the turns in the Emergency Avoid manoeuvre were based only on changes in the heading of the modelled vehicle, for example the vehicle turned immediately from a heading of 0° to 10.6° in a discontinuous way. It was hypothesised that the reason for the 309 feet disparity was due, in part, to the relatively unrealistic way in which the turns were modelled compared to the flight simulation, in which the turns were gradual and continuous. So, in order to improve the accuracy of the higher fidelity environment model the output of the simulator model was analysed to discover the turn rate of the unmanned aircraft during its two turns. It was found that the turn rate in both turns was 0.83° per second. The higher fidelity environment model was then modified to incorporate this turn rate. Running the simulation again revealed that the minimum separation distance of the unmanned aircraft and the intruder had now reduced to 929 feet – a 109 feet difference, a significant improvement over the original 309 feet difference. (Note that it would be possible to remedy the 109 feet difference through further analysis of the differences between the higher fidelity environment model and the simulator model. For example, one possible cause could be the use of a roll rate in the simulator model, which was not used in the higher fidelity environment model due to project constraints.)

After improving the accuracy of the environment model, the agent was model checked again to ensure that the 500 feet rule requirement was still satisfied for all sensor ranges between 16,700 feet and 20,000 feet.

9.6 Issues

A number of issues are raised by the work outlined in this chapter. The assumptions we make about the environment, for instance, have significant impact on the verification and potentially on the code. One of our issues here was that handling all possible inputs from the environment would have resulted not only in a significantly larger state space during verification but also in considerable code bloat in the agent – deciding what to do if informed of multiple non-sensical flight phase updates at once, for instance, or being informed both that an object was approaching and that an object had passed. Clearly though, the heavy assumptions we made about the environment here would need another form of checking for true assurance that the UAS worked as required and, as we have already mentioned, we consider an approach to this in Chapter 12.

One of the choice points we did introduce into the environment was when some sub-systems returned responses to messages. For instance, we wanted to allow there to be a delay between the agent requesting an emergency avoidance manoeuvre and the sub-system responding to say it was enacting avoidance. In our environment this was implemented as a simple choice – if a response was pending then anytime the agent polled the environment for messages it either would or would not respond. This, of course, means there is a theoretical run in which a message is never returned and meant we had to explicitly exclude consideration of this from some properties – for example, in property (9.1). Obviously we actually want to know that this can never happen – that is, that the system will always eventually respond or, ideally, that it will definitely respond within a certain time interval. In Chapter 11 we will look at an example involving vehicle platoons where timed behaviour of the system is important, but even there we do not discuss how we might construct a verification environment for a GWENDOLEN agent that explicitly excludes the possibility that a response is never received. In our example here, we could have implemented a counter in the environment which would force a response after a fixed number of message polls (at the expense of increasing the state space of the system). Whatever our solution for verification of the agent, we also need to perform some kind of verification of the route planner and emergency avoid module to ensure that they always respond, if not immediately, at least in a timely fashion.

Another issue with the various properties related to the Detect-and-Avoid behaviour is that the specific 'rule of the air', that the aircraft always turns to the right, is not captured by these properties. They simply ensure that the aircraft eventually enters an emergency avoid flight phase. Again we have to assume the existence of a sub-system that will perform the appropriate turn right behaviour whenever the emergency avoid flight phase is engaged. So our properties only partially capture the rules of the air and would need to be combined with properties established for other sub-systems in order to fully validate the system. We examine this question of compositional verification for autonomous systems in Chapter 11.

We struggled to adequately formalise the idea that the fuel level information was up-to-date. Again there is an aspect of timed behaviour here – that beliefs about fuel 'expire' after a certain point. Here we struggle not only with expressing such properties in Linear Temporal Logic, but also with the fact that the GWENDOLEN language has no concept of when beliefs were acquired, let alone any idea that beliefs might expire. Our solution was verifying the beliefs about fuel were eventually removed and implementing that removal in specific agent plans. We could possibly also have checked the absence of fuel level beliefs at specific points in the flight – for example, that the agent has no beliefs about fuel level at the point where it changes the flight phase to landed.

The work with the higher fidelity environment also reveals the importance of modelling assumptions in the results can be obtained, and highlights a need for a corroborative approach to verification (Webster et al., 2020) in which results from model-checking, simulation and testing are considered together and inform each other.

While clearly not *sufficient* for certifying UASs, this form of verification is *important* to show that the UAS does whatever a pilot _should_ do. Of course there is more to a pilot than just following the Rules of the Air in particular there are occasions when it is assumed that a pilot may deliberately break the rules of the air. We discuss this in the next chapter.

10

Ethical Decision-Making

10.1 What is the System?

As we have seen, formal verification has been used successfully to prove that specific rules of behaviour are observed when an autonomous system makes decisions.* But, in many cases, such systems must make decisions in unexpected and unplanned situations and, in some of these cases, human lives may be at risk, but even where this is not the case issues of privacy, dignity, and other ethical considerations may arise (Winfield et al., 2019). Often, in the case of a human operator or pilot there is an implicit assumption that rules can and will be broken should that be necessary in order save human lives or because of some other overriding ethical principle. Consequently, the decisions made by our system can be seen as *ethical* choices.

In this chapter we describe an extension to our basic hybrid agent approach, where ethical constraints are applied in cases when the agent has no viable predefined plans available, corresponding to unanticipated situations. In this case, our cognitive agent will fall back to constructing new plans using technologies such as path planning (Raja and Pugazhenthi, 2012), symbolic planning (Ghallab et al., 2016), or possibly by invoking some fallback system constructed using machine learning techniques (e.g., a deep neural network). It will then use ethical reasoning to decide which of these new plans to execute. We examine a number of properties that we can formally verify for this system and by extension other systems that claim to implement ethical reasoning, including that the agent never executes a plan that it believes to be unethical, unless it does

---

* The work described here was carried out in collaboration with Marija Slavkovik and Matt Webster being initially reported in Dennis et al. (2013a) then, in extended form, in Dennis et al. (2016b). It forms part of a programme of research on the formal verification of machine ethics, that also involves Alan Winfield (Dennis et al., 2015), Paul Bremner (Bremner et al., 2019), Martin Mose Bentzen, and Felix Lindner (Dennis et al., 2021) and we touch on some of this extended work here as well.

not have any other (more ethical) plan to choose. If all plan options are such that some ethical principles are violated, we verify that the agent chooses to execute the 'least unethical' plan it has available.

We will also examine a variation on this approach in an *ethical governor* architecture similar to those mentioned in Chapter 2 and again show that the governor agent always selects the least unethical option.

10.1.1 Ethical Decisions

Machine ethics is a field concerned with assessing whether, and ensuring that, the behaviour of machines (robots) towards both humans and other machines (robots) they interact with is ethical (Anderson and Anderson, 2007; Asaro, 2006; Moor, 2006). It is a continuing philosophical question as to whether machines are, or will ever be, moral agents, that is, in possession of an innate ability to distinguish between right or wrong. However, in our case, we assume no such innate ability and instead ask how a machine can be programmed to use the concepts of right and wrong in its reasoning and how such reasoning can then be verified.

The past ten years have seen many proposals for the implementation of machine ethics. See Nallur (2020) and Tolmeijer et al. (2021) for surveys of the field. These approaches can generally be divided into *top down* approaches in which there is some explicit encoding of the ethics derived in consultation with stakeholders and *bottom up* approaches in which the system itself learns the ethics by interaction with stakeholders. In this chapter we focus on a top down approach which integrates with our concept of a cognitive agent decision-maker embedded into an autonomous system and which is then amenable to formal analysis.

So, in this chapter, we consider how a cognitive agent may select amongst actions using a top-down ethical reasoning framework and look at the kind of properties we can verify for such a system. In particular we look at what happens when no ethical action is available and verify that the reasoners choose a minimally unethical course of action.

10.1.2 Up in the Air, Again

In Chapter 9, we have seen how *formal verification* can be used to assess whether or not an autonomous system for an unmanned aircraft (UAS) follows the specified 'Rules of the Air' (ROA) that a pilot *should* follow (Civil Aviation Authority, 2010). However, there are many circumstances that are not covered by the ROA. Indeed, the ROA are not intended to be exhaustive, but rather to provide a set of guidelines for pilot behaviour. It is anticipated that the ROA will be implemented by a skilled and experienced pilot whose responsibility is to ensure the safe passage of the aircraft through airspace (in our case, civil airspace). In circumstances that are *not* covered by explicit ROA, it is the responsibility of the autonomous system in control of an unmanned aircraft to make sensible, rational, safe and *ethical* decisions at all times. So, while the formal verification of safe and legal decision-making has been addressed in Chapter 9, we now focus on the formal verification of ethical decision-making within autonomous systems controlling autonomous aircraft.

Normative Ethics for Agents

Normative theories of ethics are concerned with designing ethical principles that constrain the behaviour of people within ethically desirable boundaries. An overview of the most popular normative theories can be found in Robbins and Wallace (2007). Ethical principles are rules of conduct that should guide the behaviour of moral agents when making decisions. Typically they are abstract by design allowing for applicability in a wide range of specific situations. These formal principles are intended to be subsequently made concrete, or *substantive*, providing constraints taking into account facts from the decision-making context. For example, the formal principle of 'doing no harm' could be violated by a specific action of moving 10 metres to the left when an aircraft is on the ground, therefore the aircraft should be ethically constrained from performing this action in this circumstance. The same action might not be ethically constrained when the aircraft is airborne.

How abstract principles are transformed into substantive rules that constrain behaviour is a difficult problem, even for people. Autonomous systems, and robots in particular, are being developed as specialised assistants and tools with a pre-designed domain of application. We assume therefore that these domains have abstract ethical principles developed, which express what is considered right and wrong within that domain. For example, in the biomedical domain, the principles of respect of autonomy, nonmaleficence, beneficence and justice, as summarised on pp. 13–14 of Beauchamp and Childress (2009) are considered to be the core abstract ethical principles. Given a set of high-level, formal principles, we still need the substantive constraints to actually evaluate how ethical an intended conduct is. For frequently occurring situations, the relevant institutions and governing bodies can, and do, instantiate the abstract principles into substantive rules. Thus, for instance, the abstract principle of respect for autonomy is instantiated into a rule that precisely describes when a patient's desire to refuse treatment must be observed.

In the case of a UAS therefore, we can assume that substantive ethical principles have been defined. Our task is to elaborate on how we intend to ethically constrain the reasoning process of an agent using these principles.

We treat these ethical principles not as a veto on actions, but instead as *soft constraints*. With ethical principles as soft constraints an autonomous system would be allowed to violate an ethical principle, but only under the condition that there is no ethical option available and under the assurance that the unethical option chosen is the 'least of all evils'. To represent ethical principles and rules as soft constraints we need an *ethical policy*. An ethical policy is an order over the rules that are applicable in the same situation, in terms of which rule it is better to violate when no ethical option is possible. These principles and rules are obtained from the ethical code of conduct within a given society or profession, in our case concepts of airmanship among human pilots.

Ethical Options and Planning

To construct an ethical reasoning process for machines we need to represent abstract ethical principles and specific ethical rules, paired with the context in which they apply and then invoke these at an appropriate moment in an agent's reasoning process.

As set out in Chapter 3, the reasoning of a BDI agent is controlled by its beliefs, its goals and its plans. The plans are presumed to have been supplied by a programmer. Therefore, on a trivial level, the task of ensuring that the agent acts in an ethical fashion should lie with the programmer who should ensure that the plans provided are ethical. Given our assumption of a pre-existing set of ethical rules, showing that such plans always preserve the rules can then be tackled using pre-existing verification approaches such as those we employed to show that the plans obeyed the 'Rules of the Air' from Chapter 9.

However, in many realistic scenarios, it is either not possible to provide an exhaustive set of plans that will cover all situations or, at least, not possible to provide such plans in full detail. So, for instance, a plan may need additional complex information such as the calculation of a route or schedule that is based on the situation in which it finds itself (we saw an example of this in the plans returned by the Continuous Engine in Chapter 8 and this is also true of the routes and emergency avoidance behaviour provided by the planner and autopilot in Chapter 9).

In our UAS scenario, we are particularly interested in a route planner such as that implemented in Tulum et al. (2009) which can generate different routes for a UAS to follow and these can be supplied to the agent on demand. Unlike the planner in Chapter 9, we assume that such a planner can inform an agent about the relevant *side effects* of any plan generated – in our cases whether the route violates the rules of the air (and which rule(s) are violated) and the nature of anything with which the UAS might collide.

We assume, therefore, that there are two modes of operation for our cognitive agent. In one mode the agent uses its pre-existing (ideally, pre-verified) set of plans in situations which are within its anticipated parameters. In these cases it is assumed that the programmer has taken responsibility for any ethical issues that may arise. In the other mode of operation the rational agent is working outside of these parameters but has various planning resources available to it which allow it to continue to act. In this situation it must use ethical reasoning to govern its actions.

In particular, our autonomous system needs to apply ethical reasoning when new options become available. New options are needed when:

1. no plan is available, or,
2. a plan is available, and has been attempted, but does not appear to be working.

We assume that the agent has access to some external planning mechanism from which it can obtain new plans. The new plans supplied by the external planner can then be associated with substantive ethical rules, that is, the sets of ethical principles which are violated by that plan (this work of association can be performed either by the agent or the planner). The job of the agent, then, is to determine which of the available plans is the most ethical one to invoke.

Ethical Policies

Let us begin by defining an abstract ethical principle and an ethical policy (Dennis et al., 2016b).

Definition 10.1 (Abstract ethical principle)   An abstract ethical principle is represented with $E\varphi$, where φ is a propositional logic formula. The $E\varphi$ is read as 'φ is an ethical principle in force', or alternatively 'the agent considers it unethical to allow or cause $\neg\varphi$ (to happen)'.

Definition 10.2 (Ethical policy)   An ethical policy Pol is a tuple $Pol = \langle \mathbb{E}, \geq \rangle$ where $\mathbb{E}$ is a finite set of abstract ethical principles $E\varphi$, and $\geq$ is a total (not necessarily strict) order on $\mathbb{E}$. The expression $E\varphi_1 = E\varphi_2$ denotes that violating φ_1 is as unethical as violating φ_2, while $E\varphi_1 \geq E\varphi_2$ denotes that violating φ_1 is less or at least as unethical as violating φ_2. A special type of ethical principle, denoted $E\varphi_\varnothing$, is vacuously satisfied and is included in every policy so that for any $E\varphi \in \mathbb{E}$: $E\varphi_\varnothing > E\varphi$, denoting it is always strictly more unethical to allow any of the unethical situations to occur.

We must now represent the ethical rules which are a specification of an abstract ethical principle by some context.

We define ethical rules to be context-dependent statements pairing actions with ethical principles.

Definition 10.3 (Ethical rules) Given a context c, an action a and an ethical principle E_φ, an ethical rule is the formula

$$do(a) \Rightarrow_c \neg E\varphi \qquad (10.1)$$

denoting that 'doing action a in context c counts as a violation of ethical principle φ'.

For simplicity we can consider that $do(\neg a)$ represents not doing an action. This formalization is needed to represent cases when abstaining from action is an ethical infringement, for example not calling an ambulance when witnessing a person having a heart attack.

To be able to reason about plans in terms of ethics we also need a plan selection procedure that uses the substantive policy implied by the abstract policy. We favour plans that violate the fewest concerns, both in number and in gravity. Therefore the plans are ordered using $\succeq$ (Definition 10.4) which results in a total order over plans. The agent can be in multiple contexts while determining which plan to choose, so we need to consider the rules from all the contexts that apply to the plan.

Definition 10.4 (Ethical plan order) Given a policy $Pol = \langle \mathbb{E}, \geq \rangle$, and a plan p, a violation collection for p, V_p, is a multiset (one principle can appear multiple times) of abstract ethical principles defined as:

$$V_p = \langle \varphi \mid \varphi \in \mathbb{E}, a \in p, do(a) \Rightarrow_c \neg E\varphi \rangle. \qquad (10.2)$$

For ethical plans, $V_p = \varnothing$. We define the operation $worst^1$ as follows:

$$worst(V_p) = \{\varphi \mid \varphi \in V_p \text{ and } \forall \varphi' \in V_p : \varphi' \geq \varphi\} \qquad (10.3)$$

Consider a set of available, possibly ethical, plans, $P = \{p_1, \ldots, p_n\}$. An ethical plan order $\succeq$ is a reflexive and antisymmetric relation $\succeq$ over P that satisfies the following properties. For every $p_i, p_j \in P$, it holds that $p_i \succ p_j$ if at least one of the following holds:

1. $V_{p_i} = \varnothing$ and $V_{p_j} \neq \varnothing$.
2. $E\varphi \geq E\varphi'$ for every $E\varphi \in worst(V_{p_i} \setminus V_{p_j})$ and every $E\varphi' \in worst(V_{p_j} \setminus V_{p_i})$.

---

[1] Note that $worst$ is a set since $\geq$ is not a strict order. However all the ethical principles, ϕ, appearing in $worst(V_p)$ will be equally bad wrt. $\geq$.

3. $E\varphi = E\varphi'$ for every $E\varphi \in worst(V_{p_i} \setminus V_{p_j})$, and every $E\varphi' \in worst(V_{p_j} \setminus V_{p_i})$, while $|worst(V_{p_i} \setminus V_{p_j})| < |worst(V_{p_j} \setminus V_{p_i})|$.

If none of 1, 2, or 3 holds, then p_i and p_j are equally (un)ethical, *i.e.,* $p_i \sim p_j$.

The first property (1 above) ensures that the ethical plans will always be preferred to the unethical ones. The second property (2) states that when the principles violated by both plans are disregarded, the plan that violates the worst principle is considered less ethical. Finally, the third property (3) guarantees that when the worst principles that each plan violates are different, but equally bad, the plan which violates the greater number of such principles is less ethical.

The ETHAN Extension to GWENDOLEN

We developed a BDI agent language called ETHAN for a prototype implementation of our approach. ETHAN was based on the GWENDOLEN agent programming language described earlier.

In our approach, ethical reasoning is integrated into a BDI agent programming language via the agents' plan selection mechanism. In accordance with the theory above, we assumed that the agent's existing plans are ethical *by default* and, indeed, had been formally verified as such. In the scenarios we consider below we assume the verification of the formal 'Rules of the Air' and notions of Airmanship as discussed in Chapter 9.

As discussed above we needed to ensure that an ETHAN agent:

- detects when a plan is not succeeding – for example, it has been executed but not achieved its goal;
- accesses a planning system in order to get new plans annotated with ethical principles; and
- selects the most ethical plan from a set of available plans.

For our prototype we made the simplifying assumption that the agent could only ever be in one context at a time and that, therefore, we could reason with the substantive, rather than the abstract, ethical principles. Among other things, this allowed us to avoid reasoning about ethical consequences within the agent. Instead of inspecting a plan, p, for the actions, $do(a)$, it contained (explicitly or implicitly) we were able to list the unacceptable outcomes and send these to the external planner which could evaluate the side effects of its plans for these outcomes. It is important to observe that even with additional contexts, the verification of ethical reasoning would unfold in a similar manner as in our one-context-at-a-time prototype because the choices the agent makes are still determined only by a unique ethical order over available plans. However, when multiple contextual influences are in play, verification can be used more 'deeply' and so can explore when, and why, a particular policy or rule was introduced.

For ETHAN we extended the GWENDOLEN language as follows.

- A new data structure, E, was provided for GWENDOLEN agent programs, with E consisting of a set of ethical rules. Each ethical rule in E was associated with its rank and a guard that specifies the context.

- We tracked the application of plans. Even if a plan was applicable it was excluded from the list of plans available for selection if it had already been used in attempting to achieve the current goal.

- If no (more) plans were available for a goal we requested plans from an external planner which annotated the plans with the ethical rules that risked being violated by the proposed course of action.

- In selecting plans, we prioritized those that are most ethical (according to the order $\succcurlyeq$).

In normal operation GWENDOLEN agents cycle through the deeds in their intentions. When a deed requires the generation of a new plan all applicable plans are extracted from the plan library, one is selected and converted into an intention, then the system returns to cycling though the deeds in the intentions interleaved with checking perception and messages for new beliefs, and so on. For ETHAN we added the recording of selected plans. This was achieved by storing an identifier for the plan together with the unifier that was used to match it to the current agent state; this information was linked to the particular goal the plan was expected to achieve. We extended the plan selection mechanism to select the most ethical plan (from those that were applicable) according to our ordering $\succcurlyeq$.

The most significant change for ETHAN was altering the reasoning cycle so that, if no existing plan was applicable, an external planner would be queried for new plans. This query involved sending the planner the current goal, together with the list of ethical rules relevant to the current situation in order that the planner might note any ethical rule that could be violated by a plan's execution. This extension is shown in Figure 10.1. Note that we did *not* implement a generic planning mechanism for our investigation but relied upon hard-coded pseudo-planners customised to the scenarios studied. The ETHAN reasoning cycle is shown in Figure 10.1.

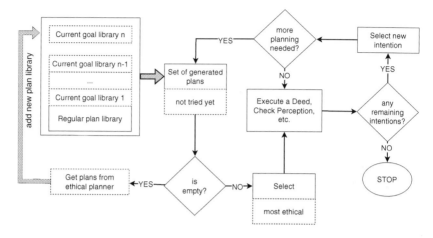

Figure 10.1 ETHAN's reasoning cycle from Dennis et al. (2016b). Dotted lines show additions to GWENDOLEN's cycle

10.2 What *Properties* Do We Want to Establish?

When we ask what properties we want to establish for an ethical reasoning system, our key desire is that it should always choose the ethically correct action. However this is difficult, if not impossible, to formalise. Instead we have identified three broad categories for formalisable properties. These are:

1. Properties to establish the correctness of the implementation of the ethical reasoning mechanism: in many cases, including ETHAN, this involves showing that the least unethical action according to the ethical theory is always chosen.

2. Properties to establish that the correct ethical rules have been identified, via the use of 'sanity checking'. For instance, in a smart home system, we might check that the system always chooses to evacuate in the case of a fire, no matter what other ethical imperatives may be at play.

3. Properties to establish that the correct ethical rules have been identified, by exploring a specific scenario in which the ethically correct action is known, to check that this action is the one chosen. This is obviously similar to sanity checking but may include more particulars about a situation.

Often a property will combine aspects of all three of these.

10.2.1 Establishing the Correctness of the Underlying Implementation

For our first category we want to define a logical property which specifies what it means for an implemented agent to reason ethically. Informally we mean that whenever an agent selects a plan, p, then all other applicable plans, p', are ethically worse (or equal), that is, that $p \succcurlyeq p'$. We could frame this in linear temporal logic as

$$\Box \, \forall p. \, (selected(p) \rightarrow \forall p'.(applicable(p') \rightarrow (p \succcurlyeq p'))). \tag{10.4}$$

Unfortunately this property involves quantification over plans which implies a potentially infinite number of possible states, particularly when plans are being supplied by some external system, and cannot be represented in AJPF's property specification language which does not contain quantifiers for this reason. Fortunately, at any point in the execution of a GWENDOLEN program we can calculate the currently selected plan and the set of applicable plans and represent these calculations as beliefs. The set of applicable plans at any one point in time of a well-engineered program should be finite (and if it is not then verification will fail with a timeout at the point in time when the calculation is attempted).

We will use $\mathcal{V}\phi$ to indicate that ethical rule ϕ is violated by the currently selected plan. This can be checked at runtime and stored as a belief.

We will also need to refer to the set of ethical principles, $W(\phi)$, that are more important than some principle ϕ – that is, it is preferable to violate ϕ than the principles in $W(\phi)$.

$$W(\phi) \equiv \{\phi' \mid E\phi{\geq}E\phi'\}.$$

We use $NaP(\Phi)$ to indicate that there is no applicable, but unselected, plan that does not violate some principle in the set Φ. Providing there are only a finite number of applicable plans at any one point, this property can be generated are runtime and stored as a belief.

We can now formulate our general property as

It is always the case that, for all ethical principles, ϕ, if the currently selected plan violates ϕ then there is no applicable, but unselected, plan that does not violate some principle that is more important than ϕ.

$$\Box \forall \phi. \, (\mathcal{V}\phi \rightarrow NaP(W(\phi))). \tag{10.5}$$

This can be instantiated for particular agent instances by enumerating the ethical concerns ϕ and the set $W(\phi)$. We will see several examples of this in the following sections.

Table 10.1 Additional atomic beliefs introduced in ETHAN

Belief	Meaning
`applicable(P)`	Plan P is applicable
`already_tried(P)`	Plan P has already been tried when attempting the current goal
`ethics_of(P, E)`	Plan P violates ethical rule E
`concern(E)`	The current selected plan violates E

Instantiating the General Property

In order to determine the truth of our general property, ETHAN stores, as explicit beliefs, its currently applicable plans, plans that have been attempted on a particular goal, and the ethical concerns violated by any selected plan. These are stored in a specialised separate belief base to distinguish them from the beliefs that are used by GWENDOLEN's planning process. The beliefs relevant to these plans are shown in Table 10.1. Therefore a check that an ETHAN agent believes `concern(E)` in AJPF's property specification language, $\mathbf{B}_{ag}$ concern(E), corresponds to a check that $\mathcal{V}E$.

Recall that GWENDOLEN programs may perform deductive reasoning on their atomic beliefs as described in their Prolog style *reasoning rules, e.g*:

```
all_well :- ~ brakesCompleteFailure
```

indicates that the program deduces that all is well if it is not the case that the brakes have failed. We used a provision in the underlying AIL implementation which allows an atom in a Prolog rule to specify that deduction should be applied to a specialised belief base rather than the default one. We extended ETHAN to use the notation, `predicate [ethics]`, to specify that a predicate should appear in the specialised *ethics* belief base containing the beliefs about the ethics of individual plans. This allows us to use Prolog style rules to deduce further beliefs allowing us to construct $NaP(\phi)$; these are shown in Code Listing 10.1.

```
other_choices_violated(T) :-                                    1
        ~ untried_plan_not_violates(T);                         2
untried_plan_not_violates(T) :-                                 3
        untried_plan(P),                                        4
        ~ an_ethic_in(P, T);                                    5
untried_plan(P) :-                                              6
        applicable(P) [applicable_plans],                       7
        ~ already_tried(P);                                     8
an_ethic_in(P, [Eth|T]) :- ethics_of(P, Eth) [ethics];          9
an_ethic_in(P, [Eth|T]) :- an_ethic_in(P, T);                  10
```

Listing 10.1 Verification Belief Rules

The predicate `others_choices_violated(L)` is deduced if all untried applicable plans violate a concern contained in the list L and so corresponds to $NaP(L)$. The beliefs about plan applicability (`applicable(P)`), plans already tried (`already_tried(P)`) and the ethical concerns of particular plans (`ethics_of(P, Eth)`) are all inserted into an agent's belief base during execution of the ETHAN reasoning cycle.

With these extensions and the rules in Listing 10.1 we were able to formally verify properties of the form

$$\mathbf{B}_{ag} \text{ concern}(\phi) \rightarrow \mathbf{B}_{ag} \text{ others\_violate}(\phi_1, \ldots, \phi_n)$$

where $\phi_1, \ldots, \phi_n$ are the set of ethical rules in $W(\phi)$. This corresponds to the general property in Equation (10.5).

10.2.2 Properties that Establish that the Correct Ethical Rules Have Been Identified

In our UAS examples we did not explore any properties of the sanity-checking variety (though we look at an example of this kind in Dennis et al. (2021) in which we check that a smart home always evacuates in the case of a fire, no matter what other ethical considerations may be in play), but we did examine a scenario probing example.

In order to establish that the correct ethical rules were identified we explored a scenario where a UAS had to make an emergency landing with the potential options of:

1. Land in field with overhead power lines, risking damage to critical infrastructure and objects on the ground (possibly other aircraft).
2. Land in a field containing people.
3. Land on an empty public road, risking damage to critical infrastructure.
4. Land in an empty field.

We then checked it would only land on the public road (formalised as it becomes perceptible that the agent has landed on the road) if the agent did not believe there was an empty field and so on:

$$\mathbf{P} \text{ land\_on\_road} \rightarrow \neg\mathbf{B}_{ag} \text{ empty\_field} \qquad (10.6)$$

$$\mathbf{P} \text{ land\_in\_field\_w\_power\_lines} \rightarrow \neg\mathbf{B}_{ag} \text{ empty\_field} \wedge \neg\mathbf{B}_{ag} \text{ road} \qquad (10.7)$$

$$\mathbf{P} \text{ land\_in\_field\_w\_people} \rightarrow \neg\mathbf{B}_{ag} \text{ empty\_field} \wedge \neg\mathbf{B}_{ag} \text{ road}$$

$$\wedge \neg\mathbf{B}_{ag} \text{ power\_lines.} \qquad (10.8)$$

10.3 ETHAN/GWENDOLEN Code

We established a (small) list of relevant *formal* ethical concerns as exemplars in order to show the method in action. The list contains: *do not harm people* (f_1), *do not harm animals* (f_2), *do not damage self* (f_3), and *do not damage property* (f_4). The (formal) ethical policy is given by comparing the concerns in terms of how unethical it is to violate them. We use the order $f_4 > f_3 > f_2 > f_1$. Recall that $f_i > f_j$ means that it is more ethical to violate f_i than f_j. Our substantive ethical policies were context-dependent refinements of the formal ethical policy.

In this prototype, each flight phase (e.g. landing, taxiing, take-off) of a UAS constitutes one context c. Since all contexts are known, and since the UAS can only be in one context at a time, the substantive concerns can be represented directly, omitting the formal-substantive relations.

We then considered three different scenarios in order to verify the ethical reasoning[2].

10.3.1 Brake Failure During Line Up

In this scenario the UAS is trying to line up on a runway prior to take-off when its brakes fail. The ethical concerns for this example, with the rank of each concern marked in brackets, are:

ϕ_1 = do not damage own aircraft (1),
ϕ_2 = do not collide with airport hardware (2),
ϕ_3 = do not collide with people (3),
ϕ_4 = do not collide with manned aircraft (4).

Code Listing 10.2 shows abridged ETHAN code for this example. During normal operation, the agent polls the vehicle's sensors and, if all is well, it requests that the planner supply routes for normal take-off. The planner does this by sending predicates naming the routes to the agent which detects them via perception. Once the agent has a route (line 26) it then delegates the actual route following to the underlying control system (`enactRoute(R)`). If the brakes fail after the vehicle's sensors are polled, all these plans become unavailable (since `all_well` ceases to be true) and, in accordance with the ETHAN reasoning cycle, an external ethical planner is contacted for options which will be assessed using ethical reasoning.

---

[2] The examples in this chapter can be found in the folder `src/examples/ethical_gwen` of the AJPF distribution.

```
: Ethical  Policy :                                                    1
E( flightPhase ( lineup ) , doNotDamageOwnAircraft , 4 )               2
E( flightPhase ( lineup ) , doNotCollideAirportHardware , 3 )          3
E( flightPhase ( lineup ) , doNotCollidePeople , 2 )                   4
E( flightPhase ( lineup ) , doNotCollideMannedAircraft , 1 )           5
                                                                       6
: Initial  Beliefs :                                                   7
flightPhase ( lineup )                                                 8
                                                                       9
: Reasoning  Rules :                                                   10
                                                                       11
all_well  :−  ∼  brakesCompleteFailure ;                              12
                                                                       13
: Initial  Goals :                                                     14
startup                                                                15
                                                                       16
: Plans :                                                              17
+!startup  :  { ⊤ }  ←   +!missionComplete ;                          18
+!missionComplete  :                                                   19
   {B  flightPhase ( lineup ) ,  ∼B  polled ( veh )  }               20
   ←  +polled ( veh ) ,  poll ( veh );                               21
+!missionComplete  :                                                   22
   {B  polled ( veh ) ,  B  all_well ,  ∼B  route (R)}               23
   ←  plan ( regularRoutes , all_well );                             24
+!missionComplete  :                                                   25
   {B  polled ( veh ) ,  B  all_well ,  B  route (R)}                26
   ←  enactRoute (R);                                                27
```

Listing 10.2 Code for Brake Failure Example

We tested this agent in a simulated environment where, at the point in time that the brakes failed, a second (manned) aircraft is crossing the runway ahead on a taxiway. To the left and right of the runway are runway lights (which can be damaged by the aircraft taxiing over them). To the right of the runway is an airport staff member who has erred onto the maneuvering area of the aerodrome.

```
+!missionComplete  :  {B  brakesCompleteFailure}          1
   ←  enactRoute ( turn_left );  [φ₁ ,  φ₂ ]               2
+!missionComplete  :  {B  brakesCompleteFailure}          3
   ←  enactRoute ( turn_right );  [φ₁ ,  φ₃ ]              4
+!missionComplete  :  {B  brakesCompleteFailure}          5
   ←  enactRoute ( continue );  [φ₄ ]                      6
```

Listing 10.3 Plans for Brake Failure Example

When the agent determines that its brakes have failed it requests new routes from the ethical planner since its current route to line-up is no longer valid.

The simulated ethical planner used for testing produced three potential routes (shown in Code Listing 10.3):

1. Turn left off the runway: this will risk damaging the unmanned aircraft (ϕ_1) and colliding with airport hardware (the runway lights, ϕ_2).
2. Turn right off the runway: this will risk damaging the unmanned aircraft (ϕ_1) and a collision with people (ϕ_3).
3. Continue straight on: this will risk a collision with a manned aircraft (ϕ_4).

We use the notation $[\phi_{i_1}, \phi_{i_2}, \ldots, \phi_{i_n}]$ to indicate the substantive ethical concerns that are violated by each plan. On receiving these plans, and assessing the ethical policy, the agent elects to turn left.

10.3.2 Erratic Intruder Aircraft

Our next example is based on the assumption that some unknown aircraft, possibly a malicious intruder, but potentially also some ill-trained new pilot, appears on a collision course with the UAS and fails to take the anticipated evasive actions. The relevant substantive ethical concerns and their ranks are as follows:

ϕ_1 = do not violate turn right rule (2);
ϕ_2 = do not violate stay above 500 feet rule (2);
ϕ_3 = do not collide with objects on the ground (3);
ϕ_4 = do not collide with aircraft (4).

The ROA (Rules of the Air) say that the UAS should turn right in the event of a potential collision, so the agent should request a route for turning right. The code for this is shown in Listing 10.4.

```
:Ethical  Policy:                                              1
E(flightPhase(eAvoid),  doNotViolateRoATurnRight,  2)         2
E(flightPhase(eAvoid),  doNotViolateRoA500Feet,  2)          3
E(flightPhase(eAvoid),  doNotCollideObjects,  3)             4
E(flightPhase(eAvoid),  doNotCollideAircraft,  4)            5
                                                              6
:Reasoning  Rules:                                            7
avoid_collision  :—  ~ das(intruder,  headOn);              8
                                                              9
:Plans:                                                      10
+!avoid_collision  :                                        11
   {B flightPhase(eAvoid),  ~B route(eAvoid,  Route)}       12
   ←  plan(reqEmergRoute,turnRight),  *route(eAvoid,  R),    13
      enactRoute(R),  wait;                                  14
                                                             15
```

```
+das(intruder, headOn) : {B flightPhase(cruise)}        16
   ← −flightPhase(cruise), +flightPhase(eAvoid),        17
     +!avoid_collision;                                 18
                                                        19
−das(intruder, headOn) : {B flightPhase(eAvoid)}        20
   ← −flightPhase(eAvoid), +flightPhase(cruise);        21
```

Listing 10.4 Code for the 'Intruder' Example

Lines 16–18 are triggered when information arrives from the detect/avoid sensor (DAS) that there is an intruder. As a result the flight phase changes from `cruise` to `eAvoid` and a new goal is set up to avoid a collision. The existing, ROA-compliant, plan for this goal is to get a route for turning right, enact that route and wait a short period to see if a collision will now be avoided. If the plan succeeds the belief that there is an intruder will vanish, the flight phase can be changed back to cruise, and the goal will be achieved since the agent now believes a collision has been avoided (see the reasoning rule in line 8).

However, in the simulation environment we used for testing this agent, the intruder turns left and so this plan fails as the detect/avoid sensor (DAS) continues to indicate that the intruder aircraft is approaching. At this point the agent knows that it has already tried to turn to the right in order to avoid the intruder. Since the intruder is still approaching its first plan has failed. The agent has no more routes (or ETHAN plans) that apply since all its plans obey the ROA and would cause the agent to turn right again. At this point the ethical planner is invoked. The planner returns the plans shown in Code Listing 10.5. The agent initially chooses to turn left. In our simulation scenario the oncoming aircraft once again matches this course change and so the agent next chooses to return to base.

```
+!avoid_collision : {B flightPhase(eAvoid)}              1
   ← enactRoute(turn_left); [φ₁]                         2
+!avoid_collision : {B flightPhase(eAvoid)}              3
   ← enactRoute(emergency_land); [φ₂,φ₃,φ₄]              4
+!avoid_collision : {B flightPhase(eAvoid)}              5
   ← enactRoute(return_to_base); [φ₄]                    6
```

Listing 10.5 Plans for the 'Intruder' Example

10.3.3 Fuel Low

In our final scenario the agent receives a 'fuel low' alert from the Fuel subsystem which causes it to request a route for performing an emergency landing. The code for this is shown in Listing 10.6.

If the UAS cannot locate a safe landing site the ethical planner is invoked and, in our simulation, this returns four options (shown with ethical concerns violated and their ranks):

1. **Land in field with overhead power lines.**
   Violates: do not cause damage to critical infrastructure (4); do not collide with objects on ground (3); 500 feet low-flying ROA (2); do not damage own aircraft (1).
2. **Land in field with people.**
   Violates: do not collide with people (5); 500 feet low-flying ROA (2).
3. **Land on an empty public road.**
   Violates: do not cause damage to critical infrastructure (4); 500 feet low-flying ROA (2).
4. **Land on an empty field.**
   Violates: 500 feet low-flying ROA (2).

The agent then chooses the most ethical – the third plan – although both the first and third plans violate an ethical concern of severity 4, the first plan also violates a concern of severity 3 while the third plan does not.

```
:Ethical  Policy:                                                    1
                                                                     2
E( flightPhase ( cruise ) ,  doNotViolateRoA500Feet ,  2)            3
E( flightPhase ( cruise ) ,  doNotCollideObjectsOnGround ,  3)       4
E( flightPhase ( cruise ) ,                                          5
      doNotCauseDamageToCriticalInfrastructure ,  4)                 6
E( flightPhase ( cruise ) ,  doNotCollidePeople ,  5)                7
                                                                     8
:Plans:                                                              9
                                                                    10
+!startup  [perform] :  {⊤} ←  +! missionComplete [achieve] ;       11
                                                                    12
// DAS (detect and avoid sensor) is polled                          13
+!missionComplete [achieve] :  {B flightPhase ( cruise ) } ←        14
   *missionComplete ;                                               15
                                                                    16
+fuel ( fuelLowEmerg ) :  {B flightPhase ( cruise )} ←             17
   +! landEmerg [achieve] ,                                        18
   −! missionComplete [achieve] ;                                  19
                                                                    20
+!landEmerg [achieve] :  {B safeToLand} ←                          21
        reqRoute ( rp ,  landEmerg ) ,                              22
        +missionComplete ;                                          23
```

Listing 10.6 Code for the 'Fuel Low' Example

10.4 Environments

We have discussed above the environments that we used for testing which had specific behaviours – such as the 'erratic intruder' choosing to match the maneuvers of the UAS. When we came to formal verification, however, following our normal practice, we implemented new environments specifically for the verification itself. We implemented a variety of environments which were related to the kinds of properties we wanted to check.

10.4.1 Brake Failure on Line-up

For the brake failure example, we replaced the ethical planner we used in our initial tests with one that contained a random component. This assumed that plans could potentially be available that violated any combination of the ethical concerns in the policy. An example of such a plan is given in Code Listing 10.7.

```
+!missionComplete  :  {B  brakesCompleteFailure}         1
   ←  enactRoutewEffects(doNotDamageOwnAircraft ,        2
      doNotCollideMannedAircraft);  [φ₁ ,  φ₄]           3
```

Listing 10.7 A Random Plan

This 'random' planner then selected a random subset of these plans and returned them to the agent. The intention here was to test that ethical reasoning was correctly implemented and the least unethical plan was always chosen.

10.4.2 Erratic Intruder

We verified the above *Erratic Intruder* scenario in a situation where the intruder aircraft might appear or disappear at any point (i.e., we used the model-checking to explore all possible scenarios where the plans in Code Listing 10.5 either succeeded or failed, thus exploring all possible orders in which these plans might be attempted). So rather than verifying every possible ethical annotation on a plan, we verified that the system continued to reason ethically as the external situation changed.

10.4.3 Fuel Low

In the *Fuel Low* scenario, we implemented a route planner which would, at random, return a subset of the four possible landing locations. Depending on which plans were available we also allowed the agent to perceive the presence of the empty field, road, and so on. The model-checking then explored all possible combinations of these plans that could be returned and we verified that the UA would always choose what we had pre-determined to be the most ethical of the possible landing sites.

10.5 Example Verification

10.5.1 Formal Verification of Brake Failure on Line-up Example

In this example we verified the agent in an environment where the returned plans could have any combination of annotations. When executed in combination with a model-checking algorithm the random choice caused the search space to branch and so the model-checking examined every possible set of plans that might be returned by the ethical planner. This allowed us to verify that the most ethical plan was always chosen. In particular we formally verified the following properties, where the ϕ_i formulae refer to the substantive ethical concerns used in the example.

$$\Box(\mathbf{B}_{ag} \, \mathsf{concern}(\phi_1) \to \mathbf{B}_{ag} \, \mathsf{others\_violate}([\phi_1, \phi_2, \phi_3, \phi_4]))$$
$$\Box(\mathbf{B}_{ag} \, \mathsf{concern}(\phi_2) \to \mathbf{B}_{ag} \, \mathsf{others\_violate}([\phi_2, \phi_3, \phi_4]))$$
$$\Box(\mathbf{B}_{ag} \, \mathsf{concern}(\phi_3) \to \mathbf{B}_{ag} \, \mathsf{others\_violate}([\phi_3, \phi_4]))$$
$$\Box(\mathbf{B}_{ag} \, \mathsf{concern}(\phi_4) \to \mathbf{B}_{ag} \, \mathsf{others\_violate}([\phi_4])).$$

Collectively these properties show that if the plan chosen violates some substantive ethical concern, ϕ, then the other available plan choices all violated some concern that was equal to, or more severe than, ϕ.

This verification demonstrates that, on this simple example at least, the underlying implementation of ethical choice was correct – the first type of property in our categorisation. Yet, the verification was costly – it took our system over 21 hours to verify each of 65,534 combinations of the 15 possible plans giving a total verification time of nearly four days for the four properties!

10.5.2 Formal Verification of the Erratic Intruder Example

In this example the plans were fixed but the behaviour of the aircraft varied. As in the previous example, we verified the following properties, where the ϕ_i formulae refer to the substantive ethical concerns used in this example.

$$\Box(\mathbf{B}_{ag} \, \mathsf{concern}(\phi_1) \to \mathbf{B}_{ag} \, \mathsf{others\_violate}([\phi_1, \phi_2, \phi_3, \phi_4]))$$
$$\Box(\mathbf{B}_{ag} \, \mathsf{concern}(\phi_2) \to \mathbf{B}_{ag} \, \mathsf{others\_violate}([\phi_1, \phi_2, \phi_3, \phi_4]))$$
$$\Box(\mathbf{B}_{ag} \, \mathsf{concern}(\phi_3) \to \mathbf{B}_{ag} \, \mathsf{others\_violate}([\phi_3, \phi_4]))$$
$$\Box(\mathbf{B}_{ag} \, \mathsf{concern}(\phi_4) \to \mathbf{B}_{ag} \, \mathsf{others\_violate}([\phi_4])).$$

Collectively these properties show that if the plan chosen violates some substantive ethical concern, ϕ, then the other available plan choices all violated some concern that was equal to, or more severe than, ϕ.

The verification of each property took between 21 and 25 seconds and explored 54 model states on 3.06 GHz iMac with 4 GB of memory.

It should be noted that this verification combines properties of checking implementation correctness – that is, our properties were all variants on checking that the least unethical option was chosen – with scenario probing – that is, the plan options were fixed and we were exploring the aircraft's behaviour as it attempted various plans and reacted to their success or failure.

10.5.3 Formal Verification of the Fuel Low Example

For this example we had pre-determined the most ethical outcome (i.e., landing in the empty field was preferable to landing on a road which was preferable to landing on a field with overhead power lines which was preferable to landing on a field containing people) and our verification property is here an example of scenario probing. We verified the properties in equations (10.6), (10.7), and (10.8) from Section 10.2.2.

The verification of each property here took between 7 and 10 seconds and explored 64 model states on 3.06 GHz iMac with 4 GB of memory.

10.6 Issues

The ETHAN approach to machine ethics forms an early example in a growing field of approaches to the problem of equipping computational systems to reason about the ethics of their choices. There are a number of aspects of the implementation itself that point to ongoing challenges faced by the field, for instance, the ordering of ethical concerns. This ordering should clearly not be provided by the agent but must come from expertise outside the system, ideally human experts. Many implementations of machine ethics face this problem – that knowledge about ethical rules, utilities or orderings must be provided by some external authority.

Then, while this approach can, and should, work with a range of planning systems it does require that the planner be able to identify which of the ethical concerns might be (or are) violated by each plan returned. Without this, the agent itself would have to make an assessment of the plans returned, something it is ill-prepared to do. We briefly consider mechanisms for a planner to assess outcomes and how this can be used by an agent in the next section.

Some issues with ETHAN are more specific to our attempt to integrate the approach within a verification framework. It is undesirable to have constructs, such as beliefs and belief rules, which can potentially affect program execution, used for verification purposes alone as is the case with the beliefs and rules in Table 10.1 and Listing 10.1. However, adapting AJPF with a more expressive property specification language was outside the scope of this work. It does raise the question, which we touched on in Chapter 4, of what extension to LTL do we need to truly reason about the behaviour of autonomous systems. LTL is adequate for many properties that we would like to prove, but there are clearly important concepts that it cannot express. We touch on potential ways AJPF can integrate with tools using more expressive logics in Chapter 11 where we consider the UPPAAL tool for representing properties related to timing and in Chapter 13 where we discuss how AJPF's models of the program can be exported in to the probabilistic model-checker, PRISM.

10.7 Cognitive Agents as Ethical Governors

Moving on from ETHAN we will now look briefly at another implementation of machine ethics to which we have applied our verification approach.

In Chapter 2 we discussed briefly governor architectures in which an agent vets the decisions made by some more opaque autonomous systems. We describe here an ethical governor architecture that not only evaluates options suggested by the other control layers but also generates and evaluates behavioural alternatives. We focus on the verification of this governor using AJPF. This governor is not implemented in GWENDOLEN but in a BDI package for the Python programming language so we only outline the high-level concepts. The full details which can be found in Bremner et al. (2019).[3]

The system consists of a task layer which contains a motion planning system developed using a machine-learning approach to select optimal paths towards some goal and an ethical layer consisting of four modules: a Simulation Module to predict the outcome of tasks (addressing the issue we mentioned above – how can a planner annotate its plans with outcomes?); a Planner Module to generate alternative tasks if those proposed by the motion planning system have ethical issues; an Ethical Decision Module to compare the simulated actions and select the most ethically appropriate using declarative BDI reasoning, and a Data Logging Module to record the situations encountered and decisions made in accordance with recommendations from Winfield and Jirotka

---

[3] The verified code can be found in the folder
    `src/examples/pbdi/naoagent/ethical_engine` of the AJPF distribution.

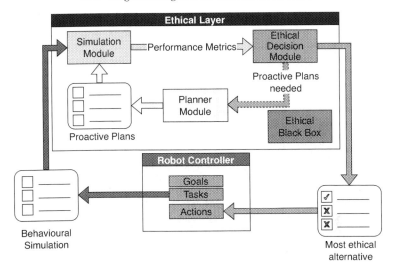

Figure 10.2 The architecture from the ethical governor system from Bremner et al. (2019). Used with permission. The task layer in the Robot Controller generates a set of tasks that might fulfil the current goal proposed by the goal layer. Before generating the actions needed for task execution, the set of proposed tasks is sent to the Ethical Layer, along with sensor data for the current situation and the goal to be achieved. The Simulation Module simulates each of the tasks (behavioural alternatives), producing a set of evaluation metrics for each, that are sent to the Ethical Decision Module. The Ethical Decision Module checks its ethical criteria to see if ethically proactive tasks are required and triggers the Planner Module if so. When triggered the Planner Module generates a set of pro-active tasks to send to the Simulation Module, and as with the controller-generated tasks they are simulated. If the Planner Module was triggered the Ethical Decision Module adds the pro-active task simulation results to its current set. The Ethical Decision Module evaluates the set of simulated task alternatives to determine the most ethically appropriate and sends this selection to the action layer for execution. A solid arrow is a flow of data, a dashed arrow is a control signal. The Ethical Black Box Module logs data from each of the other modules (for clarity these data flows are not shown).

(2017). Data flow and module integration is shown in Figure 10.2, and detailed in its caption. This is an extended version of an architecture proposed in Vanderelst and Winfield (2018), but with a more sophisticated, and transparently ethical decision process.

We considered a simple demonstration use case: A human, operating with an ethical robot in an environment containing objects which can be defined as safe or dangerous. In this context if the human is predicted to move towards a dangerous location, the Planner Module will suggest points at which the robot can intercept the human path as potential tasks to be evaluated. In this demonstration use case we treated Asimov's laws of robotics (Asimov, 1942) as a test code of ethics, despite their obvious shortcomings (see Anderson and Anderson (2007); Murphy and Woods (2009)).

Asimov's Laws of robotics are the earliest and best-known set of ethical rules proposed for governing robot behaviour. Despite originating in a work of fiction, Asimov's Laws explicitly govern the behaviour of robots and their interaction with humans. The laws are simply described as follows.

1 A robot may not injure a human being or, through inaction, allow a human being to come to harm.
2 A robot must obey the orders given it by human beings, except where such orders would conflict with the First Law.
3 A robot must protect its existence as long as such protection does not conflict with the First or Second Laws.

We supplemented Asimov's laws with additional rules that relate to the likely success of an intercept plan. These are given a lower priority than the 3rd law, so only influenced behaviour if no other law was violated.

4a If the human is far from danger prioritize waiting time at the intercept point.
4b If the human is close to danger prioritize shorter robot walking distance.

The rationale behind 4a is that the longer the wait time for the robot after arriving at the intercept location before the human arrives, the more robust the system is to errors in predicted paths and travel times. The rationale behind 4b is that walking incurs some risk of falling over. This risk increases the further the robot walks, so a shorter walking distance increases the chance of achieving the robot's goal.

These rules were represented declaratively in a BDI governor agent where the suggested tasks, the human's distance from danger and the simulator's evaluation of the outcomes of each task were represented as beliefs and the tasks were compared to each other with Asimov's laws used to order tasks in a similar way to the ordering used in our UAS example.

For the verification we created an environment which contained only the BDI component and, as per our methodology, it delivered all possible combinations of annotations on candidate tasks as well as randomly determining how much danger the human was in (i.e., our verification environment at random, returned $danger\_close$ as a belief). We considered cases where either two or three tasks were available: $task1$, $task2$, and $task3$. These tasks were then annotated showing which was preferable to which according to Asimov's laws.

For instance, in the case of $\prec_{l1}$ where $t1 \prec_{l1} t2$ means that $t1$ is preferable according to the first law (i.e., it keeps the human further away from danger) than $t2$, for each pair of tasks the environment returned either

1. $t1 \prec_{l1} t2$ or
2. $t2 \prec_{l1} t1$ or
3. neither indicating that the two tasks are equally good/bad with respect to the first law.

In the case of the movement and waiting times (rules 4a and 4b), we assumed that these imposed a strict order on tasks so that there are only two possible results.

We were able to verify that if a task was selected that violated, for instance, Asimov's third law, then this was because all other available plans violated either the first or the second law. Essentially verifying properties related to the correctness of the implementation of BDI reasoning similar to the general property for ETHAN correctness in Equation 10.4.

The Python BDI package selected no task in the case where the comparison function did not represent an antisymmetric transitive relation. This arises if there is some cycle property in the comparisons – for example, task1 is preferable to task2 which is preferable to task3 which is in turn preferable to task1. The verification environment generated many cases where this was the case. This meant that the attempt to prove the 'sanity checking' property (10.9) (Eventually either $task1$, $task2$ or $task3$ is believed to be the current task), for instance, failed rapidly with a counter-example.

$$\Diamond(\mathbf{B}_{ag} \, \text{current\_task}(\text{task1}) \vee$$
$$\mathbf{B}_{ag} \, \text{current\_task}(\text{task2}) \vee$$
$$\mathbf{B}_{ag} \, \text{current\_task}(\text{task3})). \quad (10.9)$$

This is an issue with our use of unstructured environments. While they are agnostic about the behaviour of the world and system beyond the BDI agent, and while they capture correct behaviour for all possible inputs, they usually represent over-generalisations of reality and flag up many false negatives. The solution to this is to create a structured abstraction for the environment that embodies assumptions about the behaviour of the real world.

We modified our unstructured environment with the following assumptions:

- All the predicates: $\prec_{l1}$, $\prec_{l2}$, and $\prec_{l3}$, represent transitive relations (i.e., if $t_1 \prec_{l1} t_2$ and $t_2 \prec_{l1} t_3$ then it is automatically the case that $t_1 \prec_{l1} t_3$).
- The relations for movement times and waiting times for rules 4a and 4b are antisymmetric and transitive.

This allowed us to verify (10.9) in approximately three days for the three task cases.

We note that there is no guarantee that assumptions made for structured environments are correct. It may, however, be possible to validate them through other means – for instance we were able to prove that our algorithms for calculating $\prec_{l1}$ and so on were antisymmetric and transitive given some basic assumptions about the behaviour of objects in space. In Chapter 12 we will discuss a methodology for checking the validity of our assumptions about structured environments at runtime.

While the time taken to perform verification is, as often the case with AJPF, slow, there is an automatic link between the BDI Python package and AJPF. A programmer needs to supply sensor inputs (as usual for an AJPF verification) and a list of calculations taking place outside the package – the calculation for $\prec_{l1}$ and so on, used above for instance – but does not need to perform modelling of the entire program in order to verify it with AJPF. This has advantages over many other verification techniques which require programs to be transformed by hand into some modelling language and may also require manual intervention to guide the proof process.

Part III

Extensions

11

Compositional Verification: Widening Our View beyond the Agent

Throughout this book we have been advocating an approach to the verification of autonomous systems in which the decision-making part of the autonomous system is considered as a single agent and verified as such.* However, as mentioned in Chapter 5, we also need to consider the rest of the autonomous system. Some parts of this we may verify using testing but other parts may also be amenable to formal analysis. We consider in this chapter two examples of combining verification techniques together in order to generate wider results.

11.1 Example Systems

The two systems we will consider are a vehicle platooning system and an autonomous search and rescue rover.

11.1.1 Vehicle Platooning

Although 'driverless cars' regularly appear in the media, they are usually neither 'driverless' nor fully autonomous. Legal constraints, such as the Vienna Convention (Vienna, 1968), ensure that there must always be a responsible human in the vehicle. While fully autonomous road vehicles remain futuristic, the automotive industry is working on what are variously called *road trains*, *car convoys*, or *vehicle platoons*. Here, each vehicle autonomously follows the one

---

* This chapter involves work that was carried out as part of a wider project on *Verifiable Autonomy*, that also involved Maryam Kamali, Owen McAree, and Sandor Veres. Maryam's particular expertise is in timed Automata and the UPPAAL System while Owen and Sandor are Control Engineers able to produce practical vehicles. This work was reported previously in Kamali et al. (2017).

    Leading on from this we performed work as part of three projects within the UK's 'Robots for a Safer World' programme: *Robotics and AI for Nuclear (RAIN)*, *Future AI and Robotics for Space (FAIR-Space)*, and *Offshore Robotics for Certification of Assets (ORCA)*. This work involved Rafael C. Cardoso, Marie Farrell, Matt Luckcuck, and Angelo Ferrando and was reported in Cardoso et al. (2020a), (2020b); Farrell et al. (2019).

in front of it, with the lead vehicle in the platoon/convoy/train being controlled by a human driver. This technology is being introduced by the automotive industry in order to improve both the safety and efficiency of vehicles on very congested roads. It is especially useful if the vehicles are trucks/lorries and if the road is a multi-lane highway since, in principle, a long convoy/train/platoon of vehicles can safely travel close together in a single lane.

In these platoons, each vehicle clearly needs to communicate with others, at least with the ones immediately in front and immediately behind. Vehicle-to-vehicle (V2V) communication is used at the continuous control system level to adjust each vehicle's position in the lanes and the spacing between the vehicles. Distinct categories of V2V are also used at higher levels, for example to communicate joining requests, leaving requests, or commands dissolving the platoon.

In this chapter we will consider specifically the protocols used for joining and leaving these platoons.[1] We assume that the lead vehicle serves two roles. It is controlled directly by a human driver but it also acts as the central decision-making component in platoon operations such as leaving and joining protocols. Therefore there is a software agent in the lead vehicle, in all the other vehicles in the platoon and in any vehicle wishing to join the platoon. These software agents control the enactment of the protocols for joining and leaving:

Joining the Platoon

A new vehicle can join the platoon either at the end of the platoon or in the middle with correspondingly different strategies being used. The joining procedure can be described as follows.

1. The new vehicle wishing to join first sends a joining request to the platoon leader, together with its intended joining position in the platoon.
2. If the platoon is currently in normal operation then a vehicle requesting to join the *back* of the platoon is sent an agreement by the platoon leader, so long as the maximum platoon length has not yet been reached.
3. If the platoon is currently in normal operation and if a new vehicle requests to join *in front* of vehicle X then, so long as the maximum platoon length has not been reached, the leader begins a series of steps to implement the joining. The leader sends an 'increase inter-vehicle space' command to vehicle X and, once the leader is informed that sufficient space has been created, it sends back a joining agreement to the new vehicle.

---

[1] Code for the vehicle platoon agent is not included in the MCAPL distribution but can be found at https://github.com/VerifiableAutonomy/AgentPlatooning.

4. Once receiving the agreement, the joining vehicle changes its lane (a manual procedure performed by a human driver).

5. When the vehicle is in the correct lane, its (automatic) speed controller is enabled and it undertakes a controlled approach to the vehicle in front.

6. Once the vehicle is close enough to the vehicle in front, its (automatic) steering controller is enabled and it sends a message to the leader.

7. Finally, the leader sends a 'decrease inter-vehicle space' command to vehicle X, in order to minimise space between vehicles – when the spacing is back to normal, vehicle X replies to the leader and the leader acknowledges this message.

Leaving the Platoon

A vehicle can request to leave platoon at any time. The leaving procedure is

- a platoon member sends a leaving request to the leader and waits for authorisation;
- upon receipt of 'leave' authorisation, the vehicle increases its space from the preceding vehicle;
- when maximum spacing has been achieved, the vehicle switches both its speed and steering controller to 'manual' allowing the human driver to change its lane; and, finally
- the vehicle sends an acknowledgement to the leader.

11.1.2 The Search and Rescue Rover

The search and rescue case study involves an autonomous rover deployed in a disaster situation not dissimilar to the simple examples we looked at in Chapter 3. The autonomous rover has two types of sensor: the vision sensor is used for navigation around the area while an infrared sensor detects sources of heat that might indicate an injured or trapped person. There is a route planner that works with the vision system to provide obstacle-free routes to target locations and a battery monitoring system that monitors the power level of the rover. Finally there are two agents: a goal reasoning agent which takes input from the sensors to select target locations for searching or recharging and a plan execution agent that selects and executes route plans based on battery level information and may send recharge instructions to the goal reasoning agent.[2]

---

[2] The GWENDOLEN code for these two agents can be found in Listings 11.1 and 11.2, respectively, and in the `src/examples/eass/compositional/rescue` directory of the MCAPL distribution.

11.2 Why use a Compositional Approach to Verification?

We made the case in Chapter 5 that most parts of an agent-based autonomous system can be verified using traditional approaches such as simulation or testing and do not require additional verification. However, in some cases, we do want to use additional formal techniques. We will examine this question as it applies to our two examples.

11.2.1 Vehicle Platoons

We can implement the reasoning needed to follow the leaving and joining protocols in a BDI agent programming language such as GWENDOLEN and verify properties of these agents in a manner similar to our verifications elsewhere in this book. For instance we can verify that:

If a vehicle has a goal to join a platoon but never believes it has received confirmation from the leader, then it never initiates joining the platoon.

This safety property corresponds to the first requirement of joining a platoon, as given in Section 11.1.1, and can be defined using AJPF's property specification language as:

$$\Box \mathbf{G}_{veh} \text{platoon\_m(veh, leader)}$$
$$\Rightarrow \neg \mathbf{A}_{veh} \text{perf(changing\_lane(1))} \ \text{R} \ \mathbf{B}_{veh} \text{join\_agr(veh, leader)}. \tag{11.1}$$

However we are also interested in properties of the global system, for instance we might wish to know that

If an agent ever receives a joining agreement from the leader, then the preceding agent has increased its space to its front agent.

In AJPF's property specification language this would involve both beliefs of the joining agent (that it has received an agreement) and actions of the agent in the specified place in the platoon (that space has opened up). We could, of course, verify each agent separately – for instance that the leader never *sends* an agreement message unless it believes that a space has opened but this fails to really tell us system behaviour. One approach to this problem would be to perform a multi-agent verification as we did in Chapter 7 where we have an environment that passes messages between agents and we model-check over those interactions. However we have a second problem. While it is all very well to verify that *eventually* an appropriate message is sent or an appropriate action is performed sometimes we require timing constraints on this – particularly in an environment such as a motorway where vehicles are moving at speed. So we are interested in properties like:

Given assumptions about the time taken for a vehicle to move to the correct spacing, to move to the correct place adjacent to the platoon and to change lane and for messages to be delivered then the time required for a completed join maneuver is within desired bounds

AJPF's property specification language simply cannot express these properties. While we could potentially program a `Clock` class within Java and use that to explore timing assumptions, significant work would be required to integrate this with AJPF.

Therefore we opted to use a different approach to verify global properties of the system. In this approach the agent is represented as a more simple automaton with many implementation details and edge cases associated with handling unexpected environment behaviour – such as receiving unrequested agreements – removed. This simple automaton is then used with a tool that can perform verification of timing properties. Meanwhile we use AJPF to prove desired properties of the agent implementation.

11.2.2 Search and Rescue Rover

In the case of the Search and Rescue rover we are interested in verifying system level properties such as:

If the rover needs to recharge, it will execute actions to move to the charger location.

This requires, at a minimum, formal guarantees about the behaviour of both agents and the route planning system, and ideally would also involve some analysis of the behaviour of the battery monitor.

In this case we can break this down into properties we want to hold of the individual system components and then combine these. For instance, we want to establish a couple of properties for the plan execution agent, namely:

If the plan execution agent believes the battery to be low (defined as there being no available plan to the current goal that won't leave some minimum threshold value of power in the battery) and the current goal is not the charge position then it will send a recharge message to the goal agent.

If the plan execution agent believes the current goal is the charge position and has a plan to get there then it will instruct the control system to follow the route to the charge position.

We want to establish that the goal agent has the property:

If the goal agent believes a recharge is needed then it will set the target location to be the charge position.

The route planner is not a BDI agent, but we can model the algorithm it uses and prove properties of that. For instance our route planner outputs a set of routes $\mathcal{R}$ as a sequence of waypoints, $w_0, \ldots, w_n$ so we might want to establish:

The current target location appears as a waypoint in all routes suggested by the route planner.

We then need a mechanism to combine these proofs into a system-level property.

11.3 Other Formal Tools

The tools we will be using in our additional verifications are UPPAAL and Event-B.

UPPAAL (Bengtsson et al., 1995; Behrmann et al., 2004) is a model-checker for modelling, simulating and verifying real-time systems. The systems are modelled as networks of timed automata (Alur et al., 1993) with data types for common programming constructs such as bounded integers and arrays. UPPAAL verifies properties expressed in temporal logics with *real-time* constraints.

Event-B (Abrial, 2010) is a formal method for system-level modelling and analysis. It uses a set-theoretic notation and first-order logic to model and verify state-based systems. Event-B specifications consist of *contexts*, for modelling static components, and *machines* for the dynamic components. Contexts typically define sets, constants, and axioms. Machines define variables, invariants, variants, and events.

11.4 Some Verification Results

11.4.1 The Platoon

We can visualise the overall platoon system as shown in Figure 11.1. Each agent is a GWENDOLEN program, each *Comms* component is a simple transfer protocol, and the vehicle image represents the particular vehicular system that we interact with. This is an automotive control system together with environmental interactions, which was validated both in simulation (using a TORCS automotive simulation[3]) and on physical vehicles (using Jaguar outdoor rover vehicles).

---

[3] http://sourceforge.net/projects/torcs/

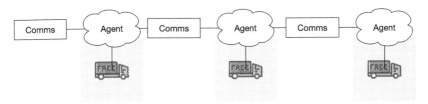

Figure 11.1 The platoon. Image from Kamali et al. (2017)

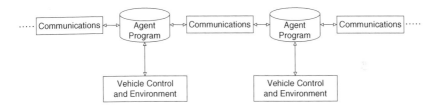

Figure 11.2 Simplified platoon architecture from Kamali et al. (2017)

We did not formally verify the vehicular control systems, and left this to standard mathematical (usually analytic) techniques from the Control Systems field (McAree and Veres, 2016). These control components, for example following a prescribed path, avoiding local obstacles, maintaining a distance from the vehicle in front, and so on, are well-established and standard. Although we ignore these in our system-level verification of the platoon protocols, the compositional verification of the search and rescue rover also in this chapter points to how such results could be integrated.

We abstract from all the vehicle control systems and environmental interactions, representing these by one (potentially complex, depending on the vehicle/environment interactions) automaton. We also use an automaton to describe the simple transfer protocol that the vehicles use for their communication. In both these cases we used *Timed Automata* (Alur et al., 1993) in order to use UPPAAL for verification. Our simplified architecture is shown in Figure 11.2 which, at least in principle, leads to the overarching formal representation shown in Figure 11.3.

In principle, though very complex, we could provide all our platoon requirements in such a logic, build structures of the above form for our platoon implementation, and then develop a model-checking approach for this combination (Konur et al., 2013). However, we can also abstract and separate the timed and agent strands, and then use AJPF for verifying the agent and UPPAAL for verifying the timed automata.

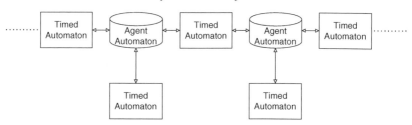

Figure 11.3 Formal platoon model from Kamali et al. (2017)

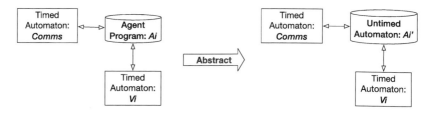

Figure 11.4 Untimed automaton representing the platoon from Kamali et al. (2017)

So, given an overall system, S, over which we wish to check φ, then we reduce $S \models \varphi$ to two problems:

1. for each individual agent, A_i, within S, verify the agent properties from φ, i.e. φ_a, on the agent within an untimed environment (an over-approximation); and

2. verify the timing properties from φ that is φ_t, on the whole system where the agent program is replaced by an untimed automaton describing solely its *input-output* behaviour (abstracting from internal BDI reasoning).

Timed Automaton $\longrightarrow$ **Untimed Automaton:** This is achieved by the over-approximating the inputs to the agent using the methodology we have used repeatedly throughout this book and which was specifically outlined in Chapter 8. We can then verify the agent behaviour using AJPF.

Agent Model $\longrightarrow$ **Untimed Automaton:** This is achieved by extracting a model of the agent program's behaviour, then removing belief/intention aspects from this (see Figure 11.4). Formal verification using UPPAAL can then be carried out on the whole system with all agents abstracted in this way.

To verify agent properties, we use the AJPF model-checker on our agent, written in the GWENDOLEN language, as above. For instance, we verified that the vehicle never initiates joining the platoon until it has received confirmation from the leader (as outlined in Equation 11.1) in the normal way.

Timed Automata Model

We model vehicle platooning in UPPAAL as a parallel composition of identical processes describing the behaviour of each individual vehicle in the platoon along with an extra process describing the behaviour of the platoon leader (the *leader* automaton). Each of these vehicle processes is a parallel composition of two timed automata, the *vehicle* and *agent*. The *agent* automaton, in turn, comprises both *Comms* and A_i' components. Our results refer to a model consisting of four vehicles.

The vehicle automaton supplies incoming perceptions for the agent automaton. It describes the sensor models and action execution. The vehicle automaton receives, and responds to, the action commands of the corresponding agent through three pairs of binary channels modelling `change-lane`, `set-space` and `join-distance` commands and responses. To model timing behaviour, we define a clock for the vehicle automaton which models the time assessments for 'changing lane', 'setting space' and 'joining distance' actions. Based on engineering analysis, actions `change-lane`, `set-space` and `join-distance` take 20 ± 5, 10 ± 5, and 10 ± 5 seconds, respectively.

We first give an example of a global property involving the coordination between the leader and the followers. Second, we evaluate timing requirements: the safe lower and upper bounds for joining and leaving activities. We observed that the verification of these properties took less than 3 seconds using UPPAAL.

Our example global property is: if an agent ever receives a joining agreement from the leader, then the preceding agent has increased its space to its front agent. This property is formulated for agent *a3* with preceding agent *a2* as follows (**A** represents 'on all paths'):

$$\mathbf{A}\square \ ((\texttt{a3.rdy\_ch\_lane \&\& l.joining\_vehicle.front} == 2) \quad\quad (11.2)$$
$$\textbf{imply} \ (\ \texttt{a2.incr\_spacing \&\& a2.spacing\_done})),$$

where *a3* is the agent which is in the *rdy_ch_lane* location, that is, the agent has received a joining agreement, variable *joining_vehicle.front* indicates the identification of the preceding agent, flag *a2.incr_spacing* models that the preceding agent has received an 'increase space' command from the leader and, finally, flag *a2.spacing_done* models whether agent *a2* has successfully increased its space. We can also verify this property for agents *a2* and *a3*.

Property 11.2 is a safety requirement ensuring that a vehicle initiates 'changing lane' only if sufficient spacing is provided.

Given the required time for a vehicle to carry out 'set spacing', 'joining distance' and 'changing lane' tasks, we are interested in verifying if an agent accomplishes joining the platoon within an expected interval (between 50 and 90 seconds, say). So if agent *a2* wishes to join the platoon this is Property 11.3.

$$A\square \ (\texttt{a2.join\_completed imply}$$
$$(\texttt{a2.process\_time} \geq 50 \ \&\& \ \texttt{a2.process\_time} \leq 90)). \tag{11.3}$$

11.4.2 Search and Rescue Rover

For the search and rescue rover we have two agents that are implemented in the EASS variant of GWENDOLEN that allows us to assume the presence of an abstraction engine which abstracts sensor data into propositions. We also have a planner module and, although this is not implemented as an agent, we do have a formal description of the planning algorithm that we can verify.

Goal Reasoning Agent

The goal reasoning agent selects a target for motion planning based on incoming information about heat values in a grid-based map. If it has been informed by the plan execution agent that the battery needs recharging, it will set the target as the recharging station, otherwise it should select the location with the highest heat value indicating an injured/trapped person. The EASS code is shown in Listing 11.1.

```
:Initial  Beliefs:                                              1
                                                                 2
chargePos(1,1)                                                   3
                                                                 4
:Reasoning  Rules:                                              5
                                                                 6
unchecked_location  :-  location(X,  Y,  H),                    7
                                ~checked(X,  Y,  H);             8
                                                                 9
:Plans:                                                         10
                                                                11
+.received(:tell,  B):  {T}  ←  +B;                             12
                                                                13
+new_goal  :  {T}  ←                                            14
        +!  select_goal  [achieve];                            15
```

```
                                                                          16
+!select_goal [achieve] :                                                 17
        { B recharge, B chargePos(X, Y) } ←                               18
                +! update_goals [perform],                                19
                + current_selection(X, Y, 0),                             20
                +select_goal;                                             21
+!select_goal [achieve] :                                                 22
        { ~B recharge, B location(X, Y, H),                               23
          ~B current_selection(X1, Y1, H1) } ←                            24
                +! update_goals [perform],                                25
                + checked(X, Y, H),                                       26
                + current_selection(X, Y, H);                             27
+!select_goal [achieve] :                                                 28
        { ~B recharge, B location(X, Y, H),                               29
          ~B checked(X, Y, H),                                            30
          B current_selection(X1, Y1, H1), H1 < H} ←                      31
                - current_selection(X1, Y1, H1),                          32
                + current_selection(X, Y, H),                             33
                + checked(X, Y, H);                                       34
+!select_goal [achieve] :                                                 35
        { ~B recharge, B location(X, Y, H),                               36
          ~B checked(X, Y, H),                                            37
          B current_selection(X1, Y1, H1), H < H1} ←                      38
                + checked(X, Y, H);                                       39
+!select_goal [achieve] :                                                 40
        { ~B recharge, ~B unchecked_location,                             41
          B current_selection(X1, Y1, H1)} ←                              42
                + select_goal;                                            43
                                                                          44
+select_goal: {B current_selection(X, Y, H)} ←                            45
        +! cleanup [achieve],                                             46
        -select_goal,                                                     47
        set_goal(X, Y);                                                   48
                                                                          49
+ atGoal :                                                                50
        {B init_pos(X, Y), ~B chargePos(X, Y),                            51
          ~B new_goal} ←                                                  52
                -location(X,Y, H);                                        53
                                                                          54
+! update_goals [perform] :                                               55
        {B atGoal, B init_pos(X, Y),                                      56
          ~B chargePos(X, Y)} ←                                           57
                -location(X,Y, H),                                        58
                -cleanup;                                                 59
+! update_goals [perform] :                                               60
        {B atGoal, B init_pos(X, Y),                                      61
          B chargePos(X, Y)} ←                                            62
                -cleanup;                                                 63
+! update_goals [perform] : {~B atGoal} ←                                 64
                -cleanup;                                                 65
+! update_goals [perform] : {~B init_pos(X, Y)} ←                         66
```

```
                  −cleanup ;                                                67
                                                                           68
+! cleanup [achieve] : {B init_pos(X, Y)} ←                                69
        −init_pos(X, Y),                                                   70
        −atGoal ;                                                         71
+! cleanup [achieve] : {B checked(X, Y, H)} ←                             72
        −checked(X, Y, H);                                                73
+! cleanup [achieve] : {B current_selection(X, Y, H)} ←                   74
        −current_selection(X, Y, H);                                      75
+! cleanup [achieve] :                                                    76
        { ∼B current_selection(X, Y, H),                                  77
         ∼B checked(X, Y, H), ∼B init_pos(X, Y)} ←                        78
              −new_goal ,                                                 79
              +cleanup ;                                                  80
```

Listing 11.1 Goal Reasoning Agent

The goal reasoning agent is activated when it perceives that a new_goal is needed. If it also perceives the need for a recharge, it sets the goal to the charge position, otherwise it removes its current position from the goal list (by performing +!update_goals) and then checks all the current goals for the one with the highest heat sensor value which it sets as the goal. Just before it sets the new target goal it performs a cleanup task (a perform goal) that essentially re-initialises its state ready for the next new_goal request to be received.

Our verification environment asserts the following at random:

1. recharge – the battery needs recharging
2. new_goal – a new target position is needed
3. init_pos(X, Y) – the initial position for the robot (from a set of three possibilities, one of which is the recharge point).
4. location(X, Y, H) – positions with heat information (from a set of three possibilities that include the recharge point)

For this agent we were able to prove:

If the agent believes a recharge is needed and that a new goal position is wanted then eventually it will set the goal to the charging position (1, 1).

$$\Box(\mathbf{B}_{goalreas} \text{ recharge} \wedge \mathbf{B}_{goalreas} \text{ new\_goal} \implies \Diamond \mathbf{A}_{goalreas}\text{set\_goal}(1,1)).$$
$$(11.4)$$

If the agent a) does not believe that a recharge is needed, b) believes that it is not at the location with the highest heat sensor reading (location (3, 4, 5)), and c) believes that a new goal location is wanted then eventually the agent will set the goal to that position with the highest heat sensor reading (3, 4).

$$\Box \neg \mathbf{B}_{goalreas} \text{ recharge } \wedge \mathbf{B}_{goalreas} \text{ location}(3,4,5) \wedge$$
$$\mathbf{B}_{goalreas} \text{ new\_goal } \wedge \neg \mathbf{B}_{goalreas} \text{ init\_pos}(3,4) \implies \qquad (11.5)$$
$$\Diamond \mathbf{A}_{goalreas} \text{set\_goal}(3,4).$$

It is worth noting here that we would have liked to prove that the agent *always* selects the position with the highest heat sensor reading without being quite so specific about the location coordinates and heat sensor value. This was challenging, given the implementation of the agent we have, though we could have used Prolog-style reasoning rules to implement a belief like `highest_heat_location` that would have let us get closer to this. However the inability of model-checking to handle infinite (or even very large) state spaces and use quantification in properties will always make it challenging to prove a property such as this. As it stands we have to justify that the scenario chosen, where we submit some arbitrary values which are tested in all combinations, adequately covers all possibilities.

Planner Module

We do not verify the implementation of the planner module but instead pursue a methodology, more common in verification, of verifying the algorithm that is run by the planner module. Our specification for the module requires that it should take input from the goal reasoning agent and some vision system that provides the locations of obstacles and outputs a set of plans, $PlanSet$, between an initial position, s_0 and the goal, g. We treat each plan as a set of coordinates (in order to avoid duplicates) that should be obstacle-free. Each plan should contain both s_0 and g, for all other grid coordinates in the plan there are two points adjacent to it. This is so that the plan can be sequentialised for execution. The planner module was modelled and verified using the Event-B formal specification language (Abrial, 2010).

We encoded a number of properties as Event-B invariants such as:

All the plans included in the plan set contain both the starting position and the goal position

$$\forall p \cdot p \in PlanSet \Rightarrow (g \in p \wedge s_0 \in p). \qquad (11.6)$$

No location in any plan in the plan set contains an obstacle.

$$\forall p, x, y \cdot p \in PlanSet \wedge (x \mapsto y) \in p \Rightarrow (x \mapsto y) \notin Obs. \qquad (11.7)$$

Here the $\mapsto$ is Event-B's tuple notation. So $(x \mapsto y)$ refers to the location (x, y) in the map grid.

All plans of length greater than or equal to 2 in the plan set contain a position adjacent to the goal.

$$\forall p \cdot p \in PlanSet \land card(p) \geq 2 \Rightarrow (\exists r \cdot r \in p \land (adjacent(r \mapsto g) = TRUE)).$$
$$(11.8)$$

All plans of length greater than or equal to 2 in the plan set contain a position adjacent to the starting position.

$$\forall p \cdot p \in PlanSet \land (card(p) \geq 2 \Rightarrow (\exists r \cdot r \in p \land (adjacent(s_0 \mapsto r) = TRUE)).$$
$$(11.9)$$

Any position in any plan of length greater than or equal to 3 in the plan set which is not the starting or goal position is adjacent to two other positions in the plan.

$$\forall p, p_0 \cdot p \in PlanSet \land p_0 \in p \land card(p) \geq 3 \land p_0 \neq g \land p_0 \neq s_0 \Rightarrow$$
$$(\exists q, r \cdot q \in p \land r \in p \land (adjacent(p_0 \mapsto q) = TRUE)$$
$$\land (adjacent(r \mapsto p_0) = TRUE)).$$
$$(11.10)$$

An Event-B machine was encoded which contained four moving events: *moveLeft*, *moveRight*, *moveUp* and *moveDown*. The four *move−* events were used to represent the addition of a new position to a 'current plan'. An *addcurrentplan* event adds the current plan to *PlanSet*. Finally an *INITIALISATION* event describes an initial state for the machine. In Event-B, events are triggered if their guards hold. For instance, the guards on the *moveLeft* event are:

$$left(currentPos) \in grid$$
$$left(currentPos) \notin Observation.$$
$$(11.11)$$

So the machine only takes a *moveLeft* action if there is a square to the left of the current position in the grid, and this square does not contain an obstacle (the set of *Observations* are the locations of obstacles). Events also include Actions which describe how variables are modified when the machine makes a transition because of the event. For instance the actions on the *moveLeft* eventare:

$$currentPlan := curentPlan \cup \{left(currentPos)\}$$
$$currentPos := left(currentPos).$$
$$(11.12)$$

So if the current position is x then after the transition the current position is $left(x)$ and $left(x)$ has been added to the current plan.

The *INITIALISATION* event creates an empty *PlanSet* and a *current Plan* containing only the starting location.

This machine describes a state machine in which a series of current plans are created, each of which takes some route from the initial position to the goal position performing obstacle-free left, right, up, and down moves until the goal is found and the current plan can be added to the plan set. In our model, even after the goal has been found, the plan can continue to be extended – it is simply *possible* to add it to the plan set at this point, not required. In a full development, such an Event-B machine could be further refined to force plans to be added to the plan set once the goal was found and to have a concept of termination after which no more plans would be explored. Refinements would also specify more directed search strategies over the space of possible plans – this model will find many routes with digressions and cycles. In many ways, this simple Event-B machine represents a basic brute-force algorithm for finding potential routes through the space which can then be refined to a more efficient algorithm through an iterative process.

A number of proof obligations were generated for the machine – for instance, requiring that each of the available events preserved the stated invariants, meaning that the invariants are properties of the output of the planner module. Some of these proof obligations could be discharged automatically, while others were proved by hand within the *Rodin* proof and development tool that supports Event-B.[4]

Plan Execution Agent

The plan execution agent takes information from the battery and a list of plans for the current goal sent by the planner module. If there is no plan that can be executed while leaving sufficient power in the battery (and the current goal is not the charging point) then the plan execution agent informs the goal reasoning agent that a recharge is needed. Otherwise it selects the shortest plan available and executes it. The plan execution agent is shown in Listing 11.2.

```
:name:  planreasoner                                              1
                                                                  2
:Initial  Beliefs:                                                3
                                                                  4
threshold(23)                                                     5
chargePos(1,  1)                                                  6
                                                                  7
:Reasoning  Rules:                                                8
                                                                  9
feasible_plan(P,  R)  :−                                          10
        current_goal(X,  Y),  chargePos(X,  Y),  plan(P,  L);     11
feasible_plan(P,  R)  :−  plan(P,  L),  [L < R];                  12
                                                                  13
cleanedup  :−  ∼plan(P,  L);                                      14
                                                                  15
```

---

[4] This development is available from https://github.com/
autonomy-and-verification/eventb-planner-module-louise.

:Initial Goals:

:Plans:

```
+select_plan  :  {B  battery(Level),  B  threshold(T)}  ←
            minus(Level,  T,  Reserve),
            +!select_plan(Reserve)  [perform];
+!select_plan(Reserve)  [perform]  :  {~  B  plan(P,  L),
            ~B  plan_selected(_,_)}  ←
                -select_plan,
                check_for_plans;
+!select_plan(Reserve)  [perform]  :
            {B  feasible_plan(P,Reserve),  B  plan(P,  L),
            ~B  plan_selected(_,_)}  ←
                +.lock,
                -plan(P,L),
                +plan_selected(P,L),
                -.lock,
                +!select_plan(Reserve)  [perform];
+!select_plan(Reserve)  [perform]  :  {B  plan(_,_),
            ~B  feasible_plan(_,Reserve)}  ←
                +.lock,
                -battery(_),
                -select_plan,
                +!cleanedup  [achieve],
                -plan_selected(_,  _),
                -.lock,
                inform_recharge;
+!select_plan(Reserve)  [perform]  :  {B  plan(P1,L1),
            B  plan_selected(P2,L2),  L1  <  L2}  ←
                +.lock,
                -plan(P1,L1),
                -plan_selected(P2,L2),
                +plan_selected(P1,L1),
                -.lock,
                +!select_plan(Reserve)  [perform];
+!select_plan(Reserve)  [perform]  :  {B  plan(P1,L1),
            B  plan_selected(P2,L2),  L2  <  L1}  ←
                -plan(P1,L1),
                +!select_plan(Reserve)  [perform];
+!select_plan  [perform]  :  {B  plan(P1,L1),
            B  plan_selected(P2,L2),  L2  ==  L1}  ←
                -plan(P1,L1),
                +!select_plan(Reserve)  [perform]  ;
+!select_plan(Reserve)  [perform]  :  {~B  plan(_,_),
            B  plan_selected(P,L),  B  chargePos(X,  Y),
            B  current_goal(X,  Y)}  ←
                +.lock,
                -plan_selected(P,  L),
                -battery(_),
```

```
                        −select_plan ,                                    67
                        −.lock ,                                          68
                        execute(P);                                       69
 +!select_plan(Reserve) [perform] : {∼B plan(_,_),                       70
        B plan_selected(P,L), B chargePos(X, Y),                         71
     ∼B current_goal(X, Y), L < Reserve} ←                              72
                        +.lock ,                                          73
                        −plan_selected(P, L),                            74
                        −battery(_),                                      75
                        −select_plan ,                                    76
                        −.lock ,                                          77
                        execute(P);                                       78
```

Listing 11.2 Plan Execution Agent

The plan execution agent is activated by the perception that it needs to select a plan. This creates a goal to select a plan that will leave at least `Reserve` battery power left. In order to establish this, it reasons about the feasibility of plans using Prolog style reasoning rules – where `feasible(P, R)` is true if plan `P` will leave reserve power, `R` or the current goal is the charge point. It then selects the feasible plan that covers the shortest distance and executes that plan.

The environment used to verify the agent asserts at random that the `battery` level is either `50` (enough for two of the plans supplied by the environment to complete without depleting the battery too much) or `24` (for which no plan could succeed without depleting the battery power below the accepted threshold) and asserts at random one of two possible current goals (one of which is the recharge point). It then supplies at random three possible plans of different lengths (plan 1 is length 30, plan 2 is length 1, and plan 3 is length 3).

Using this environment we were able to prove the following:

If the agent does not believe it has a feasible plan (i.e., one that will get it to the goal location and still leave enough reserve power) and its current goal is not (1, 1) (the charging position) then it will request a recharge.

$$\Box \neg \mathbf{B}_{planreas} \text{ feasible\_plan}(\_, \_) \land \mathbf{B}_{planreas} \text{ plan}(\_, \_) \land$$
$$\neg \mathbf{B}_{planreas} \text{ current\_goal}(1, 1) \implies \Diamond \mathbf{A}_{planreas} \text{inform\_recharge.}$$
$$(11.13)$$

If the agent believes the current target location to be (1, 1) (the charging position) and it has a plan then eventually it will execute a plan.

$$\Box \mathbf{B}_{planreas} \text{ current\_goal}(1, 1) \land \mathbf{B}_{planreas} \text{ plan}(\_, \_)$$
$$\implies \Diamond \mathbf{A}_{planreas} \text{execute}(\_).$$
$$(11.14)$$

Note that, in this second property, we do not specify which plan is executed, only that some plan is executed. We use the next three properties to check that the executed plan was the shortest plan available.

If the agent will always execute the shortest feasible plan, if it exists.

$$\Box \mathbf{B}_{planreas} \, \mathsf{feasible\_plan}(\mathsf{p_2}, \_) \implies \Diamond \mathbf{A}_{planreas} \mathsf{execute}(\mathsf{p_2}) \qquad (11.15)$$

$$\Box \mathbf{B}_{planreas} \, \mathsf{feasible\_plan}(\mathsf{p_3}, \_) \wedge \neg \mathbf{B}_{planreas} \, \mathsf{feasible\_plan}(\mathsf{p_2}, \_) \implies \\ \Diamond \mathbf{A}_{planreas} \mathsf{execute}(\mathsf{p_3}) \qquad (11.16)$$

$$\Box \mathbf{B}_{planreas} \, \mathsf{feasible\_plan}(\mathsf{p_1}, \_) \wedge \neg \mathbf{B}_{planreas} \, \mathsf{feasible\_plan}(\mathsf{p_2}, \_) \\ \wedge \neg \mathbf{B}_{planreas} \, \mathsf{feasible\_plan}(\mathsf{p_3}, \_) \implies \\ \Diamond \mathbf{A}_{planreas} \mathsf{execute}(\mathsf{p_1}). \qquad (11.17)$$

Note that we have represented the 'execute shortest feasible plan' property in a way that is specific to our verification environment by checking each of the possible plans is executed only if none of the shorter plans are feasible.

11.5 How Do We Combine These Results?

In both our case studies we now have a number of formal verification results generated using different formalisms and technologies about different parts of our system. Can we combine these results to say something about the system as a whole?

11.5.1 The Platoon

For our platooning system, we have established properties of both of the agents controlling the individual vehicles involved in the platoon with details of the communication and control behaviour abstracted away and timing properties of the system behaviour with details of the agent behaviour abstracted away. Can we combine these results?

For simplicity, we assume that our system S consists of just two agents/vehicles; this result can then easily be generalised to greater numbers of agents/vehicles.

We therefore have the following:

- V_1 and V_2 are timed automata representing the vehicle control that we used to verify properties using UPPAAL, while V_1' and V_2' are untimed abstractions of these that were used to verify properties in AJPF;

- A_1 and A_2 are BDI automata representing the agents making decisions that were used to verify properties in AJPF, while A'_1 and A'_2 are abstractions of these with BDI elements removed that were used to verify properties in UPPAAL. We assume that the time taken for A_1 and A_2 to transition between states is negligible so their behaviours can be presumed to be instantaneous; and
- *Comms12* is a timed automaton representing the inter-vehicle communications used to verify properties in UPPAAL, while *Comms12'* is an untimed abstraction of this used to verify properties in AJPF.

We use the notation $\|$ to represent the parallel combination of these automata into a system S. So $V'_i \| A_i \| Comms12'$ represents a system used to prove a property about agent, A_i, in AJPF, while $V_1 \| A'_1 \| Comms12 \| A'_2 \| V_2$ is a system consisting of two agent abstractions and communications timed automata used to prove a property about the interactions of the two agents in UPPAAL.

Our strategy is to show that the proofs we performed showing properties of the BDI agents with untimed automata can be combined with the proofs of properties of agent interaction using agent abstractions into results about a system that does not use abstractions, that is, $V_1 \| A_1 \| Comms12 \| A_2 \| V_2$. We state this in Theorem 11.1.

Theorem 11.1 Let $S == V_1 \| A_1 \| Comms12 \| A_2 \| V_2$. If

a) $V'_1 \| A_1 \| Comms12' \models \varphi_a$ and
b) $V'_2 \| A_2 \| Comms12' \models \varphi_a$ and
c) $V_1 \| A'_1 \| Comms12 \| A'_2 \| V_2 \models \varphi_t$.

then $S \models \varphi_a \wedge \varphi_t$.

Proof Note, in particular, that ϕ_a is a property expressed in terms of the beliefs, goals and actions attempted by the agent, while ϕ_t is a property expressed in terms of timed behaviour within a system.

Since V'_1 and *Comms12'* are over-approximations, then

$$V'_1 \| A_1 \| Comms12' \models \varphi_a \quad \text{implies} \quad V_1 \| A_1 \| Comms12 \models \varphi_a.$$

Similarly, (b) gives us $V_2 \| A_2 \| Comms12 \models \varphi_a$. As the agent properties in φ_a are local, we can compose these to give $V_1 \| A_1 \| Comms12 \| A_2 \| V_2 \models \varphi_a$ and so $S \models \varphi_a$.

By (c) we know that $V_1 \| A'_1 \| Comms12 \| A'_2 \| V_2 \models \varphi_t$ yet, as A_1 and A_2 have no timed behaviour (our assumption that their transitions are instantaneous, practically speaking), we know that A'_1 and A'_2 give us exactly the same timed behaviours. Consequently, $V_1 \parallel A_1 \parallel Comms12 \parallel A_2 \parallel V_2 \models \varphi_t$ and so $S \models \varphi_t$.

These two together give us $S \models \varphi_a \wedge \varphi_t$. $\qquad\qquad\qquad\square$

We now want to apply this to our early verifications using AJPF and UPPAAL. In AJPF we have proved:

If a vehicle with a goal of joining the platoon never believes it has received confirmation from the leader, then it never initiates joining to the platoon.

$$\Box \mathbf{G}_{veh}\,\mathsf{platoon\_m(veh, leader)}$$
$$\Rightarrow \neg \mathbf{A}_{veh}\mathsf{perf(changing\_lane(1))} \ \mathsf{R} \ \mathbf{B}_{veh}\,\mathsf{join\_agr(veh, leader)}. \qquad (11.18)$$

While, in UPPAAL, we have proved:

If an agent ever receives a joining agreement from the leader, then the preceding agent has increased its space to its front agent.

$$\mathsf{A}\Box\ ((\mathtt{a3.rdy\_ch\_lane}\ \&\&\ \mathtt{l.joining\_vehicle.front} == 2)$$
$$\mathbf{imply}\ (\ \mathtt{a2.incr\_spacing}\ \&\&\ \mathtt{a2.spacing\_done})). \qquad (11.19)$$

So the combined system has the property:

If a vehicle never believes it has received confirmation from the leader, then it never initiates joining to the platoon, **and** *If an agent ever receives a joining agreement from the leader, then the preceding agent has increased its space to its front agent.*

Indicating that an agent never initiates joining the platoon unless the preceding agent has increased its space to it front agent.

11.5.2 Search and Rescue Rover

In the platooning example, our combined property was expressed in a mixture of logics as used by the individual verification tools. For the Search and Rescue rover example we seek to place this kind of combination within a framework based on the concept of *contracts*.

For this system we specify contracts for each module, in the form of assumptions and guarantees and show, using first-order logic, that these contracts imply the system properties. The verifications of individual modules allow us to argue that the module fulfils its contract.

Contracts in First-Order Logic

We assume that our system consists of a set of modules, $\mathcal{M}$, and a signature, Σ, of variables.

For a given module, $C \in \mathcal{M}$, we specify its input modules, $\mathcal{I}_C \subseteq \mathcal{M}$, updates, $\mathcal{U}_C \subseteq \Sigma$, assumption, $\mathcal{A}_C : \Sigma \to Bool$ and guarantee, $\mathcal{G}_C : \Sigma \to Bool$. Taken together $\langle \mathcal{I}_C, \mathcal{U}_C, \mathcal{A}_C, \mathcal{G}_C \rangle$ form a *contract* for the module.

We use the notation $C^{\uparrow}$ to indicate that a C emits some output and $C^{\downarrow}$ to indicate that C receives an input.

We assume that all modules, C, obey the following:

$$\forall \phi, \overline{x} \cdot \overline{x} \subseteq \Sigma \backslash \mathcal{U}_C \wedge \mathcal{A}_C \wedge C^{\downarrow} \wedge \phi(\overline{x}) \Rightarrow \Diamond(\mathcal{G}_C \wedge C^{\uparrow} \wedge \phi(\overline{x})), \quad (11.20)$$

where $\Diamond$ is LTL's 'eventually' operator as used elsewhere in this book. Intuitively, this states that if, at some point, C receives an input and its assumption holds then eventually it emits an output and its guarantee holds. Moreover, for any formula, ϕ, which does not involve any of C's update variables then, if ϕ holds when C receives the input, ϕ also holds when C emits the output – that is, ϕ is unaffected by the execution of C. We will refer to this as the *module execution rule* since it describes what does and does not change as a result of module execution.

We then have a second rule that explains how inputs and outputs between two modules, C_1 and C_2, connect:

$$C_1^{\uparrow} \wedge C_1 \in \mathcal{I}_{C_2} \to C_2^{\downarrow}. \quad (11.21)$$

Intuitively this states that if C_1 emits an output and is connected to the input of C_2, then C_2 receives an input. We will refer to this as the *chain rule* since it describes how the outputs of one module chain to the inputs of another.

We will use these two rules to reason about our system.

Contracts for Our Three Modules

We therefore need to define contracts for the three modules in our system. We label our modules G (for the goal reasoning agent), P for the planner module and E for the plan execution agent. The system also gets input from H, a heat sensor, V, a vision system and B a battery monitor. We do not specify these modules here.

Our signature, Σ, is:

$$\Sigma = \{GoalSet, chargePos, recharge, PlanSet, g, plan\}, \quad (11.22)$$

where $GoalSet$ is a set of tuples $((x, y), h)$ consisting of a location in x, y coordinates and a heat value, h. This is updated by the heat sensor (which is unspecified), $chargePos$ which is the charging position for the robot. $recharge$ is a boolean value indicating whether the rover needs recharging. This is updated by the plan execution agent. $PlanSet$ is a set of plans representing obstacle-free routes through the map. This is updated by the planner module. g is the current target goal (updated by the goal reasoning module). $plan$ is the current plan (updated by the plan execution module).

Goal Reasoning Agent Contract: We define the following contract for the goal reasoning Agent, G:

> **Inputs** $\mathcal{I}_G$: $\{V, H, E\}$
> **Updates** $\mathcal{U}_G$: g
> **Assumption** $\mathcal{A}_G$: $\top$
> **Guarantee** $\mathcal{G}_G$: $(g \neq chargePos \Rightarrow$
> $\quad (\exists h \cdot h \in \mathbb{N} \wedge (g, h) \in GoalSet \wedge (\forall p, h_1 \cdot (p, h_1) \in GoalSet \Rightarrow$
> $\quad h \geq h_1))) \wedge (recharge \Longleftrightarrow g = chargePos).$

Here we see that the goal reasoning agent's inputs are the outputs of the Vision system V, the heat sensor, H and the plan execution agent, E. It updates the target goal, g. It has no assumptions ($\top$) and guarantees that:

1. If the target goal, g, (which it updates) is not the charge position then $(g, h) \in GoalSet$ for some heat signal, h, and for all other positions in the GoalSet the heat for that position is lower than h.
2. If a recharge is needed then g is the charge position.

Does the goal reasoning agent meet its contract? We previously proved, using AJPF to model-check our implementation of the goal reasoning agent, that if it believed a recharge was required then it would set the goal to be the charging position (11.4). We also proved that if recharge was not required it would select the position with the highest heat signature (11.5). Note, however, we proved this for specific assumed positions, rather than the general properties stated in the contract. Moreover it only sets a goal when it receives a set_goal percept which is not mentioned in the contract, though we can implicitly imagine this happening any time $GoalSet$ changes or a recharge is requested.

Planner Module Contract: The contract for the planner module, P, is.

> **Inputs** $\mathcal{I}_P$: $\{G\}$
> **Updates** $\mathcal{U}_P$: $PlanSet$
> **Assumption** $\mathcal{A}_P$: $\top$
> **Guarantee** $\mathcal{G}_P$: $\forall p, x, y \cdot p \in PlanSet \wedge (x, y) \in p \Rightarrow (x, y) \notin Obs$
> $\quad \wedge \forall p \cdot p \in PlanSet \cdot s_0 \in p \wedge g \in p$
> $\quad \wedge (\forall p \cdot p \in PlanSet \wedge card(p) \geq 2 \Rightarrow \exists r \cdot r \in p \wedge adjacent(r, g))$
> $\quad \wedge (\forall p \cdot p \in PlanSet \wedge card(p) \geq 2 \Rightarrow \exists r \cdot r \in p \wedge adjacent(s_0, r))$
> $\quad \wedge (\forall p, p_0 \cdot p \in PlanSet \wedge card(p) \geq 3 \wedge p_0 \in p \wedge p_0 \neq s_0 \wedge p_0 \neq g$
> $\quad \Rightarrow (\exists q, r \cdot q, r \in p \wedge adjacent(p_0, q) \wedge adjacent(r, p_0))).$

Here we see that the planner takes as input the output from the goal reasoning agent. It updates the set of plans and makes no assumptions. It guarantees the following.

- No plan takes the robot through a square containing an obstacle.
- For all plans in the set, both the agent's initial position and the target goal are contained in the plan.
- For all plans in the set, there is a location adjacent to the initial position, and a location adjacent to the target goal (provided the size of the plan is larger than 1, that is the initial position and target goal are not the same).
- If the plan is of length greater than 2 then for any point p_0 in the plan not equal to the initial position or goal position then there are points in q, r in the plan next to p_0.

Does the planner module meet its contract?: The property language of Event-B is very close to the property language used here and so the properties in the contract are, in fact, a subset of the properties we proved for the planner model. Therefore any correct implementation of that planner model will meet the contract.

Plan Execution Agent Contract: The contract for the plan execution agent is.

> **Inputs** $\mathcal{I}_E$: $\{P, B\}$
> **Updates** $\mathcal{U}_E$: $plan, recharge, execute$
> **Assumption** $\mathcal{A}_E$: $\top$
> **Guarantee** $\mathcal{G}_E$: $plan \in PlanSet \vee PlanSet = \varnothing.$
> $\qquad \wedge \forall p \cdot p \in PlanSet \Rightarrow p \neq plan \Rightarrow length(plan) \leq length(p)$
> $\qquad \wedge recharge \iff (b - t) \leq length(plan) \wedge g \neq chargePos$
> $\qquad \wedge execute = plan \iff g = chargePos \vee (b - t) > length(plan)$

Here we see that the plan execution agent takes as input the output from the planner and the battery system. It updates the current plan, the recharge value and execution target. It guarantees that:

- $plan$ is in $PlanSet$ unless there are no applicable plans.
- $plan$ has the shortest length of all the plans in $PlanSet$.
- It calls recharge if the length of $plan$ is greater than the available battery power (battery power minus some threshold value, t) and the current goal is not the charging position.
- It executes $plan$ if the current goal is the charging position or the length of $plan$ is greater than the available battery power (battery power minus some threshold value, t).

Does the plan execution Agent meet its contract? As with the goal reasoning agent we verified our implementation of the plan execution agent by model-checking in a specific scenario. In that scenario we proved that it would call a recharge if there was no feasible plan available (11.13), that it would execute the plan if it was to go to the charging position (11.14) and that it would execute the shortest feasible plan (11.15), (11.16), and (11.17). In this case the properties proved not only are specific to the scenario but also combine aspects of the contract – that is, that the plan selected is the shortest and that it is executed, if feasible. The proofs also assume that the belief `feasible_plan` correctly identifies plans that can be executed within the allowed battery limits.

System Properties

Let us consider a property that we might want to establish for the whole search and rescue rover system:

If at any point all plans sent to the plan execution agent by the planner module are longer than available battery power, then eventually the current plan will contain the charging position as the goal or there is no route to the charging position ($PlanSet = \varnothing$).

$$\Box(\mathcal{G}_P \wedge (\forall p \cdot p \in PlanSet \rightarrow length(p) > b - t) \wedge E^{\downarrow}) \Rightarrow \Diamond((g = chargePos \wedge g \in plan) \vee PlanSet \neq \varnothing)).$$

We will outline an informal proof of this property by reasoning forwards from its hypothesis until we reach the desired conclusion. The hypothesis is that the plan execution agent has received from the planner module a set of plans as input, none of which are feasible:

$$\mathcal{G}_P \wedge \forall p \cdot p \in PlanSet \rightarrow length(p) > b - t \wedge E^{\downarrow}.$$

Examining the contract for P we can see that $\mathcal{G}_P \Rightarrow \forall p \cdot p \in PlanSet \rightarrow g \in p$ – the planner agent has guaranteed that the goal appears in all the plans in the plan set. The assumption of E is trivially met. $PlanSet, b, g \notin \mathcal{U}_E$ ($PlanSet, b,$ and $g,$ are not altered by the execution of E). We can therefore use our execution rule (11.20) to deduce that:

Eventually the plan execution agent will emit an output and when it does so, its guarantee will hold, and all the plans in the plan set are longer than the available battery power and contain the goal.

$$\Diamond(\mathcal{G}_E \wedge \forall p \cdot p \in PlanSet \rightarrow length(p) > b - t \wedge \\ \forall p \cdot p \in PlanSet \rightarrow g \in p \wedge E^{\uparrow}). \tag{11.23}$$

Since the plan execution agents guarantee holds ($\mathcal{G}_E$) and all the plans in *PlanSet* are longer than the available battery power we can deduce that either the goal is the charging position, $g = chargePos$, or a recharge is called, *recharge*. We also know, again from the plan execution agent's guarantee, that *plan* $\in$ *PlanSet* and $g \in plan$ or that the plan set is empty (*PlanSet* $= \varnothing$).

If *PlanSet* $= \varnothing$ we are done. If $g = chargePos$ then since we know $g \in plan$ and *plan* $\in$ *PlanSet*, we are also done.

This leaves a case where *PlanSet* $\neq \varnothing$ and $g \neq chargePos$, implying that *recharge* is true. We will simplify (11.23) to get just the properties we are now interested in (i.e., that the plan execution agent has set *recharge* to true and has sent an output):

$$\Diamond(\mathcal{G}_E \wedge recharge \wedge E^\uparrow).$$

We use the chain rule (11.21) to deduce that the goal reasoning agent will receive an input at this point. G has a trivial assumption and *recharge* is not updated by G (*recharge* $\notin \mathcal{U}_G$). We can therefore use the execution rule (11.20) to deduce that the goal reasoning agent will emit an output that satisfies its guarantee and leaves *recharge* unchanged:

$$\Diamond(\mathcal{G}_G \wedge recharge \wedge G^\uparrow).$$

The goal reasoning agents guarantee says that if a recharge is requested then the goal will be set to the charging position: $\mathcal{G}_G \wedge recharge \rightarrow g = chargePos$ so using the chain rule (11.21) and simplifying we reach a point in time where the goal is the charging position and the planner module receives an input.

$$\Diamond(\mathcal{G}_G \wedge g = chargePos \wedge P^\downarrow).$$

Since $g \notin \mathcal{U}_P$ (the target goal is not updated by the planner module) we can use the execution rule (11.20) to deduce that the goal is still the charging position when the planner module emits an output. This leads (via the chain rule (11.21)) to the goal execution agent receiving an input where g is the charging position and the guarantee of the planner agent holds:

$$\Diamond(\mathcal{G}_P \wedge g = chargePos \wedge E^\downarrow).$$

At this point using the execution rule (11.20), we deduce that eventually the plan execution agent will omit an output where the guarantee of E holds and $g = chargePos$. This means either *PlanSet* $= \varnothing$ or *plan* $\in$ *PlanSet* $\wedge$ $g \in plan$ which was the conclusion to our original theorem.

11.6 Discussion

In this chapter we have examined two possible ways to integrate verification results about agent decision-making into wider verification of an autonomous system. In the first case, the platoon, we verified individual agents using AJPF and then verified the combined timed behaviour of multiple agents using UP-PAAL. In both cases the parts of the system omitted from the individual verifications were represented by over-approximations. This allowed us to combine the two results into a single property. However this property was expressed using two different logics that refer to the elements of the platoon in different ways – e.g., the AJPF result refers to the agents as veh while the UPPAAL result refers to individual agents, e.g., a3 etc., so the meaning of the resulting property is hard to interpret and it is possible that errors could arise in the correct specification of properties across the two verification tools.

Our second approach assumes a unifying logic for reasoning about modular systems in which each module is specified by a contract. We can reason at the contract level to establish system properties and then at the level of the individual systems to show that they meet the contract. Even here we have issues arising from the mismatch between logics, and the expressivity of our verification techniques, and have only informal arguments that the properties proved at the module level satisfy the properties specified in the contracts.

In both systems there is much work to be done – for instance, the rules for reasoning at the contract level in the second system are insufficient to handle streams of messages that may arrive at modules asynchronously, or values that might change during module execution even if they were not being changed by the module itself.

12

Runtime Verification: Recognising Abstraction Violations

So far in this book we have considered formal verification of autonomous systems in advance of deployment and so required a model of the environment to successfully accomplish the verification process.* We have recommended using a simple environment model, in which any combination of the environmental predicates that correspond to possible perceptions of the autonomous system is possible, but repeatedly throughout the book, we have been forced to constrain this model in order to manage the state space explosion and, in some cases, to ensure relevant theorems are true.

We call this most simple model an *unstructured abstraction* of the world, as it makes no specific assumptions about the world behaviour and deals only with the possible incoming perceptions that the system may react to. Unstructured abstractions obviously lead to significant state space explosion so we have explored a number of ways to structure these abstractions in order to improve the efficiency of model checking, for example specifying when specific sub-systems might send a message (Chapter 9). These *structured abstractions* of the world are grounded on assumptions that help prune the possible perceptions and hence control state space explosion.

The question that now arises is what if these environmental assumptions turn out to be wrong?

---

* This work was carried out in collaboration with Angelo Ferrando, Viviana Mascardi and David Ancona and was reported in Ferrando et al. (2018).
   This work has recently been extended in collaboration with Rafael C. Cardoso as part of the *Future AI and Robotics for Space (FAIR-Space) project*. This extension is partly covered in this chapter and was reported in Ferrando et al. (2021).

12.1 Example System

Consider an extension of our intelligent cruise control example (Example 6.1 in Chapter 6) in which the car has beliefs about when it is safe to accelerate and whether a driver has overriden the cruise control. Our autonomous vehicle can perceive the environmental predicates `safe`, meaning it is safe to accelerate, `at_speed_limit`, meaning that the vehicle has reached its speed limit, `driver_brakes` and `driver_accelerates`, meaning that the driver is braking/accelerating. This program is shown in Listing 12.1.[1]

The car has an *initial goal* to be at the speed limit (line 10). It can accelerate (line 5), if it believes it to be safe and that there are no incoming instructions from the human driver. If it has a goal to reach the speed limit (line 13), it believes it can accelerate, and it does not already believe it is accelerating or is already at the speed limit (line 14) – it removes any belief that it is braking, adds a belief that it is accelerating, performs acceleration, then waits until it no longer believes it is accelerating (line 18). If it does not believe it is safe, believe the driver is accelerating or braking, or believe it is already accelerating, then it waits for the situation to change (lines 19–23). If it believes it is at the speed limit, it maintains its speed having achieved its goal (which will be dropped automatically when it has been achieved).

If new beliefs arrive from the environment that the car is at the speed limit (line 24), no longer at the speed limit (line 28), no longer safe (line 29), or the driver has accelerated or braked (lines 33 and 39), then it reacts appropriately. Note that even if the driver is trying to accelerate, the agent only does so if it is safe.

```
:name :                                             1
car                                                 2
                                                    3
:Reasoning  Rules :                                 4
can_accelerate  :−  safe ,                          5
     ∼  driver_accelerates ,                        6
     ∼  driver_brakes ;                             7
                                                    8
:Initial  Goals :                                   9
at_speed_limit                                     10
                                                   11
:Plans :                                           12
+! at_speed_limit :                                13
```

---

[1] The examples (including verification environments and runtime monitors) in this chapter can be found in the folder `src/examples/eass/cruise_control/runtime` of the AJPF distribution.

```
              { can_accelerate ,  ~ accelerating ,   ~ at_speed_lim }   14
       ← −braking ,                                                      15
       +accelerating ,                                                   16
       perf( accelerate ),                                               17
       * ~ accelerating ;                                                18
+! at_speed_limit :  { ~ safe }  ←  *safe ;                              19
+! at_speed_limit :  { driver_accelerates }  ←                          20
       * ~ driver_accelerates ;                                          21
+! at_speed_limit :  { driver_brakes }  ←  * ~ driver_brakes ;          22
+! at_speed_limit :  { accelerating }   ←  * ~ accelerating ;           23
+at_speed_lim :  { can_accelerate ,  at_speed_lim }                      24
       ← −accelerating ,                                                 25
       −braking ,                                                        26
       perf( maintain_speed );                                          27
−at_speed_lim :  { ~ at_speed_lim }  ←  +! at_speed_limit ;             28
−safe :  { ~ driver_brakes ,  ~ safe ,  ~ braking }                     29
       ← −accelerating ,                                                 30
       +braking ,                                                        31
       perf( brake );                                                    32
+driver_accelerates :                                                   33
       { safe ,  ~ driver_brakes ,                                       34
          driver_accelerates ,  ~ accelerating }                        35
       ← +accelerating ,                                                 36
       −braking ,                                                        37
       perf( accelerate );                                               38
+driver_brakes :  { driver_brakes ,  ~ braking }                        39
       ← +braking ,                                                      40
       −accelerating ,                                                   41
       perf( brake );                                                    42
```

Listing 12.1 Example Cruise Control Agent

In order to formally verify the behaviour of the cruise control agent, we would therefore normally advocate randomly supplying subsets of {safe, at_speed_limit, driver_brakes, driver_accelerates} the generation of each subset causing branching in the state space exploration during verification so that, ultimately, all possible combinations are explored.

We would like to control the state space exploration by making assumptions about the environment. In the case of the cruise control, for instance, we might suggest that a car can never both brake and accelerate at the same time: subsets of environmental predicates containing both driver_brakes and driver_accelerates should not be supplied to the agent during the static verification stage, as they do not correspond to situations that we believe likely in the actual environment. However, since this introduces additional assumptions about environmental combinations it is important that we provide a mechanism for checking whether these assumptions are ever violated. We will describe our approach to this in the next section.

12.2 Formal Machinery

We propose to use a technology called *Runtime Verification* (Rosu and Have lund, 2005; Falcone et al., 2013) in order to monitor the environment that one of our autonomous systems finds itself in and check that this environment conforms to the assumptions used during verification. Our methodology therefore is to verify the behaviour of the program in a *structured environment* prior to deployment – we refer to this as the *static verification* of the program. Then, during testing and after deployment, we continually check that the environment behaves as we expect. If it does not then the *runtime monitor* issues a violation signal. We do not discuss in this chapter what should happen when a violation is detected but options include logging the violation for later analysis, handing over control to a human operator, or entering some fail-safe mode.

12.2.1 Trace Expressions

Trace expressions are a specification formalism specifically designed for Runtime Verification and constrain the ways in which a stream of events may occur.

An *event trace* over a fixed universe of events $\mathcal{E}$ is a (possibly infinite) sequence of events from $\mathcal{E}$. The *juxtaposition, eu*, denotes the trace where e is the first event, and u is the rest of the trace. A trace expression (over $\mathcal{E}$) denotes a set of event traces over $\mathcal{E}$. More generally, trace expressions are built on top of event types (chosen from a set $\mathcal{ET}$), rather than single events; an event type denotes a subset of $\mathcal{E}$.

A *trace expression*, τ, represents a set of possibly infinite event traces and is defined on top of the following operators:

- ε, the set containing only the empty event trace.
- $\vartheta{:}\tau$ (*prefix*), denoting the set of all traces whose first event e matches the event type ϑ ($e \in \vartheta$), and the remaining part is a trace of τ.
- $\tau_1 {\cdot} \tau_2$ (*concatenation*), denoting the set of all traces obtained by concatenating the traces of τ_1 with those of τ_2.
- $\tau_1 \wedge \tau_2$ (*intersection*), the intersection of traces τ_1 and τ_2.
- $\tau_1 \vee \tau_2$ (*union*), denoting the union of traces of τ_1 and τ_2.
- $\tau_1 | \tau_2$ (*shuffle*), denoting the set obtained by interleaving the traces of τ_1 with the traces of τ_2.
- $\vartheta \gg \tau$ (*filter*), denoting the set of all traces contained in τ, when deprived of all events that do not match ϑ.

The semantics of trace expressions is specified by the transition relation $\delta \subseteq \mathcal{T} \times \mathcal{E} \times \mathcal{T}$, where $\mathcal{T}$ denotes the sets of trace expressions. We write $\tau_1 \xrightarrow{e} \tau_2$ to mean $(\tau_1, e, \tau_2) \in \delta$. If the trace expression τ_1 specifies the current valid state of the system, then an event e is valid if, and only if, there exists a transition $\tau_1 \overset{e}{\to} \tau_2$ and τ_2 specifies the next valid state of the system. Otherwise, the event e is not valid in τ_1.

The rules for the transition functions are presented in Ancona et al. (2016). A Prolog implementation exists which allows a system's developers to use trace expressions for Runtime Verification by automatically building a trace expression-driven monitor able to both observe events taking place in the environment and execute the transition rules. If the observed event is allowed in the current state – which is represented by a trace expression itself – it is consumed and the transition function generates a new trace expression representing the updated current state. If, on observing an event, no transition can be performed, the event is not allowed. In this situation an error is 'thrown' by the monitor. When a system terminates, if the trace expression representing the current state can halt (formally meaning that it contains the empty trace), the Runtime Verification process ends successfully; otherwise an error is again 'thrown' since the system should not stop here.

12.2.2 Specifying an Environment as a Trace Expression

We can generate a verification environment for use by AJPF from a trace expression. This trace expression can then, in the actual *execution* environment, be used to check that the real world behaves as the (structured) abstraction assumes. Essentially the verification environment represents a model of the real world and a runtime monitor can be used to check that the real world is behaving according to the model.

Figure 12.1 provides an overview of this system. A trace expression is used to generate an environment in Java which is then used to verify an agent in AJPF (the dotted box on the right of the figure). Once this verification is successfully completed, the verified agent is used with an abstraction engine (as discussed in Chapter 8), and a 'thin' Java environment that handles communication to the real world or external simulator. This is shown in the dotted box on the left of the figure. If, at any point, the monitor observes an inconsistent event we can conclude that the real world is not behaving according to the assumptions used in the model during verification. Consequently, we should be less confident about any previous verification results. Depending upon the development lifecycle stage reached so far, different measures will be possible, ranging from refining the trace expression and re-executing the verification-validation steps, to involving a human or a failsafe system in the loop.

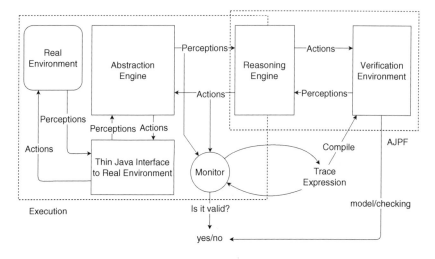

Figure 12.1 General view

Technical Details

In order to write a trace expression describing our environment model we first need to identify the events that are of interest. Since we are working with an abstraction and reasoning engine these events are the assertion and retraction of shared beliefs and the performance of actions. The following event types model events involving shared beliefs:

- $bel(b)$, where $e \in bel(b)$ iff $e = assert\_belief(b)$;
- $not\_bel(b)$, where $e \in not\_bel(b)$ iff $e = remove\_belief(b)$;

We coalesce these as event set $\mathscr{E}_b$ and define event types:

- not_action where $e \in not\_action$ iff $e \in \mathscr{E}_b$
- $action(A)$ where $e \in action(A)$ iff $e \notin \mathscr{E}_b$ and $e = A$
- $action(any\_action)$ where $e \in action(any\_action)$ iff $e \notin \mathscr{E}_b$

Abstract models in AJPF can be represented as automata, with unstructured abstractions representing their most general form. Each automaton represents a cycle of belief changes followed by actions. In an unstructured model any shared belief may be changed after an action is taken, but a structured model will place constraints on this.

We represent an abstract model of the real world as a set of possible trace expressions modelled in Prolog. The basic structure of the Prolog code is given in Figures 12.2, 12.3, and 12.4. We abuse regular expression syntax: as parentheses are used for grouping in trace expressions, we adopt [and] to represent

$$Protocol = (Cyclic\,[\,\wedge\,Whens]?\,[\,\wedge\,Befores]?\,[\,\wedge\,Causes]?) \qquad (12.1)$$
$$Cyclic = Actions\,|\,Beliefs \qquad (12.2)$$
$$Actions = [\text{defined in Figure 12.4}] \qquad (12.3)$$
$$Beliefs = [\text{defined in Figure 12.3}] \qquad (12.4)$$
$$Whens = [\text{defined in Figure 12.5}] \qquad (12.5)$$
$$Befores = [\text{defined in Figure 12.6}] \qquad (12.6)$$
$$Causes = [\text{defined in Figure 12.7}] \qquad (12.7)$$

Figure 12.2 Trace expression template for generating abstract environments

$$Beliefs = \Big|_{i=1}^{n} Bel_i \qquad (12.8)$$
$$Bel_1 = (bel(belief_1) : \epsilon) \vee (not\_bel(belief_1) : \epsilon) \cdot Bel_1 \qquad (12.9)$$
$$\dots \qquad (12.10)$$
$$Bel_n = (bel(belief_n) : \epsilon) \vee (not\_bel(belief_n) : \epsilon) \cdot Bel_n \qquad (12.11)$$

Figure 12.3 Trace expressions for beliefs.

groupings within a regular expression; similarly, since | is a trace expression operator, we use ‖ to indicate alternatives within the regular expression. Here, e? indicates zero or one occurrence of the element e. As we use Prolog, variables are represented by terms starting with an upper case letter (e.g., Act_i) and constants are represented by terms starting with a lower case letter (e.g., $belief_i$, $action_i$)). $\Big|_{i=1}^{n}$ indicates one or more trace expressions composed via the trace expression shuffle operator, |. Similarly, $\bigvee_{i=1}^{n}$ composes expressions using $\vee$ and $\bigwedge_{i=1}^{n}$ composes expressions using $\wedge$. Variables with the same name will be unified.

Protocol (12.1) in Figure 12.2 is the main body of our trace expression. *Cyclic* (12.2) consists of a shuffle between the possible beliefs and actions that can be observed. The template for the beliefs and actions are shown in Figures 12.3 and 12.4, respectively. The constraints (which are divided into *Whens*, *Befores* and *Causes* in (12.1)) add structure to the abstraction.

In this chapter we will only show examples of *Whens* type constraints – examples of the others can be found in Ferrando et al. (2021) – though we provide the Prolog templates for all of them. *Whens* constraints describe relationships between beliefs, for instance that some belief can only occur when another does, or that two beliefs cannot occur at the same time. In Figure 12.5, $B_{j,i}$ and $NB_{j,i}$ are event types, and they must meet the condition that if $B_{j,i} = bel(b_{j,i})$ then $NB_{j,i} = not\_bel(b_{j,i})$ and vice versa.

All the constraints (the *Whens* in Figure 12.5, the *Befores* in Figure 12.6 and *Causes* in Figure 12.7) consist of an intersection of trace expressions

$$Actions = \Big|_{i=1}^{n} Act_i \tag{12.12}$$

$$Act_1 = (action(action_1) : Act_1) \tag{12.13}$$

$$... \tag{12.14}$$

$$Act_n = (action(action_n) : Act_n) \tag{12.15}$$

Figure 12.4 Trace expressions for actions

$$Whens = \bigwedge_{j=1}^{n} FilterEventType_j \gg [When_j^1 \parallel When_j^4 \parallel When_j^7] \tag{12.16}$$

$$When_j^1 = ((((B_{j,1}{:}\epsilon) \vee (B_{j,2}{:}\epsilon)) \cdot When_j^1) \vee (NB_{j,1}{:}When_j^2)) \tag{12.17}$$

$$When_j^2 = ((((B_{j,2}{:}\epsilon)\vee(NB_{j,1}{:}\epsilon))\cdot When_j^2)$$
$$\vee (NB_{j,2}{:}When_j^3) \vee (B_{j,1}{:}When_j^1)) \tag{12.18}$$

$$When_j^3 = ((B_{j,2}{:}When_j^2) \vee (((NB_{j,1}{:}\epsilon) \vee (NB_{j,2}{:}\epsilon)) \cdot When_j^3)) \tag{12.19}$$

$$When_j^4 = ((B_{j,1}{:}When_j^5) \vee (B_{j,2}{:}When_j^4) \vee (NB_{j,2}{:}When_j^6)) \tag{12.20}$$

$$When_j^5 = ((((B_{j,1}{:}\epsilon) \vee (B_{j,2}{:}\epsilon)) \cdot When_j^5) \vee (NB_{j,1}{:}When_j^4)) \tag{12.21}$$

$$When_j^6 = ((B_{j,2}{:}When_j^4) \vee (((NB_{j,1}{:}\epsilon) \vee (NB_{j,2}{:}\epsilon)) \cdot When_j^6)) \tag{12.22}$$

$$When_j^7 = ((B_{j,2}{:}When_j^8) \vee (((NB_{j,1}{:}\epsilon) \vee (NB_{j,2}{:}\epsilon)) \cdot When_j^7)) \tag{12.23}$$

$$When_j^8 = ((B_{j,1}{:}When_j^9) \vee (NB_{j,2}{:}When_j^8)$$
$$\vee (((B_{j,2}{:}\epsilon)\vee(NB_{j,1}{:}\epsilon)) \cdot When_j^8)) \tag{12.24}$$

$$When_j^9 = ((((B_{j,1}{:}\epsilon)\vee(B_{j,2}{:}\epsilon)) \cdot When_j^9) \vee (NB_{j,1}{:}When_j^8)) \tag{12.25}$$

Figure 12.5 Trace expressions for the *when* constraint: $B_{j,i}$ must be the 'opposite operation' of $NB_{j,i}$

of the form $FilterEventType_j \gg [Constr_j]$. $FilterEventType_j$ is an event type which denotes only the events involved in $Constr_j$. Its purpose is to filter out any events that are not constrained by $Constr_j$. In Figure 12.5, $FilterEventType_j$ matches $bel(b_{j,1}), not\_bel(b_{j,1}), bel(b_{j,2})$ and $not\_bel(b_{j,2})$.

The equations from (12.17) to (12.25) capture the *when* constraint that $B_{j,1}$ only occurs when $B_{j,2}$ does. The constraint either starts in the state described by $When_j^1$, $When_j^4$ or $When_j^7$ depending upon whether both the constrained belief events are satisfied in the initial state ($When_j^1$), only $B_{j,2}$ is ($When_j^4$), or none of them are ($When_j^7$). The case where only $B_{j,1}$ and not $B_{j,2}$ is satisfied in the initial state is forbidden since it violates the *when* constraint.

Each equation represents a state of the formal specification where we know whether $B_{j,1}$ or $B_{j,2}$ is satisfied or not (with the opposite for their counterparts $NB_{j,1}$ and $NB_{j,2}$).

$$Befores = \bigwedge_{j=1}^{n} FilterEventType_j \gg [Before_j^1 \parallel Before_j^2] \tag{12.26}$$

$$Before_j^1 = (B_{j,1}:All^1) \vee (((NB_{j,1}:\epsilon) \vee (NB_{j,2}:\epsilon)) \cdot Before_j^1) \tag{12.27}$$

$$Before_j^2 = (Act_{j,1}:All^2) \vee ((NAct_{j,1}:\epsilon) \vee (NB_{j,2}:\epsilon) \cdot Before_j^2) \tag{12.28}$$

$$All^1 = ((B_{j,1}:\epsilon) \vee (NB_{j,1}:\epsilon) \vee (B_{j,2}:\epsilon) \vee (NB_{j,2}:\epsilon)) \cdot All^1 \tag{12.29}$$

$$All^2 = ((Act_{j,1}:\epsilon) \vee (NAct_{j,1}:\epsilon) \vee (B_{j,2}:\epsilon) \vee (NB_{j,2}:\epsilon)) \cdot All^1 \tag{12.30}$$

$$\tag{12.31}$$

Figure 12.6 Trace expressions for the *before* constraint : $B_{j,i}$ must be the 'opposite operation' of $NB_{j,i}$, and $NAct_{j,1}$ accepts every action, except $Act_{j,1}$

$$Causes = \bigwedge_{j=1}^{n} FilterEventType_j \gg [Cause_j^1] \tag{12.32}$$

$$Cause_j^1 = ((Act_{j,1}:Cause_j^2) \vee (NB_{j,1}:Cause_j^1) \vee (NAct_{j,1}:Cause_j^1)) \tag{12.33}$$

$$Cause_j^2 = (B_{j,1}:Cause_j^1) \tag{12.34}$$

Figure 12.7 Trace expressions for *cause* constraint: $B_{j,i}$ must be the 'opposite operation' of $NB_{j,i}$, and $NAct_{j,1}$ accepts every action, except $Act_{j,1}$

If we start in a $When_j^1$ where $B_{j,1}$ and $B_{j,2}$ are both satisfied, we remain in the state as long as the two beliefs keep being satisfied. We move to $When_j^2$ only when we know that $B_{j,1}$ is not satisfied anymore (this happens when $NB_{j,1}$ is observed). It is important to notice that we cannot validly observe $NB_{j,2}$ in $When_j^1$, because it would be a violation of the *when* constraint that $B_{j,2}$ is always satisfied when $B_{j,1}$ is – if $NB_{j,2}$ is observed we want the monitor to throw a violation signal and it does this if there is no valid trace.

In state $When_j^2$, $B_{j,1}$ is not satisfied, and $B_{j,2}$ is. As before, if we observe $B_{j,2}$ or $NB_{j,1}$ we do not change state. If we observe $NB_{j,2}$, we move to $When_j^3$, which represents the state where neither $B_{j,1}$ nor $B_{j,2}$ are satisfied. Finally, if we observe $B_{j,1}$, from $When_j^2$ we go back to $When_j^1$, where both $B_{j,1}$ and $B_{j,2}$ are satisfied. In contrast to $When_j^1$, all belief events are part of a valid trace in $When_j^2$. This is because the only state we wish to avoid is one where $B_{j,1}$ is satisfied while $B_{j,2}$ is not and this state cannot be reached from $When_j^2$ by the observation of a single belief event.

In state $When_j^3$, neither $B_{j,1}$ nor $B_{j,2}$ are satisfied. In this state, if we observe $B_{j,2}$, we can go back to $When_j^2$, where only $B_{j,2}$ is satisfied; if we observe $NB_{j,1}$ or $NB_{j,2}$, we stay in the same state. Just as in $When_j^1$, where we could not validly observe $NB_{j,2}$, in $When_j^3$ we cannot validly observe, $B_{j,1}$.

$When_j^i$, with $4 \leq i \leq 9$ are constructed in a similar way to express the situations where either only $B_{j,2}$ is satisfied at the start or neither $B_{j,1}$ nor $B_{j,2}$ are satisfied.

We will not describe the *Befores* or *Causes* constraints in such detail. The template for *Befores* is shown in Figure 12.6. *Befores* constraints capture the idea that some event must (or must not) occur before some other belief event can be observed (for instance that you must have attempted to accelerate before you can believe that you are at the speed limit). In this case the event that happens first can be either the addition or deletion of a belief or the performance of an action.

Finally, *Causes* constraints link actions to beliefs by specifying that, after some action is observed, some belief event must be observed. This differs from a *Befores* constraint since in this case the second event has to happen after the first, while in a *Befores* constraint the second event may or may not happen after the first, but cannot happen before it.

12.2.3 Generating the Verification Environment

Once we have created a trace expression, we translate it into Java by implementing the `generate_sharedbeliefs` method for EASS verification environments which sends the perceived beliefs to the agent during verification. We omit the involved low-level details (e.g., constructing appropriate class and package names) but just focus on the core aspects. More detail on EASS verification environments and the `generate_sharedbeliefs` method can be found in Appendix C.4. The trace expression is defined according to the template in Figure 12.2 and those that follow it. Many parts of these trace expressions are not directly translated into Java; the sub-expressions relevant to the generation of verification environments are $Cyclic$ (12.2), $Whens$ (12.16), $Befores$ (12.26) and $Causes$ (12.32).

$Cyclic$ contains a shuffle of trace expressions involving the actions and beliefs of interest. Figure 12.3 describes the belief events, Bel_i, which may occur where $Bel_i = (bel(belief_i) : \epsilon) \vee (not\_bel(belief_i) : \epsilon) \cdot Bel_i$. We define the set $\mathcal{B}(Beliefs)$ where $b_i \in \mathcal{B}(Beliefs)$ iff $(bel(b_i) : \epsilon) \vee (not\_bel(b_i) : \epsilon) \cdot Bel_i$ is one of the interleaved trace expressions in $Beliefs$. For each $b_i \in \mathcal{B}(Beliefs)$ we define a predicate in the environment class and bind it to a Java field called b_i.

$Whens$ constrain belief events by specifying pairwise exclusions between some of them. We construct a set of mutually exclusive belief events, $\mathcal{M}_x(Whens)$ from $Whens$ by analysing the constraints to extract the pair of events $(B_{j,1}, B_{j,2})$ such that after $B_{j,1}$ is observed, $B_{j,2}$ cannot be observed until after $NB_{j,1}$ has been observed – that is, we deduce from the allowable sequences of belief events that these two beliefs (or a belief and the absence of another belief) may not hold at the same time.

Once we have a set of all possible beliefs that can be observed, and a set listing mutual exclusions between them, we can then go on to describe the sets of allowable perceptions in our structured environment.

Definition 12.1 The set of possible sets of belief events for our structured environment is:

$$\mathcal{PB}(Beliefs, Whens) =$$
$$\{S \mid (\forall b_i \in \mathcal{B}(Beliefs).\, bel(b_i) \in S \vee not\_bel(b_i) \in S)$$
$$\wedge\, (\forall(B_1, B_2) \in \mathcal{M}_x(Whens).\, B_1 \in S \leftrightarrow B_2 \notin S)\} \quad (12.35)$$

Now we can move on to generating the Java code for `generate_sharedbeliefs`. Say that $\mathcal{PB}(Beliefs, Whens)$ contains k sets of belief events, S_j, $0 \le j < k$.

We generate `generate_sharedbeliefs`, as follows:

We start the method with the line:

```
int assert_random_int = random_int_generator(k);
```

where `random_int_generator` is a special method that generates random integers in a way that optimises the model checking in AJPF. For each S_j we then generate the following `if` clause:

```
if (assert_random_int == j)
  { add_percepts(S_j) }
```

Here $add\_percepts(S_j)$ adds b_i to the percept base for each $bel(b_i) \in S_j$. We do not need to handle the belief removal events, $not\_bel(b_i) \in S_j$, because AJPF automatically removes all percepts before calling `generate_sharedbeliefs`.

The other constraints we may have in the trace expression can modify these statements. More specifically, for each $Causes$ constraint denoting that an action $action$ causes a belief b, we update all the if statements that contain an S_j where $b \notin S_j$ in the following way:

```
if (assert_random_int == j &&
        !act.getFunctor().equals(action)){
    add_percepts(S_j)
}
```

where `act.getFunctor()` gives the name of the last action performed.

In this way, if a possible belief set does not contain b, it cannot be returned to the agent if the action is *action*, because otherwise the $Causes$ constraint would be violated.

The *Befores* constraint is slightly more complex. With it we can constrain the order of beliefs. Even though it is a weaker limitation than the one forced by $Whens$, it requires us to keep track of previous information. For each *Befores* constraint saying that a belief b_1 has to happen before a belief b_2; we modify all the if statements having S_j containing b_1, as follows:

```
if ( assert_random_int == j ){                                    1
    add_percepts(S_j)                                             2
    b1_observed = true ;                                          3
}                                                                 4
```

And we modify all the if statements having S_j containing b_2 as follows:

```
if ( assert_random_int == j && b1_observed ){                     1
    add_percepts(S_j)                                             2
}                                                                 3
```

In this way, we force the order on the two beliefs since we cannot generate any set of beliefs containing $b2$, unless we have already observed $b1$. This translation process from trace expressions to Java is fully implemented in SWI-Prolog.

12.3 Integration of Monitor in the MCAPL Framework

Since the MCAPL framework is implemented in Java, its integration with the trace expressions monitor (a Prolog engine that 'executes' the δ transitions) was easily achieved using the JPL interface[2] between Java and Prolog.

In order to verify a trace expression τ modelled in Prolog, we supply the runtime verification engine with Prolog representations of the events taking place in the environment. These are easily obtained from the abstraction engine and the Java environment that links to sensors and actuators. The Java environment reports instances of `assert_shared_belief`, `remove_shared_belief` and `executeAction` to the runtime verification engine which checks if the event is compliant with the current state of the modelled environment and reports any *violations* that occur during execution.

---

[2] http://jpl7.org

12.4 Verification Results

Figures 12.8 and 12.9 show the trace expression modelling the cruise control agent from Example 6.1.

Figure 12.8 specifies that the possible belief events are the assertion and removal of *safe*, *driver_accelerates* and *driver_brakes*

$$Bel_1 = ((bel(safe){:}\epsilon) \vee (not\_bel(safe){:}\epsilon) \vee \epsilon) \tag{12.36}$$

$$Bel_2 = ((bel(at\_speed\_lim){:}\epsilon) \vee$$
$$(not\_bel(at\_speed\_lim){:}\epsilon) \vee \epsilon) \tag{12.37}$$

$$Bel_3 = ((bel(driver\_accelerates){:}\epsilon) \vee$$
$$(not\_bel(driver\_accelerates){:}\epsilon) \vee \epsilon) \tag{12.38}$$

$$Bel_4 = ((bel(driver\_brakes){:}\epsilon) \vee$$
$$(not\_bel(driver\_brakes){:}\epsilon) \vee \epsilon) \tag{12.39}$$

Figure 12.8 Trace expression for the beliefs in a Cruise Control Agent.

$$When_1 = (bel(safe){:} When_2) \vee (((not\_bel(safe){:}\epsilon) \vee$$
$$(not\_bel(driver\_accelerates){:}\epsilon)){\cdot} When_1) \tag{12.40}$$

$$When_2 = (bel(driver\_accelerates){:}When_3) \vee$$
$$(((not\_bel(driver\_acclerates){:}\epsilon) \vee (bel(safe){:}\epsilon)){\cdot}$$
$$When_3) \vee (not\_bel(safe){:} When_1) \tag{12.41}$$

$$When_3 = (not\_bel(driver\_accelerates){:} When_2) \vee$$
$$(((bel(safe){:}\epsilon) \vee (bel(driver\_accelerates){:}\epsilon)){\cdot} When_3) \tag{12.42}$$

$$When_4 = (bel(driver\_accelerates){:}When_5) \vee$$
$$(((not\_bel(driver\_accelerates){:}\epsilon) \vee$$
$$(not\_bel(driver\_brakes){:}\epsilon)){\cdot} \vee$$
$$When_4)(bel(driver\_brakes){:}When_6) \tag{12.43}$$

$$When_5 = (not\_bel(driver\_accelerates){:}When_4) \vee$$
$$(((bel(driver\_accelerates){:}\epsilon) \vee (not\_bel(driver\_brakes){:}\epsilon)){\cdot}$$
$$When_5) \tag{12.44}$$

$$When_6 = (not\_bel(driver\_brakes){:}When_4) \vee$$
$$(((bel(driver\_brakes){:}\epsilon) \vee (not\_bel(driver\_accelerates){:}\epsilon)){\cdot}$$
$$When_6) \tag{12.45}$$

Figure 12.9 Trace Expression for the When Constraints on a Car where the driver only accelerates when it is safe to do so ($When_1, When_2, When_3$), and never uses both brake and acceleration pedal at the same time ($When_4, When_5, When_6$).

We have two *When* constraints in Figure 12.9. Firstly we assume that the driver never brakes and accelerates at the same time. This establishes a mutual exclusion between $bel(driver\_accelerates)$ and $bel(driver\_brakes)$. Secondly, we assume the driver only accelerates if it is safe to do so. This establishes a mutual exclusion between $bel(driver\_accelerates)$ and $not\_bel(safe)$.

From this trace expression we were able to generate a Verification Environment for the Cruise Control and compare it with performance on an unstructured abstraction. We chose to verify the property:

$$\Box(\mathbf{B}_{car}\ \mathsf{safe} \Rightarrow \Box(\Diamond(\mathbf{B}_{car}\ \mathsf{safe} \vee \mathbf{B}_{car}\ \mathsf{braking}))). \tag{12.46}$$

It is always the case that if the car believes it is safe (at some point) then it is always the case that eventually the car believes it is safe or the car believes it braking.

We need the initial $\mathbf{B}_{car}$ safe in order to exclude those runs in which the car never believes it is safe since the braking behaviour is only triggered when the belief *safe* is removed.

When model is checked using a typical hand-constructed unstructured abstraction, verification takes 4,906 states and 32:17 minutes to verify. Using the structured abstraction generated from the trace expression the proof took 8:22 minutes to prove using 1,677 states – this has more than halved the time and the state space.

Of course the structured abstraction may not reflect reality. In the original cruise control program the software could override the human driver if they attempted to accelerate in an unsafe situation. We removed this restriction. Now we had a version of the program that *was incorrect* with respect to our property in the unstructured environment model but remained correct in the structured environment model. We were then able to run our program in the motorway simulation in the MCAPL distribution where the 'driver' could accelerate whenever they liked – the runtime monitor correctly detected the violation of the environment assumption and flagged up a warning.

12.5 Discussion

We have discussed here how we can integrate a structured verification environment with a runtime monitor in order to check that the real environment matches the environmental assumptions we used for verification. We can describe this informally as continually checking that 'the world is behaving as expected' and implement fail-safe procedures to intervene if it is not. A similar process is used in Bohrer et al. (2018) where a physics model is used in a standard way as part of a feedback controller and a runtime monitor can bring the vehicle to a halt if physics is not behaving as expected – for instance if objects assumed to be static start moving.

The use of runtime monitors does not solve all our problems with structured environments – in particular our use of 'placeholder' names for plans (in Chapter 8) or tasks (in Chapter 10) and the assumptions we make about how many plans or tasks we will check over cannot at present be mitigated by the use of runtime monitoring and would require some sort of compositional or corroborative verification process in order to show that these assumptions generalise. Nevertheless, this runtime verification approach is important in both reducing verification complexity and coping with very dynamic environments.

13

Utilising External Model-Checkers

The Agent Java Pathfinder (AJPF) tool we have described in this book is a 'program' model-checker, meaning that it works directly on the program code, rather than on an abstracted model of the program's executions (as is typical for traditional model-checking).* It is built on top of Java Pathfinder (JPF), in turn, a program model-checker for Java programs (Visser et al., 2003). As we have seen, the benefits of program model-checking are that any results are directly relevant to the programs under consideration, avoiding the need for abstraction and translation via abstract mathematical models. However there are situations where we might wish to use another tool in combination with AJPF, as follows.

- AJPF uses *symbolic execution* to internally build a model to be analysed and, consequently, it is relatively slow when compared to traditional model-checkers meaning there may be situations where we would like to combine the fidelity to the program code offered by AJPF with the speed offered by another, more traditional, model-checker.
- AJPF's property specification language also lacks some concepts that we may wish to use in expressing more sophisticated properties. We looked at the inclusion of timing aspects when we discussed compositional verification with UPPAAL in Chapter 11 and in this chapter we will consider properties that involve probability.

Hunter et al. (2013) suggested using program model-checkers to generate models of agent programs that could then be passed on to other (standard) model-checkers for verification. Our aim, in this chapter, is to develop this idea and

---

* The work described in this chapter was carried out in collaboration with Matt Webster and was reported in Dennis et al. (2018). That work is, in turn, an extension of an earlier workshop paper by the same authors: Dennis et al. (2013b).
  The ethical governor case study we discuss was joint work with Alan Winfield that built on this work and was reported in Dennis et al. (2015).

show how AJPF can be adapted to output models in the input languages of both the SPIN and PRISM standard model-checkers. Overall, while model generation remains slow, and it remains inconclusive whether we have improved efficiency on individual runs, there can be significant gains especially when one generated model is reused multiple times to check different (temporal) properties. In addition, such translations give us access to a much wider range of property specification languages, allowing AJPF to be used as an automated link between agents written in BDI languages and a range of model-checkers appropriate for verifying underlying properties of those programs.

In order to describe the process of extracting models for other tools we discuss, in more depth than elsewhere in this book, the internal workings of AJPF. In particular its representation of the relevant program automata. This may be of interest to developers either extending AJPF or writing a similar tool for another language.

13.1 Example Systems

13.1.1 Satellite Control

We revisit the satellite control systems considered in Chapter 8 and, specifically, the formation control verification examples of the operation of the leader agent.

13.1.2 UAS Control

We also consider two variants of the UAS example we considered in Chapter 9. We were particularly interested with this example in assessing the effect of unreliable sensors on verification so we wanted to consider a version where the UAS's 'detect and avoid' sensor only detected approaching objects 90 per cent of the time. The inaccuracy in the sensor is modelled in the verification environment as we will discuss in Section 13.4.2 but we will briefly discuss the agent code here.[1]

```
:name: ua                                    1
                                             2
:Initial Goals:                              3
fly [perform]                                4
                                             5
:Plans:                                      6
+!fly [perform]: { ⊤ } ←  +airborne;         7
```

---

[1] The UAS examples can be found in folder `src/examples/gwendolen/uavs/prism` of the AJPF distribution.

```
+airborne: { T }                                                              8
    ← normal, +normalFlight, +direction(straight);                            9
                                                                             10
+collision: {B airborne} ← evade;                                            11
```

Listing 13.1 GWENDOLEN code for a simple unmanned aircraft

Listing 13.1 shows the code for a very simple variant of the UAS example. This BDI agent program is quite basic: the agent in control of the autonomous unmanned aircraft can only perform `normal` (normal flight) and `evade` manoeuvres.

In order to explore the capabilities of the AJPF to PRISM translator further, we used a more complex BDI agent program more closely based on the work described in Chapter 9.

This program contains two agents (one for the Executive and one for an Air Traffic Control system – ATC) with a total of 22 plans divided between the two agents (see Listing 13.2 (the Executive) and Listing13.3 (the ATC)).

```
:name: executive                                                              1
                                                                              2
:Initial Beliefs:                                                             3
waitingAtRamp                                                                 4
vicinityOfAerodrome                                                           5
                                                                              6
:Initial Goals:                                                               7
fly [perform]                                                                 8
                                                                              9
:Plans:                                                                      10
+.received(:tell, B): { T } ← +B;                                           11
+!fly [perform]: {B waitingAtRamp}                                          12
        ← .send(atc, :tell, requestingTaxiClearance);                       13
+taxiClearanceDenied: {B waitingAtRamp}                                     14
        ← .send(atc, :tell, requestingTaxiClearance);                       15
+taxiClearanceGiven: {B waitingAtRamp}                                      16
        ← −waitingAtRamp, +taxyingToRunwayHoldPosition;                     17
+taxyingToRunwayHoldPosition: { T }                                         18
        ← −taxyingToRunwayHoldPosition, +holdingOnRunway;                   19
+holdingOnRunway: { T }                                                     20
        ← .send(atc, :tell, requestingLineUpClearance);                     21
+lineUpClearanceGiven: { T }                                                22
        ← −holdingOnRunway, +linedUpOnRunway;                              23
+linedUpOnRunway: { T }                                                     24
        ← .send(atc, :tell, requestingTakeOffClearance);                    25
+takeOffClearanceGiven: { T }                                               26
        ← −linedUpOnRunway, +takingOff;                                     27
+takingOff: { T }                                                           28
```

```
            ←  take_off , +airborne ;                                    29
+airborne :  { ⊤ }                                                       30
            ←  +normalFlight , normal , +direction ( straight );        31
+collision :  {B normalFlight , B direction ( Dir )} ←                   32
            −normalFlight ,                                              33
            +oldstate ( normalFlight ),                                  34
            +olddir ( Dir ),                                             35
            +EmergencyAvoid ,                                            36
            −direction ( Dir ), +direction ( right ), evade ;           37
+collision :  {B changingHeading , B direction ( Dir )} ←               38
            −changingHeading ,                                          39
            +oldstate ( changingHeading ),                              40
            +olddir ( Dir ),                                            41
            +EmergencyAvoid ,                                           42
            −direction ( Dir ), +direction ( right ), evade ;          43
+changeHeading :  {B normalFlight , ∼B toldOtherwise ,                  44
                  B vicinityOfAerodrome }                                45
            ←  −normalFlight ,                                          46
            +changingHeading ,                                          47
            +direction ( left );                                        48
+landing :  { ⊤ } ←  land ;                                             49
+headingOK :  {B changingHeading , B direction ( Dir )}                 50
            ←  −changingHeading ,                                       51
            +normalFlight ,                                             52
            −direction ( Dir ),                                         53
            +direction ( straight );                                    54
+objectPassed :  {B emergencyAvoid , B oldstate ( State ),             55
            B olddir ( Dir ), B direction (D2)}                          56
            ←  −emergencyAvoid ,                                        57
            −oldstate ( State ),                                        58
            +State ,                                                    59
            −olddir ( Dir ),                                            60
            −direction (D2),                                            61
            +direction ( Dir );                                         62
```

Listing 13.2 A More Complex UAS Agent

```
:name :  atc                                                             1
                                                                         2
:Initial  Beliefs :                                                      3
                                                                         4
:Initial  Goals :                                                        5
                                                                         6
:Plans :                                                                 7
                                                                         8
+.received (:tell , B): { ⊤ } ←  +B;                                    9
+requestingTaxiClearance :  { ⊤ }                                       10
            ←  .send ( uav , :tell , taxiClearanceGiven );              11
+requestingTaxiClearance :  { ⊤ }                                       12
            ←  .send ( uav , :tell , taxiClearanceDenied );             13
+requestingLineUpClearance :   { ⊤ }                                    14
            ←  .send ( uav , :tell , lineUpClearanceGiven );            15
```

```
+requestingTakeOffClearance:  { ⊤ }                              16
        ← .send(uav, :tell, takeOffClearanceGiven);             17
```

Listing 13.3 An Air Traffic Control Agent

Both these programs can be found in the MCAPL distribution in `src/examples/gwendolen/uavs/prism`.

The unmanned aircraft begins on the ground (the airport ramp) at the start of its mission. The Executive agent then requests clearance to proceed to taxi from the ATC agent. Clearance is either given or denied. If it is denied, the Executive will repeatedly ask for taxi clearance until it receives permission to taxi. When the Executive receives taxi clearance it directs the unmanned aircraft into the runway holding position, which is the position to the side of the runway where the aircraft waits until it has clearance from the ATC agent to manoeuvre onto the runway itself. Once in the runway holding position the Executive will request permission to manoeuvre onto the runway ('line up'). Once this clearance is given the unmanned aircraft manoeuvres onto the runway where it lines up ready for take-off. Once again, the Executive requests clearance from the ATC, this time to take-off. When take-off clearance is given, the Executive directs the unmanned aircraft to take-off. Once in flight the Executive may receive messages from a forward-looking infrared (FLIR) sensor system on-board the unmanned aircraft, which is modelled within a Java class representing the Executive agent's environment. If the sensor detects that there is another aircraft approaching on a collision course, it contacts the Executive via a percept, `collision`, which informs the Executive agent that the unmanned aircraft is on a collision course. Upon receiving this percept the Executive directs the unmanned aircraft to perform an evasive manoeuvre using the action `evade`. Finally, the Executive will land when the navigation subsystem (again, modelled within the Java class representing the Executive agent's environment) indicates that the destination has been reached by adding a percept, `landing`.

13.1.3 Ethical Governor

We will also look at a variant on the Ethical Governor example we discussed in Chapter 10 in which a robot must move to get in the way of a human walking towards a danger. In this variant the robot does not always realise in time that the human is approaching danger, or may be faced with the task of rescuing two humans and so does not always succeed. As with the governor example in Chapter 10, this example was not modelled in GWENDOLEN but in a com-

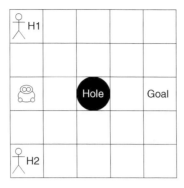

Figure 13.1 Initial state of the case study environment

bination of a simple action-based language that generated all possible actions, passed them to an ethical governor and then selected one at random from those returned by the governor, and a simple ethical governor language that would evaluate the outcomes of proposed actions, rank them and then return the set with the highest rank. This is described in Dennis et al. (2015).[2]

We created a very simple simulated environment consisting of a 5x5 grid. The grid had a hole in its centre and a robot and two humans represented in a column along one side. At each time step the robot could move to any square while there was a 50 per cent chance that each of the humans would move towards the hole. The initial state is shown in Figure 13.1. The robot cannot safely reach the goal in a single move (if it attempts this it falls into the hole) and so will move to one side or the other. At the same time the humans, H1 and H2, may move towards the hole.

The actions available to the simple agent were all of the form moveTo(X, Y) where X and Y are coordinates on the grid.

When evaluating outcomes (represented as target locations in the grid), a Breseham-based super-cover line algorithm (Dedu, 2001) was used to calculate all the grid squares that would be traversed between the robot's current position and the new one. If these included the hole then the action was negatively scored for the robot (-10) since it damaged the robot – it was also assumed that once in the hole the robot would be unable to move further. If the outcome involved traversing a square containing one of the 'humans' (but not the hole) then a negative score of -4 was generated for both robot and human as a result of the collision, after a collision the human is considered unable to move further (so a collision can be used to prevent a human from falling in the hole). If either of the 'humans' occupied a square adjacent to the hole and was

---

[2] The code for this ethical governor example can be found in the folder
src/examples/ethical_governor/human_hole of the AJPF distribution.

able to move (i.e., had not been in a collision with the robot) then a score of −10 for the human was generated representing the risk the human would fall in the hole. In the simple language used by the governor, it would prefer outcomes beneficial to the human over those beneficial to the robot. If there were outcomes with no negative scores for either, then the set of these would be returned to the action system. Otherwise the set with the best outcomes for the human would be returned and, within that set, those with the best outcomes for the robot would be selected. The intended behaviour was that the robot would move around the grid avoiding both humans and hole, unless a human was next to the hole in which case it would collide with them to prevent them falling in the hole.

13.2 Other Model-Checkers

We will consider two other model-checkers here, SPIN and PRISM.

13.2.1 SPIN

SPIN (Holzmann, 2003) is a widely used model-checking tool originally developed at Bell Laboratories in the 1980s. It benefits from this long-term development and improvement, and so is widely used in both industry and academia (Havelund et al., 2000; Kars, 1996; Kirsch et al., 2011). The input language for SPIN is the PROMELA programming language, a multi-process language with C-like syntax. As SPIN utilises a form of 'on the fly' model-checking (Gerth et al., 1996), both the program/model under analysis *and* the property being checked are represented as PROMELA structures and typically input at the same time. The properties to be assessed (technically, the negation of the property to be verified) are called 'never claims' and are essentially Büchi automata represented as a PROMELA process. Detailed development of automata is not necessary since SPIN also provides tools to convert temporal logic formulae into appropriate PROMELA code representing these never claims. Internally, SPIN works by generating C code to carry out the 'on the fly' exploration of the model relative to the appropriate property. This code can then be compiled to allow for fast exploration/checking. This, together with optimisation techniques, such as *partial order reduction*, enhance the speed of SPIN. (The work described in this chapter was carried out using SPIN version 6.2.3.)

13.2.2 PRISM

PRISM (Kwiatkowska et al., 2011) is a probabilistic symbolic model-checker itself in continuous development since 1999, primarily at the universities of Birmingham and Oxford. PRISM provides broadly similar functionality to

SPIN but also allows for the model-checking of probabilistic models, i.e., models whose behaviour can vary depending on probabilities represented in the model. Developers can use PRISM to create a probabilistic model (written in the PRISM language) which can then be model-checked using PRISM's own probabilistic property specification language, which subsumes several well-known probabilistic logics including Probabilistic Computation Tree Logic (PCTL), Probabilistic LTL (PLTL), and PCTL* (Emerson, 1990a; Hansson and Jonsson, 1994). PRISM has been used to formally verify a wide variety of systems in which reliability and uncertainty play a role, including communication protocols, cryptographic protocols and biological systems. In this chapter we use PRISM version 4.1.beta2.

The syntax of probabilistic computation tree logic, PCTL, a branching time temporal logic, is typically described by the following grammar, with ϕ representing a well-formed PCTL formula.

$$\phi ::= \texttt{true} \mid \texttt{a} \mid \phi \wedge \phi \mid \neg\phi \mid \texttt{P}^{\bullet p}[\psi]$$
$$\psi ::= \bigcirc\phi \mid \phi\texttt{U}^{\leq k}\phi \mid \phi\texttt{U}\phi,$$

where a is an atomic proposition, $\bullet$ is one of $\leq$, $<$, $\geq$, or $>$, p is a non-zero rational number, and $k \in \mathbb{N}$.

We then interpret PCTL formulae over discrete-time Markov chains (DTMCs), essentially probabilistic branching temporal structures. Instead of evaluating a formula at a particular time point i as we do for LTL, we evaluate for a state s. Paths through the DTMC structure are sequences of states $s_0(a_1, \mu_1)s_1(a_2, \mu_2)s_2 \ldots$, where a_i is the ith action taken to transform state s_{i-1} into state s_i and μ_i is the probability of that action occurring. $Paths(s)$ is the set of all paths that start in state s. The probability of a path, $\pi = s_0, s_1, \ldots$ is the product of the probability that each state in π transitions to the next state in π. The probability over a set of paths, Pr, is the sum of the probability of each individual path. The semantics is represented by the following equations evaluated at a particular state (Hansson and Jonsson, 1994):

$$\langle \mathcal{M}, s \rangle \models p \quad \textbf{iff} \quad p \in I(s) \tag{13.1}$$

$$\langle \mathcal{M}, s \rangle \models \neg\phi \quad \textbf{iff} \quad \langle \mathcal{M}, s \rangle \not\models \phi \tag{13.2}$$

$$\langle \mathcal{M}, s \rangle \models \phi \wedge \psi \quad \textbf{iff} \quad \langle \mathcal{M}, s \rangle \models \phi \quad \textbf{and} \quad \langle \mathcal{M}, s \rangle \models \psi \tag{13.3}$$

$$\langle \mathcal{M}, \pi \rangle \models \bigcirc\phi \quad \textbf{iff} \quad \langle \mathcal{M}, s_1 \rangle \models \phi \tag{13.4}$$

$$\langle \mathcal{M}, \omega \rangle \models \phi\texttt{U}^{\leq k}\psi \quad \textbf{iff} \quad \exists i \leq k.\, \langle \mathcal{M}, s_i \rangle \models \psi$$
$$\text{and } \forall j < i.\, \langle \mathcal{M}, s_j \rangle \models \phi \tag{13.5}$$

$$\langle \mathcal{M}, \pi \rangle \models \phi\texttt{U}\psi \quad \textbf{iff} \quad \exists k \geq 0.\, \langle \mathcal{M}, \pi \rangle \models \phi\texttt{U}^{\leq k}\psi \tag{13.6}$$

$$\langle \mathcal{M}, s \rangle \models \texttt{P}^{\bullet p}[\psi] \quad \textbf{iff} \quad Pr(\{\pi \in Paths(s) \mid \langle \mathcal{M}, \pi \rangle \models \psi\}) \bullet p \tag{13.7}$$

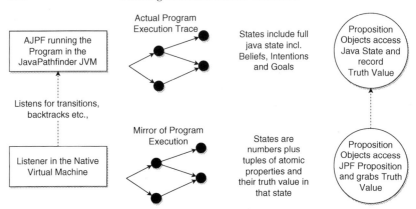

Figure 13.2 The operation of AJPF wrt. the two java virtual machines from Dennis et al. (2018)

13.3 Translation Approach

JPF is implemented via a specialised Java virtual machine which stores, among other things, choice points within the Java execution. This allows the program model-checking algorithm to explore the entire execution space of a Java program by backtracking through the alternatives. JPF is highly customisable, providing numerous 'hooks' for Java *Listeners* that monitor and control the progress of model-checking. In what follows we will refer to the specialised Java virtual machine used by JPF as the *JPFJVM*. JPF is implemented in Java itself, therefore the JPFJVM is a program that executes on an underlying native Java virtual machine. We refer to this native virtual machine as *NatJVM*. Listeners used in JPF execute in the NatJVM.

AJPF's checking process is itself constructed using a JPF Listener. As JPF executes, it labels each state explored within the JPFJVM by a unique number. The AJPF Listener tracks these numbers as well as the transitions between them and uses this information to construct a Kripke structure in the NatJVM. The LTL model-checking algorithm then works on this Kripke structure. This is partly for reasons of efficiency (the NatJVM naturally executes much faster than the JPFJVM) and also to account for the need for LTL to explore states in the model several times if the model contains a looping path and an *until expression* (e.g., true $\cup$ p) exists in the LTL.

In order to determine whether the agents being executed have particular beliefs, goals, and so on, it is necessary for the LTL model-checking algorithm to have access to these sets of *intentional* representations within the execution. However, these structures exist in the JPFJVM, not the NatJVM and so techniques (described in more detail below) are needed in order to create objects that represent propositions of interest (e.g., 'agent 1 believes the formation is a square') in the JPFJVM, and then track these from the NatJVM in order to label the states of the Kripke structure appropriately.

The steps in adapting this approach to produce a model for use with an alternative model-checker involve: (i) bypassing the LTL model-checking algorithm within AJPF[3] but continuing to generate and maintain a set of propositional objects in order to label states in the Kripke structure, and (ii) exporting the Kripke structure in a format that can subsequently be used by another model-checker, such as SPIN or PRISM.

At the start of a model-checking run AJPF analyses the property being verified (e.g., *agent 1 believes it has reached its destination, agent 2 intends to win the auction*, etc.) in order to produce a list of logical propositions that are needed for checking that property. AJPF then creates objects representing each of these propositions in both the JPFJVM and NatJVM. In the JPFJVM these propositional objects can access the state of the multi-agent system and explicitly check that the relevant propositions hold (e.g., that the Java object representing agent 1 contains, in its belief set, an object representing the formula *reached(destination)*).

The system also maintains three distinct sets of objects representing non-temporal propositions, one in the NatJVM (*native propositions*) and two in the JPFJVM (*abstract propositions* and *concrete propositions*). It is not strictly necessary to maintain two in the JPFJVM but the details of how the three different sets of propositions are created during parsing mean that abstract propositions are created first (in both JVMs) and linked by storing a reference to the JPFJVM version in the NatJVM. Once completed, native propositions are then created from the abstract propositions in the NatJVM while concrete propositions are created from them in the JPFJVM.

When the NatJVM accesses an object in the JPFJVM using a reference (this is how the native propositions access their corresponding abstract propositions), inspecting the values of its fields is straightforward providing they contain values of a primitive Java data types (such as `bool` or `int`). This is achieved using JPF's Model Java Interface (MJI) interface.

In the JPFJVM the concrete propositions have associated methods for checking their truth against the current agent system. These concrete propositions update a Boolean field in their corresponding abstract proposition whenever their own truth is checked.

---

[3] Although not strictly necessary this increases the speed of model generation and avoids the pruning of some model states based on the property under consideration.

In the NatJVM a Büchi Automaton (see Chapter 4) is constructed from the property under consideration. This is the finite-state automaton that will be used for checking the truth of the property during model-checking. When checking the truth of an individual state in the Büchi Automaton, at a particular point in an execution, only the truth value of propositions is checked, while evaluation of the truth of a temporal property is deferred to later exploration. Therefore each Büchi state maintains a list of native proposition objects, and, when the truth of the state is checked these consult the fields of their corresponding object in the JPFJVM.

Each time the interpreter for the agent programming language executes one step,[4] all of the concrete proposition objects check their truth and update the truth value field in the abstract propositions. Precisely when this occurs is the choice of the interpreter designer. It is typically either: each time a transition is taken in the operational semantics; or each time a full reasoning cycle in the operational semantics is completed.

Properties in the NatJVM are updated whenever JPF determines that a transition has been taken by the program running in the JPFJVM. When used in conjunction with simplification heuristics, such as partial order reduction, JPF typically detects a transition when there is a scheduling choice between agents (and possibly the environment) or there is branching caused by the invocation of some random choice. However, it is also possible to 'force' JPF to make a transition and we do this every time the interpreter takes a 'step' as discussed above. It is at this point, therefore, that the Native-level proposition objects examine the relevant fields in the abstract objects stored in the JPFJVM and then update their own fields. This process is illustrated informally in Figure 13.3.

13.3.1 Translation to SPIN

Both SPIN and AJPF's LTL algorithm operate on similar automaton structures so translating between the two is straightforward. In AJPF a model can be viewed as a set of model states, ms, which are a tuple of an integer, i, and a set of propositions, P. The model itself includes a function, F, that maps an integer (representing a particular model state) to a set of integers (representing all the model states which can be reached by one transition).

---

[4] The meaning of a 'step' in the semantics – as in the next point of interest to verification – is determined by the person implementing the semantics. Typically this is either the application of a single rule from the operational semantics, or of a whole reasoning cycle. This issue is discussed further in Dennis et al. (2012) and was touched on in Chapter 6. In GWENDOLEN and variants one step is by default one transition in the operational semantics although this can be changed in the configuration file.

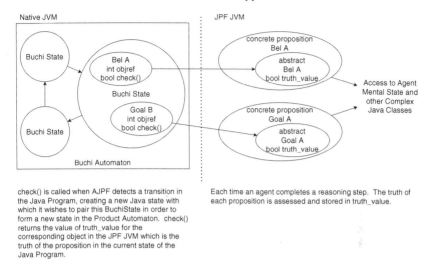

Native JVM

JPF JVM

check() is called when AJPF detects a transition in the Java Program, creating a new Java state with which it wishes to pair this BuchiState in order to form a new state in the Product Automaton. check() returns the value of truth_value for the corresponding object in the JPF JVM which is the truth of the proposition in the current state of the Java Program.

Each time an agent completes a reasoning step. The truth of each proposition is assessed and stored in truth_value.

Figure 13.3 The relationship between proposition classes in AJPF, adapted from Dennis et al. (2018)

While PROMELA has a number of language constructs, at its heart it allows the user to describe a finite state machine consisting of labelled states, the propositions that are true in each state and the next states in the transition system. Translating between AJPF's model therefore and a PROMELA model is mostly a matter of converting syntactically between AJPF's state numbers and PROMELA state labels and AJPF's propositions and PROMELA's propositions.

13.3.2 Translation to PRISM

The PRISM input language is based on probabilistic timed automata, structures that are commonly used to model systems that exhibit both timed and probabilistic behaviour, such as network protocols, sensors, biological models, etc. While we do not explicitly utilise the *timing* dimension here (see Chapter 11), we are interested in the *probabilistic* aspect. The key difference between the automata considered earlier and their probabilistic counterparts is that transitions between states are now probabilistic. Specifically, such automata typically incorporate a probability distribution to inform the choice amongst the potential transitions (Kwiatkowska et al., 2002). So instead of, as in SPIN and AJPF simply exploring all possible transitions from a state to find out which states are reachable, PRISM also considers the probability of reaching any possible state. Consequently, information about this probability distribution is important in constructing probabilistic automata and is typically modelled as labels on transitions, indicating the probability of that transition occurring.

In order to support transitions with probability labels, it was necessary to make some alterations to AJPF. JPF, and hence AJPF, is able to branch the search space when a random element is selected from a finite set. However the system does not record the probabilities of each branch created in a manner accessible to the NatJVM.

In order to address this we made use of a JPF customisation tool known as a *native peer*. The native peer of a Java object can intercept the execution of particular methods associated with the object. When a method is intercepted, alternative code associated with the native peer is executed in the NatJVM instead of the existing code associated with the object. This can allow complex algorithms to be executed natively for efficiency reasons or, as is the case here, to control branching in the program model.

We used the `Choice` class from the AIL which represents a probabilistic choice from a finite set of options and can be used in debugging AIL programs by supporting the replay of specific counter-example traces located during model-checking (this capability is discussed in Appendix A.8.2 and the use of the `Choice` class in developing environments is discussed in Appendix C.4). We developed a native peer for this class.

A `Choice` object consists of an array of `Options`. An `Option` is a tuple comprising both a probability and a value (of whatever class is needed for the results of the choice). The probabilities of the options in the array add up to one (at least in theory). At a high level, when asked to make a choice (by the system calling the class's `choose` method) the class returns one of the options from the array. When not executing in JPF, the class selects the option by using a standard 'roulette wheel' algorithm to select an option according to the probability distribution. When executing in JPF, the method that performs roulette wheel selection is intercepted and, instead, a *choice generator* is created. This sets a backtrack point in the system and, each time the execution returns to that backtrack point, a different option is selected until all choices have been explored. The `Choice` class maintains, as a field, the probability of the current choice allowing this to be accessed by the AJPF Listener and used to annotate the edges of the model.

In AJPF, a specialised Probability Listener, executing in the NatJVM, listens for invocations of the `choose` method. The listener does not replace the code in `choose` but acquires a reference to the `Choice` object itself and after execution of the method completes, it can access the value stored as the probability of that choice. This allows the Listener in the NatJVM to annotate the edge created in the automaton by the choice generator with the appropriate probability, thus annotating the relevant branch with the probability of taking that transition. Similar specialised listeners could be used to annotate branches with other information (e.g., actions, real-time estimates) were the system to be adapted for use with other model-checking systems such as UPPAAL.

In short, programming with the `Choice` class, in the normal execution of the program, simply picks an element from a set based on some probability distribution. When executed within AJPF, the `Choice` class causes the system to explore all possible choices and label each branch with its probability. These labels were then used in the translation to PRISM in order to state the probability of each transition within PRISM's input language.

13.4 Verification Results

13.4.1 Satellite Control

We tested our SPIN implementation on the verification of the leader agent for controlling formations of satellites described in Chapter 8.

Our initial hypothesis was that we would see gains in performance as the LTL property to be checked became more complex (since executing the Büchi Automata in Java could be costly). As a result we tested the system against a sequence of properties:

1. $\Box\neg\mathbf{B}_{lead}$ bad
   (The agent never believes something bad has happened).
2. $(\Box(\mathbf{B}_{lead}$ informed(ag1) $\rightarrow \Diamond\mathbf{B}_{lead}$ maintaining_pos(ag1))) $\rightarrow \Box\neg\mathbf{B}_{lead}$ bad
   (If it is always the case that when the leader has informed agent 1 of its position then eventually the leader will believe agent 1 is maintaining that position, then it is always the case that the leader does not believe something bad has happened.)

The next three properties increase in complexity by adding subformulae for agents $ag2$, $ag3$ and $ag4$. The final property adds another subformula which says that it is always the case that if the leader believes that the formation is in the shape of a square, then eventually it believes that it has informed agent $ag1$ of this.

3. $(\Box(\mathbf{B}_{lead}$ informed(ag2) $\rightarrow \Diamond\mathbf{B}_{lead}$ maintaining_pos(ag2))) $\wedge$
   $\Box(\mathbf{B}_{lead}$ informed(ag1) $\rightarrow \Diamond\mathbf{B}_{lead}$ maintaining_pos(ag1))) $\rightarrow \Box\neg\mathbf{B}_{lead}$ bad
4. $(\Box(\mathbf{B}_{lead}$ informed(ag3) $\rightarrow \Diamond\mathbf{B}_{lead}$ maintaining_pos(ag3)) $\wedge$
   $\Box(\mathbf{B}_{lead}$ informed(ag2) $\rightarrow \Diamond\mathbf{B}_{lead}$ maintaining_pos(ag2)) $\wedge$
   $\Box(\mathbf{B}_{lead}$ informed(ag1) $\rightarrow \Diamond\mathbf{B}_{lead}$ maintaining_pos(ag1))) $\rightarrow \Box\neg\mathbf{B}_{lead}$ bad

5. $(\square(\mathbf{B}_{lead}$ informed(ag4) $\rightarrow$ $\lozenge\mathbf{B}_{lead}$ maintaining_pos(ag4)) $\wedge$
   $\square(\mathbf{B}_{lead}$ informed(ag3) $\rightarrow$ $\lozenge\mathbf{B}_{lead}$ maintaining_pos(ag3)) $\wedge$
   $\square(\mathbf{B}_{lead}$ informed(ag2) $\rightarrow \lozenge\mathbf{B}_{lead}$ maintaining_pos(ag2)) $\wedge$
   $\square(\mathbf{B}_{lead}$ informed(ag1) $\rightarrow \lozenge\mathbf{B}_{lead}$ maintaining_pos(ag1))) $\rightarrow \square\neg\mathbf{B}_{lead}$ bad

6. $(\square(\mathbf{B}_{lead}$ informed(ag4) $\rightarrow$ $\lozenge\mathbf{B}_{lead}$ maintaining_pos(ag4)) $\wedge$
   $\square(\mathbf{B}_{lead}$ informed(ag3) $\rightarrow$ $\lozenge\mathbf{B}_{lead}$ maintaining_pos(ag3)) $\wedge$
   $\square(\mathbf{B}_{lead}$ informed(ag2) $\rightarrow$ $\lozenge\mathbf{B}_{lead}$ maintaining_pos(ag2)) $\wedge$
   $\square(\mathbf{B}_{lead}$ informed(ag1) $\rightarrow$ $\lozenge\mathbf{B}_{lead}$ maintaining_pos(ag1)) $\wedge$
   $\square(\mathbf{B}_{lead}$ formation(square) $\rightarrow \lozenge\mathbf{B}_{lead}$ informed(ag1))) $\rightarrow \square\neg\mathbf{B}_{lead}$ bad.

This sequence of increasingly complex properties was constructed so that each property had the form $P_1 \wedge \ldots \wedge P_n \rightarrow Q$ for some $n \geq 0$ and each P_i was of the form $(\square(P_i' \rightarrow \lozenge Q_i))$. With the addition of each such logical antecedent the property automata became considerably more complex. Furthermore, the antecedents were chosen so that we were confident that, on at least some paths through the program, P_i' would be true at some point, necessitating that the LTL checker explore the product automata for $\lozenge Q_i$. We judged that this sequence of properties provided a good test for the way each model-checker's performance scaled as the property under test became more complicated.

SPIN model-checking requires a sequence of steps to be undertaken: the LTL property must be translated to a 'never claim' (effectively representing the automaton corresponding to the negation of the required property), then it is compiled together with the PROMELA description into C, which is then compiled again before being run as a C program. We used the LTL3BA tool (Babiak et al., 2012) to compile the LTL property into a never claim since this is more efficient than the built-in SPIN compiler. In our results we present the total time taken for all SPIN operations (SPIN Time) and the total time taken overall including generation of the model in AJPF.

Table 13.1 shows the running times for model-checking the six properties on a 2.8 GHz Intel Core i7 Macbook running MacOS 10.7.4 with 8 GB of memory. Figure 13.4 shows the same information as a graph. There is no result for AJPF model-checking of the final property since the system suffered a stack overflow error when attempting to build the property automata.

The results show that as the LTL property becomes more complex, model-checking using the AJPF to PROMELA/SPIN translation tool is marginally more efficient than using AJPF alone. It should be noted that, in the SPIN case, where AJPF is not performing LTL model-checking, and is using a simple list of propositions (rather than an LTL property) the time to generate the model still increases as the property becomes more complex. This is explained

Table 13.1 Comparing AJPF with and without SPIN model-checking
from Dennis et al. (2018)

Property	AJPF	SPIN		
		AJPF model generation	SPIN Time	Total Overall Time
1	5m25s	5m17s	1.972s	5m19s
2	5m54s	5m50s	3.180s	5m53s
3	7m9s	6m28s	4.369s	6m32s
4	8m50s	7m34s	6.443s	7m40s
5	9m22s	8m27s	10.015s	8m37s
6	—	8m51s	22.361s	9m13s

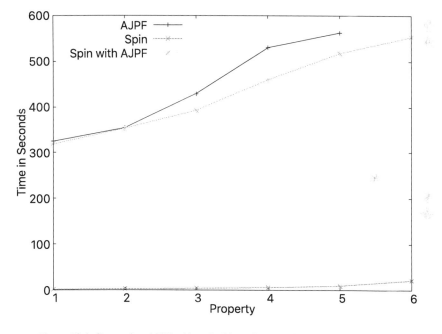

Figure 13.4 Comparing AJPF with and without SPIN model-checking from Dennis et al. (2018)

by the overhead involved in tracking the proposition objects in the JPFJVM and the NatJVM: as more propositions are involved this time increases. If only one AJPF model were to be generated then SPIN would give considerable time savings overall. (N.B. In this case it would need to be the AJPF model with all relevant propositions, i.e., the one taking nearly 9 minutes to generate.)

It is interesting to note that AJPF could not generate a property automaton for property 6. Indeed, this is a compelling argument that combining AJPF with SPIN or some other model-checker is sometimes necessary. It also illustrates the point that SPIN is optimised for working with LTL where AJPF is not.

13.4.2 UAS Control

For our two UAS implementations (from Listings 13.1 and 13.2) we are interested in the probability that the Agent will perform an 'evade' action given its sensor is unreliable. Therefore we want to track two predicates when generating the program model using AJPF: $\mathbf{P}$ collision, which means *a potential collision is perceptible in the environment*, and $\mathbf{A}_{uav}$evade, which means *the last action performed was the unmanned aircraft agent taking an evade maneouvre*. Recall that the $\mathbf{P}$ p expression refers to the environment and not to the internal state of the agent so, in this instance, $\mathbf{P}$ collision can be interpreted as meaning that, in the program itself, a collision is going to occur irrespective of whether the agent has perceived this fact. This allows us to describe properties that capture the potential unreliability of sensors.

We generated a program automaton using AJPF for the Simple UAS program (Listing 13.1) executing in an environment where its sensor had an accuracy of 90 per cent. This means there was a 90 per cent probability that if `collision` were perceptible ($\mathbf{P}$ collision) that this would be communicated to the agent as an actual perception and so become a belief ($\mathbf{B}_{uav}$ collision). From this program we extracted a model in the input language of PRISM. A fragment of the AJPF model for this program, adapted to show the probability of transitions is shown in Figure 13.5 alongside its translation into the PRISM input language.[5]

We then model-checked the Simple UAS program in PRISM against the property

$$P^{=?}\Box(\mathbf{P} \text{ collision} \rightarrow \Diamond \mathbf{A}_{uav}\text{evade}) \tag{13.8}$$

to establish that the probability that the unmanned aircraft would evade a collision, if one were possible, was 90 per cent.

In the more complex BDI agent program from Listing 13.2, the sensor was again given an accuracy of 90 per cent. Again, we were able to use the PRISM model generated by AJPF to determine that there was a 90 per cent probability that the agent would take an evade action if a collision was perceptible (Property (13.8)).

---

[5] Note that the nature of rounding in Java means that 0.1 is, in several places, represented as 0.09999999999999998.

AJPF Model

States: Edges:

```
                                               0.9 ::: 3-->4
3:  A(ua,evade()) = false;                     0.09999999999999998 ::: 3-->11
    P(collision()) = false;                    1.0 ::: 4-->5
4:  A(ua,evade()) = false;                     1.0 ::: 5-->6
    P(collision()) = true;                     ...
5:  A(ua,evade()) = false;
    P(collision()) = true;
6:  A(ua,evade()) = true;
    P(collision()) = false;
7:  A(ua,evade()) = true;
    P(collision()) = false;
 ...
```

PRISM Model

```
dtmc

module jpfModel
   state : [0 ..15] init 0;
   auaevade: bool init false;
   pcollision: bool init false;
   [] state = 2 -> 1.0:(state'=3) & (auaevade'= false)
                                  & (pcollision'= false);
   [] state = 3 -> 0.9:(state'=4) & (auaevade'= false)
                                  & (pcollision'= true)
    + 0.09999999999999998:(state'=11) & (auaevade'= false)
                                  & (pcollision'= true);
   [] state = 4 -> 1.0:(state'=5) & (auaevade'= false)
                                  & (pcollision'= true);
   [] state = 5 -> 1.0:(state'=6) & (auaevade'= false)
                                  & (pcollision'= true);
   [] state = 6 -> 1.0:(state'=7) & (auaevade'= true)
                                  & (pcollision'= false);
   ...
endmodule
```

Figure 13.5 Comparison of models for AJPF and PRISM from Dennis et al. (2018)

We can also verify the following property:

$$P^{=?}\Box(\Diamond(P\text{ collision} \land \neg(\Diamond\mathbf{A}_{uav}\text{evade}))).$$

This property expresses the probability that it is always the case that the possibility of collision is perceptible yet the UAS fails to take evasive action. PRISM calculates this probability to be 0.1, as would be expected by inspection of the model.

Therefore, these results validate the accuracy of the PRISM model generated from AJPF and verified using PRISM, at least for these properties.

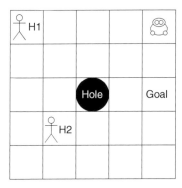

Figure 13.6 Situation where the robot cannot save the human

13.4.3 Ethical Governor System

We verified our ethical governor system within an environment which asserted the locations of the humans as percepts which then became beliefs in the agents. We do not discuss here our normal verification approach with an unstructured abstract model of the environment (although this is discussed in Dennis et al. (2013)). Here we describe a verification of our governor agent within the specific simulation of a 5 by 5 starting grid with the humans and robots placed as in Figure 13.1. In Chapter 10 we discussed the use of *scenario probing* properties for the verification of ethical reasoning and this represents a verification of this type. We were specifically interested in evaluating the robot's actions in this scenario.

We were interested in whether the humans fell in the hole, so these facts became the properties $\mathbf{B}_{governor}$ human1(hole) and $\mathbf{B}_{governor}$ human2(hole) which were used to annotate states for export to PRISM.

In the situation where both H1 and H2 move simultaneously towards the hole, the robot is unable to save them both and has to choose which to rescue and which to leave at risk. It turned out that whenever this occurred, as a result of the starting locations we had chosen for our robot and humans, that the hole was between the robot and H2 (an example of this situation is shown in Figure 13.6). This was an artefact of the fact that the humans had to make at least one move before the robot could tell they were in danger. The robot's first move was always to the far corner of the grid since this represented a point closest to the goal that the robot could safely reach. As a result the robot always selected to attempt to rescue H1. The outcome would have been different if action selection had been set up to pick at random from all the points the robot could safely reach that were equidistant from the hole.

When we exported our model to PRISM we were able to prove that

human 1 never falls in the hole

$$P^{=0}\Box(\mathbf{B}_{governor}\,\text{human1(hole)}) \tag{13.9}$$

while

human 2 falls in the hole with a probability of 0.71875 (71.8 per cent of the time) meaning equation (13.10) returns a value of 0.71875 for ?.

$$P^{=?}\Box(\mathbf{B}_{governor}\,\text{human2(hole)}). \tag{13.10}$$

The high chance of human 2 falling in the hole is caused by the robot's behaviour, moving into the far corner, as described above as its first move and hence placing the hole between itself and the second human when the human has also moved towards the hole.

13.5 Discussion

This chapter has served two key purposes. Firstly we have described how AJPF can be used, not as a model-checker in its own right, but as a tool to build a model of an agent system that can then be exported as input into another system. Secondly, in describing how this process is implemented we have thrown some light on the internal workings of AJPF which may be of interest to those seeking either to develop parts of the system themselves or to implement something similar for other languages.

What is the value of using AJPF to build models for other systems? As we have mentioned many times throughout this book, an advantage of AJPF is that it checks the behaviour of the implemented code, not that of a model of the code constructed by a human. A disadvantage of AJPF is that it is slow to build this model which, in turn, makes model-checking slow. We assert that using AJPF to generate the model removes many (though not all) of the concerns created when a human constructs a model of a system which they claim behaves as the system itself does – so using AJPF to construct the input for a model-checker from actual program code increases our level of assurance in the correctness of that code. However, as we saw in Section 13.2.1 AJPF does not run significantly faster when constructing a model as opposed to when it is constructing and checking a model. So what is the advantage here? While in an ideal world we would always state precisely the property that we wish to prove of a system, in reality, often constructing the correct property – and in particular identifying and specifying situations where the property does not hold but the system is still behaving correctly – is an iterative process. If the code itself is incorrect then clearly we would need to correct it, rebuild the model in AJPF, and export once more, but if the result of a failed model-checking attempt is simply a realisation that we need to refine our property then significant speed-ups can be achieved via this route.

Secondly, as we have shown with export to PRISM – the use of an external model-checker allows us to check properties that are not expressible in AJPF's own property specification language. This is likely to assist us in both in the verification of systems where compositional verification, as discussed in Chapter 11 is needed – imagine, for instance, exporting our AJPF model directly into the input language of UPPAAL for the platoon algorithm verifications we performed in that chapter – and can also assist in corroborative verification attempts where information from formal verification, simulation and physical testing combine and inform each other in constructing an assurance case; see (Webster et al., 2020). Here probabilistic results derived from the use of PRISM can be compared with statistical results generated by both simulation and physical experiments and, where discrepancies are revealed, work can be done to understand and reconcile those issues.

Part IV

Concluding Remarks

14

Verifiable Autonomous Systems

In this book we have advocated an approach to architecting verifiable autonomous systems by locating key high-level decisions in a declarative component based upon the BDI-model of agency and we have shown how that component can be verified.

It is undeniable, however, that most people's conception of an autonomous system, at least in 2023, when we write this, is typified by the 'driverless' cars we see in the media. While much of the software that controls such vehicles is proprietary, we do know that machine learning and deep neural networks are intrinsically involved in much of its operation and that the architecture of the system is such that it poses extreme challenges to verification. So an important question to be addressed is 'must this necessarily be the case?'. Can we only have autonomous systems with the sophistication, flexibility, and impressive performance of these driverless cars if we sacrifice our ability to perform all but the most trivial of verifications and instead must rely upon statistics derived from the number of hours driven without the need for human intervention to convince us that the car is safe, or at least safe enough?

This question is currently unanswerable, but we would argue that without making a serious attempt to architect our autonomous systems with verification in mind, we risk finding ourselves in a situation where we accept lower standards of safety because we simply have not explored the possible alternatives. While the automotive industry has a long history in which public acceptance has generally not required high degrees of assurance (although safety standards have nevertheless increased decade upon decade), other industries, such as the nuclear industry, do demand demonstrable evidence of safety. Our failure to understand how this can be delivered for autonomous systems risks becoming a barrier to development and adoption and potentially will prevent us from making use of technologies that will ultimately be beneficial.

Safety assurance tends to be an overriding concern in the development of autonomous systems, but we have also examined, in Chapter 10, how more general ethical reasoning might be incorporated in autonomous systems. In that chapter the reasoning was still primarily focused upon safety, but it is to be anticipated in the future that autonomous systems deployed in the home, such as assistive living robots, will be required to reason about issues such as privacy, dignity, and human autonomy. This is an area where not only is some form of verification of the ethics of such reasoning desirable, so too is a declarative approach that allows users and other stakeholders to examine, understand, and agree to the ethics of the system.

A key principle for ethical AI and, by extension, autonomous systems as evidenced in many publications (IEEE, 2017; Jobin et al., 2019; Winfield et al., 2021) is *transparency*. This concept has multiple interpretations from the provision of an *ethical black box* (Winfield and Jirotka, 2017) to log decisions, to the ability to provide human comprehensible explanations. However, a key observation, again, is that transparency has to be architected for. It cannot easily be retro-fitted to a deep neural network-based system. It seems probable to us that declarativity, transparency, and verifiability are concepts that naturally work together, and autonomous systems should be created to provide these features as much as possible.

This is not merely a plea that system architects, designers, and programmers consider how to create transparent and verifiable autonomous systems. It is clear that this cannot easily be done without appropriate *tools*. This book has focused primarily on the AJPF tool for model-checking agent decision-makers. While this tool is often quite slow, one of the advantages of its linkage with the GWENDOLEN programming language is that a programmer is not required to learn a specialised modelling language. Some understanding of the tool is necessary for effective use, but we would contend that, in many cases, this makes the verification of GWENDOLEN programs a straightforward matter allowing verification to become a part of the programming workflow, much as debugging tools are in other languages.

AJPF is not the only such tool aimed at enabling the verification of autonomous systems. Tools are being developed for analysing the behaviour of image classifiers (Huang et al., 2020), reasoning about control systems (Garoche, 2019), programming planning systems with defined formal properties (Lacerda et al., 2019), and validating both the models used by planning systems (Raimondi et al., 2009) and the plans produced (Howey et al., 2004). This is why the work in Chapter 11 is so critical. To truly verify an autonomous system, we need to consider all the software components that make up the system, verify each of them with the appropriate tools, and then combine those verifications together.

Not only do we need to develop the tools and theory to allow compositional verification of autonomous systems, but we must also require system engineers to create systems to which these tools can be applied.

15

The Future

Autonomous systems will be increasingly prevalent in our lives in the coming years and we should rightly ask about what kind of assurance we can gain about the behaviour of these systems. This book has primarily focused on the provision of assurance for one part of an autonomous system but what is the future for the area as a whole?

We identify key areas in need of future work:

1. We need integrated approaches to the verification of autonomous systems which account for the heterogenous nature of the software that makes up such systems and allows us to integrate the results of multiple verification tools. We outlined initial work in this area in Chapter 11. We also need approaches that integrate verifiability into all stages of the software life-cycle of these systems so that requirements and designs are created with verification in mind; the RoboStar tools (Cavalcanti, 2020) provide one approach for this kind of work. We also need *dynamic*, as well as *static*, forms of verification, reflecting the ever-changing environments in which our autonomous systems are expected to work; the work in Chapter 12 provides a start for our approach.

2. We need to better understand the properties we want these systems to have. Much work in this area, and indeed throughout this book, has focused on the safety of humans, but we also need to think about other ethical considerations, and formal properties that might apply to desiderata such as transparency and what formal properties *can* be established, for example, about the behaviour of deep neural networks even if we cannot necessarily prove that they always classify correctly. Work on capturing the required properties, together with the development of architectures and heterogeneous verification, is under way mapping a route to whole system assurance (Fisher et al., 2021).

3. We need regulatory and standards work that takes the many high-level principles for responsible or ethical AI as outlined in Jobin et al. (2019) and translates this into clear processes and guidelines to be followed in the design, development, and deployment of autonomous systems. Such work should account for the possibilities of formal verification while acknowledging the places where formal techniques currently struggle, and should develop a view on when and how more risky technologies can be deployed. For example, the IEEE's P7009 standard on 'Fail-safe Design for Autonomous Systems' (Farrell et al., 2021) is being developed targeting a particular, and critical, component allowing design and verification effort to be focused on that, rather than the whole system.

4. We need a better understanding of how autonomous systems interact with humans. Both in terms of variable autonomy in which at some points the system may hand control to the user and vice versa, and in terms of how a user's understanding of and trust in a system can affect the way the user interacts with it and what this means for outcomes. Much of this work comes under *validation* (the process of checking that the system we have designed is the one that is desired) but as our understanding of the area matures there will also be a role for verification: in checking that the system interacts with users in the correct way.

In the field of cognitive agents more work is needed to support features of autonomous systems, such as reasoning under uncertainty, actions with durations, resilience, long-term autonomy, and failure handling, and our verification methods and methodologies need to develop alongside these other advances.

Appendix A
Gwendolen Documentation

A.1 Tutorial 1: Introduction to Running Gwendolen Programs

This is the first in a series of tutorials on the use of the GWENDOLEN programming language. This tutorial covers the basics of running GWENDOLEN programs, the configuration files, perform goals and print actions. Files for this tutorial can be found in the `mcapl` distribution in the directory

```
src/examples/gwendolen/tutorials/tutorial1
```

The tutorials assume some familiarity with the Prolog programming language as well as the basics of running Java programs either at the command line or in Eclipse.

A.1.1 Hello World

In the tutorial directory you will find a GWENDOLEN program called `hello_world.gwen`. Its contents should look like Example A.1.

Example A.1

```
                                                                    1
GWENDOLEN                                                           2
                                                                    3
:name: hello                                                        4
:Initial Beliefs:                                                   5
:Initial Goals:                                                     6
   say_hello [perform]                                              7
:Plans:                                                             8
   +!say_hello [perform] : { T } ← print(hello);                   9
```

246

This can be understood as follows. Line 1 states the language in which the program is written (this is because the AIL allows us to create multi-agent systems from programs written in several different languages), in this case *GWENDOLEN*. Line 3 gives the name of the agent (hello). Line 4 starts the section for initial beliefs (there are none). Line 5 starts the section for initial goals and there is one, a *perform* goal to say_hello (we will cover the different varieties of goal in a later tutorial). Line 7 denotes the start of the agent plans. There is one plan which can be understood simply as *if the goal is to say hello, +!say_hello, then undertake the action* print (hello). There is a third component to the plan ({True}) which is a *guard* that must be true before the plan can be applied. In this case the guard is always true so the plan applies whenever the agent has a goal to perform +!say_hello.

Running the Program

To run the program you need to run the Java program ail.mas.AIL and supply it with a suitable configuration file as an argument. You will find an appropriate configuration file, hello_world.ail in the same directory as hello_world.gwen. You execute the program either from the command line, as above, or by using the Eclipse run-AIL configuration (with hello_world.ail selected in the Package Explorer window) as detailed in the MCAPL manual.

Run the program now.

A.1.2 The Configuration File

Open the configuration file, hello_world.ail, and you will see the following.

```
mas.file =
    /src/examples/gwendolen/tutorials/tutorial1/hello_world.gwen
mas.builder = gwendolen.GwendolenMASBuilder

env = ail.mas.DefaultEnvironment

log.warning = ail.mas.DefaultEnvironment
```

This is a very simple configuration file consisting of four items only. These describe:

mas.file gives the path to find the GWENDOLEN program to be executed.

mas.builder gives a Java class to be used to execute the file. In this case `gwendolen.GwendolenMASBuilder` parses a file containing one or more GWENDOLEN agents and compiles them into a multi-agent system.

env provides an environment for the agent to run in. In this case we use the default environment provided by the AIL.

log.warning sets the `ail.mas.DefaultEnvironment` class level of output. This provides a minimal level of output (namely, warnings only). We will see in later tutorials that it can be useful to prescribe more output than this.

A.1.3 Simple Exercises to Try

1. Change the filename of `hello_world.gwen` to something else (e.g., `hello.gwen`). Update `hello_world.ail` to reflect this change and check you can still run the program.
2. Edit the hello world program so it prints out `hi` instead of `hello`. Again, run and test.
3. Edit the hello world program so that the goal is called `hello` instead of `say_hello`. If you leave the plan unchanged, notice how the behaviour of the program changes. Before the next exercise, edit the program to return to the original behaviour of the agent.
4. Now change the plan to be

   ```
   +!say_hello [perform] : {True} <- print(hello), print(louise);
   ```

   and see how this changes the behaviour of the program.
5. Experiment with modifying the program to print out various different strings. Note that the parser cannot yet cope with whitespace in print statements (sorry!).

A.2 Tutorial 2: Simple Beliefs, Goals, and Actions

This is the second in a series of tutorials concerning the use of the GWENDOLEN programming language. This tutorial covers the basics of *beliefs*, *goals* and *actions* as they appear in GWENDOLEN.

The files for this tutorial can be found in the `mcapl` distribution in the directory

```
src/examples/gwendolen/tutorials/tutorial2
```

A.2.1 Pick Up Rubble

In the tutorial directory you will find a GWENDOLEN program called pickuprubble.gwen and its contents should look like Example A.2.

Example A.2

```
GWENDOLEN                                                  1
                                                           2
:name: robot                                               3
                                                           4
:Initial Beliefs:                                          5
                                                           6
:Initial Goals:                                            7
                                                           8
goto55 [perform]                                           9
                                                          10
:Plans:                                                   11
                                                          12
+!goto55 [perform] : { T } ← move_to(5,5);                13
                                                          14
+rubble(5,5): { T } ← lift_rubble;                        15
                                                          16
+holding(rubble): { T } ← print(done);                    17
```

This is a program describing a robot able to move around a simple grid based environment and pick up rubble. The robot can perform three actions in this environment, namely:

move_to(X,Y) moves to grid square (X,Y) and adds the belief at (X, Y).

lift_rubble attempts to pick up a piece of rubble and adds the belief holding(rubble) if there is indeed rubble at the robot's current location.

drop drops whatever the robot is currently holding and removes any beliefs about what the robot is holding.

The default actions (e.g., print) are also still available to the robot. The environment is constructed so there will be a block of rubble at grid square (5,5) which the robot will see if it is in square (5,5). When the robot picks something up it can see that it is holding the object. This environment is programmed in Java using the class gwendolen.tutorials.SearchAndRescueEnv.

The program in Example A.2 can now be understood as follows.

Line 1 again states the language in which the program is written.

Line 3 provides the name of the agent (`robot`).

Line 5 begins the section for initial beliefs (there are none).

Line 7 begins the section for initial goals; there is just one, a *perform* goal to `goto55`.

Line 11 denotes the start of the agent's plans; there are three. The first (line 13) states that in order to perform `goto55` the agent must move to square (5,5). The second (line 15) states that if the agent sees rubble at (5,5) it should lift the rubble, and the third (line 17) states that if the agent sees it is holding rubble then it should print 'done'.

There are three different sorts of syntax used here to distinguish between beliefs, goals and actions.

Beliefs are predicates, e.g., `rubble(5,5)`, preceded either by the '+' symbol (to indicate the addition of a belief) or the '-' symbol (to indicate the removal of a belief).

Goals are predicates preceded by an exclamation mark, e.g., `!goto55`. Again these are preceded either by the '+' symbol (to indicate the addition of a goal) or the '-' symbol (to indicate removal).

After the goal predicate there is also a label stating what *kind* of goal it is, either a *perform* goal or an *achieve* goal. We will discuss the difference between these soon.

Actions are also just predicates. Actions are performed externally to the agent and cannot be added or removed (they are just *done*).

Running the Program and Obtaining more detailed Log output

To run the program you need to call `ail.mas.AIL` and supply it with a suitable configuration file. You will find an appropriate configuration file, `pickuprubble.ail` in the same directory as `pickuprubble.gwen`. You can do this either from the command line or using the Eclipse `run-AIL` configuration as detailed in the MCAPL manual.

Run the program now.

As in Tutorial 1, all you see is the robot print the message 'done' once it has finished. However what has also happened is that the robot has moved to square (5,5), because of the *perform* goal. Once in square (5,5) it saw the rubble and so lifted it (thanks to the second plan). Once it had lifted the rubble it saw that it was holding rubble and printed 'done' (thanks to the third plan).

You can obtain more information about the execution of the program by changing the logging information in the configuration file. Open the configuration file and change

```
log.warning = ail.mas.DefaultEnvironment
```

to

```
log.info = ail.mas.DefaultEnvironment
```

Once you execute the program again, you will see logging information printed out about each action the robot takes.

If you also add the line

```
log.format = brief
```

to the configuration file you will get the log messages, but in a briefer form.

A.2.2 Perform and Achieve Goals

The program `pickuprubble_achieve.gwen` provides a slightly more complex version of the rubble lifting robot and also introduces some new concepts. It is shown in Example A.3

Example A.3

GWENDOLEN	1
	2
:**name**: robot	3
	4
:**Initial Beliefs**:	5
possible_rubble(1,1)	6
possible_rubble(3,3)	7
possible_rubble(5,5)	8
	9
:**Initial Goals**:	10
holding(rubble) [achieve]	11
	12
:**Plans**:	13
+!holding(rubble) [achieve] :	14
{B possible_rubble(X,Y), ~B no_rubble(X,Y)} ←	15
move_to(X,Y);	
	16
+at(X, Y) : {~B rubble(X,Y)} ← +no_rubble(X,Y);	17
	18
+rubble(X,Y): {B at(X,Y)} ← lift_rubble;	19
	20
+holding(rubble): {⊤} ← print(done);	21

The first changes are in lines 6–8. Here we have a list of initial beliefs. The agent believes there may possibly be rubble in one of three squares (1,1), (3,3) or (5,5). As we know, in the environment, there is actually only rubble in square (5,5).

The next change is in line 11. Here, instead of a *perform* goal, goto55 [perform] there is an *achieve* goal, holding(rubble) [achieve]. The difference between perform goals and achieve goals is as follows.

- When an agent adds a perform goal it searches for a plan for that goal, executes the plan and then drops the goal; it does not check that the plan was successful.

- When an agent adds an achieve goal it searches for a plan for that goal, executes the plan and then checks to see if it now has a belief corresponding to the goal. If it has no such beliefs it searches for a plan again, while if it does have such a belief it then drops the goal.

In the case of the above program the robot will continue executing the plan for achieving holding(rubble) until it actually believes that it is holding some rubble.

On lines 14 and 15, you can see the plan for this goal. This plan no longer has a trivial guard. Instead the plan only applies if the agent believes that there is possible rubble in some square (X,Y) and it does not (the '∼' symbol) believe there is no rubble in that square. If it can find such a square then the robot moves to it. The idea is that the robot will check each of the possible rubble squares in turn until it successfully finds and lifts some rubble. Note that, as in Prolog, we are using capital letters for variables that can be unified against beliefs.

The plan on line 17 gets the robot to add the belief no_rubble(X,Y) if it is at some square, (X,Y), and it cannot see any rubble there. By this means the plan in lines 14 and 15 will be forced to pick a different square next time it executes. Up until now all the plans we have used have simply executed actions in the plan body. This one adds a belief.

The plan at line 19 is similar to the plan in line 15 of Example A.2 only in this case we are using variables for the rubble coordinates rather than giving it the explicit coordinates (5,5).

You can run this program using the pickuprubble_achieve.ail configuration file.

A.2.3 Simple Exercises to Try

1. Instead of having the robot print 'done' once it has the rubble, get it to move to square (2,2) and then drop the rubble.

Hint: you may find you need to add a 'housekeeping' belief that the rubble has been moved to prevent the robot from immediately picking up the rubble again once it has been dropped.

2. Rewrite the program so that instead of starting with an achievement goal 'holding(rubble)', it starts with an achievement goal 'rubble(2,2)' – that is, the agent wants to believe that there is rubble in square (2,2).

   Hint: you may want to reuse the plan for achieving 'holding(rubble)' by setting it up as a subgoal. You can use this by adding the command +!holding(rubble)[achieve] in the body of a plan.

Sample solutions for these two exercises can be found at
gwendolen/examples/tutorials/tutorial2/answers

A.3 Tutorial 3: Plan Guards and Reasoning Rules

This is the third in a series of tutorials on the use of the GWENDOLEN programming language. This tutorial covers the use of Prolog-style computation rules as they appear in GWENDOLEN and also looks at plan guards in a little more detail.

Files for this tutorial can be found in the mcapl distribution in the directory

src/examples/gwendolen/tutorials/tutorial3

A.3.1 Pick Up Rubble (Again)

In the tutorial directory, you will find the GWENDOLEN program pickuprubble_achieve.gwen that looks very familiar. Its contents should look like Example A.4.

Example A.4

```
GWENDOLEN                                                        1
                                                                2
:name: robot                                                    3
                                                                4
:Initial Beliefs:                                               5
   possible_rubble(1,1)                                         6
   possible_rubble(3,3)                                         7
   possible_rubble(5,5)                                         8
                                                                9
:Reasoning Rules:                                               10
   square_to_check(X,Y) :- possible_rubble(X,Y),               11
```

```
      ~ no_rubble(X,Y);                                            12
                                                                   13
: Initial  Goals:                                                  14
  holding(rubble) [achieve]                                        15
                                                                   16
: Plans:                                                           17
  +!holding(rubble) [achieve]  :  {B square_to_check(X,Y)}         18
      ←    move_to(X,Y);                                           19
  +at(X,Y)  :  {~B rubble(X,Y)}  ←  +no_rubble(X,Y);               20
  +rubble(X,Y):  {B at(X,Y)}  ←  lift_rubble;                      21
  +holding(rubble):  { T }  ←  print(done);                        22
```

This is very similar to the second program in Tutorial 2. However, instead of
having

```
{B possible_rubble(X,Y),  ~B no_rubble(X,Y)}
```

as the guard to the first plan we have B square_to_check(X, Y) as the
guard.

We now reason about whether there is a square to check using the Prolog
style rule on line 11. The syntax is very similar to Prolog syntax but there are
a few differences. We use the symbol, ~, to indicate 'not' and we cannot use
'cuts' to control backtracking.[1]

A.3.2 Using Prolog Lists

You can use Prolog-style list structures in GWENDOLEN programs. Example A.5
shows a variation of the previous example using lists.

Example A.5

```
: name:  robot                                                     1
                                                                   2
: Initial  Beliefs:                                                3
  possible_rubble([sq(1,1),  sq(3,3),  sq(5,5)])                   4
                                                                   5
: Reasoning  Rules:                                                6
  square_to_check(X,Y)  :−  possible_rubble(L),                    7
      check_rubble(L,X,Y);                                         8
                                                                   9
```

---

[1] N.B. There is no reason in principle why we could not use *cut*, it just has not yet been
implemented.

```
check_rubble([sq(X,Y) | T],X,Y) :- ~no_rubble(X,Y);          10
check_rubble([sq(X,Y) | T],X1,Y1) :-  no_rubble(X,Y),        11
   check_rubble(T,X1,Y1);                                    12
                                                             13
:Initial Goals:                                              14
  holding(rubble) [achieve]                                  15
                                                             16
:Plans:                                                      17
  +!holding(rubble) [achieve]  : {B square_to_check(X,Y)}    18
    ←  move_to(X,Y);                                         19
  +at(X,Y)  : {~B rubble(X,Y)} ← +no_rubble(X,Y);           20
  +rubble(X,Y): {B at(X,Y)} ←  lift_rubble;                 21
  +holding(rubble): { T } ←  print(done);                   22
```

Prolog list structures can also be used in GWENDOLEN plans and a recursive style plan may sometimes provide a more efficient solution than the kind of program that relies on the failure of a plan to achieve a goal, to re-trigger the plan. Example A.6 provides an example of this style of programming where the *achieve goal* calls a *perform goal* that recurses through the list of squares, one at a time.

Example A.6

```
:name: robot                                                 1
                                                             2
:Initial Beliefs:                                            3
  possible_rubble([sq(1,1), sq(3,3), sq(5,5)])              4
                                                             5
:Reasoning Rules:                                            6
  rubble_in_current :- at(X,Y), rubble(X,Y);                7
                                                             8
:Initial Goals:                                              9
  holding(rubble) [achieve]                                  10
                                                             11
:Plans:                                                      12
  +!holding(rubble) [achieve]  : {B possible_rubble(L)} ←   13
    +! check_all_squares(L) [perform];                       14
                                                             15
  +!check_all_squares([]) [perform] : { T } ← print(done);  16
  +!check_all_squares([sq(X,Y) | T]) :                       17
    {~B rubble_in_current} ←                                 18
      move_to(X,Y),                                          19
      +!check_all_squares(T) [perform];                      20
  +!check_all_squares([sq(X,Y) | T]) :                       21
    {B rubble_in_current} ←  print(done);                   22
                                                             23
```

```
+at(X,Y) : { ∼B rubble(X,Y)} ← +no_rubble(X,Y);          24
                                                          25
+rubble(X,Y): {B at(X,Y)} ← lift_rubble;                  26
```

A.3.3 More Complex Prolog Reasoning: Grouping Predicates under a Negation

The program pickuprubble_grouping.gwen shows more complex use of *Reasoning Rules* including some syntax not available in Prolog. This is shown in Listing A.7.

Example A.7

```
GWENDOLEN                                                 1
                                                          2
:name: robot                                              3
                                                          4
:Initial Beliefs:                                         5
  possible_rubble(1,1)                                    6
  possible_rubble(3,3)                                    7
  possible_rubble(5,5)                                    8
                                                          9
:Reasoning Rules:                                         10
  square_to_check(X,Y) :− possible_rubble(X,Y),           11
    ∼ no_rubble(X,Y);                                     12
  done :− holding(rubble);                                13
  done :− ∼ (possible_rubble(X,Y), ∼ no_rubble(X,Y));    14
                                                          15
:Initial Goals:                                           16
  done [achieve]                                          17
                                                          18
:Plans:                                                   19
  +!done [achieve] : {B square_to_check(X,Y)}             20
    ← move_to(X,Y);                                       21
                                                          22
  +at(X,Y) : { ∼B rubble(X,Y)} ← +no_rubble(X,Y);         23
                                                          24
  +rubble(X,Y): {B at(X,Y)} ← lift_rubble;                25
                                                          26
  +holding(rubble): { ⊤ } ← print(done);                  27
```

In this program the agent's goal is to achieve 'done'. It achieves this either if it is holding rubble (deduced using the code on line 13), or if there is no square it thinks may possibly contain rubble that has no rubble in it (deduced using the code on line 14).

The rule on line 14

```
done :- ~ (possible_rubble(X,Y), ~no_rubble(X,Y));
```

is not standard Prolog syntax. Instead, we here group the two predicates `possible_rubble(X,Y)` and `~no_rubble(X,Y)` (from 'square_to_check') together using brackets and then negate the whole concept (i.e., there are no squares left to check).

Simple Exercises to Try

1. Try removing the initial belief that there is possible rubble in square (5,5). You should find that the program still completes and prints out done.
2. Try replacing the rule on line 14 with one that instead refers to `square_to_check`.

A.3.4 Using Goals in Plan Guards

The program `pickuprubble_goal.gwen` shows how reasoning rules can be used to reason about both goals and beliefs. This is shown in Example A.8.

Example A.8

```
GWENDOLEN                                                          1
                                                                   2
:name: robot                                                       3
                                                                   4
:Initial Beliefs:                                                  5
  possible_rubble(1,1)                                             6
  possible_rubble(3,3)                                             7
  possible_rubble(5,5)                                             8
                                                                   9
:Initial Goals:                                                   10
  rubble(2,2) [achieve]                                           11
                                                                  12
:Plans:                                                           13
  +!rubble(2,2) [achieve]: {⊤} ←                                  14
      +! holding(rubble)[achieve],  move_to(2,2),  drop;          15
                                                                  16
  +!holding(rubble) [achieve] :                                   17
      {B possible_rubble(X,Y),  ~B no_rubble(X,Y)}                18
        ←  move_to(X,Y);                                          19
                                                                  20
  +at(X,Y) : {~B rubble(X,Y)} ← +no_rubble(X,Y);                  21
```

```
                                                                        22
+rubble(X,Y):  {B at(X,Y),  G  holding(rubble)  [achieve]}              23
    ←  lift_rubble;                                                     24
```

Recall that in the exercises at the end of Tutorial 2 we had to use a belief to prevent the robot immediately picking up the rubble after it had put it down. Here we have instead added

```
        G holding(rubble) [achieve]
```

as a guard to the plan that is activated when the robot sees some rubble. In this case it only picks up the rubble if it has goal to be holding rubble.

A.3.5 Reasoning about Beliefs and Goals

The program `pickuprubble_goalat.gwen` shows how goals can be used in plan guards. This is shown in Example A.9.

Example A.9

```
GWENDOLEN                                                               1
                                                                        2
:name:  robot                                                           3
                                                                        4
:Initial  Beliefs:                                                      5
    possible_rubble(1,1)                                                6
    possible_rubble(3,3)                                                7
    possible_rubble(5,5)                                                8
                                                                        9
:Reasoning  Rules:                                                      10
    rubble_at_22  :−  holding(rubble),  at(2,2);                        11
                                                                        12
:Initial  Goals:                                                        13
    at(2,2) [achieve]                                                   14
                                                                        15
:Plans:                                                                 16
    +!at(X,Y) [achieve]: {⊤} ← +! holding(rubble)[achieve],            17
        move_to(X,Y);                                                   18
                                                                        19
    +!holding(rubble)  [achieve]  :                                     20
        {B possible_rubble(X,Y),  ∼B no_rubble(X,Y)}                    21
            ←  move_to(X,Y);                                            22
                                                                        23
    +at(X,Y) : { ∼B rubble(X,Y),  ∼B rubble_at_22}                     24
        ←  +no_rubble(X,Y);                                             25
```

```
+at(X,Y) : {B rubble_at_22} ← drop;                      26
                                                          27
+rubble(X,Y): {B at(X,Y), G rubble_at_22 [achieve]}      28
    ← lift_rubble;                                        29
```

Here the reasoning rule on line 11 is used both in the plan on line 24, in order to reason about whether the robot is holding the rubble at square (2,2), *and* in the plan on line 28 to deduce that the robot has a goal to get the rubble to square (2,2) from the fact that it has a goal to be holding rubble (added on line 17) *and* a goal to be at (2,2) (the initial goal).

Note that we cannot use reasoning rules to break down a goal into subgoals. If you gave the robot the initial goal `rubble_at_22` you would need to provide a plan specifically for `rubble_at_22`. It is no good providing a plan for holding rubble and a plan for being at (2,2) and then expecting the robot to compose these sensibly in order to achieve `rubble_at_22`.

Try changing the agent's initial goal to `rubble_at_22 [achieve]` without changing anything else in the program. You should see a warning generated that the agent cannot find a plan for the goal. At this point the program will fail to terminate. When GWENDOLEN cannot find a plan for a goal it cycles infinitely looking a plan to handle a failed goal (most programs do not include one of these). *You will need to explicitly terminate the program* (using control-C at the command line or by clicking the red stop square in Eclipse).

A.3.6 Some Simple Programs to Try

N.B. The environment `gwendolen.tutorials.SearchAndRescueEnv` situates rubble at both (5,5) and (3,4).

1. Write a program to make the robot check every square in a 5 × 5 grid (i.e., (1,1), (1,2), (1,3), etc.), until it finds some rubble at which point it stops. Try implementing this program both with, and without, using lists in plans. Not that, for the list version you may need to insert a plan that asserts a belief once the rubble is seen, in order to ensure the robot does not progress through the squares too rapidly. (See the comment about `do_nothing` in the next exercise and further discussion of this in later tutorials.)

2. Write a program to make the robot search every square in a 5 × 5 grid (i.e., (1,1), (1,2), etc.) taking all the rubble it finds to the square (2,2) until it believes there is only rubble in square (2,2).

Hints:

(a) You may see the warning similar to:

```
ail...GenerateApplicablePlansEmptyProblemGoal[WARNING|main|...
Warning no applicable plan for goal _aall_squares_checked()
```

As noted above, this warning appears if the agent cannot find any plan to achieve a goal. Sometimes this arises because of bugs in the code, but it can also happen if the agent has not had a chance to process all new perceptions/beliefs before it once again looks for a plan to achieve a goal (we will talk about this further in later tutorials).

In such cases, it may be worth adding an action do_nothing into your plan, this will act to delay the next time the agent attempts to achieve the goal giving it time to process all new beliefs.

(b) You may need to include at (2,2) in your goal in some way to ensure the agent actually takes the final piece of rubble to square (2,2).

Sample solutions for the above exercises can be found in gwendolen/examples/tutorials/tutorial3/answers

A.4 Tutorial 4: Troubleshooting

This is the fourth in a series of tutorials on the use of the GWENDOLEN programming language. This tutorial looks at some of the aspects that typically cause errors in GWENDOLEN programs and how to identify and fix such errors.

For this tutorial we will be working with files from previous tutorials but editing them to deliberately introduce errors. You may wish to create a separate folder, tutorial4, for this work and copy files into it. (Remember to update the paths in your configuration files if you do so.)

While GWENDOLEN does not have its own debugger, you can get a long way using error outputs and logging information.

A.4.1 Path Errors

If you supply the wrong path or filename in a configuration file GWENDOLEN will not be able to find the program you want to run. You will see an error similar to the following:

```
ail.mas.AIL[SEVERE|main|3:24:57]: Could not find file.  Checked:
 /src/examples/gwendolen/tutorials/tutorial3/pickup.gwen,
 /Users/lad/src/examples/gwendolen/tutorials/tutorial3/pickup.gwen,
 /Users/lad/mcapl/src/examples/.../tutorial3/pickup.gwen
```

GWENDOLEN looks for program files at the following, in order.

1. The absolute path given in the configuration file, for example

   `/src/examples/gwendolen/tutorials/tutorial3/pickup.gwen`
   above.

2. The path from the HOME environment variable (normally the user's home directory on Unix systems), for example

   `/Users/lad/src/examples/gwendolen/tutorials/tutorial3/pickup.gwen`
   above.

3. The path from the directory from which the Java program `ail.mas.AIL` is called, for example

   `/Users/lad/mcapl/src/examples/.../tutorial3/pickup.gwen` above.

4. Finally, the path from AJPF_HOME if that environment variable has been set – not shown above.

These should provide sufficient information to appropriately correct the path name.

A.4.2 Parsing Errors

Parsing errors typically arise because of failures to punctuate your program correctly, such as failing to close brackets, missing out commas or semi-colons, and so on. For example, below is the output that arises if you remove the comma between `possible_rubble(X,Y)` and `~no_rubble(X,Y)` in `pickuprubble_achieve.gwen` from Tutorial 3.

```
line 36:47 mismatched input '~' expecting SEMI
java.lang.NullPointerException
at ail.syntax.ast.Abstract_Rule.toMCAPL(Abstract_Rule.java:108)
at gwendolen.syntax.ast.Abstract_GwendolenAgent.addStructures(...
at gwendolen.syntax.ast.Abstract_GwendolenAgent.toMCAPL(Abstra...
at gwendolen.syntax.ast.Abstract_GwendolenAgent.toMCAPL(Abstra...
at ail.syntax.ast.Abstract_MAS.toMCAPL(Abstract_MAS.java:117)
at gwendolen.GwendolenMASBuilder.getMAS(GwendolenMASBuilder...
at ail.mas.AIL.AILSetup(AIL.java:80)
at ail.mas.AIL.runAIL(AIL.java:61)
at ail.mas.AIL.main(AIL.java:49)
ail.mas.AIL[SEVERE|main|3:15:19]: null
```

The first line of this output is from the parser. This identifies the line number (36) and character in the line (47) where the error was first noticed. It highlights the character that has caused the problem, '~', and then makes a guess at what it *should* have been. In this case the guess is incorrect. It suggests a semi-colon, SEMI, when a comma is actually needed. This first line is frequently the most useful piece of output from parsing errors.

We then have a Java stack trace because, in this case, the parse error has caused the whole program to fail. At the end is a log message from the Java class `ail.mas.AIL`.

It should be noted that parsing errors do not always cause the program to crash. For instance, if we delete the comma from between X and Y in the guard of the first plan of this program we get the following output:

```
line 44:51 extraneous input 'Y' expecting CLOSE
 ....GenerateApplicablePlansEmptyProblemGoal[WARNING|main|...
Warning no applicable plan for goal _aholding(rubble)()
```

In this case we once again get (some) useful output from the parser giving us the line and position in the line where the error occurred. This is followed by a warning that no plan can be found to match the goal `holding(rubble)` as this is the plan that did not parse.

Further Exercises

Experiment with adding and deleting syntax from your existing programming files and get used to the kinds of parsing errors that they generate. Remember that where a

```
no applicable plan
```

warning is generated you will often need to manually stop the program execution.

A.4.3 Why Isn't My Plan Applicable?

As mentioned in Tutorial 3, a plan can sometimes fail because the agent has not had time to process incoming beliefs and perceptions. We can get more information about the agent's operation by using log messages. Add the line

```
log.fine = ail.semantics.AILAgent
```

to the configuration file for the sample solution to Exercise 5.2 from Tutorial 3. This is in

```
.../tutorial3/answers/pickuprubble_ex5.2.ail
```

Adding this generates a *lot* of output. If you are using Eclipse you may need to set Console output to unlimited in Eclipse → Preferences → Run/Debug → Console. The output should start

```
ail.semantics.AILAgent[FINE|main|4:03:27]: Applying Perceive
ail.semantics.AILAgent[FINE|main|4:03:27]: robot
=============
After Stage StageE :
```

```
[square/2-square(1,1), square(1,2), square(1,3), square(1,4), ...
square(2,1), square(2,2), square(2,3), square(2,4), square(2,5),
square(3,1), square(3,2), square(3,3), square(3,4), square(3,5),
square(4,1), square(4,2), square(4,3), square(4,4), square(4,5),
square(5,1), square(5,2), square(5,3), square(5,4), square(5,5), ]
[]
[]
source(self)::
   *  start||True||+!_aall_squares_checked()()||[]
[]
```

This tells us that the agent is applying the Perceive rule from the agent's *reasoning cycle* called (we will discuss the reasoning cycle in a later tutorial).

Next we get the current state of the agent. It is called, robot, and we have a list of its beliefs (lots of beliefs about squares), then a list of goals (none at the start because it has not yet added the initial goal) and then a list of sent messages (also initially empty) and then its intentions. In this case the initial intention is the start intention and the intention is to acquire the goal all_squares_checked which is an achievement goal (denoted by _a at the start of the goal name) – again we will cover intentions in a later tutorial.

A little further on in the output the agent adds this as a goal:

```
ail.semantics.AILAgent[FINE|main|4:10:45]: Applying Handle Add ...
ail.semantics.AILAgent[FINE|main|4:10:45]: robot
=============
After Stage StageD :
[square/2-square(1,1), square(1,2), square(1,3), square(1,4), ...
[all_squares_checked/0-[_aall_squares_checked()]]
[]
source(self)::
   *  +!_aall_squares_checked()||True||npy()||[]
   *  start||True||+!_aall_squares_checked()()||[]
[]
```

So you can see that all_squares_checked now appears as a goal in the goal list. If we remove the action do_nothing from the first plan in pickuprubble_ex5.2.gwen then we end up with repeating output of the form:

```
ail.semantics.AILAgent[FINE|main|4:20:16]: Applying Generate App...
ail.semantics.AILAgent[FINE|main|4:20:16]: robot
=============
After Stage StageB :
[at/2-at(5,5), ,
checked/2-checked(1,1), checked(1,2), checked(1,3), ...
rubble/2-rubble(2,2), ,
square/2-square(1,1), square(1,2), square(1,3), square(1,4), ...
[all_squares_checked/0-[_aall_squares_checked()]]
[]
source(self)::
   *  x!_aall_squares_checked()||True||npy()||[]
```

```
*   +!_aall_squares_checked()||True||npy()|||[]
*   start||True||+!_aall_squares_checked()()|||[]
```

Here, x!_aall_squares_checked()||True||npy()|||[] indicates that there is some problem with the goal and that the agent is seeking to handle this. Finding where this problem first occurred in all the output is something of a chore though it can sometimes be possible to search forwards through the output for the first occurrence of x!_ or for the Warning message. Here we see the agent is in the following state:

```
ail.semantics.operationalrules.GenerateApplicablePlansEmptyProb...
ail.semantics.AILAgent[FINE|main|4:20:15]: Applying Generate Ap...
ail.semantics.AILAgent[FINE|main|4:20:15]: robot
=============
After Stage StageB :
[at/2-at(5,5), ,
checked/2-checked(1,1), checked(1,2), checked(1,3), ...
rubble/2-rubble(2,2), rubble(5,5), ,
square/2-square(1,1), square(1,2), square(1,3), square(1,4), ...
[all_squares_checked/0-[_aall_squares_checked()]]
[]
source(self)::
    *   +!_aall_squares_checked()||True||npy()|||[]
    *   start||True||+!_aall_squares_checked()()|||[]

[source(self)::
    *   +checked(5,5)||True||npy()|||[]
, source(percept)::
    *   start||True||-rubble(5,5)()|||[]
, source(percept)::
    *   start||True||+holding(rubble)()|||[]
]
```

Here we see the agent believes it is at square (5,5). It believes it has checked all the squares, but it does not yet believe it is holding any rubble. However, it *does* have an intention to hold rubble:

```
source(percept)::
    *   start||True||+holding(rubble)()|||[]
```

though it has not processed this and so has not yet added holding(rubble) to its belief base.

As you learn more about GWENDOLEN, the reasoning cycle, and intentions, you will be able to get more information from this output. However, for the moment it is important to note that this log information can be useful for seeing exactly what is in the agent's belief base and goal base at any time.

Some Further Exercises

Re-run some of your other programs with ail.semantics.AILAgent set at log level fine to get a feel for how an agent's beliefs and goals change as the program executes.

A.4.4 Tracing the Execution of Reasoning Rules

Another logger that can be useful is the one that traces the application of Prolog reasoning rules. This can also be useful for working out why a plan that *should* apply apparently does not. Try adding the line

```
log.fine = ail.syntax.EvaluationAndRuleBaseIterator
```

to `pickuprubble_achieve.ail` in Tutorial 3. If you now run the program you will get a lot of information about the unification of the reasoning rule starting with (note that some parts of the output have been elided with . . .:

```
... Checking unification of holding(rubble)() with unifier []
... Checking unification of square_to_check(X,Y)() with unifier []
... Looking for a rule match for square_to_check(X0,Y0) :- ...
... Checking unification of square_to_check(X,Y)() with unifier []
... Checking ... possible_rubble(X0,Y0) with unifier
                        [X-_VC1, X0-_VC1, Y-_VC2, Y0-_VC2]
... ... of possible_rubble(X0,Y0) and <possible_rubble(1,1), >
... Unifier for possible_rubble(X0,Y0) and <possible_rubble(1,1), >
                        is [X-1, X0-1, Y-1, Y0-1]
... ... no_rubble(X0,Y0) with unifier [X-1, X0-1, Y-1, Y0-1]
... square_to_check(X,Y)() matches the head of a rule.
... Rule instantiated with [X-1, X0-1, Y-1, Y0-1]
... Checking unification of square_to_check(X,Y)() with unifier []
... Looking for a rule match for square_to_check(X0,Y0) :- ...
... Checking unification of square_to_check(X,Y)() with unifier []
... Checking unification of possible_rubble(X0,Y0) with unifier ...
... Checking unification of possible_rubble(X0,Y0) and ...
... Unifier for possible_rubble(X0,Y0) and <possible_ ...
... Checking unification of no_rubble(X0,Y0) with unifier [X-1, ...
... square_to_check(X,Y)() matches the head of a rule.
... Rule instantiated with [X-1, X0-1, Y-1, Y0-1]
... : robot done move_to(1,1)
```

This is the selection process for the first plan in the program. We will discuss the execution line by line.

1. First it unifies with the achieve goal `holding(rubble)`. This does not instantiate any variables so there is an empty unifier, `[]`.

2. Then it checks the plan guard which is B `square_to_check(X,Y)`.

3. Since there is nothing in the belief base about this, but there is a reasoning rule, the execution now looks for a unifier between these. Notice how it has renamed the variables in the rule to X0 and Y0 – this is to avoid errors arising from unsuccessful unification explorations.

4. It then attempts to unify B `square_to_check(X,Y)` with the head of this rule.

5. As a result of this unification X and X0 are unified and Y and Y0 are unified. For technical reasons these are unified via *variable clusters*, VC1 and VC2 respectively.

6. It then checks the body of the rule starting by looking for something to unify with

```
possible_rubble(X0,Y0).
```

It finds the belief possible_rubble(1,1) which can unify with the above.

7. The unifier is reported, and all the variables are now unified with the number 1.

8. The system then checks to see if no_rubble(X0,Y0) matches with *anything* using this unifier. The rule will fail if it *does* actually match because this predicate was negated.

9. It does not match, so the negated rule *has* matched.

10. With everything unified to 1.

11. The process then repeats because of the way the reasoning rule processes transitions.

If we look later in the trace we can see the same process being run after no_rubble(1,1) was added to the belief base.

```
... Checking unification of square_to_check(X,Y)() with unifier []
... Looking for a rule match for square_to_check(X0,Y0) :- ...
... Checking unification of square_to_check(X,Y)() with unifier []
... Checking ... possible_rubble(X0,Y0) with unifier
                        [X-_VC5, X0-_VC5, Y-_VC6, Y0-_VC6]
... Checking unification of possible_rubble(X0,Y0) and
                        <possible_rubble(1,1), >
... Unifier for possible_rubble(X0,Y0) and ...
                        is [X-1, X0-1, Y-1, Y0-1]
... Checking unification of no_rubble(X0,Y0) with unifier
                        [X-1, X0-1, Y-1, Y0-1]
... Checking unification of no_rubble(X0,Y0) and <no_rubble(1,1),
... Unifier for no_rubble(X0,Y0) and <no_rubble(1,1), > is
                        [X-1, X0-1, Y-1, Y0-1]
... Checking unification of possible_rubble(X0,Y0) with unifier
                        [X-_VC5, X0-_VC5, Y-_VC6, Y0-_VC6]
... Checking unification of possible_rubble(X0,Y0) and
                        <possible_rubble(3,3), >
... Unifier for possible_rubble(X0,Y0) and <possible_rubble(3,3),
                        is [X-3, X0-3, Y-3, Y0-3]
... Checking unification of no_rubble(X0,Y0) with unifier
                        [X-3, X0-3, Y-3, Y0-3]
... Checking unification of no_rubble(X0,Y0) and <no_rubble(1,1),
... square_to_check(X,Y)() matches the head of a rule.
... Rule instantiated with [X-3, X0-3, Y-3, Y0-3]
```

Here, after a unifier is found for `no_rubble(1,1)`, that unifier for the rule has failed and the process backtracks to look for a different unifier for

`possible_rubble(X0,Y0)`.

In this instance (3,3) is found and so the rule succeeds.

A.4.5 Conclusion

This tutorial has provided some basic tools to be used for tracking errors in your GWENDOLEN programs. Although the logging facilities generate a *lot* of output that can be tiresome to read through, they are occasionally very useful for working out what is actually going wrong within a program. We will look at further debugging possibilities after we have covered the GWENDOLEN reasoning cycle in a tutorial.

A.5 Tutorial 5: Events and Intentions

This is the fifth in a series of tutorials on the use of the GWENDOLEN programming language. This tutorial looks in more depth at the GWENDOLEN concepts of *Event* and *Intention*. It is primarily theoretical but these will be important concepts for future tutorials.

For this tutorial we will be working with files from previous tutorials. You may wish to create a separate folder, `tutorial5`, for this work and copy files into it. Remember to update the paths in your configuration files if you do so.

GWENDOLEN does *not* have its own debugger, however you can get a long way using error outputs and logging information, as seen in Tutorial 4.

A.5.1 AIL: The Agent Infrastructure Layer

GWENDOLEN is implemented using the AIL Toolkit. This is mostly irrelevant to the programming of GWENDOLEN agents, but it can be useful in understanding some of the logging output that you may wish to use for debugging, since the logging is based around the underlying Java data structures rather than their specific implementation in GWENDOLEN.

The following discussion of intentions in the AIL is taken from Dennis et al. (2012).

A.5.2 Intentions

AIL's most complex data structure is that which represents an *intention*. BDI languages use intentions to store the *intended means* for achieving goals – this is generally represented as some from of *deed stack* (deeds include actions, belief updates, and the commitment to undertake goals). Intention structures in BDI languages may also maintain information about the (sub-) goal they are intended to achieve or the event that triggered them. In AIL, we aggregate this information together: an intention becomes a stack of tuples of an event, a guard, a deed, and a unifier. This AIL intention data structure is most simply viewed as a tabular structure consisting of four columns in which we record events (new perceptions, goals committed to and so forth), deeds (a plan of future actions, belief updates, goal commitments, etc.), guards (which must be true before a deed can be performed) and unifiers. These columns form an event stack, a deed stack, a guard stack, and a unifier stack. Rows associate a particular deed with the event that has caused the deed to be placed on the intention, a guard which must be believed before the deed can be executed, and a unifier. New events are associated with an empty deed, ϵ.

Example The following shows the full structure for a single intention to 'clean a room'. $!g$ indicates the goal g, and $+!g$ indicates the commitment to achieve that goal (i.e., a new goal that g becomes true is adopted). As usual, constants are shown starting with lower case letters, and variables with upper case letters.

event	guard	deed	unifier
`+!clean()`	`dirty(Room)`	`+!goto(Room)`	`Room = room1`
`+!clean()`	$\top$	`+!vacuum(Room)`	`Room = room1`

This intention has been triggered by a desire to clean – the commitment to the goal `clean()` is the trigger event for both rows in the intention. An intention is processed from top to bottom so we see here that the agent first intends to commit to the goal `goto(Room)`, where `Room` is to be unified with `room1`. It will only commit to this goal if it believes the (guard) statement, `dirty(Room)`. Once it has committed to that goal it then commits to the goal `vacuum(Room)`. In many languages the process of committing to a goal causes an expansion of the intention stack, pushing more deeds on it to be processed. So `goto(Room)` may be expanded *before* the agent commits to vacuuming the room. In this case the above intention might become

event	guard	deed	unifier
`+!goto(Room)`	$\top$	`+!planRoute(Room, Route)`	`Room = room1`
`+!goto(Room)`	$\top$	`+!follow(Route)`	`Room = room1`
`+!goto(Room)`	$\top$	`+!enter(Room)`	`Room = room1`
`+!clean()`	$\top$	`+!vacuum(Room)`	`Room = room1`

At any moment, we assume there is a *current intention* which is the one being processed at that time. The function S_{int} (implemented as a method in AIL) may be used to select an intention. By default, this chooses the first intention from the queue, though this choice may be overridden for specific languages and applications. Intentions can be *suspended* which allows further heuristic control. A suspended intention is, by default, *not* selected by S_{int}. Typically an intention will remain suspended until some trigger condition occurs, such as a message being received. Many operational semantics rules (such as those involved with perception) resume *all* intentions – this allows suspension conditions to be re-checked.

A.5.3 Events

Events are things that occur within the system to which an agent may wish to react. Typically we think of these as changes in beliefs or new commitments to goals. In many (though not all) agent programming languages, events trigger plans (i.e., a plan might be selected for execution only when the corresponding event has taken place).

In AIL there is a special event, 'start', that is used to invoke an intention which is not triggered by anything specific. This is mainly used for bootstrapping the initial goals of an agent – the intention begins as a start intention with the deed to commit to a goal. In some languages the belief changes caused by perception are also treated in this way. Rather than being added directly to the belief base, in AIL such beliefs are assigned to intentions with the event start and then added to the belief base when the intention is actually executed.

A.5.4 Intentions in GWENDOLEN

Let us recall some of the logging output generated as part of Tutorial 4.

```
ail.semantics.AILAgent[FINE|main|4:10:45]: Applying H...
ail.semantics.AILAgent[FINE|main|4:10:45]: robot
==============
After Stage StageD :
[square/2-square(1,1), square(1,2), square(1,3), ...
[all_squares_checked/0-[_aall_squares_checked()]]
[]
source(self)::
    *   +!_aall_squares_checked()||True||npy()|||[]
    *   start||True||+!_aall_squares_checked()()|||[]
[]
```

In the above agent state you can see the belief base (beliefs about squares), goal base (all_squares_checked), the empty sent messages box, and then the current intention. The main addition is the record of a *source* for the intention (in this case self – which means the agent generated the intention itself rather than getting it via external perception).

As you can see, GWENDOLEN uses the start event mentioned above for new intentions. In this case it was the intention to commit to the achieve goal !all_squares_checked. When the goal was committed to it became an event and was placed as a new row on the top of the intention. The row associated with the start event remains on the intention because this will force the agent to check if the goal is achieved when it reaches that row again. A special deed has been used npy() which stands for *no plan yet*. This means that although the goal has been committed to, the agent has not yet looked for an applicable plan for achieving the goal.

If you run the code pickuprubble_ex5.2.gwen with logging for ail.semantics.AILAgent set to fine then you will later see the intention become:

```
source(self)::
   *   +!_aall_squares_checked()||True||move_to(X,Y)()
                                    ||[X-1, X0-1, Y-1, Y0-1]
   *   start||True||+!_aall_squares_checked()()|| []
```

when an applicable plan is found the intention becomes

```
source(self)::
   *   +!_aall_squares_checked()||True||move_to(X,Y)()
                                    ||[X-1, X0-1, Y-1, Y0-1]
       +!_aall_squares_checked()||True||do_nothing()
                                    ||[X-1, X0-1, Y-1, Y0-1]
   *   start||True||+!_aall_squares_checked()()|| []
```

So now the intention is to first take a move_to action in order to get to (1,1) and then make a do_nothing action and then check if the goal has been achieved.

After the agent performs the move action, new information comes in the form of a *perception*.

```
source(percept)::
   *   start||True||+at(1,1)()|| []

[source(self)::
   *   +!_aall_squares_checked()||True||do_nothing()|| []
   *   start||True||+!_aall_squares_checked()()|| []
]
```

The first intention in this list is the *current intention* which is the one the agent will handle next. In this case it is a new intention (indicated by the start event) and the intention is to add the belief, at(1,1). The source of this intention is noted as `percept` (i.e., perception) rather than the agent itself. Since the agent had not finished processing the existing intention this is now contained in a list of other intentions.

When the agent adds the new belief, the current intention becomes empty, but GWENDOLEN actually adds yet another new intention indicating that a new belief has been adopted which allows the agent to react to this with a new plan. So the agent's intentions become

```
source(percept)::

[source(self)::
    *  +!_aall_squares_checked()||True||do_nothing()|||[]
    *  start||True||+!_aall_squares_checked()()|||[]
, source(self)::
    *  +at(1,1)||True||npy()|||[]
]
```

The current intention is empty, and there are now two intentions waiting for attention. The empty intention will be removed as the agent continues processing.

GWENDOLEN works on each intention in turn handling the top row of the intention. So the very first intention becomes the current intention again in due course:

```
source(self)::
    *  +!_aall_squares_checked()||True||do_nothing()|||[]
    *  start||True||+!_aall_squares_checked()()|||[]

[source(self)::
    *  +at(1,1)||True||npy()|||[]
]
```

After the agent has done nothing, therefore, the new intention triggered by the new belief `at(1,1)` becomes the current intention:

```
source(self)::
    *  +at(1,1)||True||npy()|||[]

[source(self)::
    *  start||True||+!_aall_squares_checked()()|||[]
]
```

If there was no plan for reacting to the new belief, the agent would just delete the intention. But, since there is a plan, the intention becomes

```
source(self)::
    *  +at(X0,Y0)||True||+checked(X0,Y0)()
                                ||[X-1, X0-1, Y-1, Y0-1]
```

```
[source(self)::
   *  start||True||+!_aall_squares_checked()()|| []
]
```

And so on.

Exercises

Run some of your existing programs with logging of `ail.semantics.AILAgent` set to fine and see if you can follow how the agent is handling events, intentions, and plans.

A.6 Tutorial 6: Manipulating Intentions and Dropping Goals

This is the sixth in a series of tutorials on the use of the GWENDOLEN programming language. This tutorial covers finer control of intentions through suspension and locking. It also looks at how goals can be discarded.

Files for this tutorial can be found in the `mcapl` distribution in the directory

```
src/examples/gwendolen/tutorials/tutorial6
```

A.6.1 'Wait For': Suspending Intentions

Recall the sample answer to the second exercise in Tutorial 3 in which we had to introduce a 'do nothing' action in order to delay the replanning of an achievement goal. In the code in Example A.10 we use, instead, some new syntax '`*checked(X,Y)`' which means *wait until* `checked(X,Y)` *is true before continuing.*

Example A.10

```
GWENDOLEN                                                         1
                                                                 2
:name: robot                                                     3
                                                                 4
:Initial Beliefs:                                                5
  square(1,1) square(1,2) square(1,3) square(1,4)                6
  square(1,5)                                                    7
  square(2,1) square(2,2) square(2,3) square(2,4)                8
  square(2,5)                                                    9
  square(3,1) square(3,2) square(3,3) square(3,4)               10
  square(3,5)                                                   11
  square(4,1) square(4,2) square(4,3) square(4,4)              12
```

```
square(4,5)                                                            13
square(5,1)  square(5,2)  square(5,3)  square(5,4)                     14
square(5,5)                                                            15
                                                                       16
:Reasoning Rules:                                                      17
  square_to_check(X,Y) :- square(X,Y), ~checked(X,Y);                  18
  no_rubble_in(X,Y) :- checked(X,Y), no_rubble(X,Y);                   19
  all_squares_checked :- ~square_to_check(X,Y),                        20
    ~holding(rubble), at(2,2);                                         21
                                                                       22
:Initial Goals:                                                        23
  all_squares_checked [achieve]                                        24
                                                                       25
:Plans:                                                                26
  +!all_squares_checked [achieve] :                                    27
    {B square_to_check(X,Y), ~B holding(rubble)}                       28
      ←   move_to(X,Y), *checked(X,Y);                                 29
  +!all_squares_checked [achieve] : {B holding(rubble)}                30
      ←   move_to(2,2), drop;                                          31
                                                                       32
  +rubble(X,Y) : {~B at(2,2)}                                          33
      ←  lift_rubble , +checked(X,Y);                                  34
                                                                       35
  +at(X,Y) : {~B rubble(X,Y)} ← +checked(X,Y);                         36
  +at(2,2) : {⊤} ← +checked(2,2);                                      37
```

We have adapted the program so that, after moving to the position (X,Y), the agent waits until it believes it has checked that square. Then we delay the addition of that belief until after the agent as lifted rubble.

If you run this program with logging for `ail.semantics.AILAgent` you will see that the intention is marked as SUSPENDED when the 'wait for' deed is encountered:

```
SUSPENDED
source(self)::
    *   +!_aall_squares_checked()||True||+*...checked(1,1)()
                                       ||[X-1, Y-1]
    *   start||True||+!_aall_squares_checked()()|||[]
```

Once such an intention is suspended it cannot become the *current* intention until it is unsuspended. In the case of the 'wait for' command this happens when the predicate that is waiting for becomes believed. Below you can see how this happens when `checked(1,1)` is added to the belief base.

```
ail.semantics.AILAgent[FINE|main|4:01:48]: robot
=============
After Stage StageC :
[at/2-at(1,1), ,
```

```
square/2-square(1,1), square(1,2), square(1,3), ...
[all_squares_checked/0-[_aall_squares_checked()]]
[]
source(self)::
   *   +at(X0,Y0)||True||+checked(X0,Y0)()
                                  ||[X-1, X0-1, Y-1, Y0-1]

[SUSPENDED
source(self)::
   *   +!_aall_squares_checked()||True||+*...checked(1,1)()
                                  ||[X-1, Y-1]
   *   start||True||+!_aall_squares_checked()()||[]
]
ail.semantics.AILAgent[FINE|main|4:01:48]: Applying ...
ail.semantics.AILAgent[FINE|main|4:01:48]: robot
==============
After Stage StageD :
[at/2-at(1,1), ,
checked/2-checked(1,1), ,
square/2-square(1,1), square(1,2), square(1,3), ...
[all_squares_checked/0-[_aall_squares_checked()]]
[]
source(self)::

[source(self)::
   *   +!_aall_squares_checked()||True||+*...checked(1,1)()
                                  ||[X-1, Y-1]
   *   start||True||+!_aall_squares_checked()()||[]
, source(self)::
   *   +checked(1,1)||True||npy()||[]
]
```

The 'wait for' command is particularly useful in simulated or physical environments where actions may take some (indeterminate) time to complete. This command allows the agent to continue operating (e.g., performing error monitoring) while waiting until it recognises that an action has finished, before continuing with what it was doing.

A.6.2 Lock and Unlock: Preventing Interleaving of Intentions

In the code in Example A.11 we have complicated our agent's situation a little. This agent has to explore squares (0,0) to (0,5) as well as the squares it was exploring previously. It also has to switch warning lights on and off before and after it lifts rubble. Finally, if a warning sounds it must stop searching and should move to position (0,0), waiting until it is able to continue searching again.

We use some new syntax here.

- At line 38 we have an empty plan. This can be useful in situations where we don't want to raise a 'no plan' warning but we don't want the agent to actually do anything.
- At line 40 we have a plan triggered by -warning. This is a plan that is triggered when something is no longer believed (in this case that the warning sound can no longer be heard).
- At line 41 we include the deed, -search_mode in a plan. This is an instruction to remove a belief.

Example A.11

```
GWENDOLEN                                                               1
                                                                        2
:name:  robot                                                           3
                                                                        4
:Initial  Beliefs:                                                      5
    square(0,0)                                                         6
    square(0,1)  square(0,2)  square(0,3)  square(0,4)                  7
    square(0,5)                                                         8
    square(1,1)  square(1,2)  square(1,3)  square(1,4)                  9
    square(1,5)                                                        10
    square(2,1)  square(2,2)  square(2,3)  square(2,4)                 11
    square(2,5)                                                        12
    square(3,1)  square(3,2)  square(3,3)  square(3,4)                 13
    square(3,5)                                                        14
    square(4,1)  square(4,2)  square(4,3)  square(4,4)                 15
    square(4,5)                                                        16
    square(5,1)  square(5,2)  square(5,3)  square(5,4)                 17
    square(5,5)                                                        18
                                                                       19
    search_mode                                                        20
                                                                       21
:Reasoning  Rules:                                                     22
    square_to_check(X,Y)  :-  square(X,Y),  ~checked(X,Y);             23
    no_rubble_in(X,Y)  :-  checked(X,Y),  no_rubble(X,Y);              24
    all_squares_checked  :-  ~square_to_check(X,Y),                    25
        ~holding(rubble),  at(2,2);                                    26
                                                                       27
:Initial  Goals:                                                       28
    all_squares_checked  [achieve]                                     29
                                                                       30
:Plans:                                                                31
    +!all_squares_checked  [achieve]  :  {~B search_mode}              32
        ←  *search_mode;                                               33
    +!all_squares_checked  [achieve]  :                                34
        {B search_mode,  B square_to_check(X,Y),                       35
        ~B holding(rubble)}                                            36
```

```
          ←   move_to(X,Y) , *checked(X,Y);            37
+!all_squares_checked [achieve] : {B holding(rubble)};  38
                                                        39
−warning: { T } ← +search_mode;                         40
+warning: { T } ← −search_mode , move_to(0,0);          41
                                                        42
+rubble(X,Y) : { ∼B at(2,2) } ←                         43
      warning_lights_on ,                               44
      lift_rubble ,                                     45
      warning_lights_off ,                              46
      move_to(2,2) ,                                    47
      drop ,                                            48
      +checked(X,Y);                                    49
                                                        50
+at(X,Y) : { ∼B rubble(X,Y)} ← +checked(X,Y);          51
+at(2,2) : { T } ← +checked(2,2);                       52
```

The agent in Example A.11 uses a belief, search_mode, to control whether
it is actively searching squares or whether it is returning to the 'safe' square
(0,0) in order to wait for the warning to switch off.

Exercise. Run the above program and see if you can spot a problem with its
execution.

Hopefully you observed an output something like:

```
...[INFO|main|10:31:44]: robot done move_to(0,1)
...[INFO|main|10:31:44]: robot done move_to(0,2)
...[INFO|main|10:31:44]: Warning is Sounding
...[INFO|main|10:31:44]: robot done warning_lights_on
...[INFO|main|10:31:44]: robot done move_to(0,0)
...[INFO|main|10:31:44]: Warning Ceases
...[INFO|main|10:31:44]: robot done lift_rubble
...[INFO|main|10:31:44]: robot done warning_lights_off
...[INFO|main|10:31:44]: robot done move_to(2,2)
```

So, *before* the robot lifts the rubble at square (0,2) it has moved to square
(0,0) because the warning has sounded. This is happening because GWEN-
DOLEN executes the *top* deed from each intention in turn. So it executes
warning_lights_on from the intention triggered by finding rubble, then
it moves to (0,0) from the intention triggered by hearing the warning, and then
it lifts the rubble (next in the intention to do with seeing the rubble).

This situation often arises where there is a sequence of deeds that need to
be performed *without interference* from other intentions such as moving to
the wrong place. To overcome this GWENDOLEN has a special deed, .lock

which 'locks' an intention in place and forces GWENDOLEN to execute deeds from that intention *only* until the intention is unlocked. The syntax +.lock locks an intention and the syntax -.lock unlocks the intention.

Exercise. Add a lock and an unlock to `pickuprubble_lock` in order to force it to pick up the rubble before obeying the warning.

N.B. As usual you can find a sample solution in

```
/src/examples/gwendolen/tutorials/tutorial6/answers
```

A.6.3 Dropping Goals

As a final note, as well as dropping beliefs as a deed in plans (as we are doing with `warning` and `search_mode` in the programs above), it is possible to drop goals with the syntax `-!goalname [goaltype]`. For example, `-!all_squares_checked [achieve]`.

Such goal drops can appear in the deeds of plans but cannot[2] be used to trigger plans.

Exercise. Write a program for picking up and moving rubble which, on hearing the warning sound, drops all its goals and leaves the area (use the action `leave`). Again you can find a sample solution in `/src/examples/gwendolen/tutorials/tutorial6/answers`.

A.7 Tutorial 7: The Gwendolen Reasoning Cycle

This is the seventh in a series of tutorials on the use of the GWENDOLEN programming language. This tutorial covers the GWENDOLEN Reasoning Cycle, looks at some simple ways to use a Java Debugger to analyse GWENDOLEN programs and sets a more significant programming challenge than suggested by previous tutorials.

Files for this tutorial can be found in the `mcapl` distribution in the directory

```
src/examples/gwendolen/tutorials/tutorial7
```

A.7.1 The GWENDOLEN Reasoning Cycle

The execution of a GWENDOLEN agent is governed by its *reasoning cycle*. This is a set of stages the agent passes through, where each stage is governed by a set of rules and the agent may choose one to execute in that stage. The

---

[2] at least not at present.

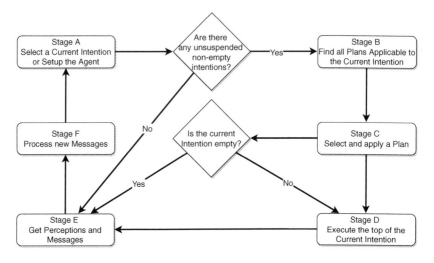

Figure A.1 The GWENDOLEN reasoning cycle

basic reasoning cycle is shown in Figure A.1 and we describe the elements within this below.

A GWENDOLEN agent starts execution in stage A.

Stage A In this stage the agent selects an intention to be the current intention. GWENDOLEN will rotate through the set of intentions ignoring any that are suspended until the current intention is locked in which case it will be reselected. If there are no unsuspended intentions, GWENDOLEN will suspend the agent. In multi-agent contexts this means that the agent will not do anything until GWENDOLEN detects that something has changed, which may mean the agent now has something to do. In single-agent contexts the program stops when the agent sleeps. At this stage GWENDOLEN also cleans up any empty intentions.

Stage B The system generates all possible plans for the current intention — if the intention has already been planned, then these are simply to continue processing the intention. If the agent cannot find a plan then it deletes the intention, unless it has been triggered by a goal, in which case it registers that there is a problem satisfying the goal and generates a warning.

Stage C GWENDOLEN has a list of plans. It here selects the first one in the list and applies it to the current intention.

Stage D GWENDOLEN executes the top deed on the current intention. This might involve taking an action, adding or removing a goal, adding or removing a belief, locking or unlocking the intention or suspending the intention using 'wait for'.

Stage E GWENDOLEN requests that the agent's environment send it a list of *percepts* (things the agent can detect) and messages. The messages are stored for processing in the agent's inbox. The percepts are compared with the agent's beliefs. If a percept is new then an intention is created to add a belief corresponding to the percept. If a previously derived belief can no longer be perceived, then an intention is created to delete the belief.

Stage F The agent sorts though its inbox and converts the messages into new intentions.

The actual code for the reasoning cycle can be found in `gwendolen .semantics.GwendolenRC`. Each of the various rules that can be used in a stage is a Java class and they can all be found in the package `ail.semantics.operationalrules`.

A.7.2 Using Java Debuggers to Debug GWENDOLEN Programs

Since the GWENDOLEN reasoning cycle is implemented in Java it is possible to use a Java debugger to debug GWENDOLEN programs. In particular it can be useful to use a Java debugger to step through a GWENDOLEN program one stage of the reasoning cycle at a time, watching to see how the state of the agent changes at each stage.

It is outside the scope of these tutorials to explain the use of Java debuggers. There are many out there and one is built into most IDEs, including Eclipse.

In our experience it is particularly useful when debugging in this way to place breakpoints in the Java `ail.semantics.AILAgent` class which is the generic class supporting agents in the Agent Infrastructure Layer (upon which GWENDOLEN is built). In particular `ail.semantics.AILAgent` has a method called `reason` which controls the progress through an agent's reasoning cycle. We recommend placing such a break point either after

```
while(! RC.stopandcheck())
```

which is the top level loop through the reasoning cycle or at `rule .apply(this)`, which is the moment that the outcome of a rule is calculated.

Exercise. Select a Java debugger (e.g., the one shipped with Eclipse) and discover how to set breakpoints using the debugger. Set a breakpoint at `rule.apply(this)` in the `reason()` method in `ail.semantics`

.AILAgent (you can find this in the src/classes/ail/semantics directory). Run one of your programs with this breakpoint in place and see what happens and experiment in seeing what information you can discover about the agent state.

A.7.3 Larger Programming Exercise

This is a fairly major programming exercise using the GWENDOLEN constructs you have already been introduced to. As usual, a sample solution can be found in the answers subdirectory for tutorial7.

In examples/gwendolen/tutorials/tutorial7 you will find a new environment, SearchAndRescueDynamicEnv.java. This extends the previous search and rescue example so that the environment may change without the agent directly taking any action. The following describes the environment.

The environment consists of a 5x5 grid of squares. The squares in the grid are numbered from (0,0) (bottom left) to (4,4) (top right). On this grid there are

- Exactly four humans which may start in any square on the grid. Some of these humans may be **injured**.
- Exactly one robot which starts in the bottom left corner of the grid.
- Up to four buildings which may appear in any square on the grid.
- Up to four pieces of rubble which may appear in any square on the grid. Any human on the same square as some rubble at the start is considered **injured** and is hidden under the rubble.

At any point the following may happen:

- A human who is not **injured** and is not **in a building** may move one square in any direction.
- A building may collapse into rubble.

The robot has the following actions available to it:

back_left If possible the robot will move one square diagonally down the grid and to the left. If not possible the robot will do nothing.

back If possible the robot will move one square down the grid. If not possible the robot will do nothing.

back_right If possible the robot will move one square diagonally down the grid and to the right. If not possible the robot will do nothing.

left If possible the robot will move one square to the left. If not possible the robot will do nothing.

right If possible the robot will move one square to the right. If not possible the robot will do nothing.

forward_left If possible the robot will move one square diagonally up in the grid and to the left. If not possible the robot will do nothing.

forward If possible the robot will move one square up in the grid. If not possible the robot will do nothing.

forward_right If possible the robot will move one square diagonally up in the grid and to the right. If not possible the robot will do nothing.

lift_rubble If the robot is not currently holding rubble then it will pick up one piece of rubble in the square revealing anything underneath it.

drop_rubble If the robot is holding rubble then it will drop it in the current square, injuring and concealing any humans if they are in the square.

assist_human If there is an injured human in the square then the robot treats them with first aid. After this activity the human is not injured.

direct_humans If there are any humans in the square then the robot tells them to leave the area immediately.

check_building If there is a building in the square then the robot looks inside it to see if there is a human there.

Other Actions Other standard actions such as `print` and `do_nothing` are also available.

The robot may perceive the following things:

holding_rubble perceived if the robot has rubble in its hands.

rubble(X,Y) perceived if the robot sees some rubble in square (X,Y). The robot can see the square it is in and one square in each direction.

building(X,Y) perceived if the robot sees a building in square (X,Y). The robot can see the square it is in and one square in each direction.

injured_human(X,Y) perceived if the robot sees an injured human in square (X,Y). The robot can see the square it is in and one square in each direction.

uninjured_human(X,Y) perceived if the robot sees an uninjured human in square (X,Y). The robot can see the square it is in and one square in each direction.

The following also holds true:

- If a human is **in a building** when it collapses then they will be **injured** and concealed by the rubble.

- If a human is **in a building** then the robot cannot see them unless it checks the building.

Humans exhibit the following behaviour:

- **injured** humans do not move.
- **directed** humans move diagonally down and left until they leave the grid. They do not enter buildings.
- If a human is not **directed** and finds itself in a square with a building then it will enter the building and stay there.
- Humans that are not **injured**, **directed** or **in a building** will move at random around the grid.

Recording and Replaying AIL Programs

We will cover recording and replaying AIL programs in more detail in a later tutorial. However some of the challenges from this tutorial will arise because of the difficultly in reproducing a specific sequence of events in the environment. In the AIL configuration file you can put the line

```
ajpf.record = true
```

This will record the sequence of events that occur in the environment (and store them in a file called `record.txt` in the folder `records`). If you want to *replay* the last recorded run of the problem then replace

```
ajpf.record = true
```

with

```
ajpf.replay = true
```

Exercise. Write a GWENDOLEN program that will get the robot to search the grid until all humans have been found, assisted if injured, and directed to leave.

A.8 Tutorial 8: Multi-Agent Systems and Communication

This is the eighth in a series of tutorials on the use of the GWENDOLEN programming language. This tutorial covers the use of communication in GWENDOLEN and also looks at setting up a multi-agent system.

Files for this tutorial can be found in the `mcapl` distribution in the directory

```
src/examples/gwendolen/tutorials/tutorial8.
```

A.8.1 Pick Up Rubble (Again)

You will find a GWENDOLEN program in the tutorial directory called simple_mas.gwen. Its contents should look like Example A.12.

Example A.12

```
GWENDOLEN                                                              1
                                                                       2
:name: lifter                                                          3
                                                                       4
:Initial Beliefs:                                                      5
                                                                       6
:Initial Goals:                                                        7
   goto55 [perform]                                                    8
                                                                       9
:Plans:                                                                10
   +!goto55 [perform]  :  { ⊤ } ←  move_to(5,5);                      11
                                                                       12
   +rubble(5,5): { ⊤ } ←  lift_rubble;                                13
                                                                       14
   +human(X,Y): { ⊤ }                                                 15
          ←  .send(medic,  :perform,  assist_human(X,Y));             16
                                                                       17
                                                                       18
:name: medic                                                           19
                                                                       20
:Initial Beliefs:                                                      21
                                                                       22
:Initial Goals:                                                        23
                                                                       24
:Plans:                                                                25
   +.received(:perform,  G): { ⊤ } ←  +!G [perform];                  26
                                                                       27
   +!assist_human(X,Y) [perform]  :  { ⊤ } ←                         28
   move_to(X,Y),  assist;
```

This is *very* similar to the first program in Tutorial 2. However there are now two agents, lifter and medic. As in Tutorial 2, the lifter robot moves to square (5,5) and lifts the rubble it finds there. However if it sees a human it performs a special kind of action which is a *send action*. This sends a message to the medic agent asking it to perform assist_human(X,Y). When the medic receives a perform instruction it converts it into a perform goal and, if it has a goal to assist a human, it moves to the relevant square and assists them.

You can run this program using simple_mas.ail. It uses a new environment SearchAndRescueMASEnv.java which is similar to SearchAndRescueEnv.java.

Syntax. A *send* action starts with the constant `.send`, followed by three arguments:

1 the name of the agent to whom the message is to be sent;
2 the performative; and
3 a logical term.

The performative can be one of `:tell`, `:perform` or `:achieve`. GWENDOLEN attaches no particular meaning to these performatives but they are often used to tell an agent to believe something, ask an agent to adopt a perform goal, or ask an agent to adopt an achieve goal.

When a message is received, GWENDOLEN turns it into an event, `.received(P, F)`, where P is the performative and F is the logical term. Since many agents interpret `:tell`, `:perform` and `:achieve` as described above, GWENDOLEN programs often include the following three plans

```
+.received(:tell, B): {True} <- +B;
+.received(:perform, G): {True} <- +!G [perform];
+.received(:achieve, G): {True} <- +!G [achieve];
```

which embody that standard interpretation. However, some programs instead choose to only handle certain performatives (e.g., only `:tell` messages) or only certain message contents, (e.g., `.received(:perform, assist_human(X,Y))` only handles messages asking the agent to perform `assist_human(X,Y)` for some X and Y).

Exercise. Amend the `simple_mas` program so that, instead of sending a *perform* message, the `lifter` agent instead sends a *tell* message and the `medic` reacts to the new belief, instead of the new goal.

N.B. It is important, for using the `SearchAndRescueMASEnv.java` environment, that the lifting agent be called `lifter` and the medic agent be called `medic`.

As usual sample solutions to all the exercises can be found in the `answers` directory for `tutorial8`.

A.8.2 Recording and Replaying AIL Programs

Now there is more than one agent in the system, you will observe that there are several paths through the program. These depend upon which agent acts when. Sometimes the `lifter` agent will go first (moving to (5,5)) and sometimes the `medic` agent will go first (sleeping).

When debugging a multi-agent program you will sometimes want to replay the exact sequence of events that occurred in the problem run. To do this you first need to record the sequence. You can get an AIL program to record its sequence of choices (in this case choices about which agent goes first) by adding the line

```
ajpf.record = true
```

To the program's AIL configuration file. By default this records the current choice path through the program in a file called `record.txt` in the directory, `records` of the MCAPL distribution. You can change the file using `ajpf.replay.file =`. There is an example of this in the configuration file `simple_mas_record.ail` within the tutorial directory.

When you wish to play back a record then include

```
ajpf.replay = true
```

in the program's AIL configuration file. Again, by default, this will replay the sequence found within `record.txt`, but will use a different file if `ajpf.replay.file =` is set. As an example, the configuration file `simple_mas_replay.ail` is set up to replay runs generated by `simple_mas_record.ail`

A.8.3 Two Ways to Create a Multi-Agent System

In the previous example we defined all the agents in the multi-agent system within one file. However you often want to separate out your agents into different files, one for each agent. This is easy to do in the AIL. You write each agent as you normally would in a separate file. Then in the `.ail` file for running the system instead of using `mas.file` you use `mas.agent.1.file` (for the file containing agent one), `mas.agent.2.file` and so on. Similarly, instead of using a MAS builder you link to individual agent builders. GWEN-DOLEN's agent builder is `gwendolen.GwendolenAgentBuilder` – so you use

```
mas.agent.1.builder =
gwendolen.GwendolenAgentBuilder
```

and so on, for each agent rather than

```
mas.builder = gwendolen.GwendolenMASBuilder.
```

Exercise. Convert `simple_mas.gwen` into a system consisting of two agents defined in different files. N.B. You will need to make sure both agent files start with the declaration GWENDOLEN to specify the language the agent is programmed in.

A.8.4 Duplicating an Agent

Occasionally, you may want to create a multi-agent system in which all agents behave identically. Ideally you would like to use the same agent code file for all these agents and just give them different names in the multi-agent system.

You can do this using files and builders, as above, with the addition of a name setting. So, for instance, mas.agent.3.name = nurse sets the name of agent 3 to nurse instead of whatever default is given in the agent file.

Exercise. Adapt the system from Exercise 2 by creating a new lifter agent that visits first square (5,5) and summons the medic to assist the human there and, after that, visits square (3,4) and summons a nurse to assist the human there. The medic and the nurse should both use the medic agent code file you developed for exercise 2. Give one of these agent's the name nurse in the .ail file.

A.9 Tutorial 9: Default Built-in Actions: Strings and Arithmetic

This is the ninth in a series of tutorials on the use of the GWENDOLEN programming language. This tutorial covers a few final elements of GWENDOLEN and the actions that come with the Default Environment. It is important to note that if a GWENDOLEN agent *is not* operating in an environment sub-classed from DefaultEnvironment then there is no guarantee that these actions will be available.

Files for this tutorial can be found in the mcapl distribution in the directory

```
src/examples/gwendolen/tutorials/tutorial9
```

A.9.1 String Handling

Recall, from Tutorial 1, that you were not able to use spaces in 'print' statements. You can actually achieve this if you use a double quotation to mark the contents as string. In the tutorial directory you will find a program called strings.gwen. It's contents should look like Example A.13.

Example A.13

```
GWENDOLEN                                                    1
                                                             2
:name:  strings                                              3
                                                             4
:Initial  Beliefs:                                           5
   string1(" hello ")                                        6
   string2(" ")                                              7
   string3(" world ")                                        8
                                                             9
:Initial  Goals:                                            10
   compose_strings  [perform]                               11
                                                            12
:Plans:                                                     13
   +! compose_strings  [perform]  :  { T }  ←              14
print(" hello  world ");
```

If you run this program you will see that it prints out `hello world` including the space without any problem.

Built-in String Actions

If you look at `strings.ail` you will see that you are using AIL's `DefaultEnvironment` class. Most GWENDOLEN environments are based on the default environment and this means they all support a set of standard actions that come with the Default Environment. The built-in actions for strings are:

toString(T,S) This will take any term, `T`, that you are passing around your program and unify the string variable, `S`, to that term.

append(S1,S2,S3) This takes two strings, `S1` and `S2` and unifies, `S3`, to the concatenation of those two strings. So, for instance, `append("gwen", "dolen",S)` will unify `S` to 'gwendolen'.

Exercise. You will notice that `strings.gwen` contains three beliefs about strings. Adapt the program so that instead of printing out `hello world` directly, it instead uses `append` to join the three strings together to print out the message.

Hint. You will need to use `append` twice.

As usual you can find sample solutions in the `answers` directory.

A.9.2 Arithmetic

GWENDOLEN can use numbers as terms but it is both fiddly and inefficient to program up arithmetic operations using Reasoning Rules. As a result the Default Environment has four simple actions for manipulating numbers.

sum(X,Y,Z) This unifies Z to be the sum of X and Y.
minus(X,Y,Z) This takes Y away from X and unifies Z to the result.
div(X,Y,Z) This divides X by Y and unifies Z to the result.
times(X,Y,Z) This multiplies X by Y and unifies Z to the result.

Exercise. In the tutorial directory you will find a partial program, arithmetic_shell.gwen. This is shown in Example A.14.

Example A.14

```
GWENDOLEN                                             1
                                                      2
:name: arithmetic                                     3
                                                      4
:Initial Beliefs:                                     5
                                                      6
:Initial Goals:                                       7
   do_maths [perform]                                 8
                                                      9
:Plans:                                               10
   +! do_maths[perform] : {⊤} ←                       11
           +! do_sum [perform],                       12
           +! do_minus [perform],                     13
           +! do_div [perform],                       14
           +! do_mult [perform];                      15
```

Implement the four missing plans so that

- do_sum adds two numbers and prints out the result as, for instance, The Sum of 1 and 5 is 6. You will need to use toString and append to generate the string you want.
- do_minus subtracts two numbers and prints out the result as, for instance, 5.5. minus 3.2. is 2.3.
- do_div divides one number by another and prints out the result as, for instance, 7 divided by 2 is 3.5.
- do_mult multiplies two numbers and prints out the result as, for instance, 100 times 2.5 is 250.

A.9.3 Using Equations in Plan Guards

Once you are using numbers in your program you quickly get to situations where you want to use equations in plan guards. GWENDOLEN has some limited support for this. It cannot perform arithmetic in the guards of plans, but it can compare numbers using '<' (less than) and '==' (equals).

Exercise. In the tutorial directory you will find a partial program, equation_shell.gwen. This is shown in Example A.15.

Example A.15

```
GWENDOLEN                                                        1
                                                                2
:name: equation                                                 3
                                                                4
:Initial Beliefs:                                               5
  number1(3)                                                    6
  number2(5)                                                    7
  number3(4.8)                                                  8
  number4(3)                                                    9
                                                               10
:Initial Goals:                                                11
  compare_numbers [perform]                                    12
                                                               13
:Plans:                                                        14
  +! compare_numbers [perform]  :                              15
    {B number1(N1), B number2(N2),                             16
     B number3(N3), B number4(N4)} ←                           17
       +!compare(N1,N2) [perform],                             18
       +!compare(N1,N3) [perform],                             19
       +!compare(N1,N4) [perform],                             20
       +!compare(N2,N3) [perform],                             21
       +!compare(N2,N4) [perform],                             22
       +!compare(N3,N4) [perform];                             23
```

Complete this program by implementing plans for the goal, compare(N1,N2), so that the program prints out the following output.

```
3 is less than 5
3 is less than 4.8
3 is equal to 3
4.8 is less than 5
3 is less than 5
3 is less than 4.8
```

A.9.4 Print Actions

GWENDOLEN's default environment has three print actions.

print(X) you have already encountered and this prints out the term, X.
printagentstate prints the current state of the agent to standard error.
printstate prints the current state of the agent to standard out.

Clearly printagentstate and printstate are virtually identical. They are mostly of use when debugging and generally either can be used, but in certain situations you may have a preference about which output channel you want to use.

Exercise. Experiment inserting printagentstate and printstate into one of your existing programs.

A.10 Tutorial 10: The EASS variant of Gwendolen

This is a tutorial on the use of the EASS variant of the GWENDOLEN language that was first developed as part of the Engineering Autonomous Space Software research project in the UK. The EASS variant is adapted for use with physical systems and simulations, such as mobile robots, satellites and unmanned aircraft. This tutorial covers the basic concepts behind the EASS variant and its differences to the GWENDOLEN language.

Files for this tutorial can again be found in the mcapl distribution in the directory

```
src/examples/eass/tutorials/tutorial1
```

The tutorial assumes familiarity with the GWENDOLEN programming language.

A.10.1 Abstraction and Reasoning Engines

Figure A.2 shows the typical architecture of an EASS Agent. The agent is actually a pair of agents, the *reasoning engine*, which is responsible for complicated reasoning tasks, and the *abstraction engine*, which is responsible for processing and filtering incoming perceptions so that only those actually needed for reasoning are passed on to the reasoning engine itself.

The reasons for this separation are primarily driven by the observation that BDI agents are unable to process incoming perceptions from real or simulated

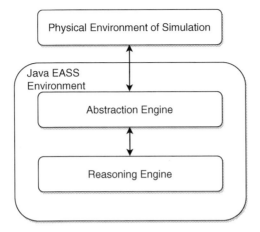

Figure A.2 The basic architecture of an EASS agent

sources fast enough and so they get 'clogged' by an ever-increasing number of beliefs and intentions related to the processing of perception.

The theoretical underpinnings of this architecture are described in Dennis et al. (2010a, 2016a). The key points are that the *reasoning engine* does not interact directly with the physical world (or a simulation) at all. It gains perceptions via *shared beliefs* which are communicated from the abstraction engine via the Java EASS environment. Similarly most of its actions (ideally all) are communicated to the abstraction engine which then reifies them (e.g., adding more low-level detail that may be required by the physical system or simulation to actually enact the action). As a rule of thumb, while perceptions and actions, as used by the physical system or simulation generally involve numeric values, reasoning generally uses logical ('yes/no') information and outputs simple non-numeric commands. Therefore the abstraction engine should be responsible for converting numeric data ('distance = 5.4m') into logical statements ('too close') and converting simple commands ('slow down') into numerical instructions ('apply a deceleration of $-1m/s^2$'). This is only a rule of thumb and the reality is that a certain amount of experimentation is often required to balance a system appropriately so that reasoning happens fast enough to adequately control the physical system.

In order for this to work, GWENDOLEN's reasoning cycle was adapted slightly; a set of dedicated actions were introduced for handling shared beliefs and delegated actions, and some new constructs were added to the language.

A.10.2 Key Differences

Perception Processing

In the GWENDOLEN language incoming perceptions are converted into intentions which contain a deed to add the perception to the belief base. In theory this gives the agent more control over the contents of its beliefs (although, as yet, no use has been made of this). However a side effect is that it takes the agent two turns of the reasoning cycle to convert a perception into a belief and this slowed down the processing of perceptions.

In the EASS variant, therefore, new perceptions are placed directly into the agent's belief base during the perception stage of the reasoning cycle.

Identifying Abstraction and Reasoning Engines

Since each agent is, in fact, a pair of agents, it is necessary to identify and link the abstraction and reasoning engines. This is done by starting the abstraction engine with the line.

```
:abstraction: agentname
```

instead of

```
:name: agentname
```

which is reserved as the start of the reasoning engine code. As long as the two agents have the same name then the environment will link them.

Shared Beliefs

The reasoning engine does not receive percepts from the outside world but only via a *shared belief* set. An abstraction engine may get perceptions both from the outside world and from the shared beliefs.

EASS environments support this communication via two dedicated actions, `assert_shared(B)` and `remove_shared(B)` which can be used to assert and remove the shared belief, `B`. Both the abstraction and reasoning engines may use these commands.

Perf

The reasoning engine may also request that the abstraction engine reify an action to be sent to some external system. It does this via the dedicated action, `perf`. This sends a message to the abstraction engine asking it to adopt a perform goal.

This means that abstraction engines need to implement plans for handling perform messages.

A.10.3 Example

Example A.16 shows a simple EASS program to control a car by making it accelerate up to the speed limit and then maintain that speed. Lines 3–27 are the abstraction engine, and lines 30-41 are the reasoning engine.

Example A.16

```
EASS                                                           1
                                                               2
: abstraction :  car                                           3
                                                               4
: Initial  Beliefs :                                           5
  speed_limit(5)                                               6
                                                               7
: Initial  Goals :                                             8
                                                               9
: Plans :                                                     10
  /* Default  plans  for  handling  messages  */              11
  +.received ( : tell ,  B ): { T } ←  +B ;                    12
  +.received ( : perform ,  G ): { T } ←  +!G [ perform ];     13
  +.received ( : achieve ,  G ): { T } ←  +!G [ achieve ];     14
                                                               15
  +started  : { T } ←      +Σ( start );                        16
                                                               17
  +yspeed(X)  : {B speed_limit(SL), SL < X}                    18
      ←  +Σ( at_speed_limit );                                 19
  +yspeed(X)  : {B speed_limit(SL), X < SL}                    20
      ←  −Σ( at_speed_limit );                                 21
                                                               22
  +! accelerate [perform] : {B yspeed(X)} ←   accelerate ;     23
  +! accelerate [perform] : { ~B yspeed(X)}                    24
      ←  print (" Waiting  for  Simulator  to  Start ");       25
  +! maintain_speed [perform] : { T } ←  maintain_speed ;      26
                                                               27
                                                               28
: name :  car                                                  29
                                                               30
: Initial  Beliefs :                                           31
                                                               32
: Initial  Goals :                                             33
                                                               34
: Plans :                                                      35
  +start : { T } ←  +!at_speed_limit [achieve ];               36
                                                               37
  +! at_speed_limit [achieve] : { T }                          38
      ←  perf ( accelerate ),  *at_speed_limit ;               39
                                                               40
  +at_speed_limit : { T } ←  perf ( maintain_speed );          41
```

As an initial belief the abstraction engine has that the speed limit on the road is 5. Every time the perception, yspeed(X) comes in (lines 18-21) the abstraction engine compares this to the speed limit and, if appropriate, asserts a shared belief (N.B., we are using $+_\Sigma(B)$ as shorthand for assert_shared(B) and $-_\Sigma(B)$ as shorthand for remove_shared(B)).

Lines 12–14 are the standard plans for handling messages. It is important that the abstraction engine has these so it correctly handles perf requests from the reasoning engine.

If the reasoning engine has a goal to reach the speed limit (line 38) then it requests that the abstraction engine perform 'accelerate'. This is passed on directly to the environment (line 23). Once the reasoning engine believes the speed limit is reached (line 41) then it requests that the abstraction engine perform 'maintain_speed'.

Finally, in order to allow time for the simulation to start, a perception 'started' is used. When the abstraction engine perceives this (line 16) it asserts the shared belief 'start' which causes the reasoning engine to adopt the goal of reaching the speed limit (line 36).

The environment passes on requests for acceleration, and so on, to the simulator and reports on the simulated speed and position using perceptions.

Running the Example

The example uses MotorwayMain which you can find in the directory

```
src/examples/eass/tutorials/motorwaysim
```

This must be run as a separate java program and must be started before the EASS program is run. When it starts you should see message:

```
Motorway Sim waiting Socket Connection
```

Now run the EASS program as normal for AIL programs. You will find the AIL configuration file in the tutorial directory. You should see the window shown in Figure A.3 (N.B. You may need to move other windows out of the way to find it!). Click on 'start' and you should see the car accelerate up to a speed of 5.

A.10.4 Exercise

eass.tutorials.tutorial1.CarOnMotorwayEnvironment provides four actions to the abstraction engine.

accelerate Accelerates the car.

Figure A.3 The motorway simulator window

decelerate Decelerates the car (if the car reaches a speed of 0 it stops).
maintain_speed Maintains the speed of the car.
calculate_totaldistance(D) unifies D with the total distance the car travelled.

The perceptions it sends to the abstraction engine are:

xpos(X) X is the x position of the car.
ypos(X) X is the y position of the car.
xspeed(X) X is the speed of the car in the x direction.
yspeed(X) X is the speed of the car in the y direction.
started The simulation has started.

The x and y positions of the car reset to 0 each time the car loops around the simulator window.

Exercise 1

Adapt `car.eass` so that the reasoning engine prints out the total distance travelled when it reaches the speed limit.

Exercise 2

Extend `car.eass` so that it accelerates to the speed limit, then continues until it has reached a total distance of 600 metres and then decelerates.

Hint. The solution does this by having the reasoning engine request an alert at 600 units. The abstraction engine then calculates the total distance each time `ypos` updates until this is reached at which point it alerts the reasoning engine. There are lots of other ways to do this but this solution maintains the idea that the reasoning engine makes decisions while the abstraction engine processes data.

Sample answers for the exercises can be found in `eass/examples/tutorials/tutorial1/answers`.

Appendix B
AIL Toolkit Documentation

B.1 Tutorial 1: Configuration Files

This is the first in a series of tutorials on the use of the Agent Infrastructure Layer (AIL). This tutorial covers the basics of configuring a multi-agent system in the AIL which can then be used within execution and/or model checking. This duplicates some material that appears in the GWENDOLEN programming language Tutorials 1 and 8 but involves a more thorough discussion of the configuration options.

Files for this tutorial can be found in the mcapl distribution in the directory

```
src/examples/gwendolen/ail_tutorials/tutorial1
```

The tutorials assume some familiarity with the basics of running Java programs either via the command line or in Eclipse.

B.1.1 Agent Java PathFinder (AJPF) and the Agent Infrastructure Layer (AIL)

Agent Java PathFinder (AJPF) is primarily designed to work with agent programming languages which are implemented using the *Agent Infrastructure Layer* (AIL). The first language implemented in the AIL was GWENDOLEN so most of the examples in these tutorials will use GWENDOLEN agents. It is not necessary to understand GWENDOLEN to use these tutorials but it is important to understand a little bit about the AIL. In particular it is important to understand AIL configuration files and how they are used to construct a multi-agent system for subsequent model checking.

297

B.1.2 An Example Configuration Files

You will find an AIL configuration file in the tutorial directory called
hello_world.ail. Its contents are shown below.

```
mas.file =
 /src/examples/gwendolen/ail_tutorials/tut1/hello_world
 .gwen mas.builder = gwendolen.GwendolenMASBuilder

env = ail.mas.DefaultEnvironment

log.warning = ail.mas.DefaultEnvironment
```

This is a very simple configuration consisting of four items only.

mas.file gives the path to the GWENDOLEN program to be run.

mas.builder gives a Java class for building the file.
> In this case gwendolen.GwendolenMASBuilder parses a file
> containing one or more GWENDOLEN agents and compiles them into
> a multi-agent system.

env provides an environment for the agent to run in.
> In this case we use the default environment provided by the AIL.

log.warning sets the level of output for the class ail.mas.
> DefaultEnvironment.
> By default, this provides a minimal level of output (warnings only).
> It is often useful to get more output than this.

You will notice that the GWENDOLEN MAS file, hello_world.gwen, is
also in this tutorial directory.

Running the Program

To run the program you need to run the Java program ail.mas.AIL and
supply it with a the configuration file as an argument. You can do this either
via the command line or by using the Eclipse run-AIL configuration (with
hello_world.ail selected in the Package Explorer window) as detailed in
the MCAPL manual.

Run the program now.

B.1.3 Configuration Files

Configuration files all contain a list of items of the form `key=value`. Agent programming languages, and even specific applications, may have their own specialised keys that can be placed in this file. However the keys that are supported by all agent programs are as follows:

env This is the Java class that represents the environment of the multi-agent system. The value should be a Java class name – for example, `ail.mas.DefaultEnvironment`.

mas.file This is the name of a file (including the path from the MCAPL home directory) describing all the agents needed for a multi-agent system in some agent programming language.

mas.builder This is the Java class that builds a multi-agent system in some language. For GWENDOLEN this is `gwendolen.GwendolenMASBuilder`. To find the builders for other languages consult the language documentation.

mas.agent.*N*.file This is the name of a file (including the path from the MCAPL home directory) which describes the *N*th agent to be used by some multi-agent system.

This allows individual agent code to be kept in separate files and allows agents to be re-used for different applications. It also allows a multi-agent system to be built using agents programmed in several different agent programming languages.

mas.agent.*N*.builder This is the Java class that is to be used to build the *N*th agent in the system. In the case of GWENDOLEN, individual agents are built using

```
gwendolen.GwendolenAgentBuilder.
```

To find the builders for other languages consult the language documentation.

mas.agent.*N*.name All agent files contain a default name for the agent but this can be changed by the configuration (e.g., if you want several agents which are identical except for the name – this way they can all refer to the same code file but the system will consider them to be different agents because they have different names).

log.severe, log.warning, log.info, log.fine, log.finer, log.finest These all set the logging level for Java classes in the system. `log.finest` prints out the most information and `log.severe` prints out the least. Most classes default to `log.warning` but sometimes, especially when debugging, you may want to specify a particular logging level for a particular class.

log.format This lets you change the format of the log output from Java's default. At the moment the only value for this is `brief`.

ajpf.transition_every_reasoning_cycle This can be `true` or `false` (by default it is true). It is used during model checking with AJPF to determine whether a new model state should be generated for every state in the agent's reasoning cycle. This means that model checking is more thorough, but at the expense of generating a lot more states.

ajpf.record This can be `true` or `false` (by default it is false). If it is set to true then the program will record its sequence of choices (all choices made by the scheduler *and* any choices made by the special `ajpf.util.choice.Choice` class). By default (unless `ajpf.replay.file` is set) these choices are stored in a file called `record.txt` in the `records` directory of the MCAPL distribution.

ajpf.replay This can be set to `true` or `false` (by default it is false). If it is set to true then the system will execute the program using a set of scheduler and other choices from a file. By default (unless `ajpf.replay.file` is set) this file is `record.txt` in the `records` directory of the MCAPL distribution.

ajpf.replay.file This allows you to set the file used by either `ajpf.record` or `ajpf.replay`.

ail.store_sent_messages This can be `true` or `false` (by default it is true). If it is false then AIL's built-in rules for message sending will not store a copy of the message that was sent. This can be useful to reduce the number of states when model checking, but obviously only if it is not important for the agent to reason about sent messages.

B.1.4 Exercises

In the tutorial directory you will find three further GWENDOLEN files (`simple_mas.gwen`, `lifter.gwen` and `medic.gwen`) and an environment (`SearchAndRescueMASEnv.java`).

simple_mas.gwen is a simple multi-agent system consisting of a lifter agent and a medic agent. The lifter explores a location (5,5). If it finds a human it will summon the medic to assist the human. If it finds some rubble it will pick up the rubble.

lifter.gwen is a single lifting agent much like the one in `simple_mas.gwen`.
It first explores location (5,5) and then (3,4) and will ask one of two
agents, `medic` or `nurse` for help assisting any humans it finds.

medic.gwen is a medic agent that assists humans if it gets sent a message
requesting help.

SearchAndRescueMASEnv.java is an environment containing two injured
humans, one at (5,5) and one at (3,4).

Exercise 1. Write a configuration file to run `simple_mas.gwen` with

`gwendolen.ail_tutorials.tutorial1.SearchAndRescueMASEnv`

as the environment. Set the log level for `ail.mas.DefaultEnvironment`
to `info`.

You should see output like

```
Jan 29, 2015 5:17:42 PM ajpf.util.AJPFLogger info
INFO: lifter done move_to(5,5)
Jan 29, 2015 5:17:42 PM ajpf.util.AJPFLogger info
INFO: lifter done send(1:human(5,5), medic)
Jan 29, 2015 5:17:42 PM ajpf.util.AJPFLogger info
INFO: medic done move_to(5,5)
Jan 29, 2015 5:17:42 PM ajpf.util.AJPFLogger info
INFO: lifter done lift_rubble
Jan 29, 2015 5:17:42 PM ajpf.util.AJPFLogger info
INFO: medic done assist
Jan 29, 2015 5:17:42 PM ajpf.util.AJPFLogger info
INFO: Sleeping agent lifter
```

N.B. the order of the actions may vary depending on which order the agents
act in.

You can find sample answers for all the exercises in this tutorial in the `answers`
directory.

Exercise 2. Write a configuration file to run `lifter.gwen` and two copies
of `medic.gwen` with

`gwendolen.ail_tutorials.tutorial1.SearchAndRescueMASEnv`

as the environment. One of the medic agents should be called `medic` and one
should be called `nurse`.

B.2 Tutorial 2: Extending the Default Environment

This is the second in a series of tutorials on the use of the Agent Infrastructure Layer (AIL). This tutorial covers creating environments for agent programs by extending the `ail.mas.DefaultEnvironment` class. Sometimes this will not be possible because of the complexity of the environments involved, or the requirements of the programming language interpreters but this is the simplest way to create an environment for an agent program to run in.

Files for this tutorial can be found in the `mcapl` distribution in the directory

`src/examples/gwendolen/ail_tutorials/tutorial2`.

The tutorial assumes a good working knowledge of Java programming and an understanding of how unification works in Prolog programs.

B.2.1 The Default Environment and the AILEnv Interface

All environments for use with language interpreters created using the AIL must implement a java interface `ail.mas.AILEnv`. This specifies some minimal functionality agents will expect the environment to provide such as the ability to deliver a set of perceptions, deliver messages and calculate the outcomes of agent actions. It also requires certain methods to be implemented for use with the AJPF property specification language.

`ail.mas.DefaultEnvironment` provides a basic level implementation of all these methods, so any environment that extends it only has to worry about those aspects particular to that environment. Typically this is just the way that actions performed by the agents are to be handled. `ail.mas.DefaultEnvironment` also provides a set of useful methods for handling changing the perceptions available to the agent that can then be used to program these action results.

B.2.2 A Survey of some of Default Environment's Methods

We note here some of the more useful methods made available by the Default Environment before we talk about implementing the outcomes of agent actions.

public void addPercept(Predicate per) This adds a percept which is perceivable by all agents in the environment. The percept has to be an object of class `ail.syntax.Predicate` (see section B.2.3).

public void addPercept(String agName, Predicate per) As above but the percept is perceivable only by the agent called `agName`.

public boolean removePercept(Predicate per) This removes a percept which is perceivable by all agents in the environment. It returns `true` if the percept existed.

public void removePercept(String agName, Predicate per) As above but the percept is perceivable only by the agent called `agName`.

public boolean removeUnifiesPercept(Predicate per) Sometimes we do not know the exact logical formulae that we want to be removed only that it unifies with some term. This method allows us to remove any percept that unifies with the argument.

public void removeUnifiesPercept(String agName, Predicate per) As above but the percept is perceivable only by the agent called `agName`.

public synchronized void clearPercepts() Removes all percepts.

public void clearPercepts(String agName) Removes all percepts perceivable only by `agName`.

public void clearMessages(String agName) Removes all messages available for `agName`.

public void addMessage(String agName, Message m) This adds a message to an agent's inbox. In general this should only be used by agent's invoking `SendAction`'s but their may be circumstances when a system requires messages to be added at other times.

B.2.3 Classes for Logical Formulae

Logical Formulae in AIL are handled by a complex hierarchy of classes. Here we are concerned only with the `ail.syntax.Predicate`, `ail.syntax.VarTerm, ail.syntax.NumberTerm, ail.syntax.NumberTermImpl` and `ail.syntax.Action` classes.

The Predicate Class

`ail.syntax.Predicate` is a basic 'work horse' class for handling logical formulae.

- You create a `Predicate` object by calling the constructor `Predicate` with a string argument that is the name of the predicate.

  So, for instance, `Predicate red = new Predicate("red")` creates a constant, *red*.

- You can add arguments to predicates using `addTerm`.

  In our example, `red.addTerm(new Predicate("box"))` changes the constant, *red* in to the predicate *red(box)*.

addTerm always adds new terms to the end of the predicate. So, for instance red.addTerm(new Predicate("train")) changes *red*(*box*) into *red*(*box, train*).

- If you want to change an argument then you need to use setTerm(int i, Term t). Thus, red.setTerm(0, new Predicate("book")) changes *red*(*box, train*) to *red*(*book, train*).

  N.B. Predicate arguments count up from zero.

- You can access the arguments of a predicate using getTerm(int i). So red.getTerm(0) applied to *red*(*book, train*) returns *book*.

  book will be returned as an object of the ail.syntax.Term interface. Most of the classes for logical terms subclass objects (usually ail.syntax.DefaultTerm) that implement this interface. Depending on the situation, a programmer may therefore need to cast the Term object into something more specific.

- getTerms() returns a list of the arguments to a term. getTermsSize() returns an integer giving the number of arguments.

- getFunctor() returns a predicate's functor as a string. So, for instance, red.getFunctor() applied to *red*(*book, train*) returns 'red'.

The VarTerm Class

ail.syntax.VarTerm is used to create variables in terms. Following Prolog conventions, all variables start with capital letters.

- You create a VarTerm object by calling the constructor VarTerm with a string argument that is the name of the variable.

  So, VarTerm v1 = new VarTerm("A") creates a variable, *A*.

- Since variables may be instantiated by unification to any logical term they subclass ail.syntax.Predicate and implement interfaces for other sorts of term, for example, numerical terms via the ail.syntax.Number Term interface mentioned below. Once instantiated to some other sort of term a variable should behave like the relevant term object.

The NumberTerm interface and the NumberTermImpl Class

ail.syntax.NumberTerm and ail.syntax.NumberTermImpl are used to work with numerical terms. NumberTermImpl implements the NumberTerm interface.

- You create a NumberTermImpl object by calling the constructor NumberTermImpl with either a string argument that is the name of the number or a double. So, for instance, NumberTermImpl value = new NumberTermImpl(2.5) creates a numerical term, 2.5.

- You convert a `NumberTerm` into a value (e.g. to be used in a simulator) using the method `solve()` which returns a double. So, for instance, `value.solve()` applied to the numerical term 2.5 returns 2.5 as a double.

  When working with predicates that have numerical arguments – for example, $distance(5.4)$ you may want to extract the argument (e.g., using `getTerm(0)`), cast it into a `NumberTerm` and then call `solve()` to get the actual number you want to work with.

Example B.1

```
if ( act . getFunctor () . equals (" move" )) {                    1
    NumberTerm distance = ( NumberTerm ) act . getTerm ( 0 );       2
    double d = distance . solve ();                                 3
    this . move ( d );                                              4
}                                                                   5
```

Example B.1 shows some sample code that takes an action such as `move(2.5)` requested by the agent extracts the distance to be moved and then calls some internal method to perform the action in the environment passing in the double as an argument.

The Action Class

Agents use `ail.syntax.Action` objects to request actions in the environment. `ail.syntax.Action` subclasses `ail.syntax.Predicate` and can generally be used just like a predicate.

Unifiers

Lastly we will briefly look at the use of unifiers with logical terms. Unifiers are represented by objects of the class `ail.syntax.Unifier`. We will use the syntax $Var - value$ to indicate that a unifier unifies the variable Var with the value $value$. We represent a unifier as a list of such variable-value pairs.

- Unifiers can be applied to any logical term (indeed to any object that implements the `ail.syntax.Unifiable` interface) by using the method `apply(Unifier u)`.

  So, for instance, suppose the Unifier, u is $[A - box]$, and `VarTerm` a is A. Then `a.apply(u)` will instantiate a as the term box.

- We can unify two terms using the `unifies(Unifiable t, Unifier u)` method.

  So, for instance, if predicate p1 is $red(A)$ and predicate p2 is $red(box)$ then `p1.unifies(p2, new Unifier u)` will turn u into the unifier $[A - box]$.

- You can extend an existing unifier in the same way.

  So, for instance, suppose u is $[A - box]$, p1 is $red(A)$ and predicate p2 is $red(B)$. Then `p1.unifies(p2, u)` will turn u into the unifier $[A - box, B - box]$.

- You can combine two unifiers using the `compose()` method (e.g., `u1.compose(u2)`. However you should be very careful about doing this unless you are certain that there is no variable unified with one term in the first unifier and a different term in the second.

B.2.4 The Message Class

This should only be relevant if you want to change the default handling of messages. This should only rarely be needed.

The message class is `ail.syntax.Message`. It has a number of fields which allow a message to specify the sender (a String), receiver (a String), propositional content (a Term), an *illocutionary force* or *performative* (an int), a message identifier (a StringTerm) and a thread identifier (a StringTerm).

It is not necessary to use all these fields when creating a message and the simplest constructor takes four arguments, the illocutionary force, sender, reciever and content, in that order. So for instance,

```
Message m = new Message(1, "ag1", "ag2", new Predicate("red"))
```

sends the message "red" from `ag1` to `ag2` with performative 1.

Each language implemented in the AIL specifies its own meanings for performative. For instance the GWENDOLEN language (and its EASS variant) define 1 as *tell*, 2 as *perform* and 3 as *achieve*. So a GWENDOLEN agent would interpret the above example message as a *tell* message.

Messages come with a set of getter methods, `getIlForce()`, `getPropCont()`, `getReceiver()`, `getSender()`, and so on, for accessing the messages field.

Message objects also have a method `toTerm()` which will convert the message to a `Predicate` object of the form: `message(msgId, threadID, sender, receiever, ilForce, propCont)`. Note that sender, receiver and ilforce are all converted to predicates (not to StringTerms and a NumberTerm) in this representation.

B.2.5 Extending executeAction

`ail.mas.DefaultEnvironment` implements a method called `executeAction`

```
public Unifier executeAction(String agName, Action act)
        throws AILexception {
```

As can be seen, `executeAction` takes the agent name and an action as parameters. The method returns a unifier. Sometimes part of the result of executing an action can be the instantiation of one of the arguments to the action predicate. This instantiation is provided by the unifier that is returned. It is this method that is called by agents when they want to perform an action.

In `DefaultEnvironment`, `executeAction` implements the default actions (discussed in Section A.9), message sending actions, updates fields relevant to model checking, and generates appropriate logging output. All these are important functions and so we *strongly recommend* that when overwriting `executeAction` you include a call to it (`super.executeAction(agName, act)`) at the end, outside of any conditional expressions. The method returns an empty unifier so this can be safely ignored or composed in subclassing environments.

Normally `executeAction` will need to handle several different actions. An easy way to do this is to use conditional statements that check the functor of the `Action` predicate (see Example B.2).

Example B.2

```
if (act.getFunctor().equals("red_button")) {                        1
    addPercept(agN, new Predicate("red_button_pressed");           2
    removePercept(agN, new Predicate("green_button_pressed");      3
} else if (act.getFunctor().equals("green_button")) {              4
    addPercept(agN, new Predicate("green_button_pressed");         5
    removePercept(agN, new Predicate("red_button_pressed");        6
}                                                                   7
```

B.2.6 Initialising and Cleaning Up

Environments get created *before* any agents are created or added to them. This can sometimes cause problems if you want the environment to be configured in some way relating to the agents (e.g., setting up a location for each agent in the environment) before everything starts running.

After environments are created they can be configured using the AIL configuration file for the multi-agent system. The key/value pairs used will be specific to the environment.

The method `public void init_before_adding_agents()` is called on environments after configuration but before any agents are added to them. This is rarely used but occasionally there is some aspect of initialisation that has to happen *after* the use of any user supplied configuration files but before agents are added.

The method `public void init_after_adding_agents()` is called after the agents have been created and added to the environment but before the environment starts running. Therefore overriding this method can be a good way in which to perform any configuration that involves agents.

Similarly `public void cleanup()` is called at the end of a run of the multi-agent system and so can be used for any final clean up of the environment or to print out reports or statistics.

B.2.7 Exercises

Exercise 1
In the tutorial directory you will find an AIL configuration file, `PickUpAgent.ail`. This is a configuration for a simple multi-agent system consisting of one GWENDOLEN agent, `pickupagent.gwen`, and the Default Environment.

The agent is programmed to continue making `pickup` actions until it believes *holding_block*. If you run the multi-agent system you will observe it making repeated actions. Because the default environment does nothing with the `pickup` action the agent sees no outcomes to its efforts and so keeps trying.

Create a new environment for the agent that subclasses `ail.mas.DefaultEnvironment` and makes the `pickup` action result in the perception that the agent is *holding_block*.

A sample answer can be found in the `answers` directory.

Exercise 2
In the tutorial directory you will find a second GWENDOLEN agent, `lucky_dip_agent.gwen`. This agent is searching for a toy in three bins which are red, green and yellow. If it does not find a toy in any of the bins it will throw a tantrum. The agent can perform three actions.

search(Colour,A) It searches in the bin of colour, *Colour* and expects *A* to be unified to whatever it finds.

drop(A) It drops A (which it will have unified with something) and then waits
until it sees A (e.g., if it does `drop(book)` it then waits until it
perceives $see(book)$ before it continues).

throw_tantrum

Create an environment for the agent that subclasses `ail.mas.Default`
`Environment` and implements the five actions in a sensible way – that is,
unifying A appropriately for the search actions (e.g., to `book` or `toy` depending which bin the agent searches in), and adding an appropriate $see(A)$ predicate. It is not really necessary for anything to happen as a result of the tantrum
action but it can if you want.

A sample answer can be found in the `answers` directory.

B.3 Tutorial 3: Dynamic and Random Environments

This is the third in a series of tutorials on the use of the Agent Infrastructure
Layer (AIL). This tutorial covers creating environments for agent programs
which contain dynamic or random behaviour. Dynamic behaviour is behaviour
that may occur without the agents doing anything to cause it. Random behaviour is when the outcome of an action, the input to a sensor, or the dynamic
behaviour of the environment has some element of chance to it.

It should be noted that the EASS variant of the GWENDOLEN language
is intended for use with dynamic and random environments and has its own
customised support for them. If you are working with the EASS variant you
may wish to skip this tutorial and use the material in Section B.5 instead.

Files for this tutorial can be found in the `mcapl` distribution in the directory

`src/examples/gwendolen/ail_tutorials/tutorial3`.

The tutorial assumes a good working knowledge of Java programming and an
understanding of the basics of constructing AIL environments.

B.3.1 Dynamic Environments

A dynamic environment is one that gets to change in some way, typically to
affect the percepts available in the system, without any agent taking any particular action. To do this the environment needs to be included in the scheduler
that is used to decide which agent gets to act next.

The schedulers all expect to pick between objects that implement the
`ajpf.MCAPLJobber` interface so the first thing a dynamic environment
needs to do is implement this interface. This interface includes implementing
a `do_job()` method which should contain the changes to be made when the

environment runs. Once this is done the environment needs to be added to the scheduler and set up to receive notifications from the scheduler. Example B.3 shows a simple dynamic environment for an agent that searches a grid in order to find a human. The agent program searches a grid by performing `move_to` actions. When the scheduler calls the environment it inserts the perception that the robot sees a human to rescue.

Example B.3

```
public class RobotEnv extends DefaultEnvironment              1
                implements MCAPLJobber {                      2
                                                              3
  public RobotEnv() {                                         4
    super();                                                  5
    getScheduler().addJobber(this);                           6
  }                                                           7
                                                              8
  @Override                                                   9
  public int compareTo(MCAPLJobber o) {                      10
    return o.getName().compareTo(getName());                 11
  }                                                          12
                                                             13
  @Override                                                  14
  public void do_job() {                                     15
    addPercept(new Predicate("human"));                      16
  }                                                          17
                                                             18
  @Override                                                  19
  public String getName() {                                  20
    return "gwendolen.ail_tutorials.tutorial3.RobotEnv";     21
  }                                                          22
                                                             23
  @Override                                                  24
  public Unifier executeAction(String agName, Action act)    25
                throws AILexception {                        26
    if (act.getFunctor().equals("move_to")) {               27
      Predicate robot_position = new Predicate("at");        28
      Predicate old_position = new Predicate("at");          29
      robot_position.addTerm(act.getTerm(0));                30
      robot_position.addTerm(act.getTerm(1));                31
      old_position.addTerm(new VarTerm("X"));                32
      old_position.addTerm(new VarTerm("Y"));                33
      removeUnifiesPercept(old_position);                    34
      addPercept(robot_position);                            35
    }                                                        36
    return super.executeAction(agName, act);                 37
  }                                                          38
}                                                            39
```

Line 2 shows that the class implements `MCAPLJobber`. At line 6 the environment is added as a jobber to the scheduler. Lines 9-23 show the three methods that need to be implemented for the `MCAPLJobber` interface. Schedulers generally compare jobbers by their names to `compareTo` implements this while `getName()` returns a name for the jobber. `do_job()` implements adding the perception of a human.

Lastly `executeAction` implements the result of the robot moving by changing the perceptions of its coordinates. This uses `removeUnifies Percept` to remove the old robot position before it then asserts the new one.

The AIL configuration file, `searcher.ail`, executes the search and rescue agent in this environment.

A Note on Schedulers

The default scheduler used by `DefaultEnvironment` is `ail.mas.ActionScheduler`. This makes a random scheduling choice from among all its jobbers each time perceptions change in the environment. In general this works well but can become a problem if one of the jobbers (either an agent or the environment) may get stuck in a run in which it never changes any perceptions – e.g., an agent never takes an action or only does print actions (or similar) which do not alter perceptions – in these situations that jobber can run indefinitely without the scheduler ever being prompted to make another choice.

One situation where this may commonly arise is if the environment modifies some underlying fields or data structures but this information only becomes available as perceptions when an agent does something (e.g., moves close enough to see the change). In this case the line

`getScheduler().perceptChanged();`

can be asserted at the end of the `do_job()` method. This will prompt the scheduler to make a new choice even though no explicit perceptions have changed.

There are other three other schedulers in the current distribution:

NActionScheduler This functions as `ActionScheduler` except every n times it is invoked it forces a choice irrespective of whether perceptions have changed. This can be particularly useful if the environment is connecting to an external system and its use is discussed in the EASS tutorials since the language is intended to work in this way. It is not advisable to use the `NActionScheduler` in verification since it contains counters that will increase the number of model-checking states.

RoundRobinScheduler This scheduler acts like `ActionScheduler` except that instead of making a random choice between jobbers, it selects each in turn.

SingleAgentScheduler This is for situations when there is only one jobber and effectively just returns that one jobber each time it is called.

If you wish to use a different scheduler in an environment then you must create the relevant scheduler object, add it to the environment (using `setScheduler(MCAPLScheduler s)` and also add it as a percept listener to the environment (using `addPerceptListener(MCAPL Percept(Listener s))`. If your environment subclasses `ail.mas.DefaultEnvironment` then you can call the method `setup_scheduler (AILEnv env, MCAPLScheduler s)` to do this for you.

B.3.2 Adding Randomness

Often we want an environment with some random behaviour to model, for instance, unreliable sensors or actuators.

It is tempting to add random behaviour to an environment simply through use of Java's `Random` class. However this will break the system's ability to record and replay runs through the program which can be very useful in debugging. The simplest way to add some random behaviour to an environment is to subclass `ail.mas.DefaultEnvironmentwRandomness` rather than `ail.mas.DefaultEnvironment`. This provides two `Choice` objects which are the mechanism the AIL manages random behaviour for recording and replaying.

The `random_booleans` object has one method, `nextBoolean()` which will return either true or false. The `random_ints` object has one method, `nextInt(int i)`, which will return a random integer between 0 and i. Example B.4 shows a sample environment for the search and rescue robot. This has a human at (1,1) in the grid and the robot has a 50 per cent chance of spotting the human if it is in the same grid square. If you run this program several times you will see that sometimes the robot finds the human quickly and sometimes it has to search the grid several times.

Example B.4

```
public class RandomRobotEnv                                          1
        extends DefaultEnvironmentwRandomness {                      2
  int human_x = 1;                                                   3
  int human_y = 1;                                                   4
                                                                     5
  public Unifier executeAction(String agName, Action act)           6
                throws AILexception {                                7
    if (act.getFunctor().equals("move_to")) {                       8
      Predicate robot_position = new Predicate("at");               9
      Predicate old_position = new Predicate("at");                10
      robot_position.addTerm(act.getTerm(0));                      11
      robot_position.addTerm(act.getTerm(1));                      12
      old_position.addTerm(new VarTerm("X"));                      13
      old_position.addTerm(new VarTerm("Y"));                      14
      removeUnifiesPercept(old_position);                          15
      addPercept(robot_position);                                  16
      if (((NumberTerm) act.getTerm(0)).solve() == human_x         17
          &&                                                        18
          ((NumberTerm) act.getTerm(1)).solve() == human_y )       19
      {                                                             20
        if (random_booleans.nextBoolean()) {                        21
          addPercept(new Predicate("human"));                      22
        }                                                           23
      }                                                             24
    }                                                               25
    return super.executeAction(agName, act);                       26
  }                                                                 27
                                                                    28
}                                                                   29
```

In example B.4 lines 20-22 add the percept, human, if random_booleans.nextBoolean() returns true.

Random Doubles

The AIL does not have support for random doubles (in part because model checking requires a finite state space) but it does let you specify a probability distribution over a set of choices. To do this you need to create your own Choice object. Say, for instance, in the above example the human is moving between the squares and could be at (0,1), (1,1) or (2,1) with a 50% chance of being at (1,1), a 30% chance of being at (2,1) and a 20% chance of being at (0,1).

Example B.5 shows an environment with this behaviour. An integer Choice object, human_location is declared as a field in line 5. This is then instantiated by the `setMAS` method in lines 28-34. This method overrides the implementation in `DefaultEnvironmentwRandomness` so first we call the super-method, then we create the `Choice` object and lastly we add the choices to it – the humans x-coordinate is 1 with a probability of 0.5, 2 with a probability of 0.3 and 0 with a probability of 0.2. It is important to note that the `Choice` object cannot be created when the class is created since it needs to be instantiated by a `MCAPLController` object [1]. Any instantiation of an Environment class that involves choice methods (e.g., placing objects at random places within the environment) should be done in the `setMAS` method after the `Choice` objects have been instantiated and *not* in the classes constructore or `initialise` method.

In line 18 you can see the call to the `Choice` object's `get_choice()` method being invoked to return the correct integer.

Example B.5

```
public  class  RandomRobotEnv2                                              1
        extends  DefaultEnvironmentwRandomness {                           2
   int  human_x = 1;                                                        3
   int  human_y = 1;                                                        4
   Choice<Integer>  human_location;                                         5
                                                                           6
   public  Unifier  executeAction(String  agName,  Action  act)            7
                       throws  AILexception {                              8
    if  (act.getFunctor().equals("move_to")) {                            9
       Predicate  robot_position = new  Predicate("at");                   10
       Predicate  old_position = new  Predicate("at");                     11
       robot_position.addTerm(act.getTerm(0));                            12
       robot_position.addTerm(act.getTerm(1));                            13
       old_position.addTerm(new  VarTerm("X"));                           14
       old_position.addTerm(new  VarTerm("Y"));                           15
       removeUnifiesPercept(old_position);                                16
       addPercept(robot_position);                                        17
       human_x = human_location.get_choice();                             18
       if  (((NumberTerm) act.getTerm(0)).solve() == human_x             19
             &&                                                           20
          ((NumberTerm) act.getTerm(1)).solve() == human_y )             21
          addPercept(new  Predicate("human"));                           22
       }                                                                  23
    }                                                                     24
    return  super.executeAction(agName, act);                             25
   }                                                                      26
```

[1] This is the object that governs the overrall behaviour of the system but which is not available when the class it created. As part of setting up a multi-agent system in the AIL the `setMAS(MCAPLController m)` from the environment will be invoked at a suitable moment after the controller has been created.

```
                                                                  27
public void setMAS(MAS m) {                                       28
    super.setMAS(m);                                              29
    human_location = new Choice<Integer>(m.getController()); 30
    human_location.addChoice(0.5, 1);                            31
    human_location.addChoice(0.3, 2);                            32
    human_location.addChoice(0.2, 0);                            33
}                                                                34
                                                                  35
}                                                                36
```

Choice objects can be created to return any object – integers, Predicates, AILAgents, and so on,[2] by being given the correct type and instantiated correctly. It is important to remember that the probabilities of the choices added by the addChoice method should add up to 1.

If you genuinely need random doubles in an AIL environment then you can use Java's Random class but be aware that the record and replay functionality will no longer work.

B.3.3 Record and Replay

When debugging a multi-agent program you sometimes want to replay the exact sequence of events that occurred in the problem run. To do this you first need to record the sequence. You can get an AIL program to record its sequence of choices (in this case choices about whether or not the agent perceives the human) by adding the line

```
ajpf.record = true
```

to the program's AIL configuration file. There is an example of this in the configuration file searcher_random_record.ail in the tutorial directory. By default this records the current path through the program in a file called record.txt in the directory, records of the MCAPL distribution. You can change the file using ajpf.replay.file =.

To play back a record you include the following in the program's AIL configuration file

```
ajpf.replay = true
```

---

[2] The sample answer to the exercise at the end of this tutorial has an example of a Choice object for a Java enum type created just for the example.

The configuration file `searcher_random_replay.ail` is set up to replay runs generated by `searcher_random_record.ail`. Again, by default, this will replay the sequence from `record.txt`, but will use a different file if `ajpf.replay.file =` is set.

B.3.4 Exercise

Obviously for complex systems you often want to combine dynamic environments with randomness.

Adapt the various search and rescue environments so that the human moves one square in a random direction each time the environment's `do_job` method is called, to simulate a human moving independently around the search grid (N.B. the search grid is 3x3 with coordinates ranging from (0,0) to (2,2) – you may assume it wraps if you wish).

You may use either `random_booleans` or `random_ints` to generate movement, however the sample answer (in the `answers` directory) creates a probability distribution over a custom Java `enum` type with the human most likely to remain stationary and least likely to move diagonally.

Since you are altering the position of the human in this environment, not the perceptions available, you will find that the scheduler will loop infinitely when selecting the environment unless you include the line

```
getScheduler().perceptChanged();
```

at the end of `do_job` or you use a different scheduler.

Check that your solution works with record and replay.

B.4 Tutorial 4: Custom Configuration and Logging

This is the fourth in a series of tutorials on the use of the Agent Infrastructure Layer (AIL). This tutorial covers using configuration and logging when programming with the AIL. These are particularly relevant for constructing environments but can be useful elsewhere.

Files for this tutorial can be found in the `mcapl` distribution in the directory

```
src/examples/gwendolen/ail_tutorials/tutorial4
```

You can find sample answers for all the exercises in this tutorial in the `answers` directory.

The tutorial assumes a working knowledge of Java programming and the implementation of logging in Java.

B.4.1 Logging

Java has a flexible API for implementing logging within programs. Unfortunately this does not work seamlessly within JPF and hence within AJPF. In order to enable logging to be used in AIL programs we have therefore provided a class `ajpf.util.AJPFLogger` which uses the native Java logging capabilities when not executed within AJPF but uses JPF's logging support when it is.

`AJPFLogger` supports the six logging levels of the Java logging framework, namely, `SEVERE`, `WARNING`, `INFO`, `FINE`, `FINER`, and `FINEST`. If you want to print a log message at a particular log level, say `info`, you call the method `AJPFLogger.info(String logname, String message)` and similarly for `severe`, `warning` etc.

When logging, Java/JPF will print out all messages for a log at the set logging level and higher. So if you have set a log at level `FINE` in your AIL or JPF configuration file you will get all messages for `FINE`, `INFO`, `WARNING`, and `SEVERE`.

The `logname` can be any string you like, though in general people use the class name for the logname. However there is no reason not to use log names associated with particular tasks your program performs or other groupings if that seems more sensible.

It is worth noting that Java's string manipulation is not particularly efficient. If you are constructing a complex string for a log message it can be worth putting the message within an if statement in order to prevent the string being constructed if it will not be printed. This can improve the speed of model checking, in particular. To help with this `AJPFLogger` provides four helper methods:

- `public boolean AJPFLogger.ltFinest(String logname)`,
- `public boolean AJPFLogger.ltFiner(String logname)`,
- `public boolean AJPFLogger.ltFine(String logname)`,
- `public boolean AJPFLogger.ltInfo(String logname)`

These return true if `logname` is set at or below a particular logging level. Therefore you can use the construction:

```
if (AJPFLogger.lfFine(logname)) {
    String s = ....
    .... code for constructing your log message ...
    AJPFLogger.fine(logname, s);
}
```

in order to ensure the string construction only takes place if the message will actually get logged.

Exercise

In the tutorial directory you will find a simple environment for a search and rescue robot (`RobotEnv.java`) together with code and a configuration file for the robot (`searcher.ail, searcher.gwen`). The robot moves around a 3 × 3 square searching for a human which may randomly appear in any square. If the human appears the robot sends a message to some lifting agent and then stops. If you run this program with the supplied AIL configuration you will see it printing out the standard messages from `ail.mas.DefaultEnvironment` noting when the robot moves and when it sends a message.

Adapt the environment with the following log messages

- If logging is set to `INFO` it prints out a message when the system first decides a human is visible,
- If logging is set to `FINE` it prints a message every time the agent is informed the human is visible (not just when the human first appears) and,
- If logging is set to `FINER` it prints a message every time the agent checks its percepts.

Experiment with setting log levels in the AIL configuration file. Note that by default anything at `INFO` or higher gets printed. If you do not want to see `INFO` level log messages then you need to configure the logger to a higher level e.g. `log.warning = gwendolen.ail_tutorials.tutorial4.RobotEnv`.

B.4.2 Customized Configuration

You can use the `key = value` mechanism inside AIL configuration files to create customisation for your own AIL programs. When the configuration file is parsed all the properties are stored in an `ail.util.AILConfig` object which is itself an extension of the Java `java.util.Properties` class.

The `Properties` class has two methods of particular note:

- `public boolean containsKey(String key)` tells you if a particular key is contained in the configuration.
- `public Object get(String key)` returns the value stored for the key. If parsed from an AIL configuration file this will return a `String`.

You can then use Java methods such as `Boolean.valueOf(String s)` and `Integer.valueOf(String s)` to convert that value into a boolean, integer, or other type if desired.

Obviously in order to add your own key/value pairs to the configuration you need to be able to access the `AILConfig` object. The easiest way to do this is via your environment. During system initialisation a method `public void configure(AILConfig config)` is called on any AIL environment. The default implementation of this method does nothing, but it is easy enough to override this in a customised environment and check any keys you are interested in.

This can be particularly useful in environments used for verification where you may wish to have a range of slightly different behaviours in the environment for efficiency reasons. Listing B.6 shows (a slightly shortened version of) the `configure` method used by `eass.verification.leo.LEOVerificationEnvironment` which was used for the Low Earth Orbit satellite verifications described in Dennis et al. (2016c). Most of the values used here are `true`/`false` values parsed into booleans but in line 30 you can see a value that is being treated as a string (where the target formation can be either `line` or `square`). In that paper you can see that different properties were proved against different sets of percepts. The `configure` method was used in conjunction with AIL configuration files for each example in order to tweak the environment to use the correct settings. You can find all the configuration files in the `examples/eass/verification/leo` directory.

Example B.6

```
public void configure(AILConf conf) {                                    1
    if (conf.containsKey("allthrusters")) {                              2
        at = Boolean.valueOf((String) conf.get("allthrusters"))          3
    }                                                                    4
                                                                         5
    if (conf.containsKey("allpositions")) {                              6
        ap = Boolean.valueOf((String) conf.get("allpositions"));         7
    }                                                                    8
                                                                         9
    if (conf.containsKey("formation_line")) {                           10
        fl = Boolean.valueOf((String) conf.get                          11
        ("formation_line"));                                            12
    }                                                                   13
                                                                        14
    if (conf.containsKey("formation_square")) {                        15
        fs = Boolean.valueOf((String) conf.get                         16
```

```
        ("formation_square");                                        17
    }                                                                18
                                                                     19
    if (conf.containsKey("all_can_break")) {                         20
        ab = Boolean.valueOf((String) conf.get                       21
        ("all_can_break"));                                          22
    }                                                                23
                                                                     24
    if (conf.containsKey("changing_formation")) {                    25
        changing_formations =                                        26
          Boolean.valueOf((String) conf.get                          27
          ("changing_formations"));                                  28
        if (changing_formations) {                                   29
            formation_line = true;                                   30
            formation_square = true;                                 31
        } else {                                                     32
            if (conf.containsKey("initial_formation")) {             33
                if (conf.get("initial_formation").equals("line"))    34
                {                                                    35
                    formation_line = true;                           36
                    formation_square = false;                        37
                } else {                                             38
                    formation_line = false;                          39
                    formation_square = true;                         40
                }                                                    41
            } else {                                                 42
                formation_line = true;                               43
                formation_square = false;                            44
            }                                                        45
        }                                                            46
    }                                                                47
}                                                                    48
```

Exercise

Adapt RobotEnv so it has a configuration option in which the robot always sees a human when it moves rather than there being a random chance of seeing a human.

B.5 Tutorial 5: Environments for the EASS Variant of GWENDOLEN

This is the second in a series of tutorials on the use of the EASS variant of the GWENDOLEN language. This tutorial covers creating environments for agent programs by extending the eass.mas.DefaultEASSEnvironment class.

Files for this tutorial can be found in the `mcapl` distribution in the directory `src/examples/eass/tutorials/tutorial2`.

The tutorial assumes a good working knowledge of Java programming, and some basic understanding of sockets. It also assumes the reader is familiar with the creation of AIL environments (see Section B.2).

B.5.1 The Default Environment and the AILEnv Interface

All environments for use with EASS must implement a java interface `eass.mas.EASSEnv`. This extends `ail.mas.AILEnv` (discussed in Section B.2) and `ajpf.MCAPLJobber` which specifies the functionality required for AJPF to include the environment in the scheduler. One of the key features of EASS environments is that they are *dynamic* – that is things may occur in the environment which are not caused by the agents. The AJPF framework uses a scheduler to switch between agents and any other *jobbers* known to the scheduler. When a dynamic environment is used the scheduler switches between agents and the environment. In fact there are a number of schedulers that can be used (See Section B.3). As well as the functionality required by the two interfaces it extends, `eass.mas.EASSEnv` requires some extra functionality to support the EASS GWENDOLEN variant, particularly managing the links between abstraction and reasoning engines and shared beliefs.

`eass.mas.DefaultEASSEnvironment` provides a basic level implementation of all these methods, so any environment that extends it only has to worry about those aspects particular to that environment. Typically this is just the way that actions performed by the agents are to be handled and the way perceptions may change in between agent actions. `ail.mas.Default EASSEnvironment` also provides a set of useful methods for handling changing the perceptions available to the agent that can then be used to program these action results. `eass.mas.DefaultEASSEnvironment` extends `ail.mas.DefaultEnvironment` (see Section B.2) so all the methods available in that class are also available to classes that subclass `eass.mas.DefaultEASSEnvironment`.

B.5.2 A Survey of some of Default EASS Environment's Methods

We note here some of the more useful methods made available by the Default Environment before we talk about implementing the outcomes of agent actions and getting new perceptions.

public static void scheduler_setup(EASSEnv env, MCAPLScheduler s)
 This takes an environment (typically one sub-classing `eass.mas.`

DefaultEASSEnvironment) and a scheduler and sets the environment and scheduler up appropriately. In general an EASS environment will want to use ail.mas.NActionScheduler – this is a scheduler which can switch between agents and the environment every time an agent takes an action but will also switch every N reasoning cycles in to force checking of changes in the environment. A good value to start N at is 100 though this will vary by application. A typical constructor for an environment may look something like Example B.7.

Example B.7

```
public MyEnvironment() {                             1
     super();                                        2
     super.scheduler_setup(this,                     3
          new NActionScheduler(100));                4
}                                                    5
```

· **public void addUniquePercept(String s, Predicate per)** It is fairly typical in the kinds of applications the EASS is used for that incoming perceptions indicate the current value of some measure – e.g. the current distance to the car in front. This gets converted into a predicate such as $distance(5.5)$ however the application only wants to have one such percept available. addUniquePercept avoids the need to use removeUnifiesPercept followed by addPercept each time the value changes. Instead addUniquePercept takes a unique reference string, s (normally the functor of the predicate – e.g., distance) and then removes the old percept and adds the new one.

public void addUniquePercept(String agName, String s, Literal pred) As above but the percept is perceivable only by the agent called agName.

B.5.3 Default Actions

Just as ail.mas.DefaultEnvironment provides a set of built-in actions, so does eass.mas.DefaultEASSEnvironment. These critically support some aspects of the EASS language:

assert_shared(B) This puts B in the shared belief set.

remove_shared(B) This removes B from the shared belief set.

remove_shared_unifies(B) This removes all beliefs that unify with B from the shared belief set. This is useful when you do not necessarily know the current value of one of a shared belief's parameters.

perf(G) This sends a message to the abstraction engine requesting it adopt G as a perform goal.

append_string_pred(S, T, V) This is occasionally useful for converting between values treated as parameters by the agent, but which need to be translated to unique actions for the application (e.g., converting from $thruster(2)$ to 'thruster_2'). It takes a string as its first argument, a term, T, as its second argument. It converts T to a string and then unifies the concatenation of the first string and the new string with V.

B.5.4 Adding Additional Actions

Adding additional actions can be done in the same way as for environments that subclass `ail.mas.DefaultEnvironment` (see Section B.2).

B.5.5 Adding Dynamic Behaviour

Dynamic behaviour can be added by overriding the method `do_job()`. This method is called each time the scheduler executes the environment. Overrides of this method can be used simply to change the set of percepts (possibly at random) or to read data from sockets or other communications mechanisms.

Once an environment is dynamic and is included in the scheduler it sometimes becomes important to know when the multi-agent system has finished running. This is not always the case, sometimes you want it to keep running indefinitely and just kill it manually when you are done, but if you want the system to shut down neatly then the scheduler needs to be able to detect when the environment has finished. To do this it calls the methods `public boolean done()` which should return `true` if the environment has finished running and `false` otherwise.

B.5.6 Example

In `CarOnMotorwayEnvironment`, you can find an example EASS environment for connecting to the Motorway Simulator over a socket in the tutorial directory. We will examine this section by section[3].

---

[3] EASS comes with a dedicated class
`eass.mas.socket.EASSSocketClientEnvironment` for environments that

Example B.8

```
public  class  CarOnMotorwayEnvironment                          1
              extends  DefaultEASSEnvironment  {                 2
                                                                 3
  String  logname  =                                             4
      "eass.tutorials.tutorial2.CarOnMotorwayEnvironment";       5
                                                                 6
  /**                                                            7
   * Socket  that  connects  to  the  Simulator.                 8
   */                                                            9
  protected  AILSocketClient  socket;                           10
                                                                11
  /**                                                           12
   * Has  the  environment  concluded?                          13
   */                                                           14
  private  boolean  finished  =  false;                         15
```

Example B.8 shows initialisation of the class. It sub-classes `DefaultEASS Environment`, sets up a name for logging and a socket. The AIL comes with some support for socket programming. `ail.util.AIL SocketClient` is a class for sockets which are clients of some server (as required by the Motorway simulator). Lastly the environment sets up a boolean to track whether it has finished executing.

Example B.9

```
public  CarOnMotorwayEnvironment()  {                            1
   super();                                                      2
   super.scheduler_setup(this,   new  NActionScheduler(100));  3
   AJPFLogger.info(logname,  "Waiting_Connection");             4
   socket  =  new  AILSocketClient();                           5
   AJPFLogger.info(logname,  "Connected_to_Socket");            6
}                                                                7
```

Example B.9 shows the class constructor. We've set the environment up with an *NActionScheduler* – this scheduler switches between jobbers every time an agent takes and action, *but also*, every n turns of a reasoning cycle. In this case

communicate with simulators via sockets. We discuss an environment implementation that does not use this class for tutorial purposes, but many applications may wish to use it.

n is set to 100. This means that the environment keeps up to date processing input from the simulator even while agent deliberation is going on. We then create the socket, we do not supply a port number for the socket. The AIL socket classes have a default port number they use and the Motorway simulator uses this port so we do not need to specify it. We are using the `AJPFLogger` class to provide output. We will cover this in future tutorials. In this instance printing messages to System Error or System out would work as well.

Example B.10

```
public void do_job() {                                           1
   if (socket.allok()) {                                         2
      readPredicatesfromSocket();                               3
   } else {                                                     4
      System.err.println("something_wrong_with_socket");       5
   }                                                             6
}                                                                7
                                                                 8
/**                                                              9
 * Reading the values from the sockets                          10
 * and turning them into perceptions.                           11
 */                                                              12
public void readPredicatesfromSocket() {                         13
   socket.readDouble();                                         14
   socket.readDouble();                                         15
   double xdot = socket.readDouble();                           16
   double ydot = socket.readDouble();                           17
   int started = socket.readInt();                              18
                                                                 19
   try {                                                         20
      while (socket.pendingInput()) {                           21
         socket.readDouble();                                   22
         socket.readDouble();                                   23
         xdot = socket.readDouble();                            24
         ydot = socket.readDouble();                            25
         started = socket.readInt();                            26
      }                                                          27
   } catch (Exception e) {                                      28
      AJPFLogger.warning(logname, e.getMessage());             29
   }                                                             30
                                                                 31
   Literal xspeed = new Literal("xspeed");                      32
   xspeed.addTerm(new NumberTermImpl(xdot));                    33
                                                                 34
   Literal yspeed = new Literal("yspeed");                      35
   yspeed.addTerm(new NumberTermImpl(ydot));                    36
                                                                 37
   if (started > 0) {                                            38
      addPercept(new Literal("started"));                       39
   }                                                             40
```

```
addUniquePercept("xspeed", xspeed);                    41
addUniquePercept("yspeed", yspeed);                    42
}                                                       43
                                                        44
```

Example B.10 shows the code that gets executed each time the environment is scheduled to run. In this case we want to get up-to-date values from the simulator by reading them off the socket. The simulator posts output in sets of four doubles and then an integer representing the x position, y position, x speed, y speed of the car and finally the integer represents whether the simulation has started or not. The code in lines 14–17 reads off these values. This particular application is not interested in the x and y position, so these are ignored but the speeds and starting information are saved as variables. Note that different methods are used to read doubles and integers, it is important to use the right methods otherwise simulator and agent environment can get out of sync since different datatypes use up different numbers of bytes on the socket. Lines 21–27 then repeat this process on a loop. socket.pendingInput() returns true if there is any data left to be read off the socket. Since the environment and simulator probably will not be entirely running in sync this loop is used to read all available data off the socket. The final assignment of values to variables will represent the most recent state of the simulation and so is probably the best data to pass on to the agent. Lines 32–26 show the environment turning the numbers read from the socket into literals for use by the agent. Finally addUniquePercept is used to add the percepts for xspeed and yspeed to the environment. We only want one value for each of these to be available to the agent so we use the special method to remove the old value and add the new one.

Example B.11

```
public Unifier executeAction(String agName, Action act)        1
    throws AILexception {                                      2
                                                               3
    if (act.getFunctor().equals("accelerate")) {               4
        socket.writeDouble(0.0);                               5
        socket.writeDouble(0.01);                              6
    } else if (act.getFunctor().equals("decelerate")) {        7
        socket.writeDouble(0.0);                               8
        socket.writeDouble(-0.1);                              9
```

```
    } else if (act.getFunctor().equals("maintain_speed")) {    10
        socket.writeDouble(0.0);                                11
        socket.writeDouble(0.0);                                12
    } else if (act.getFunctor().equals("finished")) {          13
        finished = true;                                        14
    }                                                           15
                                                                16
    return super.executeAction(agName, act);                   17
}                                                               18
```

Example B.11 shows the executeAction method. Here, as well as the actions, such as assert_shared, remove_shared, perf and .query provided by DefaultEASSEnvironment the environment offers accelerate, decelerate, maintain_speed and finished. The Motorway simulator regularly checks the socket and expects to find pairs of doubles on it giving the acceleration in the x and y directions respectively. The environment treats requests for acceleration and deceleration from the agent as requests to speed up or slow down in the y direction, but since the simulator expects a pair of values it has to write the x acceleration to the socket as well. finished is treated as a request to stop the environment and the boolean finished is set to true.

Example B.12

```
public void cleanup() {                                         1
    socket.close();                                             2
}                                                               3
                                                                4
/*                                                              5
 * (non-Javadoc)                                                6
 * @see ail.others.DefaultEnvironment#done()                    7
 */                                                             8
public boolean done() {                                         9
    if (finished) {                                            10
        return true;                                           11
    }                                                          12
    return false;                                             13
}                                                             14
```

Example B.12 shows the code used when to notify the system that the environment is finished (by overriding done) and an over-ride of the cleanup()

method which is called before the system shuts down. This is used to close the socket.

Executing the Example

The example is a variation on the one used in Section A.10 and can be executed in the same way by first starting up `MotorwayMain` and then running AIL on `car.ail`. The main difference is that the agent in this program executes the `finished` action once the car has reached the speed limit. This results in the multi-agent system shutting down and the socket being closed. These actions do not terminate the simulation which will continue executing, but you will be able to see error messages of the form `WARNING: Broken pipe` being generated by its attempts to read data from the socket.

B.5.7 Sending Messages

The `executeAction` method in the default environment simply places messages directly into the intended recipient's inbox. Obviously there will be situations, particularly if the multi-agent system needs to send messages over a socket or similar, where this will not suffice.

In fact `executeAction` calls a method, `executeSendAction`: `public void executeSendAction(String agName, Send Actionact)` so the simplest way to alter an environment's message-sending behaviour is to override this method.

The `SendAction` class has several useful methods such as:

Message getMessage(String agName) which returns the `Message` object associated with the action and takes the name of the sender as an argument.

Term getReciever() returns the name of the intended receiver of the message as a `Term`.

`Message` objects are described in Section B.2.

B.5.8 Exercises

Changing Lane

In the tutorial directory you will find an EASS program, `car_exercises.eass`. This contains a car control program that attempts to change lane (action `change_lane`) once the car has reached the speed limit. It then checks a perception, `xpos(X)` for the x position of the car until it believes it is in the next lane at which point it instructs the environment to stay in that lane (action `stay_in_lane`).

Extend and adapt `CarOnMotorwayEnvironment.java` to act as a suitable environment for this program. As normal answers (including an AIL configuration file) can be found in the `answers` directory for the tutorial.

Changing the Simulator Behaviour

It is possible to change the behaviour of the Motorway Simulator by providing it with a config file. A sample one is provided in the tutorial directory. This new configuration gets the simulator to write 7 values to the socket rather than five. These are, in order, the total distance travelled in the x direction, the total distance travelled in the y direction, the x coordinate of the car in the interface, the y coordinate of the car in the interface, the speed in the x direction, the speed in the y direction and whether the simulator has started now.

The simulator can be started in this configuration by supplying '`/src/examples/eass/tutorials/tutorial2/config.txt`' as an argument to `MotorwayMain` (If you are using Eclipse you can add arguments to Run Configurations in a tab). Adapt the environment to run `car_exercises.eass` in this environment. As normal answers (including an AIL configuration file) can be found in the `answers` directory for the tutorial.

Appendix C
AJPF Documentation

C.1 Tutorial 1: The Property Specification Language

This is the first in a series of tutorials on the use of the AJPF model-checking program. This tutorial covers the basics of configuring a model-checking run and writing properties in AJPF's property specification language.

Files for this tutorial can be found in the `mcapl` distribution in the directory

`src/examples/gwendolen/ajpf_tutorials/tutorial1`.

The tutorials assume some familiarity with the basics of running Java programs either at the command line or in Eclipse and some familiarity with the syntax and semantics of Linear Temporal Logic.

C.1.1 Setting up Agent Java Pathfinder

Before you can run AJPF it is necessary to set up your computer to use Java Pathfinder. There are instructions for doing this in the MCAPL manual (which you can find in the `doc` directory of the distribution).

The key point is that you need to create a file called `.jpf/site.properties` in your home directory on the computer you are using. In this file you need to put one line which assigns the path to the MCAPL distribution to the key `mcapl`. For instance if you have your MCAPL distribution in your home directory as folder called `mcapl` then `site.properties` should contain the line.

`mcapl = ${user.home}/mcapl`

We strongly recommend that you also set up an environment variable, `$AJPF_HOME`, set it to the path to the MCAPL directory and add this to your `.bashrc` or equivalent start-up files.

C.1.2 A Simple Model-Checking Attempt

To run AJPF you need to run the program `gov.jpf.tool.RunJPF` which is contained in `lib/3rdparty/RunJPF.jar` in the MCAPL distribution. Alternatively you can use the `run-JPF` (MCAPL) Run Configuration in Eclipse.

You need to supply a JPF Configuration file as an argument. You will find a sample file in

```
src/examples/gwendolen/ajpf_tutorials/lifterandmedic.jpf.
```

If you run this you should see output like the following:

```
JavaPathfinder v7.0 (rev ${version}) - (C) RIACS/NASA A...


=============================== system under test
ail.util.AJPF_w_AIL.main("/Users/lad/mcapl/src/...

=============================== search started: 02/...

=============================== results
no errors detected

=============================== statistics
elapsed time:          00:00:12
states:                new=96, visited=116, backtr...
search:                maxDepth=16, constraints hit=0
choice generators:     thread=1 (signal=0, lock=1, sh...
heap:                  new=761483, released=752805, ...
instructions:          122799365
max memory:            495MB
loaded code:           classes=316, methods=4705

=============================== search finished: 02/...
```

Note this will take several seconds to generate. We will discuss in future tutorials how to get more detailed output from the model-checker.

At the moment the key point is the fact that it states `no errors detected`. This means that the property supplied to the model-checker was true for this program.

C.1.3 JPF Configuration Files

`lifterandmedic.jpf` is a JPF Configuration file. There are a large number of configuration options for JPF which you can find in the JPF documentation.[1] We will only discuss a handful of these options. If you open `lifterandmedic.jpf` you should see the following:

```
@using = mcapl

target = ail.util.AJPF_w_AIL
target.args = ${mcapl}/src/examples/.../answers/ex2.ail,
          ${mcapl}/src/examples/.../tutorial1/lifterandmedic.psl,1
```

We explain each line of this below.

@using = mcapl Means that the proof is using the home directory for `mcapl` that you set up in `.jpf/site.properties`.

target = ail.util.AJPF_w_AIL This is the Java file containing the main method for the program to be model-checked. By default when model-checking a program implemented using the AIL, you should use `ail.util.AJPF_w_AIL` as the target. For those who are familiar with running programs in the AIL, this class is very similar to `ail.mas.AIL` but with a few tweaks to set up and optimise model-checking.

target.args = ... This sets up the arguments to be passed to `ail.util.AJPF_w_AIL`. `ail.util.AJPF_w_AIL` takes three arguments. In the configuration file these all have to appear on one line, separated by commas (but *no spaces*). This means you cannot see them all in the file printout above. In order the arguments are:

1. The first is an AIL configuration file. In this example the file is

   `${mcapl}/src/examples/..../answers/ex2.ail`

   which is a configuration file for a multi-agent system written in the GWENDOLEN language. Note some of the path has been elided with `....`.

2. The second argument is a file containing a list of properties in AJPF's property specification language that can be checked. In this example this file is `lifterandmedic.psl` in the directory for this tutorial.

3. The last argument is the name of the property to be checked, `1` in this case.

---

[1] Currently to be found at `http://babelfish.arc.nasa.gov/trac/jpf`.

C.1.4 The Property Specification Language

Syntax The syntax for property formulæ ϕ is as follows, where ag is an 'agent constant' referring to a specific agent in the system, and f is a ground first-order atomic formula (although it may use _, as in Prolog, to indicate variables which may match any value):

$$\phi ::= \quad \mathbf{B}_{ag}\, \mathsf{f} \mid \mathbf{G}_{ag}\mathsf{f} \mid \mathbf{A}_{ag}\mathsf{f} \mid \mathbf{I}_{ag}\mathsf{f} \mid \mathbf{ID}_{ag}\mathsf{f} \mid \mathbf{P}\,\mathsf{f} \mid$$
$$\phi \vee \phi \mid \phi \wedge \phi \mid \neg\phi \mid \phi\, \mathsf{U}\, \phi \mid \phi\, \mathsf{R}\, \phi \mid \Diamond\phi \mid \Box\phi.$$

Here, $\mathbf{B}_{ag}\,\mathsf{f}$ is true if ag believes f to be true, $\mathbf{G}_{ag}\mathsf{f}$ is true if ag has a goal to make f true, and so on (with $\mathbf{A}$ representing actions, $\mathbf{I}$ representing intentions, $\mathbf{ID}$ representing the intention to take an action, and $\mathbf{P}$ representing percepts, that is, properties that are true in the environment).

The following representation of this syntax is used in AJPF's property specification files:

$$\phi ::= \quad \mathtt{B}\,(ag,\ f) \mid \mathtt{G}\,(ag,\ f) \mid \mathtt{D}\,(ag,\ f) \mid$$
$$\mathtt{I}\,(ag,\ f) \mid \mathtt{ItD}\,(ag,\ f) \mid \mathtt{P}\,(f)$$
$$\phi' ::= \quad \phi \mid \sim \phi \mid \phi' \mid\mid \phi' \mid \phi' \, \& \, \phi' \mid \phi'\, \mathtt{U}\, \phi' \mid \phi'\, \mathtt{R}\, \phi' \mid <>\phi' \mid [\,]\phi'.$$

Note, in particular, that in property specification files 'not' ($\sim$) must always appear in an innermost position next to one of the BDI agent properties such as $\mathtt{B}\,(ag,\ f)$.

It is also possible to use $\phi\mathord{-}\mathord{>}\psi$ as shorthand for $\neg\phi \vee \psi$ in property specification files.

Semantics We summarise semantics of property formulæ. Consider a program, P, describing a multi-agent system and let MAS be the state of the multi-agent system at one point in the run of P. MAS is a tuple consisting of the local states of the individual agents and of the environment. Let $ag \in MAS$ be the state of an agent in the MAS tuple at this point in the program execution. Then

$$MAS \models_{MC} \mathbf{B}_{ag}\, \mathsf{f} \quad \text{iff} \quad ag \models \mathbf{B}_{ag}\, \mathsf{f},$$

where $\models$ is logical consequence as implemented by the agent programming language. The semantics of $\mathbf{G}_{ag}\mathsf{f}$, $\mathbf{I}_{ag}\mathsf{f}$, and $\mathbf{ID}_{ag}\mathsf{f}$ similarly refer to internal implementations of the language interpreter.[2] The interpretation of $\mathbf{A}_{ag}\mathsf{f}$ is:

$$MAS \models_{MC} \mathbf{A}_{ag}\mathsf{f}$$

---

[2] We briefly cover the GWENDOLEN implementation in Section C.1.6.

if, and only if, the last action changing the environment was action f taken by agent ag. Finally, the interpretation of **P** f is given as:

$$MAS \models_{MC} \mathbf{P}\,f$$

if, and only if, f is a percept that holds true in the environment.

The other operators in the AJPF property specification language have standard PLTL semantics Emerson (1990) and are implemented as Büchi Automata as described in Gerth et al. (1996); Courcoubetis et al. (1992). Thus, the classical logic operators are defined by:

$$MAS \models_{MC} \varphi \vee \psi \quad \text{iff} \quad MAS \models_{MC} \varphi \text{ or } MAS \models_{MC} \psi$$
$$MAS \models_{MC} \neg \phi \quad \text{iff} \quad MAS \not\models_{MC} \phi.$$

The temporal formulae apply to runs of the programs in the JPF model-checker. A run consists of a (possibly infinite) sequence of program states MAS_i, $i \geq 0$ where MAS_0 is the initial state of the program (note, however, that for model-checking the number of *different* states in any run is assumed to be finite). Let P be a multi-agent program, then:

$MAS \models_{MC}$	$\varphi \cup \psi$	iff	in all runs of P there exists a state MAS_j such that $MAS_i \models_{MC} \varphi$ for all $0 \leq i < j$ and $MAS_j \models_{MC} \psi$.
$MAS \models_{MC}$	$\varphi \mathrel{R} \psi$	iff	either $MAS_i \models_{MC} \varphi$ for all i or there exists MAS_j such that $MAS_i \models_{MC} \varphi$ for all $0 \leq i \leq j$ and $MAS_j \models_{MC} \varphi \wedge \psi$.

Conjunction $\wedge$ and the common temporal operators $\Diamond$ (eventually) and $\Box$ (always) are, in turn, derivable from $\vee$, $\cup$ and R in the usual way Emerson (1990).

C.1.5 Exercises

If you look in `lifterandmedic.psl` you should see the following:

```
1: [] (~B(medic, bad))
```

So this file contains one formula, labelled, 1 and the formula is equivalent to $\Box \neg \mathbf{B}_{medic}$ bad – which means it is always the case the medic agent does not believe the formula bad (or alternatively that the medic agent never believes *bad*).

As noted previously the multi-agent system in `ex2.ail` is a GWENDOLEN program and is, in fact, the one described in Section A.8. It is not necessary, for this tutorial, to understand the implementation of the BDI modalities (belief, goal, intention etc.) in the GWENDOLEN interpreter but a brief discussion is included in Section C.1.6.

Adapt the JPF configuration file and extend the property specification file in the tutorial directory in order to verify the following properties of the multi-agent system. You can find sample answers in the `answers` directory.

1. Eventually the lifter believes $human(5, 5)$.

$$\Diamond \mathbf{B}_{\texttt{medic}} \, \mathsf{human}(5, 5).$$

2. Eventually the medic has the goal $assist\_human(5, 5)$.

$$\Diamond \mathbf{G}_{\texttt{medic}} \mathsf{human}(5, 5).$$

3. Eventually the lift believes $human(3, 4)$ and eventually the lifter believes $holding(rubble)$.

$$\Diamond \mathbf{B}_{\texttt{lifter}} \, \mathsf{human}(3, 4) \wedge \Diamond \mathbf{B}_{\texttt{lifter}} \, \mathsf{holding}(\mathsf{rubble}).$$

4. If the lifter has the intention to $goto55then34$ then eventually the medic will have the goal $assist\_human(5, 5)$.

$$\mathbf{I}_{\texttt{lifter}} \mathsf{goto55then34} \Rightarrow \mathbf{G}_{\texttt{medic}} \mathsf{assist\_human}(5, 5).$$

5. It is always the case that if the lifter does $move\_to(5, 5)$ then $human(5, 5)$ becomes perceptible.

$$\Box(\mathbf{A}_{\texttt{lifter}} \mathsf{move\_to}(5, 5) \Rightarrow \mathbf{P} \, \mathsf{human}(5, 5)).$$

6. Eventually the lifter intends to move to (5, 5).

$$\Diamond \mathbf{ID}_{\texttt{lifter}} \mathsf{move\_to}(5, 5).$$

7. Eventually the lifter intends to send the medic a perform request to assist the human in some square.

$$\Diamond \mathbf{ID}_{\texttt{lifter}} \mathsf{send}(\texttt{medic}, 2, \mathsf{assist\_human}(\_, \_)).$$

C.1.6 Implementation of BDI Modalities in GWENDOLEN

In GWENDOLEN the BDI modalities of the AJPF property specification language are implemented as follows.

- $\mathbf{B}_{ag}$ f. An agent, ag, believes the formula, f, if f appears in its belief base or is deducible from its belief base using its reasoning rules.

- $G_{ag}f$. An agent, ag, has a goal f, if f is a goal that appears in the agent's goal base.
- $I_{ag}f$. An agent, ag, has an intention f, if f is a goal in the goal base a plan has been selected to achieve or perform the goal.
- $ID_{ag}f$. An agent, ag, intends to do f, if f is an action that appears in the deed stack of some intention.

Intending to Send a Message

GWENDOLEN uses a special syntax for send actions (`.send(ag, :tell, c)`) which is not recognised by the property specification language. If you want to check that a GWENDOLEN agent intends to send a message then you need to use the syntax `send(agname, number, c)` where `agname` is the name of the recipient, `number` is

1 For `:tell`,
2 For `:perform`,
3 For `:achieve`

and `c` is the content of the message.

C.2 Tutorial 2: JPF Configuration Files: Troubleshooting Model-Checking

This is the second in a series of tutorials on the use of the AJPF model-checking program. This tutorial covers JPF configuration files in more detail as well as techniques for troubleshooting model-checking.

Files for this tutorial can be found in the `mcapl` distribution in the directory

`src/examples/gwendolen/ajpf_tutorials/tutorial2`.

The tutorials assume some familiarity with the basics of running Java programs either at the command line or in Eclipse and some familiarity with the syntax and semantics of Linear Temporal Logic, and the use of Büchi Automata in model-checking.

C.2.1 JPF Configuration Files

As mentioned in Section C.1, JPF has an extensive set of configuration options which you can find in the JPF documentation.[3] We only examined the most basic there but in this tutorial we will cover a few more that are useful, particularly when debugging a program you are attempting to model-check.

---

[3] Currently to be found at `http://babelfish.arc.nasa.gov/trac/jpf`.

In the tutorial directory you will find a simple GWENDOLEN program, `twopickupagents.gwen`. This contains two agents, one holding a block and one holding a flag. Each agent puts down what they are holding. If the agent with the block puts it down before the agent with the flag puts the flag down, then the agent with the flag will pick up the box. The agent with the flag also performs an action with random consequences after it puts down the flag.

TwoPickUpAgents_basic.jpf

`TwoPickUpAgents_basic.jpf` is a minimal configuration file containing only options discussed Section C.1. This generates the following output (ignoring some initial system information):

```
JavaPathfinder core system v8.0 - (C) 2005-2014 Unite....


===============================================....
ail.util.AJPF_w_AIL.main("/Users/louisedennis/eclipse....

===============================================....
MCAPL Framework 2020
ANTLR Tool version 4.4 used for code generation does ...
===============================================....
no errors detected

===============================================....
elapsed time:          00:00:05
states:                new=31,visited=32,backtracked=63,...
search:                maxDepth=7,constraints=0
choice generators:     thread=1 (signal=0,lock=1,shared...
heap:                  new=412761,released=409463,...
instructions:          28180407
max memory:            437MB
loaded code:           classes=326,methods=5084

===============================================...
```

This is obviously sufficient as output in situations where the model-checking completes quickly and with `no errors detected` but gives the user very little to go on if there is a problem or the model-checking is taking a long time and they are not sure whether to kill the attempt or not.

TwoPickUpAgents_ExecTracker.jpf

`TwoPickUpAgents_ExecTracker.jpf` adds the configuration option:

```
listener+=,.listener.ExecTracker
et.print_insn=false
et.show_shared=false
```

Adding listener.ExecTracker to JPF's listeners means that it collects more information about progress as it goes and then prints this information out. The next two lines suppress some of this information which is generally less useful in AJPF. With these settings the following output is generated (only the start is shown):

```
# choice: gov.nasa.jpf.vm.choice.ThreadChoiceFromSet {...
# garbage collection
------------------------------- [1] forward: 0 new
# choice: gov.nasa.jpf.vm.choice.IntChoiceFromSet[...
# garbage collection
------------------------------- [2] forward: 1 new
# choice: gov.nasa.jpf.vm.choice.IntChoiceFromSet[...
# garbage collection
------------------------------- [3] forward: 2 new
# choice: gov.nasa.jpf.vm.choice.IntChoiceFromSet[...
# garbage collection
------------------------------- [4] forward: 3 new
# choice: gov.nasa.jpf.vm.choice.IntChoiceFromSet[...
# garbage collection
------------------------------- [5] forward: 4 new
# choice: gov.nasa.jpf.vm.choice.IntChoiceFromSet[...
# garbage collection
------------------------------- [6] forward: 5 new
# choice: gov.nasa.jpf.vm.choice.IntChoiceFromSet[...
# garbage collection
------------------------------- [7] forward: 6 visited
------------------------------- [6] backtrack: 5
# choice: gov.nasa.jpf.vm.choice.IntChoiceFromSet[...
# garbage collection
------------------------------- [7] forward: 7 visited
------------------------------- [6] backtrack: 5
------------------------------- [6] done: 5
------------------------------- [5] backtrack: 4
# choice: gov.nasa.jpf.vm.choice.IntChoiceFromSet[...
# garbage collection
------------------------------- [6] forward: 8 new
# choice: gov.nasa.jpf.vm.choice.IntChoiceFromSet[...
# garbage collection
------------------------------- [7] forward: 6 visited
------------------------------- [6] backtrack: 8
```

Every time JPF generates a new state for model-checking it assigns that state a number. In the output here you can see it generating new states 0 through to 7 and advancing forward to each state. You then see it backtracking back to state 5 (which is fully explored done) and then state 4 at which point it finds a branching point in the search space and advances to state 8 and then again to state 6 which it has visited already and so backtracks to 8.

Typically search space branching is caused whenever a random value is generated. This happens most often when the multi-agent system scheduler must choose between several agents.

Random value generation activates an `IntChoiceFromSet` choice generator (which picks a random integer from a set – usually picking one number from a range). The scheduler keeps track of the agents which are awake and assigns an integer to them. Since there are only two agents, there is no choice if one is asleep, but you can see when the choice is between 0 and 1.

The numbers in square brackets – `[7]`, `[6]`, and so on, indicate the depth that model-checking has reached in the search tree. If these numbers become very large without apparent reason then it may well be the case that the search has encountered an infinite branch of the tree and needs to be killed.

Logging

JPF suppresses the logging configuration you have in your AIL configuration files so you need to add any logging configurations you want to the JPF configuration file. Useful classes when debugging a model-checking run are

ail.mas.DefaultEnvironment At the `info` level this prints out any actions the agent performs. Since the scheduler normally only switches between agents when one sleeps or performs an action this can be useful for tracking progress on this model-checking branch.

ajpf.MCAPLAgent At the `info` level this prints information when an agent sleeps or wakes. Again this can be useful for seeing what has triggered a scheduler switch. It can also be useful for tracking which agents are awake and so deducing which one is being picked from the set by the `IntChoiceFromSet` choice generator.

ajpf.product.Product At the `info` level this prints out the current path through the search tree being explored by the agent. This can be useful just to get a feel for the agents' progress through the search space. It can also be useful, when an error is thrown and in conjunction with some combination of logging actions, sleeping and waking behaviour and (if necessary) internal agent states, to work out why a property has failed to hold.

It also prints the message `Always True from Now On` when exploration of a branch of the search tree is halted because the system deduces that the property will be true for the rest of that branch. This typically occurs when the property is something like $\Diamond\phi$ (i.e., ϕ will eventually occur) and the search space is pruned once ϕ becomes true.

ajpf.psl.buchi.BuchiAutomaton At the `info` level this prints out the Büchi Automaton that has been generated from the property that is to be proved. Again this is useful, when model-checking fails, for working out what property was expected to hold in that state.

ail.semantics.AILAgent At the `fine` level this prints out the internal agent state once every reasoning cycle. Be warned that this produces a lot of output in the course of a model checking run.

In general, when working on a program for model checking it is useful to have the ExecTracker listener enabled and `ajpf.MCAPLAgent`, `ajpf.product.Product` and any environment loggers (so typically `ail.mas.DefaultEnvironment` and any sub-classes of that you are using) set at info. This provides a useful starting point for accessing information about model checking.

`TwoPickUpAgents_Logging.jpf` has this set up. Its output starts

```
[INFO] Adding 0 to []
------------------------------------ [1] forward: 0 new
  # choice: gov.nasa.jpf.vm.choice.IntChoiceFromSet[...
[INFO] ag2 done putdown(flag)
  # garbage collection
[INFO] Adding 1 to [0]
------------------------------------ [2] forward: 1 new
  # choice: gov.nasa.jpf.vm.choice.IntChoiceFromSet[...
  # garbage collection
[INFO] Adding 2 to [0, 1]
------------------------------------ [3] forward: 2 new
  # choice: gov.nasa.jpf.vm.choice.IntChoiceFromSet[...
[INFO] Block 1 is visible
  # garbage collection
[INFO] Adding 3 to [0, 1, 2]
------------------------------------ [4] forward: 3 new
  # choice: gov.nasa.jpf.vm.choice.IntChoiceFromSet[...
[INFO] Block 2 is visible
[INFO] ag2 done random
  # garbage collection
[INFO] Adding 4 to [0, 1, 2, 3]
------------------------------------ [5] forward: 4 new
  # choice: gov.nasa.jpf.vm.choice.IntChoiceFromSet[...
[INFO] Sleeping agent ag2
[INFO] Waking agent ag2
[INFO] ag1 done putdown(block)
  # garbage collection
[INFO] Adding 5 to [0, 1, 2, 3, 4]
------------------------------------ [6] forward: 5 new
  # choice: gov.nasa.jpf.vm.choice.IntChoiceFromSet[...
[INFO] Sleeping agent ag2
  # garbage collection
[INFO] Adding 6 to [0, 1, 2, 3, 4, 5, 6]
[INFO] Always True from Now On
------------------------------------ [7] forward: 6 visited
```

```
-------------------------------- [6] backtrack: 5
# choice: gov.nasa.jpf.vm.choice.IntChoiceFromSet[...
[INFO] Sleeping agent ag1
# garbage collection
[INFO] Adding 7 to [0, 1, 2, 3, 4, 5, 7]
[INFO] Always True from Now On
-------------------------------- [7] forward: 7 visited
-------------------------------- [6] backtrack: 5
-------------------------------- [6] done: 5
-------------------------------- [5] backtrack: 4
# choice: gov.nasa.jpf.vm.choice.IntChoiceFromSet[...
[INFO] ag1 done putdown(block)
# garbage collection
[INFO] Adding 8 to [0, 1, 2, 3, 4]
-------------------------------- [6] forward: 8 new
# choice: gov.nasa.jpf.vm.choice.IntChoiceFromSet[...
[INFO] Sleeping agent ag2
# garbage collection
[INFO] Adding 6 to [0, 1, 2, 3, 4, 8]
-------------------------------- [7] forward: 6 visited
-------------------------------- [6] backtrack: 8
# choice: gov.nasa.jpf.vm.choice.IntChoiceFromSet[...
[INFO] Sleeping agent ag1
# garbage collection
[INFO] Adding 7 to [0, 1, 2, 3, 4, 8]
-------------------------------- [7] forward: 7 visited
-------------------------------- [6] backtrack: 8
-------------------------------- [6] done: 8
-------------------------------- [5] backtrack: 4
-------------------------------- [5] done: 4
-------------------------------- [4] backtrack: 3
# choice: gov.nasa.jpf.vm.choice.IntChoiceFromSet[...
[INFO] Block 2 is not visible
[INFO] ag2 done random
# garbage collection
[INFO] Adding 9 to [0, 1, 2, 3]
-------------------------------- [5] forward: 9 new
# choice: gov.nasa.jpf.vm.choice.IntChoiceFromSet[...
[INFO] Sleeping agent ag2
[INFO] Waking agent ag2
[INFO] ag1 done putdown(block)
# garbage collection
[INFO] Adding 10 to [0, 1, 2, 3, 9]
-------------------------------- [6] forward: 10 new
```

You can see the additional information provided by the loggers here, in terms of printing out the current path through the search tree, reporting on sleeping and waking behaviour, and so on.

Important Note: While the additional output information can be very useful for understanding what is happening during a model-checking run, printing output slows down the computation. If speed of model-checking is important then it is best to turn off all logging and the `ExecTracker`.

Saving the log to a file

It is possible to save log messages generated by the AIL to a file by including `log.output = filename` (where `filename` is the name of the file you want to use) in your JPF configuration file. Unfortunately this does not save the output of the `ExecTracker` to the file but may nevertheless be useful.

C.2.2 What to Do When Model-Checking Fails

`TwoPickUpAgents_FalseProp.jpf` attempts to prove the property $\Diamond B_{ag2}$ hold(block) which is not true. The configuration file uses the normal loggers but does not have the `ExecTracker` listener.[4] The following output is generated.

```
====================================================== system...
ail.util.AJPF_w_AIL.main("/Users/lad/Eclipse/mcapl/src/...

====================================================== search s...
[INFO] Adding 0 to []
[INFO] ag2 done putdown(flag)
[INFO] Adding 1 to [0]
[INFO] Adding 2 to [0, 1]
[INFO] Block 1 is visible
[INFO] Adding 3 to [0, 1, 2]
[INFO] Block 2 is visible
[INFO] ag2 done random
[INFO] Adding 4 to [0, 1, 2, 3]
[INFO] Sleeping agent ag2
[INFO] Waking agent ag2
[INFO] ag1 done putdown(block)
[INFO] Adding 5 to [0, 1, 2, 3, 4]
[INFO] Sleeping agent ag2
[INFO] Adding 6 to [0, 1, 2, 3, 4, 5]

====================================================== error 1
ajpf.MCAPLListener
An Accepting Path has been found:
[MS: 0, BS: 2, UN: 0], [MS: 1, BS: 2, UN: 0],
[MS: 2, BS: 2, UN: 0], [MS: 3, BS: 2, UN: 0],
[MS: 4, BS: 2, UN: 0],
[MS: 5, BS: 2, UN: 0], [MS: 6, BS: 2, UN: 0],

====================================================== snap...
no live threads

====================================================== results
error #1: ajpf.MCAPLListener "An Accepting Path has been found...
```

---

[4] Largely to keep the output compact.

As can be seen at the end of the failed run this prints out the accepting path that it has found that makes the property false. This path is a sequence of triples consisting of the state in the model, MS, the state in the Büchi automaton generated from the negation of the property, BS, and lastly a count of the number of until statements that have been passed in this branch/loop of the search space (This counter is explained in (Gerth et al., 1996) – it is not normally useful for debugging properties but is included for completeness).

So we can see that the accepting path through the model is 0,1,2,3,4,5,6 and we can work out what happens on that path from the logging output: ag2 puts down the flag, both blocks becomes visible, ag2 does random and then sleeps, ag1 puts down the block, waking ag2 which then sleeps again. All these states in the model are paired with state 2 in the Büchi Automaton. To see the Büchi Automaton you have to add ajpf.psl.buchi.BuchiAutomaton to the logging.

If you do this you get the following print out at the start:

```
[INFO] Number: 2
Incoming States: 0,2,
True in this State: ~B(ag2,hold(block())),~T R ~B(ag2...
True in next State: ~T R ~B(ag2,hold(block())),
```

The property has created a very simple Büchi Automaton. It has been given the number 2 in the automaton generation process. It has two incoming states 0 (which is the start state) and 2 (i.e., itself). It has two properties that hold in that state $\neg \mathbf{B}_{ag2}$ hold(block) (ag2 does not believe it is holding the block) and $\neg \top \mathbf{R} \neg \mathbf{B}_{ag2}$ hold(block) (false ($\neg \top$) released by ag2 does not believe it is holding the block – which under standard LTL transformations means $\Box \neg \mathbf{B}_{ag2}$ hold(block) (it is always the case that ag2 does not believe it is holding the block)). In the next state this should also hold. For debugging failed model-checking runs it is normally safe to ignore the properties that should hold in the next state, and any temporal properties that should hold in the current state, so this automaton can be visualised as in figure C.1.

That is, a single-state automaton in which $\mathbf{B}_{ag2}$ hold(block) is never true. The model-checking has failed because this state is true for every state in the model along the path 0,1,2,3,4,5,6 (you can look in the program to see why).

C.2.3 Replaying a Counterexample

When model-checking fails the branch it has failed on has essentially generated a counterexample for the property. Sometimes you will want to replay this counter-example in the AIL without performing model-checking. AJPF has *record* and *replay* functionality to assist with this.

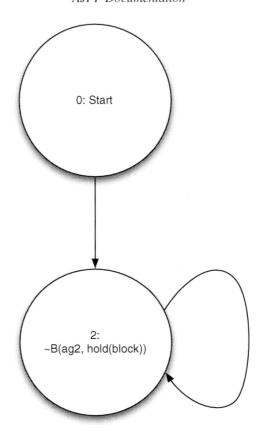

Figure C.1 The property automaton for $\neg\Diamond\mathbf{B}_{ag2}\,\text{hold}(\text{block})$

To obtain a record of a model-checking run you will need to set *logging mode* in the AIL *configuration file* (using ajpf.record = true) and then set the logging level to fine in ajpf.util.choice.ChoiceRecord). TwoPickupAgents_Recording.txt has this setup. Its output starts:

```
# choice: gov.nasa.jpf.vm.choice.ThreadChoiceFromSet ...
# garbage collection
-------------------------------- [1] forward: 0 new
# choice: gov.nasa.jpf.vm.choice.IntChoiceFromSet[...
[FINE] Record: [0]
[FINE] Record: [0, 0]
# garbage collection
-------------------------------- [2] forward: 1 new
# choice: gov.nasa.jpf.vm.choice.IntChoiceFromSet[...
[FINE] Record: [0, 0, 0]
```

```
[FINE] Record: [0, 0, 0, 0]
# garbage collection
------------------------------ [3] forward: 2 new
# choice: gov.nasa.jpf.vm.choice.IntChoiceFromSet[...
[FINE] Record: [0, 0, 0, 0, 0]
# garbage collection
------------------------------ [4] forward: 3 new
# choice: gov.nasa.jpf.vm.choice.IntChoiceFromSet[...
[FINE] Record: [0, 0, 0, 0, 0, 0]
# garbage collection
------------------------------ [5] forward: 4 new
# choice: gov.nasa.jpf.vm.choice.IntChoiceFromSet[...
[FINE] Record: [0, 0, 0, 0, 0, 0, 0]
[FINE] Record: [0, 0, 0, 0, 0, 0, 0, 0]
[FINE] Record: [0, 0, 0, 0, 0, 0, 0, 0, 0]
[FINE] Record: [0, 0, 0, 0, 0, 0, 0, 0, 0, 0]
# garbage collection
------------------------------ [6] forward: 5 new
# choice: gov.nasa.jpf.vm.choice.IntChoiceFromSet[...
[FINE] Record: [0, 0, 0, 0, 0, 0, 0, 0, 0, 0, 0]
[FINE] Record: [0, 0, 0, 0, 0, 0, 0, 0, 0, 0, 0, 0]
[FINE] Record: [0, 0, 0, 0, 0, 0, 0, 0, 0, 0, 0, 0, 0]
[FINE] Record: [0, 0, 0, 0, 0, 0, 0, 0, 0, 0, 0, 0, 0, 0]
# garbage collection
------------------------------ [7] forward: 6 visited
------------------------------ [6] backtrack: 5
# choice: gov.nasa.jpf.vm.choice.IntChoiceFromSet[...
[FINE] Record: [0, 0, 0, 0, 0, 0, 0, 0, 0, 0, 1]
[FINE] Record: [0, 0, 0, 0, 0, 0, 0, 0, 0, 0, 1, 1]
[FINE] Record: [0, 0, 0, 0, 0, 0, 0, 0, 0, 0, 1, 1, 0]
[FINE] Record: [0, 0, 0, 0, 0, 0, 0, 0, 0, 0, 1, 1, 0, 0]
# garbage collection
```

The lines starting [FINE] Record: show the record of choices at that point. To replay a particular branch through the search tree in AIL without model-checking do the following:

1. Paste the relevant record list, for example [0, 0, 0, 0, 0, 0, 0, 0, 0, 0, 1] into the file record.txt in the records directory of the MCAPL distribution.
2. Replace the line ajpf.record = true in your AIL configuration file with the line ajpf.replay = true.
3. Run the program in AIL as normal.

If you want to use a different file to record.txt to store the record for replay you can, but you will need to set ajpf.replay.file in the AIL configuration file appropriate in order to replay that record.

(Use of Random) Please note: that it is important for record and replay to work correctly that all choice points in the program are used in the record. Among other things this means that Java's `Random` class **cannot** be used in constructing environments and AJPF's `Choice` class should be used instead.

C.2.4 Forcing Transitions in the Agent's Reasoning Cycle

In the examples considered so far in this tutorial, AJPF has only generated new states for the model when JPF would generate a state. This has been when there has been a scheduling choice between the two agents. While this is often sufficient for many model-checking problems it does mean that the property is only checked when the agent program has done significant processing. This means that states of interest can sometimes be omitted for checking – particularly in the case of the $ID_{ag}f$ properties where you are interested in whether the agent ever has an intention that contains a particular action, the action may well have been removed from the intention before the property is checked.

By default, in fact, AJPF generates a new model state every time the agent advances its reasoning cycle. `TwoPickUpAgents_EveryTransition.jpf` runs the above examples in this mode. If you run it you will notice that there are a lot more states in the model and that most of them are generated by a `NewAgentProgramState` choice generator that does not actually cause any branching. This behaviour can be switched off by including `ajpf.transition_every_reasoning_cycle = false` in the AIL configuration file (Note this has to be the *AIL configuration file* not the *JPF configuration file*).

C.3 Tutorial 3: Using AJPF to Create Models for Other Model-Checkers

This is the third a series of tutorials on the use of the AJPF model-checking program. This tutorial covers the use of AJPF in conjunction with other model-checkers, specifically SPIN and PRISM. AJPF is used to create a model of the program which is then verified by another tool. The main purpose of this is to enable model checking with more expressive logics (as can be done with the PRISM implementation), but there may also be efficiency gains in outsourcing property checking to another tool.

Files for this tutorial can be found in the `mcapl` distribution in the directory

`src/examples/gwendolen/ajpf_tutorials/tutorial3`.

This tutorial assumes familiarity with the operation of AJPF as described Sections C.1 and C.2 and familiarity with the theory of model-checking. Unlike most tutorials, this tutorial is not standalone and assumes the user has access to both SPIN and PRISM.

This tutorial explains how to use the tools described in Chapter 13.

C.3.1 Separating out Model and Property

In normal operation, the AJPF system is performing two tasks at once. Firstly it is building a *model* of the program execution. This is a graph (or Kripke structure) of states. These are numbered and labelled with the facts that are true in each state (e.g., 'agent 1 believes holding_block', 'agent 2 has a goal pickup_block' and so on). At the same time it is checking this graph against a property (e.g., 'eventually agent 2 believes holding_block'). It does this by converting the property into an automaton, combining the property automaton with the Kripke structure on-the-fly (following Gerth et al. (1996); Courcoubetis et al. (1992)) and then checking for accepting paths through this product automaton.

In this tutorial we demonstrate how AJPF can be used to produce just the Kripke structure without creating the property automaton or the product automaton.

C.3.2 Using AJPF with SPIN

SPIN Holzmann (2003) is a popular model-checking tool originally developed by Bell Laboratories in the 1980s. It has been in continuous development for over thirty years and is widely used in both industry and academia (e.g., Havelund et al. (2000); Kars (1996); Kirsch et al. (2011)). SPIN uses an input language called PROMELA. Typically a model of a program and the property (as a 'never claim' – an automaton describing executions that violate the property) are both provided in PROMELA, but SPIN also provides tools to convert formulae written in LTL into never claims for use with the model-checker. SPIN works by automatically generating programs written in C which carry out the exploration of the model relative to an LTL property. SPIN's use of compiled C code makes it very quick in terms of execution time, and this is further enhanced through other techniques such as partial order reduction. The examples in this tutorial were checked using SPIN version 6.2.3 (24 October 2012).

To complete this tutorial you will need to download, install and run SPIN. SPIN can be downloaded from http://spinroot.com where you can also find documentation in its use.

```
@using = mcapl

target = ail.util.AJPF_w_AIL
target.args = ${mcapl}/src/examples/gwendolen/ajpf_tut...

ajpf.model_only = true
ajpf.target_modelchecker = spin
ajpf.model.location = stdout

listener+=,.listener.ExecTracker
et.print_insn=false
et.show_shared=false
```

Figure C.2 A configuration file for use with SPIN

Why Use SPIN?

SPIN and AJPF are both LTL model-checkers so it may seem odd to use AJPF only to produce the model and then use SPIN to create the property automaton. There are a couple of advantages to this however. Firstly SPIN has more powerful tools for producing property automata and so there are some properties that AJPF cannot handle which SPIN can. Secondly SPIN's LTL model-checking algorithms are more efficient than AJPF's so in theory the whole process could be quicker by using SPIN. In practice it has been demonstrated (see Chapter 13) that the major cause of slow performance in AJPF is in generating the Kripke structure of the program model and any gains in efficiency from using SPIN are often lost in converting AJPF's program model into PROMELA. However there may nevertheless be situations where efficiency gains can be made.

In terms of this tutorial, looking at the process of exporting models to SPIN forms a useful preliminary first step before we turn our attention to PRISM.

Configuring AJPF to Output SPIN Models

In order to configure AJPF to use another model-checker you need to tell it:

1. to produce *only* a program model,
2. which other model-checker to target and,
3. where to output the program model.

This is done in the JPF configuration file.

We will use the same program that was used in Section C.2. In the directory for tutorial 3 you will find the configuration file TwoPickUpAgents_Spin. jpf that is shown in Figure C.2.

This configuration file tells AJPF to produce a model only (ajpf.model_only = true), to target the SPIN model-checker

```
bool bag1holdblock

active proctype JPFModel()
{
state0:
bag1holdblock = true;
if
:: goto state1;
:: goto state37;
fi;
state1:
bag1holdblock = true;
if
:: goto state2;
:: goto state24;
fi;
```

Figure C.3 Model output for SPIN

```
state8:
bag1holdblock = false;
goto end_state3;
end_state9:
bag1holdblock = false;
printf("end state\n");
```

Figure C.4 Further states in the SPIN model

(ajpf.target_modelchecker = spin), and to print the model to standard out (ajpf.model.location = stdout). If you execute it in AJPF you get a print out of the model after AJPF has finished executing. The start of this print out is shown in Figure C.3. In this, the first state (state 0) in the AJPF model has become state0 in the PROMELA model. This state can transition to either state 1 (state1) or state 37 (state77) and so on.

This model also records one proposition bag1holdblock which is true in both states 0 and 1. If we look further into the model (shown in Figure C.4) we see that bag1holdblock is false in state 8 and end_state9 which is an end state in the model.

The property The property is, in fact, the AJPF property $\mathbf{B}_{ag1}$ hold(block)) and this has been stated in the property specification language file as property 1.

When using AJPF to generate only a program model, the property in the property specification language file should be a conjunction of the atomic properties that will appear in the property checked by the external system. In the property specification language, the atomic properties are those about the mental state of the agent, or the perceptions in the environment, that is, those of the form $\mathbf{B}_{ag}$ f, $\mathbf{G}_{ag}$f, $\mathbf{A}_{ag}$f, $\mathbf{I}_{ag}$f, ID_{ag}f, and $\mathbf{P}$ ag$f$.

Printing the Output to a file You can obviously cut and paste the PROMELA model from the AJPF output into a file for use with SPIN. Alternatively you can set `ajpf.model.location` to the path to an output file. The path should be relative to your `HOME` directory.

If you want to give the absolute file name you need to set `ajpf.model.path` as well as `ajpf.model.location` in the configuration file. The system will then join these to create the absolute path to the file you want to use.

The file `TwoPickUpAgents_SpinToFile.jpf` will print the model to a file `tutorial3_spin.pml` in the tutorial directory.

Model-checking the program in SPIN In the tutorial directory you will find a file `spinprop.pml` which is a PROMELA file containing the *never claim* for $\neg\Diamond\mathbf{B}_{ag1}$ hold(block). SPIN searches for a contradiction, so the model-checking succeeds if it can find no path through the model where $\mathbf{B}_{ag1}$ hold(block) does not eventually hold.

You can take the file containing your program model, plus `spinprop.pml` and compile them (using `spin -a -N spinprop.pml` *modelfile*) to get a C file, `pan.c`. This needs to be compiled then executed in order to check the program. More details on this process can be found in the SPIN documentation.

Exercise

You will find a second file in the tutorial directory, `spinprop2.pml`, which contains a never claim for the property $\neg(\Diamond\mathbf{B}_{ag1}$ hold(block) $\wedge \Diamond\neg\mathbf{B}_{ag2}$ hold(block)).

In order to verify this property you will need to adapt the property in `PickUpAgent.psl` so that it contains a conjunction of $\mathbf{B}_{ag1}$ hold(block) and $\mathbf{B}_{ag2}$ hold(flag) and then regenerate the model and check in SPIN. As usual a solution file can be found in the answers directory.

C.3.3 Using AJPF with PRISM

PRISM (Kwiatkowska et al., 2011) is a probabilistic symbolic model-checker in continuous development, primarily at the Universities of Birmingham and

Oxford, since 1999. PRISM provides broadly similar functionality to SPIN but also allows for the model-checking of probabilistic models, that is, models whose behaviour can vary depending on probabilities represented in the model. Developers can use PRISM to create a probabilistic model (written in the PRISM language) which can then be model-checked using PRISM's own probabilistic property specification language, which subsumes several well-known probabilistic logics including PCTL, probabilistic LTL, CTL, and PCTL*. PRISM has been used to formally verify a variety of systems in which reliability and randomness play a role, including communication protocols, cryptographic protocols, and biological systems. The examples in this tutorial were checked using PRISM version 4.3.

To complete this tutorial you will need to download, install and run PRISM. PRISM can be downloaded from http://www.prismmodelchecker. org where you can also find documentation on its use.

Configuring AJPF to Output PRISM Models

As mentioned in Section C.3.2, in order to configure AJPF to use another model-checker you need to tell it:

1. to produce *only* a program model,
2. which other model-checker to target and,
3. where to output the program model.

Because PRISM also includes probabilistic information in the model, when using AJPF with PRISM it is also important to use a *listener* that records such information when a choice in the java execution is governed by a probability.

This is done in the JPF configuration file. Initially we will, once again, use the same program that was used in Section C.2. In the directory for tutorial 3 you will find the configuration file TwoPickUpAgents_Prism.jpf that is shown in Figure C.5.

This configuration file tells AJPF to produce a model only (ajpf.model_only = true), to target the PRISM model-checker (ajpf.target_modelchecker = prism), to print the model to standard out (ajpf.model.location = stdout), and to use a probability listener (listener=ajpf.MCAPLProbListener). If you execute it in AJPF you get a print out of the model after AJPF has finished executing. The start of this print out is shown in Figure C.6.

There is no specifically probabilistic behaviour in this example, however there are two agents and the system, by default, assumes each agent has an equal chance of running every time the scheduler makes a decision. We can see here, therefore, that in state 0 there is a 50 per cent change that the system will

```
@using = mcapl

target = ail.util.AJPF_w_AIL
target.args = ${mcapl}/src/examples/gwendolen/ajpf_...

ajpf.model_only = true
ajpf.target_modelchecker = prism
ajpf.model.location = stdout

listener=ajpf.MCAPLProbListener

listener+=,.listener.ExecTracker
et.print_insn=false
et.show_shared=false
```

Figure C.5 A Configuration file for PRISM

```
dtmc

module jpfModel
state : [0 ..89] init 0;
bag1holdblock: bool init true;
[] state = 0 -> 0.5:(state'=1) & (bag1holdblock'= true) + 0.5:...
[] state = 1 -> 0.5:(state'=2) & (bag1holdblock'= true) + 0.5:...
[] state = 2 -> 0.5:(state'=3) & (bag1holdblock'= true) + 0.5:...
[] state = 3 -> 0.5:(state'=4) & (bag1holdblock'= true) + 0.5:...
[] state = 4 -> 0.5:(state'=5) & (bag1holdblock'= true) + 0.5:...
[] state = 5 -> 0.5:(state'=6) & (bag1holdblock'= false) + 0.5:...
[] state = 6 -> 1.0:(state'=89) & (bag1holdblock'= false);
[] state = 8 -> 1.0:(state'=88) & (bag1holdblock'= false);
```

Figure C.6 A Model for PRISM

transition to state 1 and a 50 per cent chance that it will transition to state 37. As with the SPIN example we are interested in one property, bag1holdblock ($\mathbf{B}_{ag1}$ hold(block))) and this is true in all the initial states of the model but is false after state 5.

The property Just as when using AJPF with SPIN, the property in the AJPF property specification file should be a conjunction of the atomic properties that will be used in the final property to be checked. In the property specification language, the atomic properties are those about the mental state of the agent, or the perceptions in the environment, that is, those of the form $\mathbf{B}_{ag}f$, $\mathbf{G}_{ag}f$, $\mathbf{A}_{ag}f$, $\mathbf{I}_{ag}f$, $\mathrm{ID}_{ag}f$, and $\mathbf{P}$ ag$f$.

Printing the Output to a file You can obviously cut and paste the PRISM model from the AJPF output into a file for use with PRISM. Alternatively you can set `ajpf.model.location` to the path to an output file. The path should be relative to your HOME directory.

If you want to give the absolute file name you need to set `ajpf.model.path` as well as `ajpf.model.location` in the configuration file. The system will then join these to create the absolute path to the file you want to use.

The file `TwoPickUpAgents_PrismToFile.jpf` will print the model to a file `tutorial3_prism.pm` in the tutorial directory.

Model-checking the program in PRISM In the tutorial directory you will find a file `prismprop1.pctl` which is a PRISM file containing the PCTL property for $P^{=?}\Box\Diamond\mathbf{B}_{ag1}$ hold(block).

You can take the file containing your program model, plus `prismprop1.pctl` and run them in PRISM (using `prism` *model file* `prismprop1.pctl`). This property is actually false and you should get a result of 0 probability:

`Result: 0.0 (value in the initial state)`.

More details on this process can be found in the PRISM documentation.

C.3.4 Model-Checking Agent Systems with Probabilistic Behaviour

We will now look at a program with probabilistic behaviour. This program is a modified version of one used in Section B.3. The program consists of a robot, `searcher.gwen`, which searches a 3x3 grid in order to find a human and an environment, `RandomRobotEnv`, in which a human is moving between the squares and could be at (0, 1), (1, 1) or (2, 1) with a 50 per cent chance of being at (1, 1), a 30 per cent chance of being at (2, 1) and a 20% chance of being at (0, 1). The robot only finds the human if it is in the same square as the robot and it immediately leaves the area once it finds the human (if it has checked every square without finding the human then it checks every square again) therefore there is a chance that the robot will never check the last square (2, 2).

In the directory for tutorial 3 you will find the JPF configuration file `searcher.jpf` for this program, that is shown in Figure C.7.

This file target's the PRISM model-checker and prints the model to standard out. It uses the listener `ajpf.MCAPLProbListener` to record probabilistic information as the model is built. If you execute it in AJPF you get a print out

```
@using = mcapl

target = ail.util.AJPF_w_AIL
target.args = ${mcapl}/src/examples/gwendolen/ajpf_...

log.info = ail.mas.DefaultEnvironment,ajpf.product.Product

ajpf.model.location = stdout
ajpf.model_only = true
ajpf.target_modelchecker = prism

listener=ajpf.MCAPLProbListener

listener+=,.listener.ExecTracker
et.print_insn=false
et.show_shared=false
```

Figure C.7 Configuration file for the searcher program

```
dtmc

 module jpfModel
state : [0 ..80] init 0;
bse2020: bool init false;
[] state = 0 -> 0.5:(state'=1) & (bse2020'= false) + 0.3:(st...
[] state = 1 -> 0.5:(state'=2) & (bse2020'= false) + 0.3:(st...
[] state = 2 -> 0.5:(state'=3) & (bse2020'= false) + 0.3:(st...
[] state = 3 -> 0.3:(state'=66) & (bse2020'= false) + 0.2:(st...
[] state = 4 -> 0.2:(state'=65) & (bse2020'= false) + 0.5:(st...
[] state = 5 -> 1.0:(state'=80) & (bse2020'= false);
```

Figure C.8 PRISM model for the searcher program

of the model after AJPF has finished executing. The start of this is shown in Figure C.8.

In this state 0 can transition to three states representing the movement of the human: state 1 (probability 0.5), state 72 (with probability 0.3) and state 73 (with probability 0.2), and so on.

This model also records one proposition bse2020 (shortened from bsearcherempty2020) which is false in all the early states but if you look further into the model you will see it becomes true when state 10 transitions to state 11.

The property The property is the AJPF property $\mathbf{B}_{searcher}$ empty$(2, 2)$ and this has been stated in the property specification language file as property 1.

Model-checking the program in PRISM In the tutorial directory you will find a file `prismprop2.pctl` which is a PRISM file containing the PCTL property for $P^{=?}\Diamond\mathbf{B}_{searcher}$ empty$(2, 2)$. If you run your PRISM model with this file you should find that the property has a 35 per cent chance of being true – that is, the robot has roughly a 35 per cent chance of checking the final square.

In the property specification file there is a second property for $\mathbf{B}_{searcher}$ found (that the searcher has found the human). If you generate a model for this property and check it in PRISM you will find its probability is 1, even though there is an infinite loop where the robot never finds the human. However the probability that the robot will remain in this infinite loop forever is infinitesimally small.

A Note on Creating Environments with Probabilistic Behaviour

In order for AJPF's probability listener to work correctly, all randomness (and probabilistic behaviour) should be created using AIL's `Choice` classes as documented in Section B.3.

It is important that probabilistic choices cause *unique* transitions in the model. If, for instance, you generate four choices each with, say, a 25 per cent probability but two of them end up leading to the same next state then AJPF will only annotate the transition with one of the probabilities (not the sum of both) and this will lead to PRISM generating an error. For instance say you have four choices each representing a direction some human could move in, north, east, south or west. If you are working in a grid world and if the selected direction were to take the human off the grid then you might choose to have the human remain in the same place instead. In this situation, when the human is in the corner of the grid, two of those choices will lead to the same result (the human remains in place) however only the probability for one of these occurring will be annotated on the transition and PRISM will warn that the probabilities of the transitions in this state do not sum to 1.

Exercise

You will find, in the tutorial directory an AIL program, `pickuprubble.ail`. This controls a robot (called `robot`) that searches a small 2×3 grid for injured humans. There is one human in the grid who moves around it randomly and one building in the grid that may collapse. If the building collapses onto the human then they will be injured. The robot systematically searches the grid. If it encounters the human it will direct them to safety and if it finds them injured it will assist them. However once the robot has reached the top corner of the grid it will stop searching. There is, therefore, a chance that the robot will never encounter the human and, what is more, that the human will visit the building after the robot has checked and will be injured by the building collapsing.

We are interested therefore in discovering the probability that if a human is injured then, eventually they are assisted by the robot. The file `prismprop_ex.pctl` in the tutorial directory contains the property $P^{=?}\Box(\mathbf{P}\text{ injured\_humans} \Rightarrow \Diamond\mathbf{A}_{robot}\text{assist\_humans})$.

Create a JPF configuration file and property specification file that will generate a PRISM model for this program and property. You should be able to discover that there is an 88 per cent chance of the robot assisting any injured human. Note that the AJPF model build will take several minutes to run (it generates 3,546 states).

As usual solution files can be found in the answers directory.

C.4 Tutorial 4: Verifying Reasoning Engines

This is the third in a series of tutorials on the use of the EASS variant of the GWENDOLEN language. This tutorial covers verifying EASS reasoning engines as described in Dennis et al. (2016); Fisher et al. (2013).

Files for this tutorial can be found in the `mcapl` distribution in the directory

```
src/examples/eass/tutorials/tutorial3.
```

The tutorial assumes a good working knowledge of Java programming. It also assumes the reader is familiar with the basics of using AJPF to verify programs (see AJPF Tutorials 1 and 2).

C.4.1 Overview

The process for verifying an EASS reasoning engine is to first analyse the agent program in order to identify all the shared beliefs that are sent from the abstraction engine to the reasoning engine. In multi-agent systems it is also necessary to identify all messages that the reasoning engine may receive from other agents in the environment. This is discussed in some detail in Dennis et al. (2016). Once a list of shared beliefs and messages has been identified, an environment is constructed for the reasoning engine alone in such a way that every time the agent takes an action the set of perceptions and messages

available to it are created *at random*. When model-checking the random selection causes the search tree to branch and the model-checker to explore all
possibilities.

C.4.2 Example

As an example we will consider the accelerating car controller we looked at
in EASS tutorial 1. The full code for this is shown in Example C.1 and from
this we can see there are two shared beliefs used by the program, start and
at_speed_limit.

Example C.1

```
EASS                                                             1
                                                                2
: abstraction :  car                                            3
                                                                4
: Initial  Beliefs :                                            5
                                                                6
speed_limit (5)                                                 7
                                                                8
: Initial  Goals :                                              9
                                                               10
                                                               11
: Plans :                                                      12
/* Default  plans  for  handling  messages */                 13
+.received (: tell ,  B):  { T }  ←  +B;                        14
+.received (: perform ,  G):  { T }  ←  +!G [ perform ];       15
+.received (: achieve ,  G):  { T }  ←  +!G [ achieve ];       16
                                                               17
+started  :  { T } ←                                           18
        +Σ( start );                                           19
                                                               20
+yspeed (X)  :  {B speed_limit (SL),  SL < X} ←               21
        +Σ( at_speed_limit );                                 22
+yspeed (X)  :  {B speed_limit (SL),  X < SL} ←               23
        −Σ( at_speed_limit );                                 24
                                                               25
+! accelerate  [ perform ]  :  {B yspeed (X)}  ←  accelerate ; 26
+! accelerate  [ perform ]  :  { ∼B yspeed (X)}  ←            27
print (" Waiting  for  Simulator  to  Start ");
+! maintain_speed  [ perform ]  :  { T }  ←  maintain_speed ; 28
                                                               29
: name :  car                                                 30
                                                               31
: Initial  Beliefs :                                          32
                                                               33
: Initial  Goals :                                            34
                                                               35
```

```
: Plans :                                                    36
                                                             37
+start : { T } ←                                             38
         +!at_speed_limit[achieve];                          39
                                                             40
+! at_speed_limit [achieve] : { T } ←                        41
         perf(accelerate),                                   42
         *at_speed_limit;                                    43
                                                             44
+at_speed_limit: { T } ←                                     45
         perf(maintain_speed);                               46
```

For verification purposes, we are only interested in the reasoning engine so we create a file containing just the reasoning engine. This is car_re.eass in the tutorial directory. You will also find an AIL configuration file car.ail, a JPF configuration file, car.jpf and a property specification file, car.psl in the tutorial directory.

The environment for verifying the car reasoning engine is shown in example C.2. This subclasses eass.mas.verification.EASSVerificationEnvironment which sets up a basic environment for handling verification of single reasoning engines. In order to use this environment you have to implement two methods, generate_sharedbeliefs (String AgName, Action act) and generate_messages (String Ag Name, Action act). It is assumed that these methods will randomly generate the shared beliefs and messages of interest to your application. EASSVerificationEnvironment handles the calling of these methods each time the reasoning engine takes an action. It should be noted that EASSVerificationEnvironment ignores assert_shared and remove_shared actions, assuming these take negligible time to execute – this is largely in order to keep search spaces as small as possible. generate_sharedbeliefs and generate_messages both take the agent's name and the last performed action as arguments. These are used if creating *structured environments* which are not discussed here.

In the example verification environment, generate_messages returns an empty set of messages because we did not identify any messages in the program. generate_sharedbeliefs is responsible for asserting at_speed_limit and start. EASSVerificationEnvironment provides random_bool_generator which is a member of the ajpf. util.choice.UniformBoolChoice class and random_int_ generator which is a member of the ajpf.util.choice.

Example C.2

```java
/**                                                                      1
 * An environment for verifying a simple car reasoning engine.          2
 * @author louiseadennis                                                3
 *                                                                       4
 */                                                                      5
public class VerificationEnvironment extends                            6
                    EASSVerificationEnvironment {                       7
                                                                         8
    public String logname = "tutorial3.VerificationEnvironment";        9
                                                                        10
    public Set<Predicate>                                               11
            generate_sharedbeliefs(String AgName, Action act) {         12
        TreeSet<Predicate> percepts = new TreeSet<Predicate>();         13
        boolean assert_at_speed_limit =                                 14
                random_bool_generator.nextBoolean();                    15
        if (assert_at_speed_limit) {                                    16
            percepts.add(new Predicate("at_speed_limit"));              17
            AJPFLogger.info(logname, "At_the_Speed_Limit");             18
        } else {                                                        19
            AJPFLogger.info(logname, "Not_At_Speed_Limit");             20
        }                                                               21
                                                                        22
        boolean assert_start = random_bool_generator.nextBoolean();     23
        if (assert_start) {                                             24
            percepts.add(new Predicate("start"));                       25
            AJPFLogger.info(logname, "Asserting_start");                26
        } else {                                                        27
            AJPFLogger.info(logname, "Not_asserting_start");            28
        }                                                               29
        return percepts;                                                30
    }                                                                   31
                                                                        32
    public Set<Message> generate_messages() {                           33
        TreeSet<Message> messages = new TreeSet<Message>();             34
        return messages;                                                35
    };                                                                  36
}                                                                       37
```

UniformIntChoice class. These can be used to generate random boolean and integer values. In this case random_bool_generator is being used to generate two booleans, assert_at_speed_limit and assert_start. If these booleans are true then the relevant predicate is added to the set returned by the method while, if it is false, nothing is added to the set. An AJPFLogger is used to print out whether the shared belief was generated or not – this can be useful when debugging failed model-checking runs.

There are four properties in the property specification file:

1 $\Box \neg \mathbf{B}_{car}$ crash – The car never believes it has crashed. We know this to be impossible – no such belief is ever asserted – but it can be useful to have a simple property like this in a file in order to check the basics of the model-checking is working.

2

$$\Box(\mathbf{A}_{car}\,perf\,(\text{accelerate}) \Rightarrow$$
$$(\Diamond \mathbf{A}_{car}\,perf\,(\text{maintain\_speed}) \vee \Box \neg \mathbf{B}_{car}\,\text{at\_speed\_limit}))$$

– If the car ever accelerates then either eventually it maintains its speed, or it never believes it has reached the speed limit.

3 $\Box(\mathbf{B}_{car}\,\text{at\_speed\_limit}) \Rightarrow \Diamond \mathbf{A}_{car}\,perf\,(\text{maintain\_speed})$ – If the car believes it is at the speed limit then eventually it maintains its speed. Properties of this form are often not true because $\mathbf{A}_{ag}a$ only applies to the last action performed and beliefs are often more persistent than that so the agent acquires the belief, b, does action a, and then does something else. At this point it still believes b but unless it does a again the property will be false in LTL. In this case, however, the property is true because `perf(maintain_speed)` is the last action performed by the agent.

4 $\Box \neg \mathbf{B}_{car}$ start $\Rightarrow \Box \neg \mathbf{A}_{car}\,perf\,(\text{accelerate})$ – If the car never believes the simulation has started then it never accelerates.

The JPF configuration file in the tutorial directory is set to check property 3. It is mostly a standard configuration, as discussed in Section C.2. However it is worth looking at the list of classes passed to `log.info`. These are:

ail.mas.DefaultEnvironment As discussed in Section C.2, this prints out the actions that an agent has performed and is useful for debugging.

eass.mas.verification.EASSVerificationEnvironment This prints out when an agent is just about to perform an action, before all the random shared beliefs and messages are generated. If both this class and `ail.mas.DefaultEnvironment` are passed to `log.info` then you will see a message before the agent does an action, then the search space branching as the random shared beliefs and messages are generated and then a message when the action completes. You may prefer to have only one of these print out.

eass.tutorials.tutorial3.VerificationEnvironment As can be seen in Example C.2 this will cause information about the random branching to get printed.

ajpf.product.Product As discussed in Section C.2, this prints out the current path through the AJPF search space.

C.4.3 Messages

Normally there is no need to construct messages in environments since this is handled by the way `ail.mas.DefaultEnvironment` handles send actions. However for EASS verification environments, where messages must be constructed at random, it is necessary to do this in the environment.

The important class is `ail.syntax.Message` and the main constructor of interest is `public Message(int ilf, String s, String r, Term c)`. The four parameters are

ilf This is the *illocutionary force* or the *performative*. For EASS agents this should be 1, for a tell message, 2 for a perform message and 3 for an achieve message. If in doubt you can use the static fields `EASSAgent.TELL`, `EASSAgent.PERFORM` and `EASSAgent.ACHIEVE`.

s This is a string which is the name of the sender of the message.

r This is a string which is the name of the receiver of the message.

c This is a term for the content of the message and should be created using the AIL classes for `Predicates` and so on.

Where messages are to be randomly generated a list of them should be created in `generate_messages`.

C.4.4 Exercises

Exercise 1

Take the sample answer for Exercise 2 in Section B.5, and verify that if the car never gets an alert then it never stops. As usual you can find a sample answer in the `answers` sub-directory.

Exercise 2

In the tutorial directory you will find a reasoning engine, `car_re_messages.eass`. This is identical to `car_re.eass` apart from the fact that it can process tell messages. Provide a verification environment where instead of `start` being asserted as a shared belief, the agent receives it as a tell message from the simulator. Check you can verify the same properties of the agent. As usual you can find a sample answer in the `answers` sub-directory.

References

Abrial, Jean-Raymond. 2010. *Modeling in Event-B*. Cambridge University Press.

Aitken, Jonathan M., Veres, Sandor M., and Judge, Mark. 2014. Adaptation of System Configuration under the Robot Operating System. *Proceedings of 19th World Congress of the International Federation of Automatic Control (IFAC)*.

Aitken, Jonathan M., Shaukat, Affan, Cucco, Elisa et al. 2017. Autonomous Nuclear Waste Management. *IEEE Intelligent Systems*, 33(6), 47–55.

Alur, Rajeev, Courcoubetis, Costas, and Dill, David. 1993. Model-Checking in Dense Real-Time. *Information and Computation*, **104**, 2–34.

Alur, Rajeev, Courcoubetis, Costas, Halbwachs, Nicolas et al. 1995. The Algorithmic Analysis of Hybrid Systems. *Theoretical Computer Science*, **138**(1), 3–34.

Ammann, Paul, and Offutt, Jeff. 2008. *Introduction to Software Testing*. Cambridge University Press.

Ancona, Davide, Ferrando, Angelo, and Mascardi, Viviana. 2016. Comparing Trace Expressions and Linear Temporal Logic for Runtime Verification. Pages 47–64 of: Erika Ábrahám, Marcello Bonsangue, and Einar Broch Johnsen (eds), *Theory and Practice of Formal Methods: Essays Dedicated to Frank de Boer on the Occasion of His 60th Birthday*. Lecture Notes in Computer Science, vol. 9660. Springer.

Anderson, Michael, and Anderson, Susan. 2007. Machine Ethics: Creating an Ethical Intelligent Agent. *AI Magazine*, **28**(4), 15–26.

Arkin, Ronald C. 2008. Governing Lethal Behavior: Embedding Ethics in a Hybrid Deliberative/Reactive Robot Architecture. Pages 121–128 of: Terry Fong, Kerstin Dautenhahn, Matthias Scheutz, and Yiannis Demiris (eds), *Proceedings of 3rd ACM/IEEE International Conference on Human Robot Interaction (HRI)*. ACM.

Asaro, Peter M. 2006. What Should We Want From a Robot Ethic? *International Review of Information Ethics*, **6**, 9–16.

Asimov, Isaac. 1942. Runaround. In *Astounding Science Fiction*. Street & Smith.

Babiak, Tomás, Kretínský, Mojmír, Rehák, Vojtech, and Strejcek, Jan. 2012. LTL to Büchi Automata Translation: Fast and More Deterministic. Pages 95–109 of *Proceedings of 18th International Conference on Tools and Algorithms for the Construction and Analysis of Systems (TACAS)*. Lecture Notes in Computer Science, vol. 7214. Springer.

Baltag, Alexandru, Gierasimczuk, Nina, and Smets, Sonja. 2019. Truth-Tracking by Belief Revision. *Studia Logica*, **107**(5), 917–947.

Beauchamp, Tom L., and Childress, James F. 2009. *Principles of Biomedical Ethics.* Sixth ed. Oxford University Press.

Behrmann, Gerd, David, Alexandre, and Larsen, Kim Guldstrand. 2004. A Tutorial on Uppaal. Pages 200–236 of: *International School on Formal Methods for the Design of Computer, Communication, and Software Systems, Revised Lectures.* Lecture Notes in Computer Science, vol. 3185. Springer.

Bengtsson, Johan, Larsen, Kim G. Larsson, Fredrik, Pettersson, Paul, and Yi, Wang. 1995. UPPAAL – A Tool Suite for Automatic Verification of Real–Time Systems. Pages 232–243 of: *Proceedings of Workshop on Verification and Control of Hybrid Systems III.* Lecture Notes in Computer Science, no. 1066. Springer.

Berthon, Raphaël, Maubert, Bastien, Murano, Aniello, Rubin, Sasha, and Vardi, Moshe Y. 2021. Strategy Logic with Imperfect Information. *ACM Transactions on Computational Logic,* **22**(1), 5:1–5:51.

Bierce, Ambrose. 2001. *The Enlarged Devil's Dictionary.* Penguin Modern Classics. www.thedevilsdictionary.com.

Blackburn, Patrick, van Benthem, Johan, and Wolter, Frank (eds). 2006. *Handbook of Modal Logic.* Elsevier.

Bohrer, Brandon, Tan, Yong Kiam, Mitsch, Stefan, Myreen, Magnus O., and Platzer, André. 2018. VeriPhy: Verified Controller Executables from Verified Cyber-Physical System Models. Pages 617–630 of: *Proceedings of ACM SIGPLAN Conference on Programming Language Design and Implementation (PLDI).* PLDI 2018. Association for Computing Machinery.

Bond, Alan H., and Gasser, Les (eds). 1988. *Readings in Distributed Artificial Intelligence.* Morgan Kaufmann.

Bonner, Michael C., Taylor, Robert M., and Miller, Christopher A. 2004. Tasking Interface Manager: Affording Pilot Control of Adaptive Automation and Aiding. Pages 70–74 of: McCabe, P. T., Hanson, M. A., and Robertson, S. A. (eds), *Contemporary Ergonomics 2000.* CRC Press.

Bordini, R., Dastani, M., Dix, J., and El Fallah-Seghrouchni, Amal (eds). 2005. *Multi-Agent Programming: Languages, Platforms and Applications.* Springer.

Bordini, Rafael H., Dastani, Mehdi, Dix, Jürgen, and El Fallah-Seghrouchni, Amal (eds). 2009. *Multi-Agent Programming: Languages, Tools and Applications.* Springer.

Boutilier, Craig, Shoham, Yoav, and Wellman, Michael P. 1997. Economic Principles of Multi-Agent Systems. *Artificial Intelligence,* **94**(1–2), 1–6.

Bratman, Michael E. 1987. *Intentions, Plans, and Practical Reason.* Harvard University Press.

Bratman, Michael E., Israel, David J., and Pollack, Martha E. 1988. Plans and Resource-Bounded Practical Reasoning. *Computational Intelligence,* **4**, 349–355.

Bredin, Jonathan, Kotz, David, Rus, Daniela et al. 2003. Computational Markets to Regulate Mobile-Agent Systems. *Autonomous Agents and Multi-Agent Systems,* **6**(3), 235–263.

Bremner, Paul, Dennis, Louise A., Fisher, Michael, and Winfield, Alan F. T. 2019. On Proactive, Transparent, and Verifiable Ethical Reasoning for Robots. *Proceedings of the IEEE,* **107**(3), 541–561.

Brooks, Rodney A. 1986. A Robust Layered Control System for a Mobile Robot. *IEEE Journal of Robotics and Automation,* **2**(10).

Brooks, Rodney A. 1999. *Cambrian Intelligence: The Early History of the New AI.* MIT Press.

Bull, Robert A., and Segerberg, Krister. 1984. Basic Modal Logic. Pages 1–88 of: Gabbay, D., and Guenthner, F. (eds), *Handbook of Philosophical Logic (II)*. Synthese Library, vol. 165. Reidel.

Cameron, Neil, Webster, Matthew, Jump, Mike, and Fisher, Michael. 2011. Certification of a Civil UAS: A Virtual Engineering Approach. In *AIAA Modeling and Simulation Technologies Conference (AIAA-2011-6664)*.

Cardoso, Rafael C., Farrell, Marie, Luckcuck, Matthew, Ferrando, Angelo, and Fisher, Michael. 2020a. Heterogeneous Verification of an Autonomous Curiosity Rover. Pages 353–360 of: *Proceedings of 12th International NASA Formal Methods Symposium (NFM)*. Lecture Notes in Computer Science, vol. 12229. Springer.

Cardoso, Rafael C., Dennis, Louise A., Farrell, Marie, Fisher, Michael, and Luckcuck, Matthew. 2020b. Towards Compositional Verification for Modular Robotic Systems. In *Proceedings of 2nd International Workshop on Formal Methods for Autonomous Systems (FMAS 2020)*.

Cavalcanti, Ana. 2020. Modelling and Verification of Robotic Platforms for Simulation Using RoboStar Technology. Pages 3–5 of: Raschke, Alexander, Méry, Dominique, and Houdek, Frank (eds), *Rigorous State-Based Methods*. Springer International.

Chatila, Raja, Dignum, Virginia, Fisher, Michael, et al. 2021. Trustworthy AI. Pages 13–39 of: Braunschweig, Bertrand, and Ghallab, Malik (eds), *Reflections on Artificial Intelligence for Humanity*. Springer.

Civil Aviation Authority. 2010. *CAP 393 Air Navigation: The Order and the Regulations.* www.caa.co.uk/docs/33/CAP393.pdf.

Cohen, Philip R., and Levesque, Hector J. 1990. Intention is Choice with Commitment. *Artificial Intelligence*, **42**, 213–261.

Collins, John, Faratin, Peyman, Parsons, Simon, et al. (eds). 2009. *Agent-Mediated Electronic Commerce and Trading Agent Design and Analysis (AMEC/TADA) — Selected and Revised Papers from AAMAS Workshops*. Lecture Notes in Business Information Processing, vol. 13. Springer.

Corera, Jose Manuel, Laresgoiti, Iñaki, and Jennings, Nicholas R. 1996. Using Archon, Part 2: Electricity Transportation Management. *IEEE Expert*, **11**(6), 71–79.

Courcoubetis, Costas, Vardi, Moshe Y., Wolper, Pierre, and Yannakakis, Mihalis. 1992. Memory-Efficient Algorithms for the Verification of Temporal Properties. *Formal Methods in System Design*, **1**(2), 275–288.

Crick, Christopher, Jay, Graylin, Osentosiki, Sarah, Pitzer, Benjamin, and Jenkins, Odest Chadwicke. 2011. Rosbridge: ROS for Non-ROS Users. In *15th International Symposium on Robotics Research (ISRR 2011)*.

Dash, Rajdeep K., Vytelingum, Perukrishnen, Rogers, Alex, David, Esther, and Jennings, Nicholas R. 2007. Market-Based Task Allocation Mechanisms for Limited-Capacity Suppliers. *IEEE Transactions on Systems, Man, and Cybernetics, Part A*, **37**(3), 391–405.

Davis, Randall, and Smith, Reid G. 1983. Negotiation as a Metaphor for Distributed Problem Solving. *Artificial Intelligence*, **20**(1), 63–109.

Dedu, Eugen. 2001. *A Bresenham-Based Super-Cover Line Algorithm.* http://lifc.univ-fcomte.fr/home/~ededu/projects/bresenham. [Online; 29 September 2014].

Demri, Stéphane, Goranko, Valentin, and Lange, Martin. 2016. *Temporal Logics in Computer Science: Finite-State Systems.* Cambridge Tracts in Theoretical Computer Science. Cambridge University Press.

Dennis, Louise A. 2018. The MCAPL Framework including the Agent Infrastructure Layer and Agent Java Pathfinder. *The Journal of Open Source Software*, **3**(24), 617.

Dennis, Louise A., Fisher, Michael, Lincoln, Nicholas K., Lisitsa, Alexei, and Veres, Sandor M. 2010a. Declarative Abstractions for Agent Based Hybrid Control Systems. Pages 96–111 of: *Proceedings of 8th International Workshop on Declarative Agent Languages and Technologies (DALT).* Lecture Notes in Computer Science, vol. 6619. Springer.

Dennis, Louise A., Fisher, Michael, Lincoln, Nicholas K., Lisitsa, Alexei, and Veres, Sandor M. 2010b. Reducing Code Complexity in Hybrid Control Systems. In *Proceedings of 10th International Symposium on Artificial Intelligence, Robotics and Automation in Space (i-Sairas).*

Dennis, Louise A., Fisher, Michael, Lisitsa, Alexei, Lincoln, Nicholas K., and Veres, Sandor M. 2010c. Satellite Control Using Rational Agent Programming. *IEEE Intelligent Systems*, **25**(3), 92–97.

Dennis, Louise A., Fisher, Michael, Webster, Matthew P., and Bordini, Rafael H. 2012. Model Checking Agent Programming Languages. *Automated Software Engineering*, **19**(1), 5–63.

Dennis, Louise A., Fisher, Michael, Slavkovik, Marija, and Webster, Matthew. 2013a. Ethical Choice in Unforeseen Circumstances. Pages 433–445 of: *Proceedings of 14th Towards Autonomous Robotic Systems (TAROS).* Lecture Notes in Computer Science, vol. 8069. Springer.

Dennis, Louise A., Fisher, Michael, and Webster, Matthew. 2013b. Using Agent JPF to Build Models for Other Model Checkers. Pages 273–289 of: *Proceedings of International Workshop on Computational Logic in Multi-Agent Systems (CLIMA).* Lecture Notes in Computer Science, vol. 8143. Springer.

Dennis, Louise A., Fisher, Michael, and Winfield, Alan F. T. 2015. Towards Verifiably Ethical Robot Behaviour. In *Proceedings of AAAI-15 Workshop on AI and Ethics.* https://arxiv.org/abs/1504.03592.

Dennis, Louise A., Aitken, Jonathan M., Collenette, Joe et al. 2016a. Agent-Based Autonomous Systems and Abstraction Engines: Theory Meets Practice. Pages 75–86 of: Alboul, Lyuba, Damian, Dana, and Aitken, M. Jonathan (eds), *Proceedings of 17th Annual Conference on Towards Autonomous Robotic Systems (TAROS).* Springer.

Dennis, Louise A., Fisher, Michael, Slavkovik, Marija, and Webster, Matthew P. 2016b. Formal Verification of Ethical Choices in Autonomous Systems. *Robotics and Autonomous Systems*, **77**, 1–14.

Dennis, Louise A., Fisher, Michael, Lincoln, Nicholas K., Lisitsa, Alexei, and Veres, Sandor M. 2016c. Practical Verification of Decision-Making in Agent-Based Autonomous Systems. *Automated Software Engineering*, **23**(3), 305–359.

Dennis, Louise A., Fisher, Michael, and Webster, Matthew. 2018. Two-Stage Agent Program Verification. *Journal of Logic and Computation*, **28**(3), 499–523.

Dennis, Louise A., Bentzen, Martin Mose, Lindner, Felix, and Fisher, Michael. 2021. Verifiable Machine Ethics in Changing Contexts. *Proceedings of the AAAI Conference on Artificial Intelligence*, **35**(13), 11470–11478.

Dinmohammadi, Fateme, Fisher, Michael, Flynn, David et al. 2018. Certification of Safe and Trusted Robotic Inspection of Assets. *Proceedings of Prognostics and System Health Management Conference (PHM-Chongqing)*, 276–284.

Doghri, Ines. 2008. Formal Verification of WAHS: An Autonomous and Wireless P2P Auction Handling System. Pages 1–10 of: *Proceedings of 8th International Conference on New Technologies in Distributed Systems (NOTERE)*. ACM.

Downing, Troy, and Meyer, Jon. 1997. *Java Virtual Machine*. O'Reilly Media.

Durfee, Edmund H., Lesser, Victor R., and Corkill, Daniel D. 1989. Trends in Cooperative Distributed Problem Solving. *IEEE Transactions on Knowledge and Data Engineering*, **1**(1), 63–83.

Emerson, E. Allen. 1990a. Temporal and Modal Logic. Pages 995–1072 of: van Leeuwen, J. (ed), *Handbook of Theoretical Computer Science*, vol. B. Elsevier Science.

Emerson, E. Allen. 1990b. *The Role of Büchi's Automata in Computing Science*. Springer-Verlag.

Fagin, Ronald, Halpern, Joseph Y., Moses, Yoram, and Vardi, Moshe Y. 1996. *Reasoning About Knowledge*. MIT Press.

Falcone, Yliès, Havelund, Klaus, and Reger, Giles. 2013. A Tutorial on Runtime Verification. Pages 141–175 of: Manfred Broy, Doron Peled, and Georg Kalus (eds), *Engineering Dependable Software Systems*. IOS Press.

Farrell, Marie, Cardoso, Rafael C., Dennis, Louise A. et al. 2019. *Modular Verification of Autonomous Space Robotics*. http://arxiv.org/abs/1908.10738.

Farrell, Marie, Luckcuck, Matt, Pullum, Laura et al. 2021. Evolution of the IEEE P7009 Standard: Towards Fail-Safe Design of Autonomous Systems. In *Proceedings of 32nd Symposium on Software Reliability Engineering 2021 [Industry Track]*.

Ferrando, Angelo, Dennis, Louise A., Ancona, Davide, Fisher, Michael, and Mascardi, Viviana. 2018. Verifying and Validating Autonomous Systems: Towards an Integrated Approach. Pages 263–281 of: Colombo, Christian, and Leucker, Martin (eds), *Runtime Verification*. Lecture Notes in Computer Science, vol. 11237. Springer.

Ferrando, Angelo, Dennis, Louise A., Cardoso, Rafael C. et al. 2021. Toward a Holistic Approach to Verification and Validation of Autonomous Cognitive Systems. *ACM Transactions on Software Engineering and Methodology*, **30**(4), 43:1–43:43.

Ferrère, Thomas, Maler, Oded, Nickovic, Dejan, and Pnueli, Amir. 2019. From Real-time Logic to Timed Automata. *ACM Journal*, **66**(3), 19:1–19:31.

FIPA. 2002. *FIPA Communicative Act Library Specification*. Tech. rept. FIPA00037. Foundation for Intelligent Physical Agents. http://fipa.org/specs/fipa00037.

Firby, R. James. 1990. *Adaptive Execution in Complex Dynamic Worlds*. Yale University.

Fisher, Michael. 2011. *An Introduction to Practical Formal Methods Using Temporal Logic*. John Wiley & Sons.

Fisher, Michael, Dennis, Louise A., and Webster, Matthew P. 2013. Verifying Autonomous Systems. *ACM Communications*, **56**(9), 84–93.

Fisher, Michael, Mascardi, Viviana, Rozier, Kristin Yvonne et al. 2021. Towards a Framework for Certification of Reliable Autonomous Systems. *Autonomous Agents and MultiAgent Systems*, **35**(1), 8.

Fortnow, Lance, Riedl, John, and Sandholm, Tuomas (eds). 2008. *Proceedings of 9th ACM Conference on Electronic Commerce (EC)*. ACM.

Franklin, Stan, and Graesser, Arthur. 1996. Is it an Agent, or just a Program?: A Taxonomy for Autonomous Agents. Pages 21–35 of: Müller, J.P., Wooldridge, M.J., and Jennings, N.R. (eds), *Intelligent Agents III (Proceedings of 3rd International Workshop on Agent Theories, Architectures, and Languages)*. Lecture Notes in Computer Science, vol. 1193. Springer.

Gabbay, Dov M., Kurucz, Agnes, Wolter, Frank, and Zakharyaschev, Michael. 2003. *Many-Dimensional Modal Logics: Theory and Applications*. Studies in Logic and the Foundations of Mathematics, vol. 148. Elsevier Science.

Garoche, Pierre-Loïc. 2019. *Formal Verification of Control System Software*. Princeton University Press.

Gerth, Rob, Peled, Doron, Vardi, Moshe Y., and Wolper, Pierre. 1996. Simple on-the-fly Automatic Verification of Linear Temporal Logic. Pages 3–18 of: Piotr Dembiński, and Marek Średniawa (eds), *Proceedings of 15th IFIP WG6.1 International Symposium on Protocol Specification, Testing and Verification XV*. Chapman & Hall.

Ghallab, Malik, Nau, Dana, and Traverso, Paolo. 2016. *Automated Planning and Acting*. Cambridge University Press.

Ghidini, Chiara, and Serafini, Luciano. 2014. Multi-context Logics - A General Introduction. Pages 381–399 of: Brézillon, Patrick, and Gonzalez, Avelino J. (eds), *Context in Computing - A Cross-Disciplinary Approach for Modeling the Real World*. Springer.

Halpern, Joseph Y. 2003. *Reasoning About Uncertainty*. MIT Press.

Hansson, Hans, and Jonsson, Bengt. 1994. A Logic for Reasoning about Time and Reliability. *Formal Aspects of Computing*, **6**, 102–111.

Haque, Nadim, Jennings, Nicholas R., and Moreau, Luc. 2005. Resource Allocation in Communication Networks using Market-Based Agents. *Knowledge-Based Systems*, **18**(4–5), 163–170.

Havelund, Klaus, Lowry, Mike, Park, SeungJoon et al. 2000. Formal Analysis of the Remote Agent Before and After Flight. In *Proceedings of 5th NASA Langley Formal Methods Workshop, Virginia, USA*, 163–174.

Havelund, K., Pressburger, T. 2000. Model checking JAVA programs using JAVA PathFinder. *STTT 2*, 366–381. https://doi.org/10.1007/s100090050043.

Henzinger, Thomas A., Ho, Pei-Hsin, and Wong-Toi, Howard. 1997. HYTECH: A Model Checker for Hybrid Systems. *International Journal on Software Tools for Technology Transfer*, **1**(1–2), 110–122.

Hierons, Robert M., Bogdanov, Kirill, Bowen, Jonathan P. et al. 2009. Using Formal Specifications to Support Testing. *ACM Computing Surveys*, **41**(2), 1–76.

Holzmann, Gerard J. 2003. *The Spin Model Checker: Primer and Reference Manual*. Addison-Wesley.

Howey, Richard, Long, Derek, and Fox, Maria. 2004. VAL: Automatic Plan Validation, Continuous Effects and Mixed Initiative Planning using PDDL. Pages 294–301 of: *Proceedings of ICTAI*, IEEE.

Huang, Xiaowei, Kroening, Daniel, Ruan, Wenjie et al. 2020. A Survey of Safety and Trustworthiness of Deep Neural Networks: Verification, Testing, Adversarial Attack and Defence, and Interpretability. *Computer Science Review*, **37**, 100270.

Hughes, George E., and Cresswell, Max J. 1984. *A Companion to Modal Logic*. Methuen (UP).

Hunter, Josie, Raimondi, Franco, Rungta, Neha, and Stocker, Richard. 2013. A Synergistic and Extensible Framework for Multi-Agent System Verification. Pages 869–876 of: Maria L. Gini, Onn Shehory, Takayuki Ito, and Catholijn M. Jonker (eds), *Proceedings of 13th International Conference on Autonomous Agents and Multiagent Systems (AAMAS)*. IFAAMAS.

IEEE. 2017. *The Global Initiative on Ethics of Autonomous and Intelligent Systems. Ethically Aligned Design: A Vision for Prioritizing Human Well-being with Autonomous and Intelligent Systems, Version 2*. Tech. rept.

Jobin, Anna, Ienca, Marcelo, and Vayena, Effy. 2019. The Global Landscape of AI Ethics Guidelines. *Nature Machine Intelligence*, 1, 389–399.

Jones, Cliff B. 1986. *Systematic Software Development Using VDM*. Prentice Hall International.

Kamali, Maryam, Dennis, Louise A., McAree, Owen, Fisher, Michael, and Veres, Sandor M. 2017. Formal Verification of Autonomous Vehicle Platooning. *Science of Computer Programming*, **148**, 88–106.

Kars, Pim. 1996. *The Application of Promela and Spin in the BOS Project (Abstract)*. http://spinroot.com/spin/Workshops/ws96/Ka.pdf.

Kirsch, Michael T., Regenie, Victoria A., Aguilar, Michael L. et al. 2011. *Technical Support to the National Highway Traffic Safety Administration (NHTSA) on the Reported Toyota Motor Corporation (TMC) Unintended Acceleration (UA) Investigation*. NASA Engineering and Safety Center Technical Assessment Report.

Klemperer, Paul. 2004. *Auctions: Theory and Practice*. Princeton, USA: Princeton University Press. www.nuff.ox.ac.uk/users/klemperer/VirtualBook/VBCrevisedv2.asp.

Konishi, Hideo, and Ray, Debraj. 2003. Coalition Formation as a Dynamic Process. *Journal of Economic Theory*, **110**(1), 1–41.

Konur, Savas, Fisher, Michael, and Schewe, Sven. 2013. Combined Model Checking for Temporal, Probabilistic, and Real-time Logics. *Theoretical Computer Science*, **503**, 61–88.

Kowalski, Robert A. 1979. Algorithm=Logic+Control. *Communications of the ACM*, **22**(7), 424–436.

Kwiatkowska, Marta, Norman, Gethin, Segala, Roberto, and Sproston, Jeremy. 2002. Automatic Verification of Real-time Systems with Discrete Probability Distributions. *Theoretical Computer Science*, **282**, 101–150.

Kwiatkowska, Marta, Norman, Gethin, and Parker, David. 2011. PRISM 4.0: Verification of Probabilistic Real-time Systems. Pages 585–591 of: Ganesh Gopalakrishnan, and Shaz Qadeer (eds), *Proceedings of 23rd Conf. Computer Aided Verification*. Lecture Notes in Computer Science, vol. 6806. Springer.

Lacerda, Bruno, Faruq, Fatma, Parker, David, and Hawes, Nick. 2019. Probabilistic Planning with Formal Performance Guarantees for Mobile Service Robots. *International Journal of Robotics Research*, **38**(9), 1098–1123.

Lincoln, Nicholas K., and Veres, Sandor M. 2006. Components of a Vision Assisted Constrained Autonomous Satellite Formation Flying Control System. *International Journal of Adaptive Control and Signal Processing*, **21**(2–3), 237–264.

Lincoln, Nicholas K., Veres, Sandor M., Dennis, Louise A., Fisher, Michael, and Lisitsa, Alexei. 2013. Autonomous Asteroid Exploration by Rational Agents. *Computational Intelligence*, **8**(4), 25–38.

Lorini, Emiliano, and Herzig, Andreas. 2008. A Logic of Intention and Attempt. *Synthese*, **163**(1), 45–77.

Manna, Zohar, and Pnueli, Amir. 1992. *The Temporal Logic of Reactive and Concurrent Systems: Specification*. Springer.

McAree, Owen, and Veres, Sandor M. 2016. Lateral Control of Vehicle Platoons with on-board Sensing and Inter-Vehicle Communication. In *Proceedings of European Control Conference (ECC)*.

Mehlitz, Peter C., Rungta, Neha, and Visser, Willem. 2013. A Hands-on Java PathFinder Tutorial. Pages 1493–1495 of: David Notkin, Betty H. C. Cheng, and Klaus Pohl (eds), *Proceedings of 35th International Conference on Software Engineering (ICSE)*. IEEE / ACM.

Moor, James. 2006. The Nature, Importance, and Difficulty of Machine Ethics. *IEEE Intelligent Systems*, **21**(4), 18–21.

Murphy, Robin, and Woods, David D. 2009. Beyond Asimov: The Three Laws of Responsible Robotics. *IEEE Intelligent Systems*, **24**(4), 14–20.

Muscettola, Nicola, Nayak, P. Pandurang, Pell, Barney, and Williams, Brian C. 1998. Remote Agent: To Boldly Go Where No AI System Has Gone Before. *Artificial Intelligence*, **103**(1–2), 5–48.

Nallur, Vivek. 2020. Landscape of Machine Implemented Ethics. *Science and Engineering Ethics*, **26**(5), 2381–2399.

Patchett, Charles, Jump, Mike, and Fisher, Michael. 2015. Safety and Certification of Unmanned Air Systems. *Engineering and Technology Reference*, 1–6. http://doi.org/10.1049/etr.2015.0009.

Pauly, Marc. 2002. A Modal Logic for Coalitional Power in Games. *Journal of Logic and Computation*, **12**(1), 149–166.

Peled, Doron. 1993. All from One, One for All: on Model Checking Using Representatives. Pages 409–423 of: Costas Courcoubetis (ed), *Proceedings of 5th International Conference on Computer Aided Verification (CAV)*. Lecture Notes in Computer Science, vol. 697. Springer.

Platzer, André. 2010. *Logical Analysis of Hybrid Systems: Proving Theorems for Complex Dynamics*. Springer.

Plotkin, Gordon. 1981. *A Structural Approach to Operational Semantics*. Tech. rept. DAIMI FN-19. Department of Computer Science, Aarhus University.

Quigley, Morgan, Conley, Ken, Gerkey, Brian P. et al. 2009. ROS: An Open-source Robot Operating System. In *Proceedings of ICRA Workshop on Open Source Software*.

Raimondi, Franco, Pecheur, Charles, and Brat, Guillaume. 2009. PDVer, a Tool to Verify PDDL Planning Domains. In *Proceedings of ICAPS'09*.

Raja, P., and Pugazhenthi, S. 2012. Optimal Path Planning of Mobile Robots: A Review. *International Journal of Physical Sciences*, **7**(9), 1314–1320.

Rao, Anand S. 1998. Decision Procedures for Propositional Linear-Time Belief-Desire-Intention Logics. *Journal of Logic and Computation*, **8**(3), 293–342.

Rao, Anand S., and Georgeff, Michael P. 1991. Modeling Agents within a BDI-Architecture. Pages 473–484 of: James F. Allen, Richard Fikes, and Erik Sandewall (eds), *Proceedings of 2nd International Conference on Principles of Knowledge Representation and Reasoning (KR&R)*. Morgan Kaufmann.

Rao, Anand S., and Georgeff, Michael P. 1992. An Abstract Architecture for Rational Agents. Pages 439–449 of: Bernhard Nebel, Charles Rich, and William R. Swartout (eds), *Proceedings of 3rd International Conference on Principles of Knowledge Representation and Reasoning (KR&R)*. Morgan Kaufmann.

Rao, Anand S., and Georgeff, Michael P. 1995. BDI Agents: From Theory to Practice. Pages 312–319 of: Victor Lesser, and Les Gasser (eds), *Proceedings of 1st Int. Conf. Multi-Agent Systems (ICMAS)*. MIT Press.

Reeves, Daniel M., Wellman, Michael P., MacKie-Mason, Jeffrey K., and Osepayshvili, Anna. 2005. Exploring Bidding Strategies for Market-Based Scheduling. *Decision Support Systems*, **39**(1), 67–85.

Robbins, Russell W., and Wallace, William A. 2007. Decision Support for Ethical Problem Solving: A Multi-Agent Approach. *Decision Support Systems*, **43**(4), 1571–1587. (Special Issue on Clusters).

Rosu, Grigore, and Havelund, Klaus. 2005. Rewriting-Based Techniques for Runtime Verification. *Automated Software Engineering*, **12**(2), 151–197.

Russell, Stuart, and Norvig, Peter. 2003. *Artificial Intelligence, A Modern Approach (2nd ed.)*. Prentice Hall.

Sandholm, Tuomas, and Lesser, Victor R. 1997. Coalitions Among Computationally Bounded Agents. *Artificial Intelligence*, **94**(1–2), 99–137.

Sastry, Shankar, and Bodson, Marc. 1994. *Adaptive Control: Stability, Convergence, and Robustness*. Prentice Hall.

Searle, John R. 1969. *Speech Acts: An Essay in the Philosophy of Language*. Cambridge University Press.

Shaukat, Affan, Gao, Yang, Kuo, Jeff A., Bowen, Bob A., and Mort, Paul E. 2015. Visual Classification of Waste Material for Nuclear Decommissioning. *Robotics and Autonomous Systems*, 75, 365–378.

Shoham, Yoav. 1993. Agent-Oriented Programming. *Artificial Intelligence*, **60**(1), 51–92.

Sistla, A. Prasad, Vardi, Moshe Y., and Wolper, Pierre. 1987. The Complementation Problem for Büchi Automata with Applications to Temporal Logic. *Theoretical Computer Science*, **49**, 217–237.

Sterling, Leon, and Shapiro, Ehud. 1987. *The Art of Prolog*. MIT Press.

Tolmeijer, Suzanne, Kneer, Markus, Sarasua, Cristina, Christen, Markus, and Bernstein, Abraham. 2021. Implementations in Machine Ethics: A Survey. *ACM Computing Surveys*, **53**(6), 132:1–132:38.

Tulum, Kamil, Durak, Umut, and Yder, S. Kemal. 2009. Situation Aware UAV Mission Route Planning. Pages 1–12 of: *Proceedings of IEEE Aerospace Conference*. IEEE.

Ueda, Kazunori. 1985. *Guarded Horn Clauses*. Tech. rept. TR-103. ICOT.

van der Hoek, Wiebe, and Wooldridge, Michael J. 2005. On the Logic of Cooperation and Propositional Control. *Artificial Intelligence*, **164**(1–2), 81–119.

Vanderelst, Dieter, and Winfield, Alan F. T. 2018. An Architecture for Ethical Robots Inspired by the Simulation Theory of Cognition. *Cognitive Systems Research*, **48**, 56–66.

Vardi, Moshe Y., and Wolper, Pierre. 1994. Reasoning About Infinite Computations. *Information and Computation*, **115**(1), 1–37.

Vickrey, William. 1961. Counterspeculation, Auctions, and Competitive Sealed Tenders. *The Journal of Finance*, **16**(1), 8–37.

Vienna. 1968. *Vienna Convention on Road Traffic*. www.unece.org/trans/conventn/crt1968e.pdf.

Visser, Willem, Havelund, Klaus, Brat, Guillaume P., Park, Seungjoon, and Lerda, Flavio. 2003. Model Checking Programs. *Automated Software Engineering*, **10**(2), 203–232.

Walsh, William E., and Wellman, Michael P. 1998. A Market Protocol for Decentralized Task Allocation. Pages 325–332 of: *Proceedings of 3rd International Conference on Multiagent Systems (ICMAS)*. IEEE Computer Society.

Webster, Matthew, Fisher, Michael, Cameron, Neil, and Jump, Mike. 2011. Formal Methods and the Certification of Autonomous Unmanned Aircraft Systems. Pages 228–242 of: Flammini, F., Bologna, S., and Vittorini, V. (eds), *Proceedings of 30th Int. Conf. Computer Safety, Reliability and Security (SAFECOMP)*. Lecture Notes in Computer Science, vol. 6894. Springer.

Webster, Matthew, Cameron, Neil, Fisher, Michael, and Jump, Mike. 2014. Generating Certification Evidence for Autonomous Unmanned Aircraft Using Model Checking and Simulation. *Journal of Aerospace Information Systems*, **11**(5), 258–279.

Webster, Matthew, Western, David, Araiza-Illan, Dejanira. et al. 2020. A Corroborative Approach to Verification and Validation of Human–Robot Teams. *The International Journal of Robotics Research*, **39**(1), 73–99.

Webster, Matthew P., Dennis, Louise A., and Fisher, Michael. 2009. *Model-Checking Auctions, Coalitions and Trust*. Tech. rept. ULCS-09-004. University of Liverpool, Department of Computer Science. www.csc.liv.ac.uk/research/.

Winfield, Alan. 2012. *Robotics: A Very Short Introduction*. Oxford University Press.

Winfield, Alan F. T., and Jirotka, Marina. 2017. The Case for an Ethical Black Box. Pages 262–273 of: Gao, Yang, Fallah, Saber, Jin, Yaochu, and Lekakou, Constantina (eds), *Proceedings of 18th Annual Conference on Towards Autonomous Robotic Systems (TAROS)*. Lecture Notes in Computer Science, vol. 10454. Springer.

Winfield, Alan F. T., Michael, Katina, Pitt, Jeremy, and Evers, Vanessa. 2019. Machine Ethics: The Design and Governance of Ethical AI and Autonomous Systems [Scanning the Issue]. *Proceedings of the IEEE*, **107**(3), 509–517.

Winfield, Alan F. T., Booth, Serena, Dennis, Louise A. et al. 2021. IEEE P7001: A Proposed Standard on Transparency. *Frontiers in Robotics and AI*, **8**, 225.

Winikoff, Michael, Dennis, Louise, and Fisher, Michael. 2019. Slicing Agent Programs for More Efficient Verification. Pages 139–157 of: Weyns, Danny, Mascardi, Viviana, and Ricci, Alessandro (eds), *Proceedings of 6th International Workshop on Engineering Multi-Agent Systems (EMAS)*. Lecture Notes in Computer Science, vol. 11375. Springer.

Woodman, Roger, Winfield, Alan F. T., Harper, Christopher J., and Fraser, Mike. 2012. Building Safer Robots: Safety Driven Control. *International Journal of Robotics Research*, **31**(13), 1603–1626.

Wooldridge, Michael, Ågotnes, Thomas, Dunne, Paul E., and van der Hoek, Wiebe. 2007. Logic for Automated Mechanism Design – A Progress Report. Pages 9–17 of: *Proceedings of 22nd Conference on Artificial Intelligence (AAAI)*. AAAI Press.

Wooldridge, Michael J. 2002. *An Introduction to Multiagent Systems*. John Wiley & Sons.

Wooldridge, Michael J., and Rao, Anand S. (eds). 1999. *Foundations of Rational Agency*. Applied Logic Series. Kluwer Academic.

Index

Printed in the United States
by Baker & Taylor Publisher Services